A THREAT TO LIFE

The Impact of Climate Change on Japan's Biodiversity

Compiled and Edited by
Akiko Domoto, Kunio Iwatsuki,
Takeo Kawamichi and Jeffrey McNeely

with the assistance of
Cindy Termorshuizen, Mieko Kawamichi,
Kei Inami, and Nobuo Takeshita

Foreword by
Jeffrey McNeely

The designation of geographical entities in this book, and the presentation of the material, do not imply the expression of any opinion whatsoever on the part of IUCN concerning the legal status of any country, territory, or area, or of its authorities, or concerning the delimitation of its frontiers or boundaries.

The views expressed in this publication do not necessarily reflect those of IUCN.

Publication of this book was aided by grants from EXPO'90 Foundation, The Toyota Foundation, and ÆON Group Environment Foundation.

Published by:
Tsukiji-Shokan Publishing Co., Ltd, Japan and IUCN, Gland, Switzerland and Cambridge, UK

Copyright:
©2000 Biodiversity Network Japan

Reproduction of this publication for educational or other non-commercial purposes is authorized without prior written permission from the copyright holder provided the source is fully acknowledged and the copyright holder receives a copy of the reproduced material.
Reproduction of this publication for resale or other commercial purposes is prohibited without prior written permission of the copyright holder.

Citation:
Akiko Domoto et al. (2000). A Threat to Life: The Impact of Climate Change on Japan's Biodiversity. Tsukiji-Shokan Publishing Co., Ltd., Japan and IUCN, Gland, Switzerland and Cambridge, UK. Includes bibliographical references and index.

ISBN: 4-8067-1217-5

Printed by Tsukiji-Shokan Publishing Co., Ltd., Japan

Paper:
Printed on 100% recycled paper with soy-based inks.

Available from:
IUCN Publications Services Unit
219c Huntingdon Road, Cambridge CB3 ODL, United Kingdom
Tel: +44 1223 277894, Fax: +44 1223 277175
E-mail: info@books.iucn.org; www.iucn.org/bookstore/
A catalogue of IUCN publications is also available

発行所：
築地書館株式会社
〒104－0045　東京都中央区築地7－4－4－201
電話 03－3542－3731　ファクス 03－3541－5799
Eメール：JDH07647@nifty.ne.jp
ホームページ：www.tsukiji-shokan.co.jp

Figure 1.
Distribution of change in temperature at ground level in 100 years (Chapter 3; Meteorological Agency).

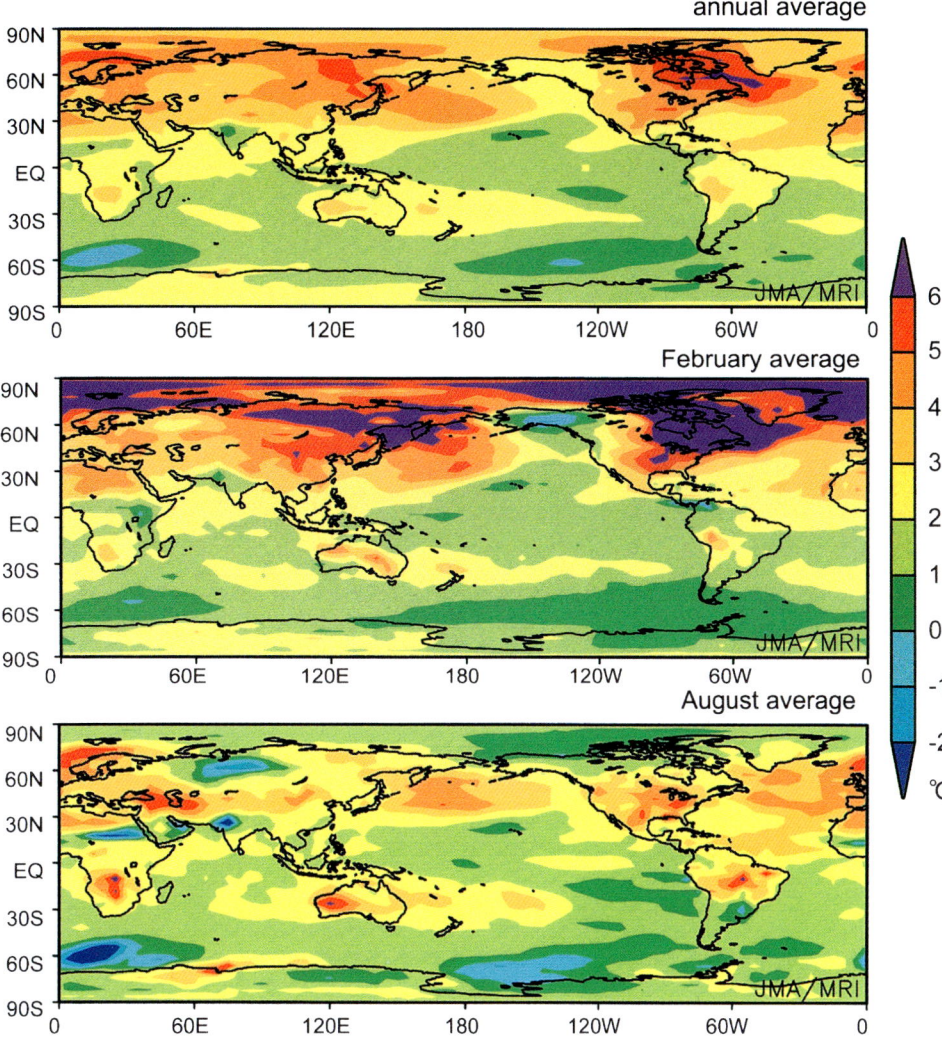

Figure 2.
Change in the distribution of sea ice in the Northern Hemisphere. The distribution of ice is shown in terms of the percentage (%) of area covered by sea ice 30, 50, 70, and in 100 years (Chapter 3; Meteorological Agency).

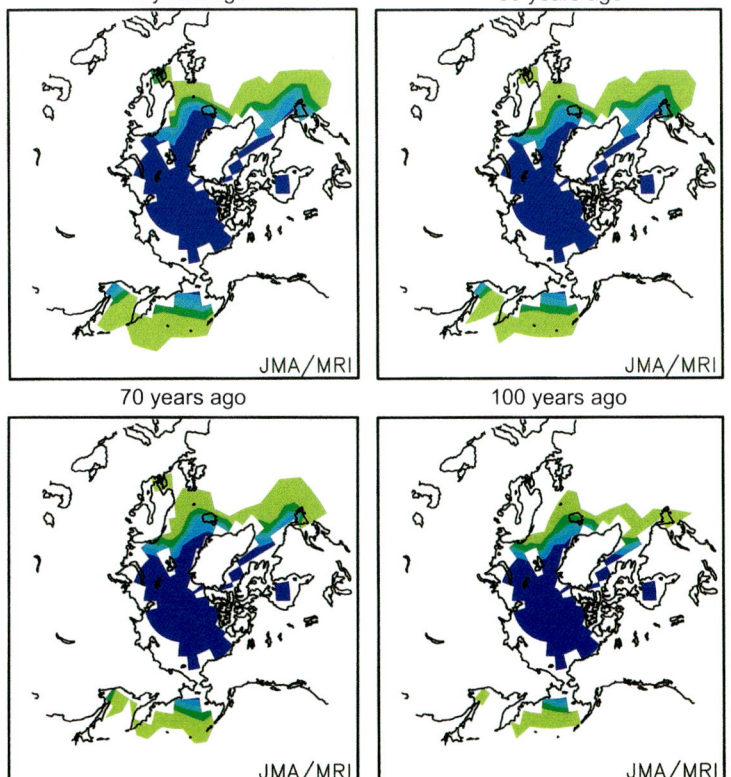

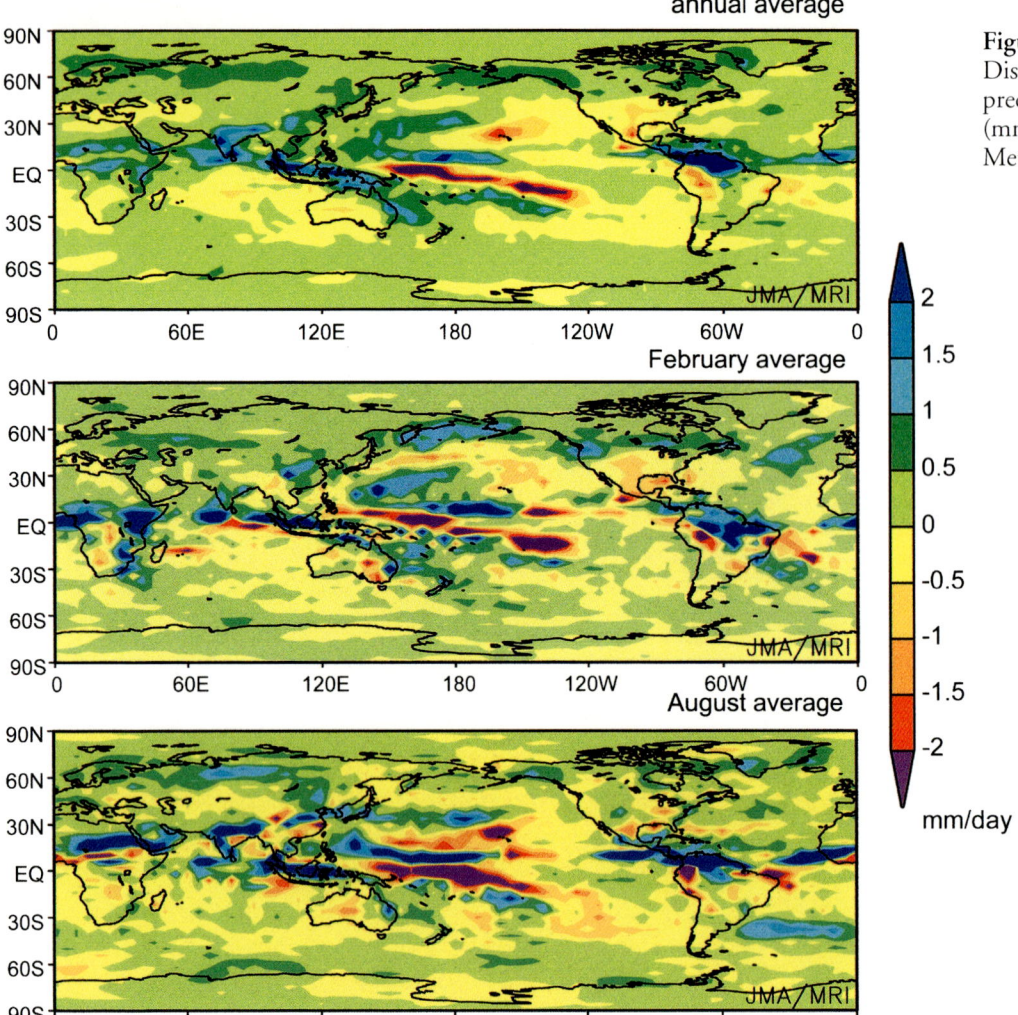

Figure 3.
Distribution of change in precipitation in 100 years (mm/day) (Chapter 3; Meteorological Agency).

Figure 4.
Distribution of change in the sea level in 100 years (Chapter 3; Meteorological Agency).

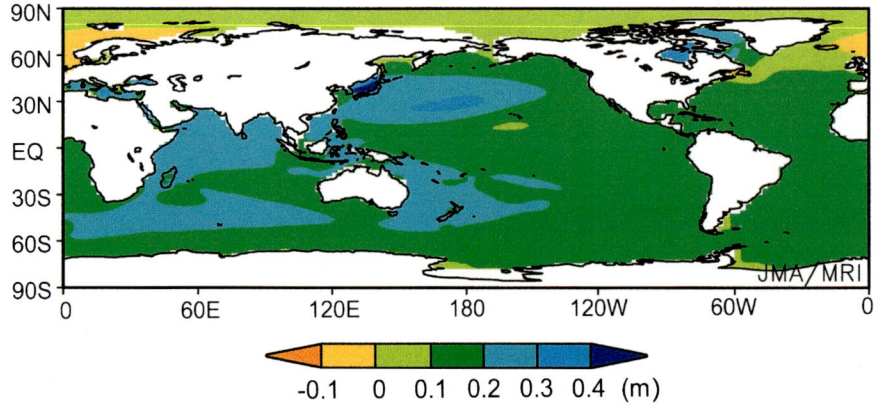

Figure 5.
Bleached colonies of the branching species of *Acropora* on the reef of Tokashiki Island, Okinawa. The brown area to the right is a dead portion, overgrown by filamentous algae (Chapter 16; photo by Tsuyoshi Uehara, 23 Sep. 1998).

Figure 6.
Potential distribution of the world's major biomes under present climate conditions as calculated by the Atmosphere-Plant-Soil System model (MAPSS). Potential distribution means natural vegetation that is expected to exist based on precipitation, temperature, humidity, and wind speed at each place (Chapter 20; Environmental Agency).

Figure 7.
Distribution of the world major biomes forecast by calculating the influence of doubled CO_2 - equivalent concentrations (Overall circulation model by GFDL/NOAA---Global Fluid Mechanics Institute, National Oceanic and Atmospheric Agency) including the direct influence of CO_2 to plant physiology (Chapter 20; Environmental Agency).

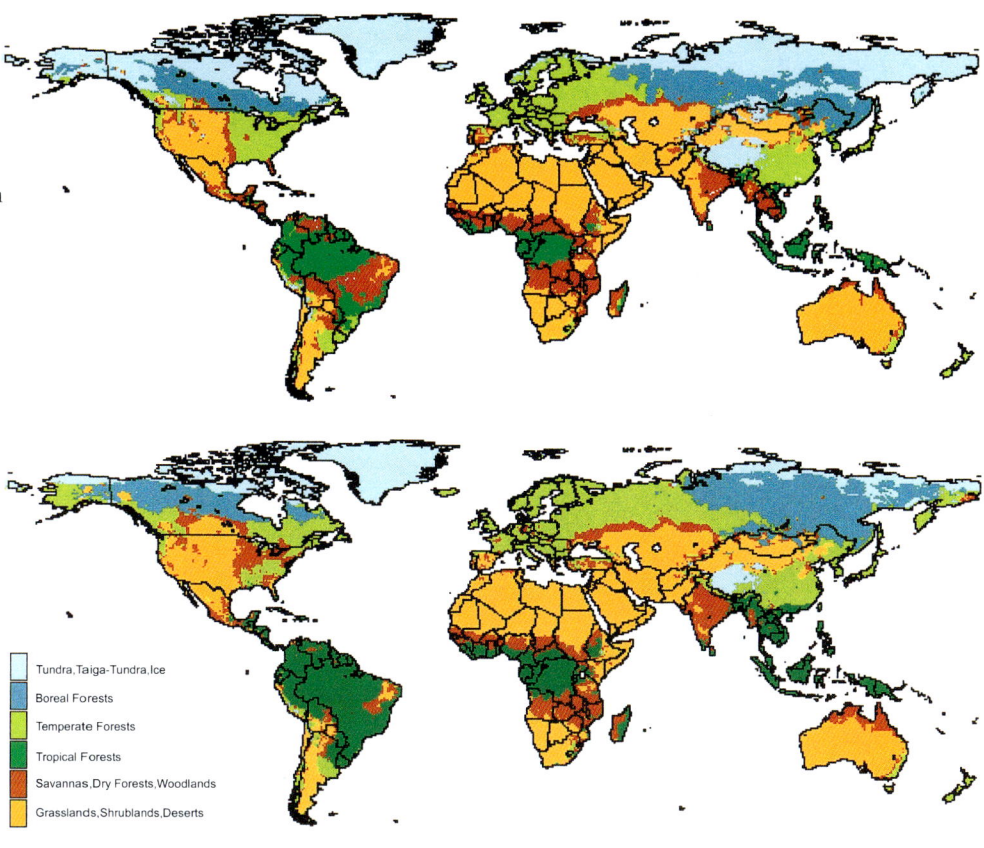

Figure 8.
Mangrove forest in Iriomote Island. The soil is rich in organic matter (photo by Gisuke Kubo).

Figure 10.
Parnassius eversmanni in the Taisetsu Mountains (Chapter 12; photo by Nobunori Hoda).

Figure 9.
Alpine meadow in the Taisetsu Mountains. A number of alpine plants are growing like mosaics (Chapter 9; photo by Takehiro Masuzawa).

Figure 11.
Japanese pika *Ochotona hyperborea yesoensis* in the Taisetsu Mountains (Chapter 21; photo by Nozomu Kojima).

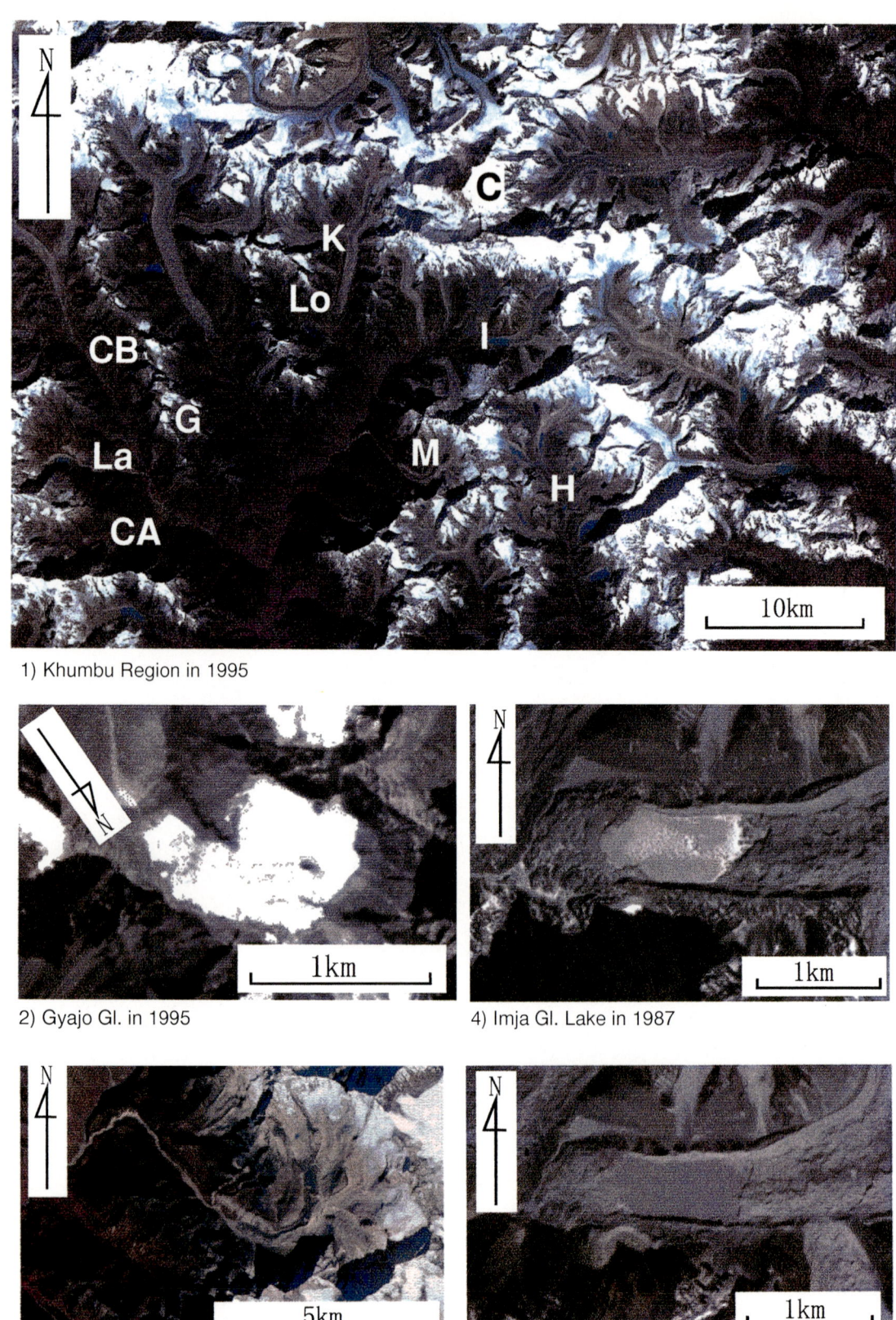

1) Khumbu Region in 1995
2) Gyajo Gl. in 1995
3) Mingbo Valley in 1995
4) Imja Gl. Lake in 1987
5) Imja Gl. Lake in 1993

Figure 12.
SPOT (Systeme Pourl' Observation de la Terre) images of the Khumbu district, eastern Nepal.
c: chomolungma (Mt. Everest) (Chapter 8).

Foreword

Like other highly industrialised modern states, Japan is highly dependent on fossil fuels to support its economy. These fossil fuels, primarily oil, have many advantages as a source of energy, and Japan is a world leader in the efficient use of them. But it has also become clear in recent years that the burning of such fossil fuels is also leading to increases in atmospheric carbon dioxide, that this in turn can lead to significant changes in climate and that these changes can have profound effects on both ecosystems and their component species.

Japan, therefore, has a deep interest in assessing the impact of climate change on the biodiversity of the country. Considerable work has been done on this topic in Japan over the past decade or so, but much of this work has been in the Japanese language and is not readily available to the global community. Given the increasing interest around the world in the linked topics of climate change and biodiversity, this book is an extremely useful contribution that demonstrates the depth of Japanese concern about climate change issues, and especially its impact on biological diversity. This book therefore contributes to the implementation of the two most important results of the 1992 United Nations Conference on Environment and Development, the so-called "Earth Summit": the Framework Convention on Climate Change and the Convention on Biological Diversity.

While Japan's industrial base provides much of its prosperity, it remains dependent on nature in a part of the world that is especially vulnerable to the impacts of volcanoes, tsunamis, earthquakes, and typhoons. Maintaining healthy forests, coastal zones, and agricultural lands are important elements for maintaining the capacity to adapt to changing conditions. Of course, people are interested especially in the impact of climate change on people, but many of these impacts will be felt through changes in biological diversity, including on fisheries, wild plant communities, and agriculture.

This book, which contains numerous examples and figures, presents the latest and best of Japanese research on climate change and particularly its impacts on marine ecosystems, insects, birds, and vegetation. It therefore demonstrates the important contributions that Japanese scientists can make to global discussions on climate change and its impacts on global biological diversity. It places Japanese science firmly in the mainstream of research in this important field, and demonstrates how seriously Japan is taking its global responsibilities.

As Chief Scientist at IUCN, I have had the pleasure of working with Japanese colleagues for over 30 years. The contribution of Japanese scientists to field work in the Himalayas and in many parts of Africa has been particularly noteworthy in its relevance to the major conservation issues of the day. I am particularly pleased, therefore, that we have been able to work together with colleagues in Japan to produce a book that so effectively demonstrates the level of concern, commitment, and competence of the research being done by Japanese scientists, both in Japan and more broadly. We hope and expect that this will be the first of many such publications to be produced collaboratively over the coming years, helping to mobilise support in all countries for the critical conservation challenges that are facing humanity as we enter the exciting and challenging times of the 21st century.

Jeffrey A. McNeely
Gland, Switzerland
8 June 2000

Preface

Of the nine planets of our solar system, it is only the Earth which has oceans. It is from these very oceans that life was born some 3.8 to 4 billion years ago. Since then, living creatures have both directly effected the Earth and adjusted to those very effects over a long period of time. In this way, life and the planet have evolved together. About 10,000 years ago, at the end of the last ice-age, temperatures were 5 degrees Centigrade lower than now. Over a period of around 1,000 years, temperatures rose to current levels and then were stable for about 9,000 years. But since the industrial revolution and the establishment of modern industrial society, this stability has been destroyed and average temperatures have been increasing at an extremely rapid rate. For hundreds of thousands of years, the Earth's delicate balance was maintained, and in a mere 100-200 years, human activities have seriously threatened this balance as they directly and indirectly contribute to an alarming rate of climate change.

Indeed, the speed at which climate change is occurring may soon surpass the speed at which life itself can adapt. We are seeing an unnatural rise in sea levels, increasing frequency of floods, and desertification. The immense impact of climate change on the balance of ecosystems is undeniable. If current trends continue, by the year 2100, temperatures could rise by 2 degrees Centigrade, which could cause sea levels to rise from 60 to 100 centimeters. Okinawa Prefecture's famous Shiraho coral reef could be irreversibly damaged, Tottori Prefecture's sand dunes would disappear, and the beauty of Japan's shoreline would be lost. With a one meter rise in sea level, 90% of Japan's sandy beaches would be submerged, turning Japan into a beachless archipelago.

Considering the potentially irreversible damage to the earth's ecosystems by continued climate change, Biodiversity Network Japan, a Japanese non-governmental organization (NGO) whose members are scientists and experts on biodiversity, believes strongly that more attention must be given to the impacts of climate change on biodiversity.

Before the United Nations Framework Convention on Climate Change held its Third Conference of the Parties (COP3) in Kyoto in December 1997, the world's attention was turned to numbers. Numerical targets for the reduction of greenhouse gas emissions and the number of gases to be included in reduction calculations were the focus of much heated debate. Though numerical targets were undoubtedly an issue of concern, Biodiversity Network Japan felt an important element was missing from discussions leading to COP3. We saw an urgent need to examine the effects of climate change on biodiversity and were disturbed that this topic of central importance was not to be given any treatment during the Conference of Parties. It was with this sense of urgency that, together with IUCN-The World Conservation Union, we organized a series of symposiums before the COP3.

The first took place in Tokyo on the theme of climate change and forests. The second was in Nagoya on global warming and infectious diseases. The third symposium was entitled "Global Warming and the Crisis of Biodiversity," and the final was in Kyoto on the links between global warming, wetlands, and coral reefs. Many experts were asked to give presentations at these symposiums, and we were surprised that not a single person declined. It was clear that these specialists were also noting irregularities in their fields which were explainable by the effect of climate change. The many positive responses we received from the speakers as well as those who attended the symposiums led to the idea to compile a book on the effects of climate change on biodiversity. The book, completed in Japanese and entitled *The Threat of Climate Change to Biodiversity*, was completed just in time for COP3.

We took the book to COP3, and many people expressed great interest in its contents. With their encouraging remarks and the desire of Japanese scientists to share their work with others around the world, we were inspired to create this English edition, *A Threat to Life: The Impact of Climate Change on Japan's Biodiversity*.

We hope that readers will find this book interesting, as it provides information from Japan, and useful in illustrating some examples of the interrelationship between climate change and biodiversity. This is an area which has not yet been adequately addressed by international organizations. Science in the 20th century has been largely oriented around the physical sciences—those which can be explained with mathematics or produce quantitative evidence for their theories. To quantify the effects of climate change on biodiversity, however, is extremely difficult.

When we have not yet even mastered the art of weather forecasting, we cannot expect to precisely predict changes in climate over the next few decades. We also do not know in exact terms how living creatures react to changes in climate. Quantifying the interrelationship between two very unpredictable and little understood sciences will require more time than we have. We do know, however, that changes are occurring, and scientists are noticing irregularities in the biological tendencies which have been consistent over hundreds of years.

Perhaps someday we will have enough quantitative information to prove how climate change is affecting biodiversity. But by this time, it will be much too late. We now require a different approach. The 21st century will be the century of biological sciences as we are hit with a natural resources crisis and increasing attention is given to such areas as genetics and biosafety. To understand the interrelationship between climate change and biodiversity will require a biological science approach. In an effort to contribute to the development of this approach, Biodiversity Network Japan published its first book in Japanese and has now succeeded in the release of this English edition.

Akiko Domoto
Member, House of Councillors
Cofounder, Biodiversity Network Japan
Vice President and Regional Councillor,
IUCN-The World Conservation Union
JAPAN

Acknowledgements

A book covering as vast a territory as this one could not have been compiled without the help of many committed individuals. In addition to the authors, we are grateful to all of those who translated, proofread, edited, provided data and photos, created tables and figures, and peer reviewed this volume. For their time and linguistic talents, we thank our translators Keiko Funanami, Mutsuko Inui, Naoya Ishizawa, Kazuko Jinguji, Naoko Miyazaki, Madoka Onizuka Chase, Masako Oshima, Manabu Sakamoto, Cindy Termorshuizen and Laura Samartin. For their careful editing, we thank Barnaby Briggs, Yuki Fukuda, Tim Groves, Mieko Kawamichi, Jason Minton, Elizabeth Platt, Richard B. Primack, Maggie Suzuki, Nobuo Takeshita, Emily Wood and Kei Inami. For providing unpublished data, our gratitude goes especially to Sidney Dunkle, Naoya Ishizawa, Shigeto Koike, and Dennis Paulson. Without the figures and photos that brighten the following pages, this book would be rather pale and colourless. We are particularly grateful, therefore, to Gisuke Kubo, Nobuki Yasuda, Nozomu Kojima, and Dexter Sear for providing photographs, to Hiroto Shimazaki and Masayuki Tamura for creating a number of the figures, and to Masako Ishizaki for preparing for publication all of the figures in this volume. For co-ordinating the peer review of this book, we thank Brett Orlando of IUCN-US. We do not know their names, but we are grateful to the many scholars who heeded Brett's call for peer reviewers and took time out of their busy schedules to comment on the various chapters of this book. Last, but not least, we are thankful to Elaine Shaughnessy and her team at the IUCN Publications Services Unit for making sure that this book finally made it into print.

Production of the *A Threat to Life: The Impact of Climate Change on Japan's Biodiversity* would not have been possible without the support of grants from EXPO'90 Foundation, The Toyota Foundation, and ÆON Group Environment Foundation.

Editorial Board, Biodiversity Network Japan

Contents

Foreword   Jeffrey McNeely
Preface   Akiko Domoto
Acknowledgments

Section I : Toward a Biospheric Approach
Advancing from the Intersection of the Two Rio Conventions

Chapter 1 Creating Synergy in Environmental Policy
Bridging the Gaps between the Framework Convention on Climate Change
and the Convention on Biological Diversity
Akiko Domoto   1

Chapter 2 Global Climate Change and Biodiversity
Richard B. Primack   9

Section II : An Overview of Climate Change
From the Past to the Future

Chapter 3 Projections Concerning Climate Change
Hiroshi Nirasawa   14

Chapter 4 Greenhouse Gas Emission Scenarios
Mikiko Kainuma, Tsuneyuki Morita and Yuzuru Matsuoka   19

Chapter 5 Ecosystems and the Carbon Cycle
Takehisa Oikawa   24

Chapter 6 Influence of Decreased Snowfall due to Warming Climate Trends
on the Water Quality of Lake Biwa, Japan
Hiroji Fushimi   35

Chapter 7 Sudden Global Warming and Sea Level Change in Holocene Japan
Arata Momohara   38

Chapter 8 Recent Changes in Glacial Phenomena in the Nepalese Himalayas
Hiroji Fushimi   42

Section III: The Impact of Global Warming on Flora and Fauna

Chapter 9 How Will Communities of Alpine Plants be Affected by Global Warming ?
Takehiro Masuzawa   46

Chapter 10 Aquatic Plants at Risk
Yasuro Kadono   52

Chapter 11 Warming and Japanese Seagrasses
Keiko Aioi and Yuji Omori   57

Chapter 12 The Impact of Global Warming on Insects
Hidenori Ubukata   61

Chapter 13 Global Warming and Alpine Moths in Raised Bogs in Eastern Hokkaido
Masahiko Nakatani   71

Chapter 14 Global Warming and Forest Insect Pests-An Example from Hokkaido
    Kenji Fukuyama   76

Chapter 15 What Will Happen to Marine Organisms in the Future?
    Masayuki M. Takahashi   83

  Box 1 How will the Expansion of Deserts Affect the Sea?
    Masayuki M. Takahashi   91

  Box 2 How will Ice Algae be Affected by Rapid Changes Induced by Global Warming?
    Masayuki M. Takahashi   91

  Box 3 The Blessings of Floating Ice
    Nobuo Gouchi   92

Chapter 16 Global Warming and Coral Reefs
    Kiyoshi Yamazato   95

Chapter 17 Potential Impacts of Global Warming on Freshwater Ecosystems in Japan
    Hiromi Kobori   102

Chapter 18 The Influence of Global Warming on Fish
    Seiichi Mori   110

Chapter 19 The Impact of Global Warming on Sea Turtles
    Naoki Kamezaki   120

Chapter 20 What Will Happen to the Birds?
    Nobuo Takeshita and Masayuki Kurechi   127

Chapter 21 Can Pikas on High Mountains Survive the Greenhouse Effect?
    Takeo Kawamichi   136

Chapter 22 Global Warming and Increases in Human Infectious Diseases
    Takayuki Ezaki   141

Chapter 23 Global Warming and the Dynamics of Biodiversity
    Kunio Iwatsuki   147

Postscript

Global Warming and Biodiversity - The Situation in Japan
    Harufumi Nishida   152

Index   156
Contributors   162

Chapter 1

Creating Synergy in Environmental Policy

Bridging the Gaps between the Framework Convention
on Climate Change and the Convention on Biological Diversity

Akiko Domoto

The Earth Summit which took place in Rio de Janeiro in June 1992 was a time of near euphoria. One hundred eighty-three states and 20,000 NGOs and individuals gathered for the event whose highlights were the signing of a number of ground breaking environmental agreements, including the United Nations Framework Convention on Climate Change (UNFCCC) and the Convention on Biological Diversity (CBD). The key objective of the UNFCCC is to achieve "stabilisation of greenhouse gas concentrations in the atmosphere at a level that would prevent dangerous anthropogenic interference with the climate system" (Article 2). The CBD, the first convention to address in a comprehensive fashion all genes, species, and ecosystems, is aimed at "the conservation of biological diversity, the sustainable use of its components and the fair and equitable sharing of the benefits arising out of the utilisation of genetic resources" (Article 1). The two conventions, both signed by over 150 countries, were intended to contribute to the establishment of a systematic, legal mechanism capable of balancing the need for development with environmental protection and conservation (Glowka, 1994).

Important strides have been made in implementing these conventions over the years. In the context of the UNFCCC, the 1997 Kyoto Protocol established binding emissions reduction targets for the so-called Annex I countries. The Protocol obliges Japan to cut its greenhouse gas emissions by 6% of 1990 levels by 2010; the EU and the US are to cut theirs by 7% and 8%, respectively. Under both conventions, many countries have made progress in reporting, public education, and the creation of national action plans. Of great import-ance as well, a significant amount of funding has been made available through the Global Environ-ment Facility (GEF) and other mechanisms to aid developing countries in their efforts to implement these conventions.

While the importance of these achievements should not be minimized, what has not been achieved is a comprehensive system for the protection of both the biosphere and atmosphere. This is evident in continued high levels of species extinction and increasing carbon dioxide emissions. Worldwide, 100,000 species are lost annually (Peters and Myers, 1992). In Japan, 2,096 species are listed as endangered or vulnerable (Environment Agency, 1998). Carbon dioxide levels have risen by 30% since the beginning of the Industrial Revolution and continue to rise (Watson, 1998). In Japan, emissions rose by 30 million tons, or 8.9%, between 1990-1996 alone (Environment Agency, 1998).

The roots of this alarming level of environmental degradation lie, to a significant extent, in the mechanistic world view which continues to prevail in modern society. This world view, which arose in the 16th century and was expanded upon by great scientist-philosophers like Descartes and Newton, holds that the world can be seen as a "multitude of separate objects assembled into a huge machine" (Capra, 1982). Problems occurring in such a world can be solved by breaking them up into fragments and addressing these fragments individually. Following this school of thought, separate pieces of legislation and institutions have been created to address supposedly unrelated problems.

In an age of increasing economic and political globalization and increasingly shared environmental problems, however, this way of thinking is more inappropriate than ever. Crucial linkages between the environment and poverty, gender equity and other socio-economic issues often go largely unaddressed in both policy development and implementation. More specifically, a failure to create linkages between environmental problems has led to piecemeal approaches to environmental degradation, overlaps and gaps in monitoring and reporting mechanisms, waste of funds, failures in communication, and a myriad of other problems.

The following chapter focuses on the present fragmented approach toward environmental problems, particularly climate change and the loss of biodiversity. It begins with a discussion on the importance of building synergies between multilateral environmental agreements such as the CBD and the UNFCCC. It then points out five key areas where the lack of synergy between the CBD and the UNFCCC is evident and briefly discusses the reasons behind this state of affairs. Finally, it suggests possible actions that could be taken to strengthen the links between the Conventions and bring about a more holistic approach to environmental conservation. Many of these actions can take place by building on strengths inherent in the Conventions or their implementing bodies. Though the focus is on 'synergizing' the UNFCCC and the CBD, the proposed solutions may very well be applicable to the numerous other environmental agreements and conventions in existence, particularly the United Nations Convention to Combat Desertification (CCD).

The importance of synergies

In the 1970s and 1980s, synergies among multilateral environmental agreements and their implementing agencies were generally sought in order to promote more efficient use of resources, to further internal policy coordination, and to avoid environmental impacts across sectors (Kimball, 1999). However, it has been argued that in the 1990s two additional rationales have been added to the above three: the need to ensure that the commitments of governments to implement a wide range of environmental agreements are not contradictory, and that these environmental agreements both contribute to sustainable development and enhanced international trade (Kimball, 1999).

While all of these are important factors, this chapter focuses on the need to ensure that the CBD and the UNFCCC jointly promote the conservation of the earth's biological diversity and the stabilization of atmospheric greenhouse gas concentrations in the context of sustainable development. Where synergies in negotiations, data gathering, project implementation and other areas advance this goal, they should be pursued. Synergies that do not clearly advance this goal, should not, however, as the considerable financial and human resource commitments needed to establish coordinated mechanisms could perhaps be used to better effect elsewhere (Hyvarinen, 1999).

Synergy gaps

A lack of synergy between the United Nations Frame-work Convention on Climate Change and the Convention on Biological Diversity is evident in the timing and interpretation of the scientific research underpinning the conventions, the process by which the conventions were drawn up, the content of the resulting conventions, the implementation of the conventions, and the direction taken in the negotiations for further protocols to the conventions.

The science

The scientific links between climate change and biodiversity loss have become increasingly well understood over the past decade. Already in 1987, Our Common Future, the report of the World Commission on Environment and Development, acknowledged these links. Though it presented no in-depth analysis of the matter, the report noted that "[widespread climate changes] will produce considerable stress for all ecosystems, making it particularly important that natural diversity be maintained as a means of adaptation" (WCED, 1987). A World Wildlife Fund-sponsored Conference on the Consequences of the Greenhouse Effect for Biological Diversity, held in October 1988, was the first major conference to focus specifically on the impact of global warming on natural ecosystem conservation. One of its objectives was to ensure that scientific study as well as policy discussions on global warming would focus adequate attention on natural ecosystems (Peters and Lovejoy, 1992). In addition, the Intergovernmental Panel on Climate Change (IPCC), the world's most influential body of researchers on climate change, stressed the impact that climatic change would have on terrestrial and marine ecosystems in its 1990 Impacts Assessment and again in its 1995 Second Assessment Report.

Country level studies have also gone far to elucidate linkages between climate change and biodiversity. In Japan, for instance, the effects of climate change on the marine environment are likely to be severe. According to a model developed by the Meteorological Agency, the doubling of atmospheric CO_2 concentrations from their 1990 level will result in a $1.6°C$ rise in sea surface temperatures along the Japan Sea Coast, and a 20 - 40 cm rise in sea level. The Environment Agency calculates that a 30 cm sea level rise would result in the loss of 57% of Japan's sandy beaches (Environment Agency, 1997). This, in turn, would result in serious habitat loss for many species of shellfish, sea weed, sea turtle, and shore bird. The impact of climate change on Japan's terrestrial environment is also likely to be severe. The Environment Agency estimates that a $3°C$ rise in temperature over the 21th century would necessitate a 500 km shift in latitude or 500 m shift in altitude for the country's ecosystems. There are many factors determining the success of such a shift, from competition with existing species to urban development (Environment Agency, 1997) to the adaptability of individual species (Peters and Myers, 1992).

Finally, thematic studies have shed considerable light on the links between climate change and biodiversity. Studies of wetlands have been particularly fruitful in this regard. Hydrological changes resulting from climate change may lead to the lowering of water levels in wetlands, with serious implications for biodiversity in these areas and possible further climate impacts. Wetlands, as a whole, are a larger carbon reservoir than tropical forests and have the potential to release massive amounts of carbon into the atmosphere as a result of lowered water levels and soil oxidation (Parish and Looi, 1999). Studies of coral reefs also suggest that the impact of climate change on the biological diversity of these ecosystems will be negative (IUCN, 1998).

While much of this knowledge regarding the links between biodiversity loss and climate change existed already in the late 1980s, it played only a limited role in the drafting of the UNFCCC and the CBD. In part this was because of the timing of scientific research, particularly in the case of the CBD. While the UNFCCC was drafted on the basis of interdisciplinary research conducted by the IPCC, the drafters of the CBD had no such scientific body to which to refer. It was not until after the adoption of the CBD that UNEP launched a two and a half year project resulting in the Global Biodiversity Assessment. It can be argued that the very limited references to climate change in the CBD result from this fact.

The process

The CBD and the UNFCCC were drafted during essentially the same period, but in relative isolation from each other.

The Convention on Biological Diversity

In the early 1980s, international experts began to call for an overarching convention to protect biodiversity. The idea was first discussed at the Third World Conference on National Parks in 1982 in Bali, Indonesia (Holdgate, 1999). Work on the CBD within the UN system began in earnest in 1987 when the UNEP Governing Council recognized a need to consolidate existing instruments and streamline various efforts to protect biodiversity. An *ad hoc* working group was set up to this end and, at its first meeting in Nairobi in November 1988, examined the possibility of consolidating more topic-specific conventions such as the Convention on International Trade in Endangered Species of Wild Fauna and Flora (CITES), the Convention concerning the Protection of the World Cultural and Natural Heritage (World Heritage Convention), and the International Convention on Wetlands (Ramsar Convention) under one umbrella convention. The group concluded that this would not be effective, and decided in 1990 that a framework convention addressing the conservation of biodiversity as a global environmental issue should be established.

The *ad hoc* working group went on to prepare various elements to be included in a convention using work done by IUCN-The World Conservation Union as well as the Food and Agriculture Organization. On this basis, the UNEP Secretariat and a small group of legal experts prepared the first draft of the Biodiversity Convention. In February 1991, a formal negotiating process began, and the UNEP working group was renamed the Intergovernmental Negotiating Committee for a Convention on Biological Diversity (INC). Meetings of the *ad hoc* group and the INC continued over four years, and the last meeting of the INC was held in May 1991 in Nairobi, just before the Earth Summit.

The original purpose of the convention was the conservation of the earth's ecosystems, species, and genetic diversity, but the creation of such a convention proved difficult in practice. Debate surrounding biotechnology, in particular, was polarized. Industrialized countries wanted intellectual property rights over genetic resources they had developed. Developing countries, on the other hand, insisted that since those resources are predominately found in developing nations, it is not the North which should have claim to intellectual property rights, but the South's sovereign right to control the use of their own genetic resources (Domoto, 1995). In order to address these points of contention, a number of provisions relating to biotechnology and use of genetic resources were added to the draft. Negotiations concerning conservation also shifted to sustainable use. With these changes, the draft of the Convention was adopted and thereby made available for signature at the Earth Summit in June, 1992.

The United Nations Framework Convention on Climate Change

One of the first comprehensive reports addressing global environmental issues was commissioned by US President Carter. The resulting Global 2000 Report to the President of the US was published in 1980 and provided a comprehensive overview of current problems and future trends. In the context of a chapter on the importance of synergies, it is important to note that this report pointed out the links between population, resources, and the environment, and indicated that projections regarding each of these must take into consideration the manner in which they are connected.

In its discussion of climate change, the report outlined three possible scenarios. The first assumed that temperatures would change at the same rate as they had for the past 30 years. The second assumed that temperatures would change at a faster rate, and the third assumed they would change at a slower rate (Barney, 1980). Gradually, it came to be thought that the second scenario of rapid global warming given in The Global 2000 Report was most likely, and the issue was taken up in the United States thanks to the efforts of key senators from both major parties.

At the same time in Europe, a large population of seals suddenly died along the Baltic Sea, and in South America large areas of tropical forest were destroyed. These factors contributed to an increasing concern for the environment in Europe. It was in this context that *Our Common Future* was released, bringing global recognition to the "risks of global warming" (WCED, 1987) and to the wider concept of sustainable development.

The first time extensive discussion on the threats of global warming formally occurred was at a meeting of a group of scientists in Villach, Austria in 1985. In 1987, the Bellagio Conference was held in Italy involving both scientists and policy makers who began discussion on measures necessary to stop global warming. Immediately after the G7 Summit in Toronto in 1988, the Canadian government organized another international conference where scientists and policy makers met in their individual capacities and continued the discussion on ways to prevent the progression of global warming. Participants agreed to make efforts to reduce CO_2 emissions by 20% of 1988 levels. The Toronto conference was given wide coverage by the media (Takeuchi, 1998), and contributed greatly to public awareness regarding the issue.

In the same year, the IPCC was established, with Professor Bert Bolin of the University of Stockholm as its first Chairperson. In 1990, the IPCC issued its first Assessment Reports which formed the foundation for intergovernmental negotiations. Parallel to this, an intergovernmental negotiating committee began work on drafting the UNFCCC with Jan Ripert as Chairperson.

Debate on climate change also took place at the highest political level. At the invitation of the USS's President Gorbachev, Foreign Minister Shevardnaze proposed to the UN General Assembly that a new organization on global environment such as an "Environment Council" be established. In 1989, France's Mitterand worked with the Dutch Prime Minister Lubbers and completed the Noordwijk Declaration. In the same year, the UNEP Governing Council decided to begin negotiations for a Framework Convention on Climate Change. Japan, led by its Ministry of International Trade and Industry and joined by the US, then the Soviet Union, China, and the UK, opposed the setting of numerical targets in the Convention, arguing that such targets would need to be set by the IPCC and could not be determined politically (Takeuchi, 1998).

Between 1991 and 1992, six meetings of the INC were held, during which Europe, in particular, showed strong leadership. This, combined with scientific backup and public support, allowed for the completion of the UNFCCC in two years, in time for submission to the Earth Summit.

The content

Though the two conventions were drafted separately, it should be noted that neither the UNFCCC nor the CBD completely ignore the synergies between climate change and biodiversity loss. The UNFCCC already in Article 2 notes that greenhouse gas concentrations should be reduced "within a time-frame sufficient to allow ecosystems to adapt naturally to climate change...". The Preamble and Articles 1 and 4, as well, make specific references to the need to protect ecosystems from changes in climate, and the need to prepare natural systems to adapt to climate change. Article 1, for example, defines "adverse effects of climate change" as "changes in the physical environ-ment or biota resulting from climate change which have significant deleterious effects on the composi-tion, resilience or productivity of natural and managed ecosystems or on the operation of socio-economic systems or on human health and welfare". The Convention also implicitly recognizes the impact that alteration of natural ecosystems can have on the climate, and thus calls for the promotion of sustai-nable management and conservation of ecosystems that act as sinks and reservoirs for greenhouse gases (Article 4 (d)). *The CBD,* though not referring to climate change specifically, does call for integrated planning (Article 6) and the monitoring of activities likely to have impacts on conservation (Article 7). These statements could be interpreted to include climate change impacts.

National and regional action plans, legislation, public education, reporting and other requirements included in the two conventions, however, do not specify any integrated approach to climate change and biodiversity loss. Thus, for instance, the Government of Japan's *First National Report under the Convention on Biological Diversity* contains not a single reference - either direct or indirect - to the impact of climate change on the country's flora and fauna. The report does not even mention the potentially serious impact of sea level rise in its treatment of biodiversity in coastal areas (Government of Japan, 1997).

The implementation

Given the fragmented approach of the two conven-tions to climate change and biodiversity loss, it should come as little surprise that their implementation has not been marked by integrated approaches to the two issues. At the international level, the problem is exacerbated by the location of the two secretariats on different continents: the UNFCCC Secretariat is in Bonn (Germany) and the CBD Secretariat is in Montreal (Canada). Furthermore, the Conferences of the Parties to these conventions are separate and have entirely separate timetables. At the national level, the implementation of the two conventions is often the responsibility of different ministries, or at best different departments within one ministry, making cooperation difficult. In Japan the national focal points for the UNFCCC and the CBD are both located within the Environment Agency. However, the former is located within the Global Environment Department of the Planning and Coordination Bureau, while the latter is in the Nature Conservation Bureau. Communication and personnel exchange between these two areas of the Environment Agency is limited.

As a result of such fragmentation, there has been a failure in most countries to re-evaluate existing policies and laws from a perspective which holistically considers the relationship between climate change and biodiversity. In this regard, it is instructive to look at Japan's failure to re-evaluate key pieces of legislation in response to its ratification of the CBD. At the time of ratification, a number of domestic laws were inconsistent with the Convention and should have been amended. There was (and still is), for example, a clause which exempts many public works projects from the country's Species Preservation Law. Thus, agricultural development and infrastructure projects which threaten endangered species have often taken precedence over affected species, rendering the law ineffective.

During two parliamentary committee meetings, the author - who is also a member of the House of Councillors - insisted upon the necessity of revising legislation like the Species Preservation Law in order to comply with the CBD. In the end, however, despite Article 6 (b) of the Convention, which states that each contracting party "shall integrate, as far as possible and as appropriate, the conservation and sustainable use of biological diversity into relevant sectional or cross-sectional plans, programmes and policies", such revision of domestic law was declared inappropriate. Given this experience with the CBD, it is clear that an holistic revision of existing legislation in light of the CBD and the UNFCCC remains both a pressing priority and a serious political challenge.

The follow-up

Negotiations that have taken place subsequent to the signing of the conventions have focused so as to widen the gap between them. This is especially obvious in the negotiations on protocols to each convention. The protocols have not been the result of an holistic approach to the environment, but of priority placed on protecting national interests.

In the case of the UNFCCC, the Kyoto Protocol focuses largely on numerical targets and flexibility mechanisms such as emissions trading and the Clean Development Mechanism. In addition, its definition of sinks - namely, "direct human-induced land-use changes and forestry activities, limited to afforestation, reforestation and deforestation since 1990" (Article 3.3) - and provisions allowing for the subtraction of carbon dioxide absorbed by these sinks from a country's actual emissions to produce a net emissions figure are particularly problematic from a biodiversity perspective. Under this definition of sinks, countries with existing tropical forests are given no incentive to conserve these forests, but do stand to benefit financially from planting fast growing plantations (UNU/GEIC/IAS 1998). The potential negative impact of this provision on biodiversity is clear.

Negotiations on the first protocol to the CBD, known as the Cartagena Protocol on Biosafety, were similarly narrow and focused exclusively on the transboundary movement of Living Modified Organisms. Perhaps as a result of their narrowness and failure to take into sufficient consideration related environmental and socio-economic considerations (Egziabher, 1999), no final agreement could be reached on the wording of a protocol during February 1999 negotiations in Cartagena, Columbia. The Biosafety Protocol was not adopted until January 2000 in Montreal, Canada. In short, while targets for emissions reductions and rules for the movement of LMOs are extremely important, the failure to create synergy in the follow-up to the two conventions greatly limits their effectiveness.

Building synergies

The challenges involved in integrating the implementation of the UNFCCC and the CBD are immense. Nonetheless, there are important strengths that can be built upon to synergize the Conventions and ensure that they begin to function jointly for the protection of both the atmosphere and the biosphere in the context of sustainable development.

The science

The existence of the IPCC, which provides constant up-to-date scientific information upon which sound policy on climate change can be based, is a boon to the UNFCCC. To strengthen the scientific underpinnings of the CBD, the creation of a scientific body similar to the IPCC, but focused on biological diversity, is an idea worthy of consideration. This idea was first put forward on a formal basis in 1992 in the Global Biodiversity Strategy. The Strategy called for "a mechanism such as an International Panel on Biodiversity Conservation, including scientists, non-governmental organizations, and policy-makers to provide guidance on priorities for the protection, understanding, and sustainable and equitable use of biodiversity" (VGBF, 1999). Were such a body to be created, a system institutionalizing information exchange between it and the IPCC should be put in place.

In the interim, fuller use could be made of the Global Biodiversity Forum (GBF), a forum established by the 1994 General Assembly of the IUCN- World Conservation Union in order to "analyze and debate ecological, economic, institutional and social issues to further the development and implementation of the Convention on Biological Diversity" (Resolution 19.36). The Global Biodiversity Forum has been held in conjunction with meetings of the Conferences of the Parties of the CBD, UNFCCC, CITES, and the Ramsar Convention as well as on other occasions, and has played a significant role in promoting scientific and policy discussion on the inter-linkages between multilateral environmental agreements. Its role and impact could be expanded by ensuring that its participants include scientists, policymakers, and NGO representatives, and by encouraging discussion and the exchange of ideas between these groups.

The content

In the Framework Convention on Climate Change, there are a significant number of references to ecosys-tem impacts and the need for mitigating these. The Convention on Biological Diversity, however, contains no explicit reference to climate change. The inadequacy of the latter Convention in this area needs to be recognized and addressed. Parties to both Conventions must be encouraged to consider the implications for biodiversity of decisions made regarding climate change policy and visa versa. Such consideration must occur in the context of the quest for sustainable development. This would be an incentive for cooperation and information exchange between ministries, NGOs and local communities - both in industrialized and developing countries - involved in climate change and biodiversity- related policy development and implementation.

The implementation

On the level of implementation, more coordination of effort is needed at both the international and national levels. At the international level, for instance, the coordination of reporting requirements among the convention secretariats would provide for more efficient use of time and resources and would ensure that the links between climate change and biodiversity loss were better recognized by the relevant govern-ment ministries and agencies. The World Conserva-tion Monitoring Centre in the UK has already done a feasibility study to identify opportunities for harmonizing information management amongst five biodiversity related agreements (Harrison and Collins, 1999). A similar study could be undertaken for the CBD and UNFCCC. Delegates to the Expert Meeting on Synergies among the Conventions, convened by the United Nations Development Program in Sede Boqer, Israel in early 1997 suggested that coordination could be facilitated if the Conference of the Parties (COPs) of the various conventions instruct their secretariats to work together (UNDP, 1997). This suggestion was taken up in May 1998 at COP4 of the CBD. There, Parties requested the CBD Executive Secretary to strengthen relations with the UNFCCC and the Kyoto Protocol (Parish and Looi, 1999). The GEF is also in a position to promote synergies as it is the key funding mechanism for both conventions.

At the national level, delegates to the 11th Global Biodiversity Forum held in Buenos Aires in November 1998 noted in their Summary Report that implementation would be enhanced if responsibility for implementation and compliance were to reside in the same institution of government, particularly if that institution had strong lines of communication with other parts of government and to the society at large. In the short term, this could be difficult to achieve, as ministries are sometimes in competition or more interested in one convention than others. These problems could be mitigated in part by ensuring that regular exchanges take place between ministries. In the long term, the formation of a national committee or even the creation of a single institution with authority over both the UNFCCC and the CBD (and possibly other conventions, such as the UN Convention to Combat Desertification) could be envisioned.

In Japan, for instance, the Inter-ministerial Coordinating Committee to the CBD could be a model upon which to base a UNFCCC/CBD Coordinating Committee. The Inter-ministerial Coordinating Committee to the CBD, established in January 1994 to promote the implementation of the CBD, is comprised of Directors-General or officials of an equivalent rank from all Ministries and Agencies with jurisdiction over the conservation and sustainable use of biological diversity. It was largely responsible for drafting the country's National Strategy for the Implementation of the CBD

(Government of Japan, 1997). In one sense the Coordinating Committee has been a negative force, as it has allowed the Ministry of Construction and other traditionally 'anti-environmental' ministries to pull discussion down to the lowest common denominator. At the same time, however, it has made such ministries aware of 'biodiversity', forcing them to actually read the Convention and to consider it when planning projects. Bearing in mind the weaknesses of the present Coordinating Committee, a similar UNFCCC/CBD Coordinating Committee, perhaps established so that the present Inter-ministerial Coordinating Committee to the CBD becomes a sub-committee to it, could be envisioned.

The benefits of a coordinated approach could be significant for both biodiversity protection and climate change mitigation. It would, for example, increase the probability of climate change being taken into account in the selection and management of protected areas. As protected areas will need to adapt to climate change, the potential impacts of climate change will need to be taken into consideration (McNeely, 1997). One way to do this would be to ensure that corridors are maintained between protected areas to allow wildlife to migrate in response to climate change.

Protected areas could also be specifically designed to both conserve habitat and serve as a carbon offset. An example of such an approach is the Noel Kempff Mercado pilot carbon offset project in Bolivia which extends the Noel Kempff Mercado National Park by 634,000 ha and is designed to both preserve the region's biodiversity and function as a sink for greenhouse gases (Nelson, 1997). Projects like this which address both biodiversity and climate change concerns would likely become more common were UNFCCC/CBD Coordinating Committees to become a standard feature in countries that are signatories to both agreements.

The follow-up

Though the Kyoto Protocol and the Cartagena Protocol on Biosafety have been extremely important follow-up activities to the UNFCCC and the CBD respectively, future discussion on these protocols as well as the negotiation of any new protocols need to explicitly address the links between biodiversity loss and climate change. Without such synergized follow-up, the Conventions will not be able to move beyond piecemeal responses.

National governments can promote synergized follow-up by coordinating the positions of relevant national authorities involved in international negotiations on linked issues (Hyvarinen, 1999). If these national authorities operate transparently and draw upon the expertise of non-governmental organizations and local communities, the positions which they go on to argue at the international level will also likely reflect more accurately the inherent linkages between environmental problems and the social and economic spheres in which they occur. And these are, ultimately, the linkages that need to be addressed (McNeely, 1995).

Conclusion

Biodiversity loss and climate change are inextricably linked in the natural environment, particularly in climatically sensitive ecosystems. The legacy of the mechanistic world view, however, has resulted in piecemeal approaches to these problems. The two conventions that now exist to address climate change and biodiversity loss, namely the Framework Convention on Climate Change and the Convention on Biological Diversity, are sadly not designed to address the interface between the two problems. Greater synergy is needed between the science, content, implementation of, and follow-up to these two conventions. In the absence of an holistic approach, it is unlikely that the UNFCCC and the CBD will truly be able to help bring about the now desperately needed balance between development and environmental protection and conservation.

References

Barney, G. O. 1980. *The Global 2000 Report to the President of the U.S: Entering the 21st Century.* Pergamon, New York.

Capra, F. 1982. *The Turning Point: Science, Society, and the Rising Culture.* Simon and Schuster, New York.

Domoto, A. 1995. *Biodiversity.* Iwanami Shoten, Tokyo. (in Japanese)

Egziabher, T. B. G. 1999. Of power affirmed to men and of safety denied to life. Third World Resurgence, No. 106: 2-3.

Environment Agency. 1997. *Environment White*

Paper. Tokyo. (in Japanese).

Global Biodiversity Forum 11. 1998. Workshop on coordinating national strategies and action plans under the UNFCCC, the CBD, and the UNCCD (Summary Report). Buenos Aires, Argentina. November 1998.

Glowka, L., F. Burhenne-Guilmin, et al. 1994. *A Guide to the Convention on Biological Diversity. Environmental Policy and Law Paper* No.30. IUCN Environmental Law Centre.

Government of Japan. 1997. The first national report under the convention on biological diversity. www.biodiv.org/natrep/Japan/Japan.pdf

Harrison, J. and M. Collins. 1999. Harmonizing the information management infrastructure for biodiversity-related treaties. Background paper for Inter-linkages: International Conference on Synergies and Coordination between Multilateral Environmental Agreements, United Nations University, Tokyo, Japan, 14 - 16 July 1999.

Holdgate, M. 1999. *The Green Web: A Union for World Conservation*. Earthscan Publications, London.

Hyvarinen, J. 1999. Synergies and co-ordination of international instruments in the area of oceans and seas. Background paper for Inter-Linkages: International Conference on Synergies and Coordination between Multilateral Environmental Agreements, United Nations University, Tokyo, Japan, 14 - 16 July 1999.

IPCC. 1995. *Climate Change: The Science of Climate Change*. Contribution of Working Group I to the Second Assessment Report of the Intergovernmental Panel on Climate Change.

IUCN-The World Conservation Union. 1998. Coral Reefs Dying from Heat-Stroke. Press Release.

Kimball, L. A. 1999. Institution linkages among multilateral environmental agreements: a structured approach based on scale and function. Background paper for Inter-Linkages: International Conference on Synergies and Coordination between Multilateral Environmental Agreements, United Nations University, Tokyo, Japan, 14 - 16 July 1999.

McNeely, J. A. 1995. Strange bedfellows: why science and policy don't mesh, and what can be done about it. Presented to Living Planet in Crisis: Biodiversity Science and Policy, American Museum of Natural History, New York City, 9 - 10 March 1995.

McNeely, J. A. 1997. Linking the biodiversity and climate change conventions. Report of the Ninth Global Biodiversity Forum, Kyoto, Japan, 20 - 23.

Nelson, T. 1997. Bolivia: Noel Koempff Mercado climate action project. Report of the Ninth Global Biodiversity Forum, Kyoto, Japan, 31 - 32.

Parish, F. and C. C. Looi. 1999. Options and needs for enhanced linkage between the Ramsar Convention on Wetlands, Convention on Biological Diversity and UN Framework Convention on Climate Change. Background paper for Inter-Linkages: International Conference on Synergies and Coordination between Multilateral Environmental Agreements, United Nations University, Tokyo, Japan, 14-16 July 1999.

Peters, Robert L. and Thomas E. Lovejoy (eds.). 1992. *Global Warming and Biological Diversity*. Yale University Press, New Haven.

Peters, R. L. and J. P. Myers. 1992. Preserving biodiversity in a changing climate. Issues in Science and Technology, vol. VIII (no.2): 66 - 72.

Takeuchi, K. 1998. *The Politics of Global Warming*. Asahi Shinbunsha, Tokyo. (in Japanese)

UNU/GEIC/IAS. 1998. Global climate governance: a report on the inter-linkages between the Kyoto Protocol and other multilateral regimes.

UNDP. 1997. Synergies in National Implementation: The Rio Agreements.

Virtual Global Biodiversity Forum (VGBF). 1999. What is GBF? http://real.geog.ucsb.edu/vgbf/information.html.

Watson, R. et al. 1998. *Protecting Our Planet, Securing Our Future*. UNEP, NASA, World Bank.

World Commission on Environment and Development (WCED). 1987. *Our Common Future*. Oxford University Press, Oxford.

Chapter 2

Global Climate Change and Biodiversity

Richard B. Primack

Over the 21st century, as much as 10% to 20% of the world's species may go extinct as a result of human activities. Until recently, the threats to species were primarily local in nature; over-harvesting of species in one place or the destruction of a habitat in another place. Being local in nature, the methods for dealing with threats to species were local in nature also, such as setting up a nature reserve or stopping a local source of pollution. Global climate change differs from these threats to biological diversity in several regards. First, global climate change will affect every species and biological community in the world in some way (Gates, 1993). Second, dealing with the problem requires co-operation among nations on a scale rarely seen in international relations. And third, because greenhouse gases reside in the atmosphere for many years, when global climate change begins to affect many biological communities, it will take at least several decades for the atmosphere to be restored. There has been considerable debate about global climate change, whether or not it has started, whether it will be a serious problem, and what we should do about it.

What are the facts?

1. Carbon dioxide levels have risen dramatically over the 19th century as a result of burning of fossil fuels by people (IPCC, 1996). CO_2 levels will continue to rise at least into the 21st century due to a continued use of these fuels.
2. Plants respond to changing CO_2 levels as shown by numerous greenhouse studies. Because CO_2 is taken up in plants through the photosynthetic process and is often in short supply, rising CO_2 levels will change plant communities in predictable and unpredictable ways (Bazzaz and Fajer, 1992).
3. Rising temperatures and higher CO_2 concentrations have already resulted in a longer growing season and greater productivity in boreal environments (Myeni et al., 1997).
4. In temperate areas, detailed phenological studies have documented earlier flowering in the spring (Birdlife International and WWF, 1997). Tropical forests appear to be in flux, with higher rates of tree death and recruitment than occurred previously. In alpine areas, species appear to be migrating higher on slopes as conditions warm.
5. Global warming is also affecting the ocean, as seen by reduction in the polar ice caps and rising sea water levels throughout the world. Studies of the ocean show that despite its vast volume, it is also affected by global climate patterns. Past glacial periods have reduced marine biological diversity.

The changes that have already occurred, including rising temperatures, rising CO_2 levels, altered patterns of plant phenology and growth, plant migrations, and an altered marine environment, will continue into the 21st century and may even accelerate.

Many threats to biological diversity

Global climate change is just one of many assaults to the integrity of biological communities (Vitousek, 1994; Meyer, 1996). All of these threats need to be dealt with and some are far more immediate and threatening than global climate change.

Habitat destruction. Certain habitats that are rich in species are being destroyed at a tremendous rate by direct human intervention (Meyer and Turner, 1994). These include tropical forests, temperate grasslands, freshwater wetlands, such as lakes, rivers, and swamps, coastal marine environments, such as coral reefs, mangroves, and estuaries. Protecting examples of these communities as nature reserves and restoring degraded habitats are immediate needs.

Degradation. Biological communities are often gradually degraded by human activities. Industrial and residential areas produce acid rain and other forms of air pollution. Water pollution is often a result of fertiliser runoff from lawns and agricultural areas and of sewage from residential areas. Factories, agriculture, mining, and other human activities can release toxic chemicals such as pesticides, herbicides, and toxic metals. Pollution control is the obvious, but expensive, way of dealing with these threats to the environment.

Fragmentation. As a result of human activities, such as road building, residential development, agriculture, and industrial activities, what was formerly a large, continuous expanse of habitat becomes divided into smaller fragments. These smaller habitat fragments are often drier, hotter, and windier than large expanses of similar habitat, and the migration of animals across the landscape is inhibited. As a result, these fragments gradually lose species that are not replaced.

Over-harvesting. People are removing far more of the natural world for our use than is produced each year. As a result, huge numbers of species are threatened with extinction. Examples of over-harvesting include tropical fish for the aquarium trade, tigers and bears for traditional medicines, orchids, cacti, and other unusual plants for horticulturists, and parrots and other exotic animals for the pet trade (Hemley, 1994). Entire seas are being stripped of animals to supply our diets with seafood, while poor people in tropical areas eat every animal that they can shoot, trap or net. We now have the phenomenon of the "empty forest;" the trees are still there, but the animals have been removed. Over-harvesting includes having too many domestic animals, such as cattle, sheep, and goats on rangelands, resulting in the loss of vegetation, massive soil erosion, and the degradation of the biological and physical environment.

Introduced species. In many cases, species have been introduced deliberately or accidentally, outside of their natural range, by human activities. Introduced plants and animals have frequently taken over in their new location, displacing and eliminating the native species (Vitousek et al., 1996). One example is the brown tree snake, which has eliminated most of the native bird species since its introduction to Guam.

Disease. Many rare and endangered species have become susceptible to disease. In some cases, environmental stress caused by habitat destruction and degradation have made the native species more susceptible to disease. In other cases, new diseases have come in with introduced species, spreading to native species and killing them in the process.

These factors have a powerful impact on biological diversity, not only by themselves, but in synergy with each other. For example, a species living in a degraded environment will often be more susceptible to competition from exotic species and to disease. Global climate change will increase the vulnerability of species to these threats.

How will global climate change affect biological diversity?

Rising CO_2 levels will completely restructure biological communities. CO_2 is necessary for photosynthesis and is sometimes in short supply. As carbon dioxide levels rise, plant species that can use the increased supply to grow more rapidly will increase in abundance within their communities, while other species will decline in abundance. Animal populations will similarly change, as many species of insects are specialised for feeding on a particular plant species. The relative abundance of species in a community will change, and it is probable that many rare species will go locally extinct.

CO_2 levels will not be the only challenge that plants face. Increasing levels of ozone at ground level, increasing UV light caused by high-altitude ozone depletion, continuing acid rain, and atmospheric nitrogen deposition will also rearrange biological communities. While some species may increase in abundance, other species will not be able to tolerate the new conditions. Many species which are sensitive to acidity, excess nitrogen, UV light, or ozone will be lost. Global climate change will result in increased temperatures over much of the earth's surface, particularly in more temperate and polar latitudes. In addition to the overall warming, there will be a greater number of extreme events, such as hurricanes, intense rainstorms, heavy snowstorms, and periods of intense summer heat (Karl et al., 1997). Many areas of the world will become wetter or drier than they currently are.

As conditions change, protected areas that currently exist will lose species, as many species will no longer be able to survive at that place. Species adapted to a moist, mild summer environment may not be able to tolerate a drier, hotter summer. Species adapted to moderate snow levels may not be able to survive if rain falls instead. Protected areas established to protect particular rare species may not be effective at protecting those species any longer.

As global climate changes, species will tend to migrate to conditions that are more suitable for them. For many animals, the mode of this migration is direct: they can walk, fly or swim. For plants, migration is more passive and random; the wind blows the seeds, animals eat fruits and deposit seeds elsewhere, and water carries seeds along. In response to increasing temperatures and changing rainfall patterns, species will tend to migrate toward the poles and up the slopes of mountains in order to remain within the same optimum environmental conditions for the species. As species migrate out from an area, other species, more suited to the new conditions and themselves displaced, will migrate in.

In the past, species migrated in response to periods of global warming and cooling associated with episodes of glaciation. Why can't species do it now, just as they did in the past? The reason is that the environmental changes associated with this present global climate change will be ten times faster than the changes associated with past glacial episodes. The species of today have never faced such rapid changes, and it is doubtful if many of them could migrate fast enough to keep pace with the changing climate.

Also, human activities create many barriers to species migration. Whereas species may have formerly migrated across plains or forested regions, they are now halted by impassable human barriers, such as roads, canals, farmland, ranches, plantations, mining sites, and residential areas. Potential future migration patterns will be most severely disrupted where there is only a narrow migration corridor intensively broken up by human activities. For example, coastal areas are often densely settled by people, presenting many effective barriers to species migration. River valleys aligned north to south may have formerly been effective dispersal routes but may now be blocked by farmland.

Species at risk

Some species that are effective at long-distance dispersal will be able to migrate in response to global climate change, particularly migrating birds. But certain types of species will be vulnerable to an altered climate:

Isolated species. Species which occur in small, distinctive habitats may not be able to migrate out of those habitats because of the surrounding inhospitable habitat. Species that occur on isolated mountain peaks, in lakes, in desert oases, and on unusual mineral outcrops, may be vulnerable. Species that occur on islands are extreme examples of species that will likely die off if the climate changes rapidly; many island species have lost their dispersal ability, and exotic species may thrive under altered conditions. Also, populations of species at the extreme of a species' range may be most susceptible to local extinction. Altered climate conditions may be just sufficient to make the site unsuitable for the species.

Rare species. Species with few individuals may go rapidly extinct within their present range. Such species may not have sufficient numbers of individuals to migrate outwards and locate new suitable sites.

Species with poor dispersal abilities. Many plant species depend on animals for seed dispersal. As bird and mammal species have declined in abundance and even gone extinct in some cases, many plants are no longer effectively dispersed over long-distances. Many ground-dwelling animals, particularly those that live in the soil, such as spiders, beetles, rodents, and salamanders, often have poor dispersal abilities and may be vulnerable to extinction if the climate changes.

Species occupying a specific coastal habitat. As sea levels rise, coastal vegetation will tend to be shifted landward. However, this migration will be blocked by intensively settled zones of human occupation. Extensive areas of coastal habitat will be lost between the rising tide and the dikes erected to keep back the sea.

Species dependent on sea-ice. In polar zones, many species are linked to sea-ice for their survival. The sea-ice provides structure for numerous animals and algae, and is linked to the productivity of the ecosystem. If sea-ice is melted or significantly reduced in area, it could have major impacts on polar habitats.

Global warming may put people and other species into increased competition for survival. People may need to take over more land for agriculture to feed an expanding population or to replace land lost to altered climate. People may need to take over more coastal areas for aquaculture. Yet these same areas may be crucial to the survival of other species. Reconciling these conflicting imperatives will be a great challenge.

What can be done to protect biological diversity from global warming?

At the most basic level, the production of CO_2 and other greenhouse gases needs to be reduced. This may be possible to some extent in fuel-efficient countries with a stable population such as Japan. It is eminently possible in fuel-efficient countries, such as the U.S.A., but not likely due to domestic political considerations, that is a public that wants cheap oil. But it is probably not possible to reduce CO_2 emissions in countries that have increasing populations, such as India, or a high level of economic growth, such as China. In short, if global climate change is caused by rising CO_2 levels, then the climate is going to change and CO_2 levels are going to continue to rise.

Strong efforts to limit CO_2 production will result only in minimising the magnitude of that change. These efforts include requiring (or encouraging) industries to reduce fuel consumption, increasing fuel prices through taxation, improving home insulation, building more fuel-efficient cars, and providing better public transportation. These policies could be readily implemented if the public is willing to accept the need for change. Political leaders and scientists have a responsibility to educate the public on the need for changes.

Over the next few decades, the most immediate threats to biological diversity will continue to be the obvious ones that are driving species to extinction today, in particular habitat destruction and degradation and over-harvesting (Primack, 1998). In addition to planning for the impact of global warming, we need to take strong actions to deal with the immediate threats to biological diversity:

Habitat destruction. Additional protected areas need to be established and then managed effectively. Areas established for production, such as forestry plantations and rangelands, need to be managed with species protection as an important objective. Protecting marine habitats and wetlands deserves a high priority, because they are fragile, poorly understood, and often neglected.

Fragmentation. Habitat fragmentation damages biological diversity. Forces that act to divide up continuous habitat, such as road building and development, should be resisted. Where possible, roads should be closed in conservation areas, and the natural ecological processes re-established. Managers of protected areas should work together with other land-owners, both private and governmental, to protect biological diversity at larger scales, known as ecosystem management or bioregional management.

Pollution. Biological communities are destroyed by pollution. Air and water pollution need to be dramatically reduced. Air pollution not only harms human health, but hurts biological communities. Water pollution needs to be cleaned up by reducing the quantity of sewage and building new sewage treatment facilities. Not only does water pollution damage freshwater systems, but people are increasingly damaging huge areas of the marine environment. Pollution of the environment often makes animals more susceptible to disease and creates conditions suitable for the outbreak of introduced species.

Over-harvesting. Tigers, bears, macaws, tropical orchids, cacti, tropical fish, tuna, and shell-fish, to name only a few, are being over-harvested today to the point where their future existence is in question. Dealing with this unsustainable over-harvesting is an immediate priority, regardless of global warming.

So what to do about global climate change?

By the time global climate change starts to have a serious impact on biological communities, many species may have already been lost. We need to take action to deal with the immediate threats to species and whole communities. While global climate change is an important threat to biological diversity, it should not be used as a ploy or a camouflage to hide the need for immediate action dealing with the immediate problems faced by species.

What actions are needed to protect biological diversity in the face of global climate change ?

1. Continue to acquire protected areas, and expand the size of existing protected areas, because the more populations of a species that are protected, and the larger those populations are, the greater the chance that species will be able to survive somewhere. Where possible, new protected areas should include elevational gradients to allow species to migrate to higher altitudes.

2. Protected areas should be acquired that protect known or possible migration routes of the species. In the Northern Hemisphere, species will need to migrate northward or to higher altitudes to maintain the same environmental condition. North-south corridors that link existing protected areas should be developed. This might involve acquiring small "stepping stone" reserves between existing protected areas.

3. Detailed monitoring programs need to be established in order to track the location and population size of rare and endangered species, as well as critical habitats and ecosystem processes. Such a monitoring system can be used to determine the health of species, and to determine if management actions are needed. Monitoring of the marine environment is particularly critical because migration patterns and ecological processes are poorly understood.

4. Where species appear to be headed toward extinction in the wild, an active conservation program is called for. This may include modifying an existing habitat to better suit the species, or removing competing species, particularly when they are introduced species. The species can also be bred in captivity, and the captive population used to start new populations in the wild. New populations could be started beyond the current range of the species, in areas made suitable by global climate change, particularly at higher elevations and toward the poles.

Conclusion

Global climate change is an enormous problem that will be dealt with by humanity over the next decades and centuries. It requires serious attention on the part of scientists, governments, businesses, and the general public. The global community will need to come together to avoid the potential destruction caused by global climate change. However, we also need to focus our attention on the human activities that are destroying biological diversity right now. If we ignore these immediate threats, then vast numbers of species will be lost over the 21st century regardless of our actions on the issue of global climate change.

Reducing the production of carbon dioxide and other greenhouse gases needs to be linked to monitoring species, biological communities, and ecosystem processes. Field work and monitoring provide the crucial reality check to tell us whether biological diversity is really being protected. New protected areas need to be acquired and managed effectively. Protecting biological diversity needs to be addressed at local, national and international levels. International treaties to reduce carbon dioxide emissions and air pollution need to be written and enforced; governments need to establish new protected areas; and citizens, biologists, and conservation organisations need to watch what is happening in their immediate environment and act in a vigilant and responsible way.

In the end, a clean environment, including clean water, clean air, and clean soil is not only better for protecting the global climate, but it provides immediate help to biological diversity. Also, this healthy environment is better for human health and the quality of life. Cleaner air and water mean less asthma, cancer, and respiratory infections for people, as well as more frogs, trees, birds, dragonflies, wildflowers and fish. It makes sense in both the short-term and the long-term to protect the environment.

References

Bazzaz, F. A. and E. D. Fajer. 1992. Plant life in a CO_2-rich world. Scientific American 266: 68-74.

Bird Life International and WWF. 1997. *Climate Change and Wildlife: a Summary of an International Workshop*. Royal Society for the Protection of Birds, Bedfordshire.

Gates, M. 1993. *Climate Change and its Biological Consequences*. Sinauer Associates, Sunderland, MA.

Hemley, G. (ed.) 1994. *International Wildlife Trade: a CITES Sourcebook*. Island Press, Washington, D.C.

IPCC. 1996. *Climate Change 1995: the Science of Climate Change*. World Meteorological Organisation and United Nations Environmental Program.

Karl, T., N. Nichols, and J. Gregory. 1997. The coming climate. Scientific American 276: 78-83.

Meyer, W. B. 1996. *Human Impact on the Earth*. Cambridge University Press, Cambridge.

Meyer, W. B. and B. L. Turner II. 1994. *Changes in Land Use and Land Cover: a Global Perspective*. Cambridge University Press, Cambridge.

Myeni, R. B., C. D. Keeling, C. J. Tucker, G. Asrar, and R. R. Nemani. 1977. Increased plant growth in the northern high latitudes from 1981 to 1991. Nature 386: 698-702.

Primack, R. 1998. *Essentials of Conservation Biology*. 2nd ed. Sinawuer Associates, Sunderland, MA.

Vitousek, P. M. 1994. Beyond global warming: ecology and global change. Ecology 75: 1861-1876.

Vitousek, P. M., C. M. D'Antonio, L. L. Loope, and R. Westerbrooks. 1996. Biological invasions as global environmental change. American Scientist 84: 468-478.

Chapter 3

Projections Concerning Climate Change

Hiroshi Nirasawa

The influence of global warming on organisms is being assessed through recourse to projections concerning changes in temperature and precipitation. The only method of quantitatively projecting future climatic conditions is a numerical simulation method called a climate model. Climate models have been developed in the United States, Britain, Germany, and Japan.

The Japan Meteorological Agency (JMA) is now publicizing the results of its models under the title "Global Warming Projection" in order to make them easily available to people who are charged with assessing the effects of global warming.

The mechanism of global warming

I will begin by briefly explaining the mechanism that drives this phenomenon (Figure 3.1). The earth is warmed by sunlight, mostly in the form of visible light, and as a result its surface emits infrared radiation into space. Gases such as carbon dioxide (CO_2) and methane (NH_4) are transparent to visible light but strong absorbers of infrared wavelengths, so in the atmosphere these gases absorb infrared radiation emitted from the ground. This absorption warms up the gas molecules, causing them to re-emit radiation at infrared wavelengths. Part of the infrared re-emission is directed downwards, causing further warming of the Earth's surface.

The greenhouse effect itself is not harmful to life on Earth. If the Earth's atmosphere was not subject to any greenhouse effect at all, it has been calculated that the average surface temperature would be around -28°C, a very harsh environment for living organisms. Actually, the average temperature of the earth is around 15°C, which is a suitable environment for the survival of living organisms. Global warming, which is now recognized as a serious problem, is an increase in global temperature caused by the accumulation of greenhouse gases due to human activities.

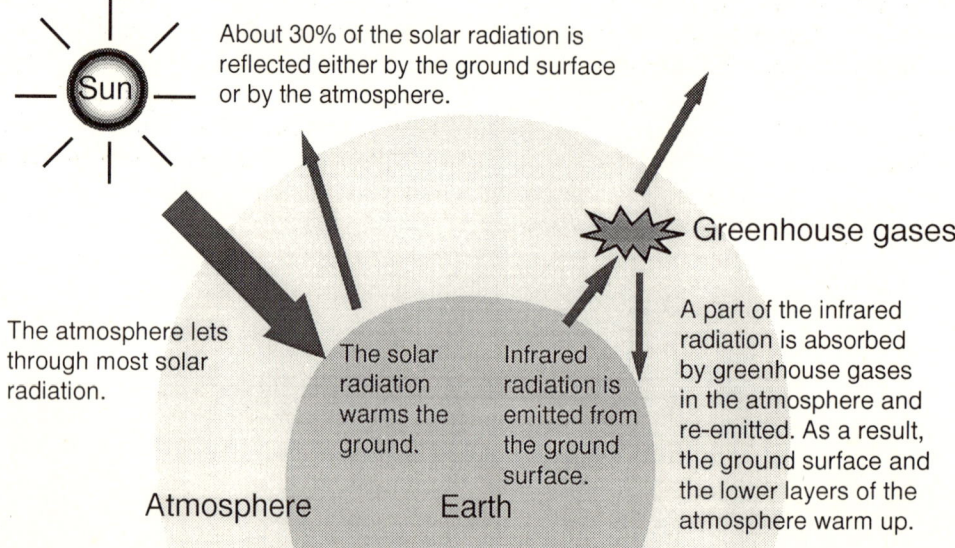

Figure 3.1. General concept of global warming.

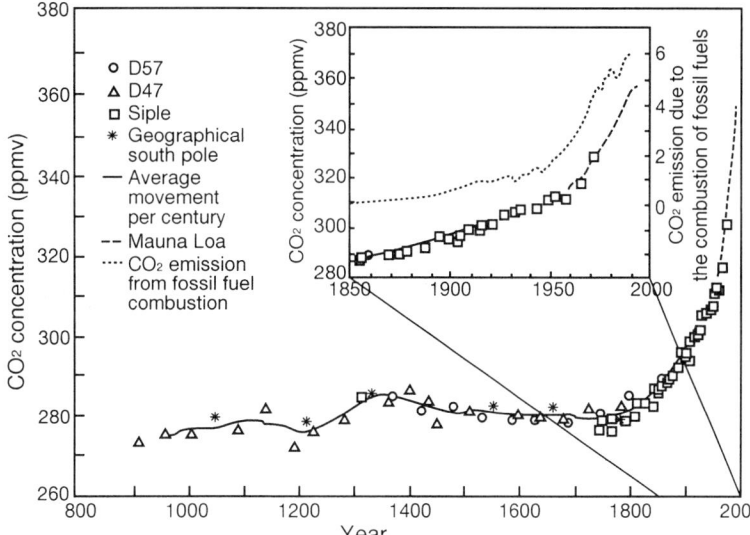

Figure 3.2.
Atmospheric CO_2 concentration over the past 1000 years (IPCC, 1995). D57 (○), D47 (△), Sipl (□), and the geographical south pole (*) are the points where ice was sampled in the Antarctic. The solid line shows the average movement per century based on values from each point. The broken line shows observations made at Mauna Loa, Hawaii (since 1958). The broken line in the magnified graph covering the period from 1850 onwards shows CO_2 emissions due to the combustion of fossil fuels (the unit Gt C/year is equivalent to one billion tons of carbon per annum).

Trends in the atmospheric carbon dioxide concentration

Gases such as CO_2, CH_4, nitrous oxide (N_2O) and halocarbons, which contribute to the greenhouse effect, are known as greenhouse gases. CO_2 has the largest influence on the greenhouse effect on a global scale due to its high concentration in the atmosphere, and consequently a great deal of attention is paid to the trends in its emission and atmospheric concentration.

Figure 3.2 shows historical changes in atmospheric CO_2 concentration based on air contained in Antarctic ice core samples and on atmospheric observations made in Hawaii. Until the late eighteenth century, when the Industrial Revolution began, the atmospheric CO_2 concentration was stable at around 280 ppmv (parts per million volume). Since then, it has risen steadily as a result of human activities such as the combustion of fossil fuels, including coal and oil.

The JMA has been observing the atmospheric concentration of CO_2 at Ryori station in Sanriku Town, Iwate Prefecture, since 1987. The average concentration recorded at this observatory in 1996 was 365.5 ppmv. The average increase over the nine years since observations began has been 1.7 ppmv per annum, which represents an increase of 0.5% per year.

The Intergovernmental Panel on Climate Change (IPCC) was set up in order to make scientific assessments of global warming. The latest report (IPCC, 1996) predicted that if future anthropogenic CO_2 emissions were stabilized at the 1994 level, the atmospheric concentration of CO_2 would continue to rise steadily for at least the next 200 years. By the end of the 21st century it would reach 500 ppmv, a level double that at the start of the Industrial Revolution.

The IPCC has also estimated that if anthropogenic CO_2 emissions were reduced to 1990 levels within 40 years, 110 years, or 240 years, and then further reduced to well below 1990 levels, the resulting atmospheric CO_2 concentration would stabilize at 450, 650, and 1000 ppmv, respectively.

Climate change outlook in the case of an annual 1% rise in atmospheric CO_2 concentration

The projections introduced in this section assume a 1% annual rise in the atmospheric CO_2 concentration over 100 years. In predictive calculations using a climate model, the extent of climate change caused by greenhouse gases other than CO_2 is accounted for by adjusting the CO_2 figure according to the "equivalent CO_2 concentration" of these gases. The 1% annual rise in atmospheric CO_2 concentration, therefore, is the rate of increase in all greenhouse gases.

In order to use the projections obtained by means of the climate model correctly, one important point should be noted. Climate models numerically formulate processes within a system (called the climate system) which is influenced by the atmosphere, oceans, land, snow and ice, and the biosphere, based on physical laws. Further, the climate model is programmed to calculate the future climate such as temperature and precipitation in numerical values. When calculating using computers, the conditions of the atmosphere and ocean, which are naturally continuous, are expressed as physical values (wind direction and velocity, temperature, oceanic current velocity, etc.) at each point on a three-dimensional grid (Figure 3.3). In the climate model used by the JMA, for example, the atmosphere is

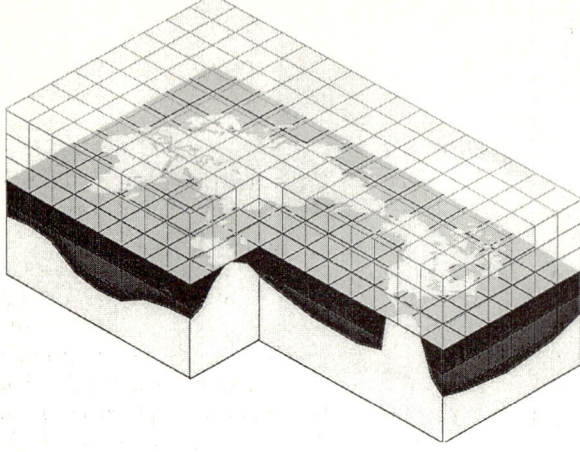

Figure 3.3.
Concept underlying climate models. The atmosphere and ocean are divided into three-dimensional grids and physical values (temperature, wind direction, and velocity) at each grid point are used in calculations.

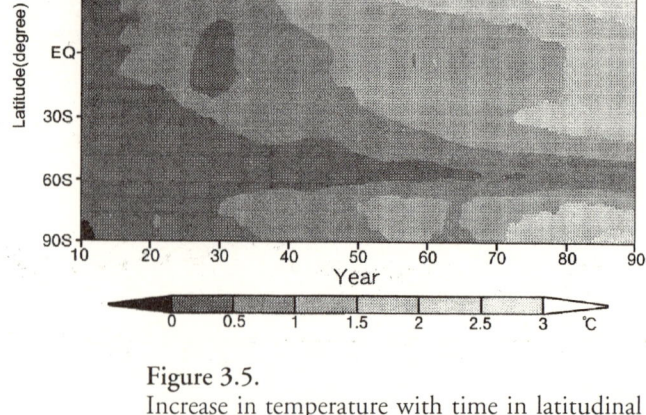

Figure 3.5.
Increase in temperature with time in latitudinal average zones. This graph shows the 11-year average movement of the amount of increase in the ground temperature (°C) averaged latitudinally.

expressed as points on a grid spaced at 4 degrees longitude and 5 degrees latitude apart, while the ocean is expressed as points spaced at 2 degrees longitude and 2.5 degrees latitude apart. However, the grid points for the oceans are made narrower in the latitudinal direction close to the equator.

Since phenomena on scales smaller than the utilized grid intervals cannot be expressed, such models cannot predict detailed future climate changes in areas as small as those of the Japanese region. Thus, when applying the results of global scale climate models to regional climate change projections, they should be used only for reference.

Changes in ground temperature

A rise of 1.6°C in global average ground temperature is projected over the next 70 years (Figure 3.4). During this same period, a doubling of atmospheric CO_2 concentrations is predicted. In 100 years, the ground temperature is projected to be 2.5°C higher than at present. In average ground temperature in different latitudinal blocks over time (Figure 3.5), it can be seen that the temperature rise in the Southern Hemisphere is lower than that in the Northern Hemisphere. This is because the circulation of the ocean reaches deeper in the Southern Hemisphere, causing warm water near the surface to sink further

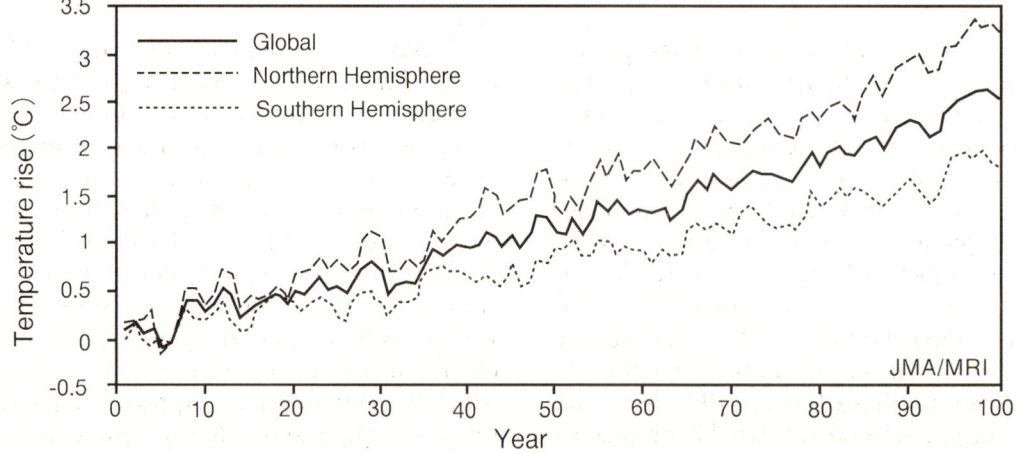

Figure 3.4.
Changes in the ground temperature (°C) between the present and one century from now.

and thereby minimizing the change in the surface temperature of the ocean. This, in turn, limits changes in atmospheric temperatures.

The geographic distribution of average ground temperatures for February and August 100 years from now (Frontispiece 1) shows that global warming is more marked in winter. In the vicinity of Japan, there is a noteworthy temperature rise around the Sea of Okhotsk. This reflects the supposition that since there will be almost no winter ice formation in the Sea of Okhotsk even before the atmospheric CO_2 concentration doubles about 70 years from now (Frontispiece 2), a significant rise in temperature can be expected to occur in this region in winter. The projected timing of the cessation of sea ice formation can be viewed as an indication of the quantitative accuracy of the model, and close attention will need to be paid to this point. However, the projection that sea ice formation in the Sea of Okhotsk will cease at a relatively early stage seems appropriate, given that the Sea of Okhotsk is the lowest latitude at which sea ice currently forms in winter.

Changes in the amount of precipitation

Frontispiece 3 shows the geographical distribution of average daily precipitation for February and August 100 years from now. Changes in precipitation will occur on a smaller scale than is the case with ground temperature, and will be greatly affected by fluctuations in the surface temperature of the oceans at low latitudes. In general, precipitation will tend to increase in areas that are currently subject to large amounts of precipitation.

In seasonal trends, for example, the annual average daily precipitation will increase in the region extending from northern Australia and Indonesia to the Indian Subcontinent. The increase in northern Australia and Indonesia will occur in the Northern Hemisphere winter, whereas that of the Indian Subcontinent will occur in summer. Increases in precipitation in the northern part of South America centered on Brazil will occur in the Northern Hemisphere winter, and those affecting the African Continent at latitudes between 10 and 15 degrees will occur in the Northern Hemisphere summer.

In and around Japan, the temperature is expected to increase slightly in winter, but no remarkable increase is projected for the annual average temperature. Winter precipitation will increase in the region bordering the Sea of Okhotsk, where there will also be a conspicuous rise in temperature. Because there are large differences between the major global climate models with respect to changes in the amount of precipitation, further study is required.

Changes in sea level

Frontispiece 4 shows the expected change in sea level in 100 years. Sea level changes are estimated by combining global average changes using climate models and local-scale average changes. Changes in sea level are caused mainly by changes in sea water density and water balance, but contributions from glaciers and icecaps are not included in these models. These changes in sea level have been projected mainly with reference to changes in sea water density. Although local changes in the sea level can also occur due to changes in oceanic circulation, approximate values were obtained using changes in sea water density distribution within the ocean.

The global average increase in sea level is expected to be about 20 cm over the next 100 years. If it is assumed that changes in water balance, resulting mainly from icecap changes, affect the sea water density (IPCC, 1990) and these are added to the results of the JMA climate model, the overall rise in sea level will be in the region of 40 cm. On a regional scale, there will be larger than average sea level rise in the Sea of Japan, the Mediterranean Sea, and Hudson Bay. The calculation method for working out changes in sea level is the same as that described in the IPCC report (1996). However, in sea level changes on a local scale, further improvements are required, such as detailed investigations of the processes acting on sea water.

Typhoon trends

Typhoons cause major damage in Japan, yet are also a very important source of fresh water. There is, therefore, a high level of interest in projections of how the occurrence and scale of typhoons will change in response to global warming. However, the resolution and scale of physical processes that present climate models can handle are too crude to allow typhoon trends to be directly obtained from climate model results. There have been studies aimed at predicting typhoon trends using high-resolution models of the atmosphere, together with sea surface temperature figures obtained from general climate models, and some results have been reported. However, these results are inconsistent and are not yet reliable. The development of higher-resolution climate models will be necessary in order to predict the effects of global warming on typhoons with a high degree of confidence.

El Niño trends

El Niño is a phenomenon occurring at intervals of several years in which the sea surface temperature in the Pacific equatorial zone, extending from off the

South American coast to the vicinity of the International Date Line, rises by several degrees. El Niño affects the weather in Japan and consequently, there is interest in Japan in how its behavior will be influenced by global warming. According to several studies using climate models, the scale of the fluctuations in sea surface temperature will remain unchanged or will decrease. It is still uncertain whether this result is a natural phenomenon or due to global warming. As in the case of typhoons, further research is required in order to assess the effect of global warming on El Niño.

Conclusion

In this chapter, I have introduced parts of the Global Warming Projection published by the JMA. In order to assess global warming quantitatively, it is essential to have climate models which can model complex processes in the climate system and use the results to predict future changes in the global climate. The information such models produce is useful provided that we remember to take account of the uncertainties inherent in their results.

The development of high-resolution climate models and regional climate models is progressing and promises to make available more reliable predictions. For regional climate models, a region is taken out of the general climate model and the climate change within the region is then calculated in greater detail. In the near future it may be possible to predict changes in local conditions, such as the amount of snowfall in areas close to the Sea of Japan coast in winter.

References

Japan Meteorological Agency 1997. *Global Warming Projection Vol. 1.* Printing Bureau, Ministry of Finance, Japan. 82 pp. (in Japanese)

IPCC. 1990. *Climate Change* (J. T. Houghton, G. J. Jenkins, and J. J. Ephraums, eds.). The IPCC Scientific Assessment. Cambridge University Press, New York, 365pp

IPCC 1996. *Climate Change 1995: the Science of Climate Change.* (J.T. Houglton, L. G. Meira Filho, B. A. Callander, N. Harris, A. Kattenberg, and K. Maskell, eds.). Cambridge University Press, Cambridge, 572pp.

Chapter 4

Greenhouse Gas Emission Scenarios

Mikiko Kainuma, Tsuneyuki Morita and Yuzuru Matsuoka

In order to identify possible future climate change impacts and to uncover opportunities to stabilize the global climate, a very large number of scenarios have been prepared for utilization in efforts to forecast greenhouse gas emissions. For the most part, these emission scenarios have been quantified using computer simulation models, which in turn utilize numerous assumptions with respect to such factors as population growth, GDP growth, technological efficiency improvements, land use changes and energy resource base projections.

Emission scenarios form the basis for discussions of various climate change-related issues and the possibility of mounting future responses to them. The scenarios have been used to determine the future atmospheric concentrations of the greenhouse gases which cause radiative temperature forcing, and future climate changes have also been simulated by inputting the resulting radiative forcing trends into the General Circulation Model. At the same time, identifying feasible methods of reducing emissions remains a fundamental criterion for climate policies.

This chapter will introduce some of the latest research results from the field of emission scenario studies, with special reference to the long-term global scenarios that were reviewed by the authors and also to the Japanese scenarios that were estimated using our model.

Global emission scenarios

Hundreds of scenarios for greenhouse gas emissions have been published since the 1980s, and some of these scenarios were used as input assumptions for the General Circulation Model. Current climate change predictions are mostly based on a scenario called IS92a, which was established by the IPCC Supplement Report in 1992. Global emission scenarios including IPCC scenarios were reviewed in the IPCC Special Report "Climate Change 1994" using several databases established by IIASA, PNL, NIES, IEW and EMF. However, since 1994 new emission scenarios have been prepared in response to changes in economic conditions and other factors related to climate change, as well as to new requests from the academic and policy fields. These scenarios are stored in computer files or in other media, but they are not yet systematically managed.

The authors have developed a new database system that can be used to manage the huge amount of data related to the recently published greenhouse gas emission scenarios. In addition, we have collected previous data, including literature and other information related to the emission scenarios, and filed this data in the new database. The first incentive in establishing this database is to support a new IPCC activity, the Special Report on Emission Scenario (SRES), which has been established to prepare new emission scenarios. The current database collection includes the results of a total of 428 scenarios from 176 sources. These scenarios were mainly produced after 1994. Of the 428 scenarios, 290 were global emission scenarios estimating greenhouse gas emissions comprising 177 non-intervention scenarios and 113 intervention scenarios.

Using the data stored in the database, global carbon emissions are plotted in Figure 4.1. Emissions are indexed to 1990, when actual global energy-related CO_2 emissions were equivalent to about 6 GtC. In all, 232 scenarios are included in the figure. The two vertical bars on the right-hand side indicate the ranges for scenarios with emission control measures (labeled "CONTROL") and for those without controls (labeled "NON-CONTROL").

In general, the level of CO_2 emissions from the combustion of fossil fuels can be explained by assumptions about population, per capita GDP, energy efficiency improvements and fuel carbon intensity. In order to assess the CO_2 emission scenarios more thoroughly, rather detailed analyses need to be conducted of the elasticities of price-induced energy substitution, the international adjustment processes, backstop technologies, and other technological and socio-economic assumptions. These factors influence the carbon intensity and energy intensity and determine the resulting carbon

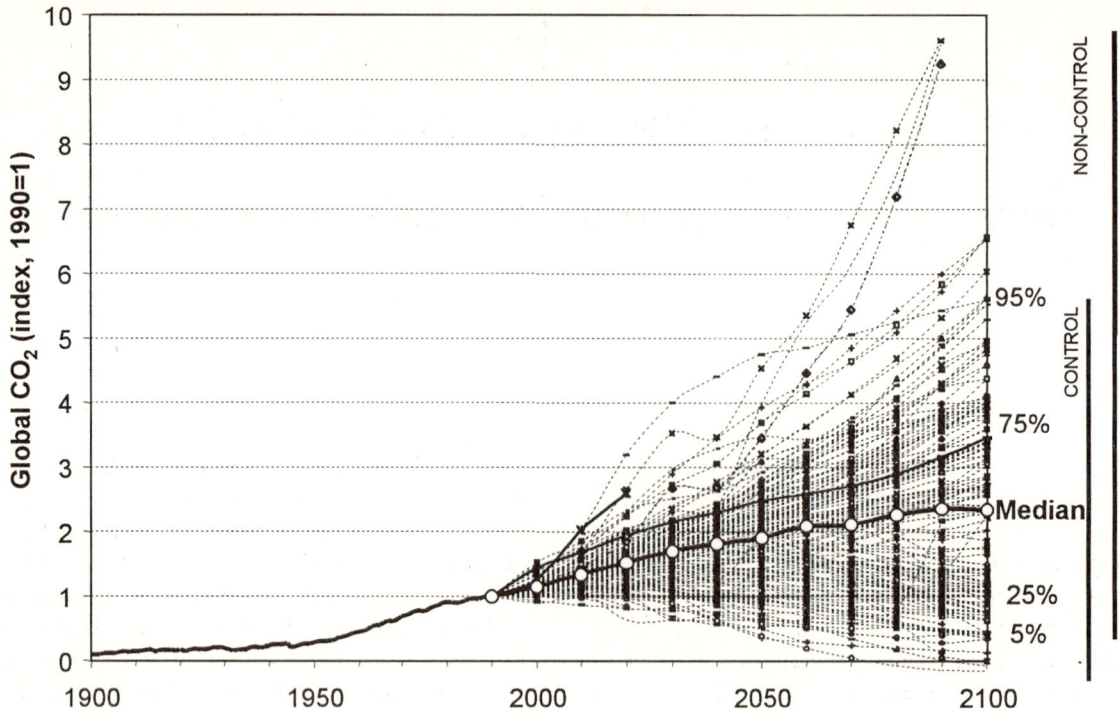

Figure 4.1. Global carbon emissions: Historical development and scenarios.

emissions. Carbon intensity represents carbon dioxide emissions per unit energy and is an index of energy mix. Energy intensity is energy per unit output and changes according to technology development. The carbon emission values of the various scenarios are affected by the different assumptions and model parameters used to determine carbon intensity and energy intensity.

Several key points can be deduced from Figure 4.1. The range of scenarios is very wide. The maximum CO_2 emission levels projected are equivalent to more than ten times the current emission level and the minimum level is about half the current level in the NON-CONTROL case. The median is about 2.3 times the current level. The range distribution of the new scenarios is approximately the same as that of the pre-1994 scenarios and encompasses the IS92 scenario range. These emission scenarios were input into a simple climate model of AIM for estimating global temperature change. It was found that even the lowest emission scenario in the NON-CONTROL case could not stabilize the global climate. This means that it is very difficult to prevent global warming.

Several characteristics can be observed from an OECD/non-OECD comparison. Both the OECD and non-OECD scenarios embrace a wide range of emission level projections. The range distribution among the scenarios for the non-OECD nations is wider than in the case of the OECD nations. In percentage terms, the projected growth in the CO_2 emissions of non-OECD nations is generally larger than that of OECD nations. This is mainly the result of larger expected percentage-based GDP increases in the non-OECD nations. The range of scenarios for carbon intensity is very wide for both OECD and non-OECD nations. There is a high degree of uncertainty in predicting the future carbon intensity levels for both groups. The uncertainty range for energy intensity is larger in the case of non-OECD than OECD nations. This is a result of the many indefinite factors associated with improving energy efficiency in developing nations.

It is very difficult to come to any general conclusions in making regional comparisons, as the ranges involved in regional scenarios are extraordinarily large. Moreover, except for the USA, Europe, the former Soviet Union and China, the number of available scenarios is limited. However, some general trends can be identified in association with the medium ranges of the scenarios. For Asian countries, GDP growth is the most significant factor, resulting in increasing levels of energy use and CO_2 emissions. Energy efficiency improvements are assumed to be the most significant factor in scenarios relating to China. By contrast, carbon intensity reductions are expected to be very large in Africa, Latin America, and southeast Asia because of drastic energy mix changes.

Japanese emission scenarios

There is a wide range of global emission projections. These differences come from assumptions regarding socio-economic scenarios and technology develop-ment. At the Kyoto Conference on climate change in 1997, parties agreed to reduce greenhouse gas emissions of Annex I countries by at least 5% below 1990 levels in the commitment period 2008 to 2012. The target is different region by region. Japan has to reduce emissions by 6% of 1990 levels. Our main concern is to determine the extent to which Japan can reduce emissions without decreasing productive activities or lowering living standards. The AIM model is used to simulate Japanese CO_2 emissions.

When one looks at Japan over the long-term, that is, in the first half of the 21st century, one should bear in mind the considerable uncertainty regarding anticipated changes in the social structure, particularly with regard to demographic trends. For example, the Japanese population will peak in 2010 and then begin to decrease. In addition, the post-war baby boom generation will be approaching retirement age at around that time. It is possible that such changes will greatly affect people's lifestyles and the direction of the nation's economic development.

Furthermore, if the trend toward economic globalisation continues during the 21st century, by 2030 China and other East Asian nations can be expected to reach the economic standard attained by Japan in the 1970s. As a result, the industrial structure of Japan will change significantly. On the other hand, widespread environmental impacts, such as acid rain from the burning of coal in China, may become apparent in East Asia from the beginning of the 21st century. Consequently, it seems likely that investment in environmental pollution control will increase rapidly and that the cost of the required technologies will decrease very quickly.

This type of structural change will have a significant impact on the scale of future CO_2 emissions. However, the extent of such changes is difficult to predict. For this reason, it is necessary to adopt a perspective that incorporates a sufficient degree of uncertainty.

Let us now assume two scenarios for Japan's future. The first scenario is one in which little structural change occurs and present consumption-dependent lifestyles as well as existing manufacturing activities are maintained as much as possible. We will call this scenario the "contemporary materialistic nation scenario". The other scenario is one in which the Japanese social structure undergoes a radical shift toward knowledge-based production systems and creative lifestyles, and in which structural changes occur on a significant scale. We will call this the "creative/knowledge-intensive nation scenario".

If one assumes for each of these scenarios parameters with respect to the economic growth rate, the industrial structure and goods shipments, required office space, transportation, etc., the projected amount of CO_2 emitted can be estimated. On the basis of these assumptions, we have conducted a computer simulation analysis.

The AIM model first estimates energy service demands based on socio-economic factors such as population, economic growth, industrial structure and lifestyle, and then calculates what kinds of technology will be used to what extent. Energy services include the production of steel, cement, and plastics, cooling and heating, lighting, and transportation as well as steam and electricity that are used to produce such energy services. Technologies such as blast furnaces, air conditioners and automobiles offer energy services by using energy such as oil, coal and gas. To compare energy technologies, detailed technological and energy databases are used. Once the kind of energy technology to be used is known, the model calculates the energy necessary to provide the energy services and the amount of CO_2 emissions produced when each type of technology operates. In our analysis, five sectors (industrial, residential, commercial, transportation and energy conversion) are used and more than 200 technologies are considered for forecasting CO_2 emissions from Japan.

Figure 4.2 shows future prospective CO_2 emissions in the case of the "contemporary materialistic nation scenario" and the "creative/knowledge-intensive nation scenario". If consumers and businesses do not acknowledge the advantages of saving fuel through energy-saving measures and new technology does not spread (frozen efficiency case), CO_2 emissions will increase by 47% by 2030 in comparison with 1990 in the "contemporary materialistic nation scenario" and by 31% in the "creative/knowledge-intensive nation scenario".

If the cheapest technology spreads based on market principles (profitable potential case), the increase in CO_2 emissions by 2030 will be 28% and 16%, respectively. Even if energy-saving technology remains somewhat expensive, the spread of the technology will proceed because it is possible to recover the initial costs through fuel savings within a relatively short period. However, the computer model used does not take into account flawed information with respect to the market, or other social factors, so it is possible that energy efficiency improvements are overestimated. One must therefore assume that actual CO_2 emissions will be higher than these estimates.

In either case, if no special countermeasures such as government intervention occur, CO_2 emissions will continue to increase. Swift action is necessary if CO_2 emissions are to be stabilized and ultimately reduced.

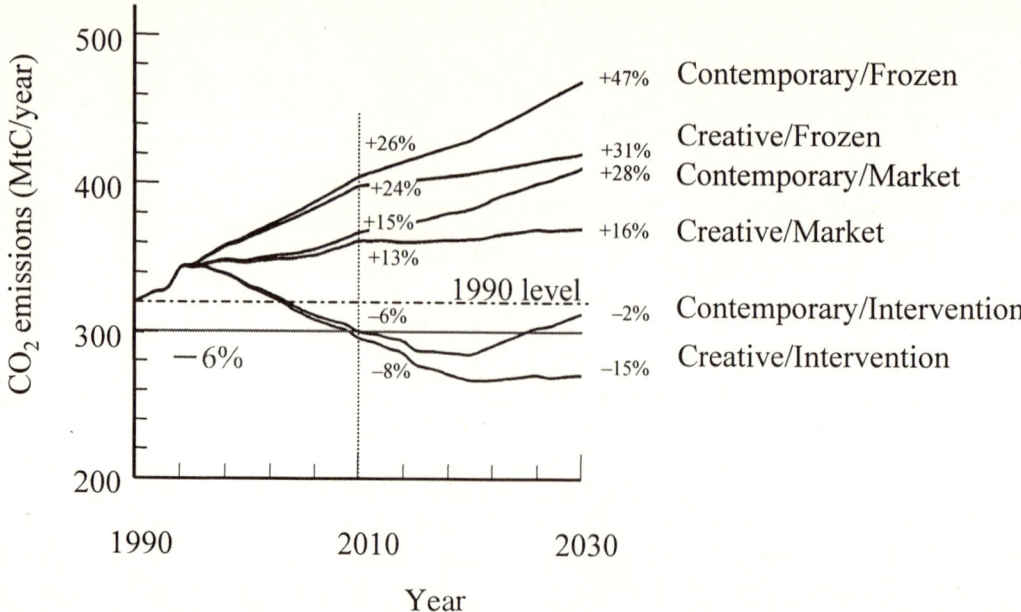

Figure 4.2. Forecasts of Japanese carbon dioxide emissions.

To what extent can CO_2 emissions be reduced through countermeasures? Without decreasing production levels and lowering living standards as assumed under the two scenarios, we used the same model to simulate the extent to which CO_2 emissions could be reduced through the introduction of more efficient technology alone. To be more precise, with respect to energy-saving and recycling technologies that are not market-competitive at projected energy prices, we propose the levying of a carbon tax of, 30,000 yen (US$240) per ton of carbon to promote the technologies concerned. However, if we assume that this tax is to be returned to companies and households in the form of subsidies for the introduction of energy-saving and recycling technology, a carbon tax of 3,000 yen (US$24) per ton of carbon would be sufficient. This would add the equivalent of 2 yen (US$0.016) to the retail price of a liter of gasoline and would accelerate the introduction of energy-saving technology across a variety of fields.

Through such measures, it would become possible to reduce Japan's CO_2 emissions by the year 2020 by 15% as compared to the 1990 level in the case of the "creative/knowledge-intensive nation scenario" and by 10% in the case of the "contemporary materialistic nation scenario". Even without decreasing productive activities or lowering living standards, a reduction in CO_2 emissions is possible.

Concluding remarks

This chapter brings together some of the most recent information on global CO_2 emissions projections and compares their future trends including their driving forces. Japanese CO_2 projections are studied in more detail based on future socio-economic assumptions and policy intervention. The following observations are made:

(1) Recent emission scenarios embrace a wide range of future emission trends. They vary from half to ten times the 1990 level in 2100. However, even the lowest emission scenario in the non-control case cannot prevent a future increase of global temperature.

(2) The diversity of assumptions with respect to energy resources and supply technologies results in very wide ranges for CO_2 emission among the various scenarios. The uncertainty of future GDP and energy efficiency improvement also explains the wide range of CO_2 projections. The major driving force behind CO_2 emissions is economic growth, including that resulting from population growth and technological change. Carbon and energy intensities change differently over time and region, due to different assumptions about driving forces and other factors, such as the elasticities of energy substitution. These also add uncertainty to CO_2 projections.

(3) An overview of future trends extrapolated from the various scenarios shows greater divergence in the predicted ranges for developing countries than for developed nations. This is mainly the result of larger expected percentage-based GDP increases in the developing nations. The wide range of scenarios for energy intensity also leads to uncertainty in CO_2 projections for developing nations.

(4) More research needs to be done on regional disparities. With respect to future regional trends, there is little consensus among existing scenarios.

The following observations also emerged from the Japanese CO_2 emission study:

(1) It is possible to decrease CO_2 emissions without scaling back productive activities or reducing living standards in Japan. However, if one relies on the market mechanism alone, this will not occur. Our analysis shows that it is necessary to introduce new policies and measures such as a carbon tax and increased subsidies for introducing energy-saving technology.

(2) If Japan attempts to reduce CO_2 emissions even further, the costs will inevitably become larger. There will certainly be costs for the companies and households that will have to bear the burden of reducing CO_2 emissions. However, there will be an increase in the effective demand for energy-saving technology. It is estimated that the indirect cost of CO_2 emission reductions for Japan as a whole will be extremely small as a result of the growth of environment-related industries. Moreover, the business opportunities for these industries will increase further as joint projects with developing countries to reduce CO_2 emissions are implemented.

(3) The likelihood is high that in the 21st century, social-structural change will transform Japan from a "contemporary materialistic nation" to a "creative/knowledge-intensive nation". This transformation will make it relatively easy to control CO_2 emissions and take countermeasures to protect the global environment. It can be argued that the social system of Japan is changing in such a way as to make it more advantageous to introduce environmental policies.

Although the predictions we have examined are fraught with uncertainties, large and long-lasting climate changes are certain to occur. It is possible to tackle global warming, but this will require a new level of policy integration. The sooner this occurs, the more effective such action will be.

References

Alcamo, J., A. Bouwman, J. Edmonds, A. Gruebler, T. Morita, and A. Sugandhy. 1995. An Evaluation of the IPCC IS92 Emission Scenarios. In: *Climate Change 1994, IPCC*. Pp.233-304. Cambridge University Press, Cambridge.

IPCC. 1998. Special Report on Emission Scenarios (SRES) Open Process.

Leggett, J., W. J. Pepper, and R. J. Swart. 1992. Emissions scenarios for the IPCC: an update. In: *Climate Change 1992, IPCC*. Pp.69-95. Cambridge University Press, Cambridge.

Morita, T. and H. C. Lee. 1998. IPCC SRES Database, Version 0.1. Emission Scenario Database prepared for IPCC Special Report on Emission Scenarios.

Chapter 5

Ecosystems and the Carbon Cycle

Takehisa Oikawa

Essentially, ecosystems both in the oceans and on land are formed and maintained by photosynthesis, which is carried out by green plants. The chemical reaction involved in photosynthesis, which is common to all plants, from very small phytoplankton to huge trees is shown in the following equation:

$$6CO_2 + 6H_2O \xrightarrow{Light} C_6H_{12}O_6 + 6O_2 \qquad Eq.~(1)$$

As can be understood from Eq.(1), plants synthesize glucose from CO_2 (Carbon dioxide) and H_2O (water) using sunlight as an energy source, emitting O_2 (oxygen) into the environment as a byproduct. Plant photosynthesis is highly active both in the oceans and on land, and makes a major contribution to the global carbon cycle. Respiration involves the reverse reaction of that shown in Eq.(1), and creates energy by oxidizing organic compounds with O_2. CO_2 and H_2O are emitted into the environment during this process.

Estimating the total biomass of plants and their productivity was a major research theme of the International Biological Program (IBP) implemented from 1965 to 1974. Thus, the total biomass of all existing plants on land and in the oceans as well as their biological productivity was estimated.

Ecosystems and the global carbon cycle

First of all, we introduce marine ecosystems, terrestrial ecosystems, and their relationship to the carbon cycle (Figure 5.1).

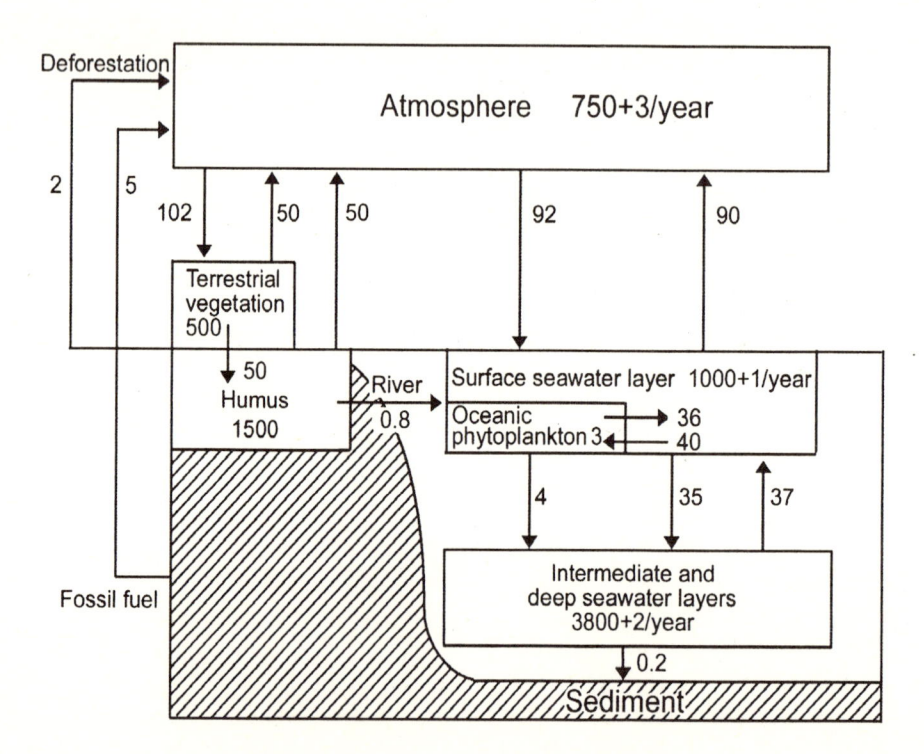

Figure 5.1. Global carbon cycle (IPCC, 1990).

Carbon reserves in the biosphere move between three major reservoirs: the atmosphere, marine ecosystems and terrestrial ecosystems. The amounts of carbon contained in these reservoirs, in Pg units (1 Pg (Petagram) = 1 Gt (Gigaton) = 10^{15} g), are as follows: 750 in the atmosphere (+3/year), 1,000 in the ocean surface layer (+1/year), 3,800 in the ocean's intermediate and deep layers (+2/year), with just 3 in phytoplankton living in the surface layer. Regarding the amount of carbon contained in terrestrial plants, 550 are contained in vegetation, while the soil is estimated to contain 1,500.

Large amounts of carbon in the form of CO_2 are actively exchanged in both directions between the atmosphere and marine ecosystems as well as between the atmosphere and terrestrial ecosystems. The rate of carbon exchange between the atmosphere and the oceans is in proportion to the difference in the CO_2 partial pressure between the atmosphere and the ocean surface layer. The direct exchange of CO_2 between the atmosphere and the oceans is a purely physical process. When the CO_2 partial pressure is higher in the atmosphere than in the oceans, CO_2 in the atmosphere is absorbed by the oceans (A), but when the CO_2 partial pressure is lower in the atmosphere than in the oceans (E), the reverse process occurs in which CO_2 in the oceans is emitted to the atmosphere. The IPCC estimates A as equal to 92 PgC/year and E as 90 PgC/year. The mechanism for determining the CO_2 partial pressure in the oceans is very complicated because this is influenced by the pH, temperature, and salinity of sea water. The productivity of phytoplankton also affects the CO_2 partial pressure in the surrounding sea water.

CO_2 exchange between the atmosphere and terrestrial ecosystems is achieved mainly through biological processes. That is, plants carry out photosynthesis and make organic compounds, in the process fixing CO_2 from the atmosphere (gross primary production: GPP). At the same time, CO_2 is emitted as plants respire (plant respiration: R) and bacteria and fungi decompose organic compounds in the soil (soil respiration: D). According to the IPCC (1990), the amounts of GPP, R, and D are estimated at 102, 50, and 50 PgC/year, respectively. Deforestation is estimated to emit 2 PgC/year. CO_2 emitted into the atmosphere through the combustion of fossil fuel is eventually distributed to each reservoir through the processes described above, and the CO_2 concentration in the atmosphere is determined accordingly. The estimates of CO_2 amounts and the scale of exchange between each reservoir in Figure 5.1 include significant uncertainties, except the CO_2 concentration in the atmosphere (750 PgC) and the amount of CO_2 emitted through fossil fuel consumption (5 PgC/year).

The carbon cycle in the oceans and marine life

The oceans cover approximately 70% of the earth's surface. The average depth of the oceans is 3,800 m and the deepest point is 10,924 m. Consequently, the volume of sea water is calculated as $1,370 \times 10^6 \, km^3$. Na, Cl and many other inorganic ions are dissolved in sea water. The salinity produced by these ions averages 35‰ and the pH of sea water is 8.3 (weak alkalinity).

The ocean surface layer and the intermediate and deep layers must be considered separately (Figure 5.1). The surface layer is well mixed by wind action and the temperature is very stable (Figure 5.2). CO_2 exchange between the surface layer and the atmosphere is active. Beneath the surface layer lies the thermocline, with the intermediate and deep layers further below. The thermocline has a structure which ensures that the rate of exchange of water and soluble substances across it is very slow. It takes as long as 1,500 years for the layers on either side of the thermocline to reach equilibrium, so human activities that take place over a time scale of 100 to 200 years, even if they are on a significant scale, are too short-lived to influence the intermediate and deep ocean layers.

When considering the issue of CO_2 in the oceans, the dissociation equilibrium has to be taken into account.

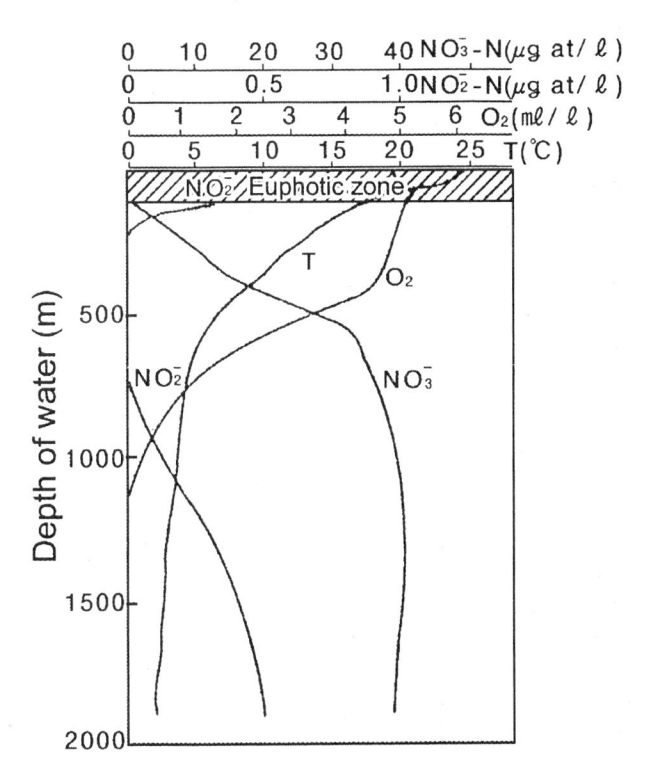

Figure 5.2.
Vertical distribution of water temperature, oxygen partial pressure, nitric acid ions, and nitrous acid ions in the ocean (Hattori, 1972).

$$CO_2 + H_2O \rightleftarrows H^+ + HCO_3^-$$
$$HCO_3^- \rightleftarrows H^+ + CO_3^{2-}$$

In the formula, gaseous CO_2, bicarbonate ions (HCO_3^-) and carbonic ions (CO_3^{2-}) are dissolved in the sea water, and the total amount is called the total carbonate (ΣCO_2). Of these three, gaseous CO_2 is directly related to CO_2 exchange with the atmosphere. The ratio of these three forms of CO_2 varies greatly depending on pH, making the issue very complicated. In sea water with a salinity of 35‰ and at pH 8.3, HCO_3^- is the dominant form (about 86%) and most of the rest is CO_3^{2-}. Gaseous CO_2 accounts for less than 0.5% of the total. It should be noted that the CO_2 ratio is particularly sensitive around pH 8.3. At this point, if the pH changes by about 3% toward acidity, the concentration of CO_2 in sea water doubles. On the contrary, if the value shifts by 3% toward alkalinity, the CO_2 concentration drops by half. This chemical characteristic is important from the standpoint of examining the buffer effect of the oceans against changes in the CO_2 concentration in the atmosphere. For example, if CO_2 is added to the atmosphere which is in a state of equilibrium with the oceans in terms of CO_2 concentration, a certain portion of the additional CO_2 will dissolve into the sea water and the pH value of the sea water will accordingly shift toward acidity because CO_2 is slightly acidic. Consequently, about 10% of the CO_2 which was added to the atmosphere is absorbed by the oceans and the other 90% remains in the atmosphere. The CO_2 absorption capacity of the oceans is limited by the buffer effect. Over a long period, on the order of 1000 years or more, however, the CO_2 concentration will reach equilibrium throughout the oceans as a whole including not just the surface layer but also intermediate and deep layers. The amount of CO_2 eventually absorbed by all layers of the oceans will be very large, equivalent to about 84% of all the CO_2 added to the atmosphere.

The surface layer of the oceans is involved in active CO_2 exchange with the atmosphere, and its uppermost portion, where sunlight penetrates in sufficient quantity to allow phytoplankton to carry out photosynthesis, is called the euphotic zone. A large amount of O_2 generated by photosynthesis is present in the euphotic zone (Figure 5.2). On the other hand, there are almost no nutrients such as NO_3^- and NO_2^-, which are crucial for the growth of the phytoplankton, in the euphotic zone. Although the biomass of phytoplankton in the surface layer as a whole is only 3 PgC, the amount of CO_2 that these phytoplankton fix by photosynthesis is estimated to be 40 PgC/year (Figure 5.3). This is more than 40% of the physical CO_2 flux between the atmosphere and the ocean.

The rate of vertical exchange of water and soluble substances across the thermocline between the ocean surface layer and the intermediate and deep layer is very slow. The intermediate and deep layers are a dark world in which organic substances are rapidly decomposed, and during this process the available O_2 is consumed completely. NO_3^-, NO_2^-, and other nutrients which are produced by decomposition accumulate in high concentrations (Figure 5.2).

The rate of vertical movement of sea water is very slow in most parts of the oceans. Nevertheless, there are some areas where such movements take place rapidly. For example, sea water sinks from the surface layer to intermediate and deep layers in the northern part of the North Atlantic Ocean. Close to the Polar Regions, sea water is cooled and then sinks because its density increases due to the cooling. Also, when sea water is frozen its salinity increases, again increasing its density. The resulting physical flow is called a solubility pump. The amount of inorganic carbon transferred downward by solubility pump effects is estimated to be 35 Pg/year.

On the contrary, there are upwelling zones in which sea water rises from the intermediate and deep layers to the surface layer carrying carbon along with it. The upwelling zones are found mainly along the coasts of continents and in equatorial areas. The amount of inorganic carbon transferred upward by upwelling is estimated to be 37 Pg/year.

The elemental composition of phytoplankton is very stable irrespective of the type. The average is C : N : P = 80 : 15 : 1. This is called the Redfield ratio. Sea water acts as a buffer for CO_2; thus, phytoplankton never encounter a lack of Carbon (C). Because sea water contains only very small amounts of nitrogen (N) and phosphorus (P), the growth of phytoplankton is limited by the concentration of N and P, as well as of silicon (Si), iron (Fe) and other elements. In upwellings, however, sea water from the intermediate and deep layers rich with C, N, P, and other elements rises into the euphotic zone. The primary productivity of phytoplankton is very high in such places. The world's four richest fishing grounds - the North Sea and northeastern part of the North Atlantic Ocean, the northern and northwestern parts of the North Atlantic off the North American coast, the northwestern Pacific including the sea near Japan, and the eastern Pacific off the coast of Peru in South America - are all upwelling zones, and the fish caught in these zones account for nearly half of the world's total fish catch. This is a reflection of the high primary productivity of phytoplankton in these zones.

As is typically observed in the upwelling zones, the primary production of the ocean is maintained mainly by the flow of nutrients carried from intermediate and deep layers to the euphotic zone. Production created in this way is called new production. Production

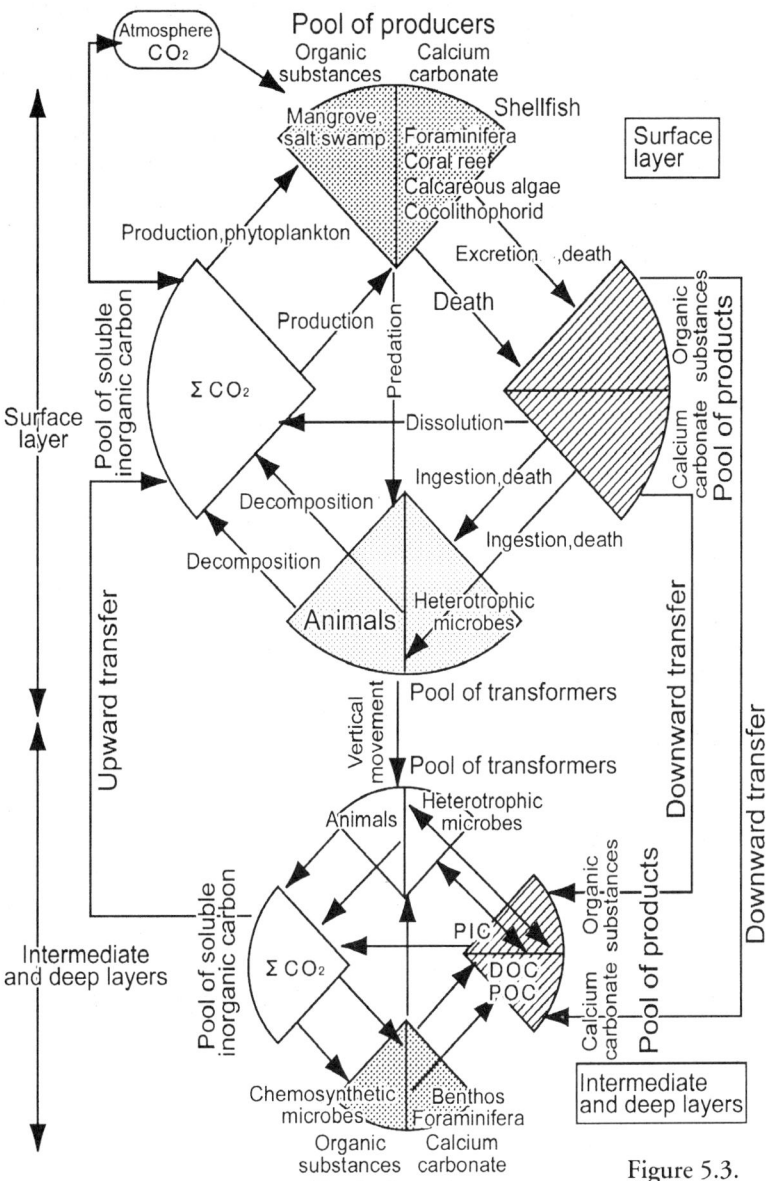

Figure 5.3.
New model of the carbon cycle in the ocean (Suzuki et al., 1997).

created by the circulation of nutrients within the euphotic zone is called reproduction. New production is estimated to account for approximately 20% of the total primary production of the oceans.

The thermocline is a determinant of the exchange of soluble substances between the surface layer and intermediate and deep layers. Particulate organic carbon (POC) materials such as the remains of dead phytoplankton and the excreta of zooplankton are heavy, and sink rapidly into the intermediate and deep layers. The transfer of substances generated by organisms is called the biological pump. The total amount of organic carbon transferred to the intermediate and deep layers by the biological pump is estimated to be 4 Pg/year.

A new theory of the carbon cycle in the oceans

In addition to the processes shown in Figure 5.3, another biological process plays an important role in the global carbon cycle. Suzuki et al. (1997) have summarized the carbon cycle focusing on the activities of ocean dwelling organisms (Figure 5.3). Each of two circles is divided into producer, products, transformer, and soluble inorganic carbon. The exchange of organic carbon and inorganic carbon is shown as closely related within biological processes. For example, cocolithoporid, a kind of phytoplankton, and calcareous algae, a kind of seaweed, produce organic substances by photosynthesis as well as particulate inorganic carbon (PIC) materials containing calcium carbonate. Fermatypic corals which are coelenterates produce calcium carbonate in the form of coral reefs as well as organic substances, because the zooxanthella inhabiting corals carry out photosynthesis.

Photosynthesis carried out in the oceans essentially fixes soluble inorganic carbon and reduces the overall carbonate concentration (ΣCO_2). Consequently, the ΣCO_2 partial pressure in the sea water is also reduced. When calcium carbonate is produced, however, Ca^{2+} is also eliminated from the sea water along with CO_2. Therefore, the CO_2 partial pressure increases and CO_2 may be emitted into the atmosphere. Increases in atmospheric CO_2 concentration can be suppressed by facilitating the growth of coral reefs. This may, however, have the opposite effect to that which is intended. In any case, increased production of organic substances and calcium carbonate would change the carbon structure and significantly affect the carbon cycle in the oceans.

In Figure 5.3, organic substances and calcium carbonate are included in the pool of products. The productivity of the oceans is not directly limited by photosynthesis, but by the processes in which organic substances are formed from elements including the products of photosynthesis, N, and P, as in the growth process of phytoplankton. It has been established that the products of photosynthesis carried out by phytoplankton are discharged into the nutrient-poor environment of the euphotic zone. Soluble organic substances (DOCs) discharged in this way are the organic materials of the production pool. DOCs are quickly consumed because they are favored by the bacteria inhabiting the euphotic zone. Consequently, it is very difficult to measure directly the rate at which phytoplankton discharge DOCs.

This situation has forced researchers to begin to consider that actual primary productivity includes the productivity of bacteria. When existing primary productivity estimates are reviewed from this viewpoint, overall primary productivity is found to increase 10 - 70%. Although the extent to which these results can be generalized is not yet clear, the primary productivity of the oceans shown in Figure 5.1 may have to be significantly revised.

Biomass in terrestrial ecosystems and carbon flux

Terrestrial plants synthesize organic substances from CO_2 and water (Eq. (1)). The total amount of organic substances synthesized by the terrestrial ecosystem as a whole is gross primary production (GPP). Terrestrial plants emit CO_2 into the atmosphere through respiration (R_P). GPP minus R_P is net primary production (NPP), and is used to form new plants. Animals are not physiologically capable of synthesizing organic substances. Herbivores feed on plant materials, while carnivores eat herbivores. Through this food chain, all animals utilize the products of plant photosynthesis to stay alive. NPP is the amount of organic production that can be utilized by animals. Therefore, NPP is an indicator of plant productivity as well as of the scale of an ecosystem. This is why NPP is also referred to as the biospheric carrying capacity.

The flow of carbon in terrestrial ecosystems can be expressed as follows:

$$NPP = GPP - R_P \quad (2.1)$$
$$= \triangle W + L + G \quad (2.2)$$

Where $\triangle W$ represents the increased amount of carbon contained in plants during a given period, L represents the amount of organic carbon that plants contribute to the land in the form of fallen leaves and branches, and G represents the amount of organic carbon contained in plants eaten by animals.

The NPP of a given ecosystem can be obtained from Eq. (2.2). For example, to obtain the NPP of a forest, the diameters of all trees within certain area are measured at time t_1 and again one or two years later at time t_2. The biomass values W_1 and W_2 can be estimated from t_1 and t_2, respectively. $\triangle W = W_2 - W_1$. Fallen leaves and branches have to be regularly collected by litter traps installed on the ground over the period from t_1 to t_2. L can be obtained from the amount of material collected. G is generally very small, and therefore, can be neglected for the purpose of this calculation. $\triangle W + L = NPP$. Estimated NPP vales and present organic material amounts in different ecosystems are obtained by this method (Table 5.1).

Forests contain large amounts of organic material in the form of wood. From tropical rain forests to boreal coniferous forests, forests cover approximately one third of the Earth's land surface. The present amount of carbon contained in forests is 743 Pg, about 90% of the amount of carbon on land as a whole (827 Pg). The area occupied by the tropical rain forests is only 11% of the total land area, yet the present amount of carbon stored in these forests accounts for 41% of the total in all terrestrial ecosystems. The NPP of tropical rain forests expressed in terms of carbon is 15.3 Pg/year, 32% of the total for all terrestrial ecosystems. The substantive biomass and high biological productivity of the tropical rain forests are due to warm climate and sufficient sunlight and water throughout the year. The productivity of a terrestrial ecosystem is primarily determined by its temperature and humidity conditions, while in marine ecosystems sea water nutrient conditions are the most important factor. Within certain limits the temperature plays only a minor role.

Figure 5.1 summarizes the present amount of carbon and the carbon flux on a global scale as

Table 5.1. Biomass, net primary productivity and soil organic mass of different types of ecosystems (partially modified from Whittaker and Likens, 1973; Schlesinger, 1977)

	Area (10⁶km²)	Average biomass (GgC/km²)	Total biomass (PgC)	Net primary productivity (MgC/km²·yr)	Net primary production (PgC/yr)	Soil organic mass (GgC/km²)	Soil organic mass accumulation (PgC)
Tropical rain forest	17	20	340	900	15.3 }	10.4	259
Tropical seasonal forest	7.5	16	120	675	5.1 }		
Temperate evergreen forest	5.0	16	80	585	2.9 }	11.8	157
Temperate deciduous forest	7.0	13.5	95	540	3.8 }		
Boreal forest	12	9.0	108	358	4.3	14.9	203
Woodland	8.5	2.6	22	259	2.2	6.9	61
Savanna	15	1.8	27	315	4.7	3.7	58
Temperate grassland	9	0.7	6.3	225	2.0	19.2	175
Tundra, alpine belt	8	0.3	2.4	65	0.5	21.6	177
Shrub desert	18	0.3	5.4	32	0.6	5.6	101
Desert, rocky areas, icebound areas	24	0.01	0.2	1.5	0.04	0.1	3
Cultivated areas	14	0.5	7.0	290	4.1	12.7	179
Marsh	2	6.8	13.6	1.125	2.2	68.6	140
Total	147	5.6	827	324	47.7	10.3	1,513

1Mg = 10⁶ g, 1Gg = 10⁹ g, 1Pg = 10¹⁵ g

Table 5.2. Mean amount of litter fall and nutrient supply in each forest ecosystem (Mg/km^2/year)(Tsutsumi, 1989)

	No.	Dry materials (Mean± SE)	N	P	K	Ca	Mg
Tropical rain forest	32	987 ± 236	14.4	0.79	5.65	12.6	3.55
Evergreen forest	13	651 ± 81	7.3	0.48	2.50	7.2	0.98
Temperate deciduous broad-leaved forest	40	407 ± 100	4.5	0.41	1.60	5.3	0.79
Temperate evergreen coniferous forest	41	457 ± 142	3.3	0.28	0.93	3.3	0.46
Northern coniferous forest	4	423 ± 97	3.0	0.26	0.71	2.7	0.27

Approximately 45% of dry materials consist of cafbon.
No. is the number of forests surveyed.

calculated based on Table 5.1. It should be noted that the biomass of terrestrial vegetation is 550 Pg, which is more than 180 times that of ocean organisms (3 Pg). With regard to GPP, however, the total value of terrestrial ecosystems is 102 Pg/year, only 2.5 times that of marine ecosystems (40 Pg/year). The major reason for this is that for the most part the present terrestrial vegetation consists of the trunks and branches in forests, which are not directly involved in production. The relatively slow rate of organic material rotation, and the long life span of terrestrial vegetation - which is much longer than that of phytoplankton and can in some instances extend to several thousand years, as in the Japanese cedar *Cryptomeria japonica* on Yaku Island - are among the causes of this phenomenon.

Soil organic mass and its decomposition

The flow of substances from plants into the soil takes place in the form of litter fall (L) expressed in Eq. (2.2). Table 5.2 indicates L according to the type of forest and the amount of nutrient value it contains (Tsutsumi, 1989). These values can differ even within the same type of forest. In general, however, tropical rain forests have much larger L and nutrient values than other types of forests. From Eq.(2.2), L is a factor in NPP. As a forest becomes more mature, $\triangle W$ approaches 0 and L approaches the NPP value. L, an indicator of NPP, declines linearly from 1090 Mg/km^2/year in tropical rain forests to 10 Mg/km^2/year in subarctic forests.

L is very large in tropical rain forests. The organic mass accumulated per unit of soil, however, is not very large. The organic mass in the soil of tropical rain forests is 10.4 GgC/km^2, while in the soils of temperate forests and northern coniferous forests in the subarctic zone this increases to 11.8 GgC/km^2 and 14.9 GgC/km^2, respectively (Table 5.1). The higher the latitude, the colder the climate and the shorter the annual growing period, the less litter fall. However, more organic substances accumulate in a given area of soil. This indicates that the soil organic mass is determined by the rate of decomposition of organic substances in the soil. As Schlesinger (1991) has summarized, the average remaining period for litter (the amount of litter on the ground in forests / the annual amount of L) is as long as 353 years in boreal coniferous forests, falling to just 0.4 year in tropical rain forests. This difference is more than 800 times (Table 5.3).

It should be also noted that the total soil organic mass is much greater than the total biomass throughout the world (Table 5.1). The decomposition of litter proceeds slowly in temperate grasslands and tundra zones due to dryness and low temperatures, and this allows a large amount of organic mass to accumulate. Soil is a significant reservoir of organic mass in the carbon cycle in terrestrial ecosystems.

The carbon flux within terrestrial ecosystems is

Table 5.3. Average residence time of organic materials and nutrient salts in litter in each forest ecosystem (in years)(Schlesinger and Melack, 1981)

	Organic materials	N	P	K	Ca	Mg
Tropical rain forest	0.4	2.0	1.6	0.7	1.5	1.1
Mediterranean forest	3.8	4.2	3.6	1.4	5.0	2.8
Temperate deciduos foresta	4	5.5	5.8	1.3	3.0	3.4
Temperate coniferous foresta	17	17.9	15.3	2.2	5.9	12.9
Northern coniferous foresta	353	230	324	94	149	455

The average residence time is the value abtained by dividing the amount of litter accumulated on the ground by the amount of annual litter fall.

expressed as follows:

$$\begin{align} NEP &= NPP - D - D_f & (3.1) \\ &= GPP - R_p - D - D_f & (3.2) \\ &= 102 - 50 - 50 - 2 & (3.3) \\ &= 0 & (3.4) \end{align}$$

If NEP (net ecosystem production) is positive, the terrestrial ecosystem is a net sink of CO_2. If NEP is negative, the terrestrial ecosystem is a net source of CO_2. According to the IPCC's estimate (1990), NEP is zero. Therefore, the terrestrial ecosystem is considered to be neither a sink nor a source of CO_2.

The IPCC estimate (1990) challenges the common idea that the terrestrial ecosystem is a net source of CO_2. One of the reasons is that the carbon flux caused by deforestation (D_f) is not as large as was previously thought; Woodwell et al. (1978) estimated D_f at 4 - 8 PgC/year, equivalent to the amount of carbon released by fossil fuel combustion. However, the CO_2 sinks of oil and coal are yet missing.

Formation of terrestrial ecosystems and their environmental conditions

The wide variety of terrestrial ecosystems on earth (Table 5.1) is essentially determined by the humidity and temperature of a specific location. The radiative dryness index advocated by Budyko (1973) is a useful indicator of humidity for plants. It is obtained by the formula: $Rn/\lambda P$; where Rn represents the net annual radiation at a specific place, P represents annual precipitation and λ represents the heat of vaporization.

Different levels of the radiative dryness index are closely correlated with different natural types of terrestrial ecosystem. In Figure 5.4, areas with a radiative dryness index of 1 or less are occupied by forests, those with an index between 1 and 2 with grassland such as Savannah or steppe, those with an index between 2 and 3 with semi-deserts, and those with an index of 3 or more with deserts.

Humidity is not the only important factor in the interrelationship between the radiative dryness index and terrestrial ecosystems. Soil conditions also change along with humidity. The formation of soil is closely related to climate and vegetation. In moist areas in which the radiative dryness index is small, only a part of precipitation evaporates and the rest flows into rivers and eventually into the oceans. Therefore, humid, high-temperature zones in which the radiative dryness index is small, for example, tropical rain forest areas, tend to have more water flowing underground. Subterranean water removes Na (sodium), K (potassium), Mg (magnesium), and other basic salts and also erodes the soil itself. Consequently, the soil in tropical rain forests is prone to acidification and easily loses nutrients.

In areas in which the radiative dryness index is large, evaporation from the soil surface is active and large quantities of salts concentrate near the soil

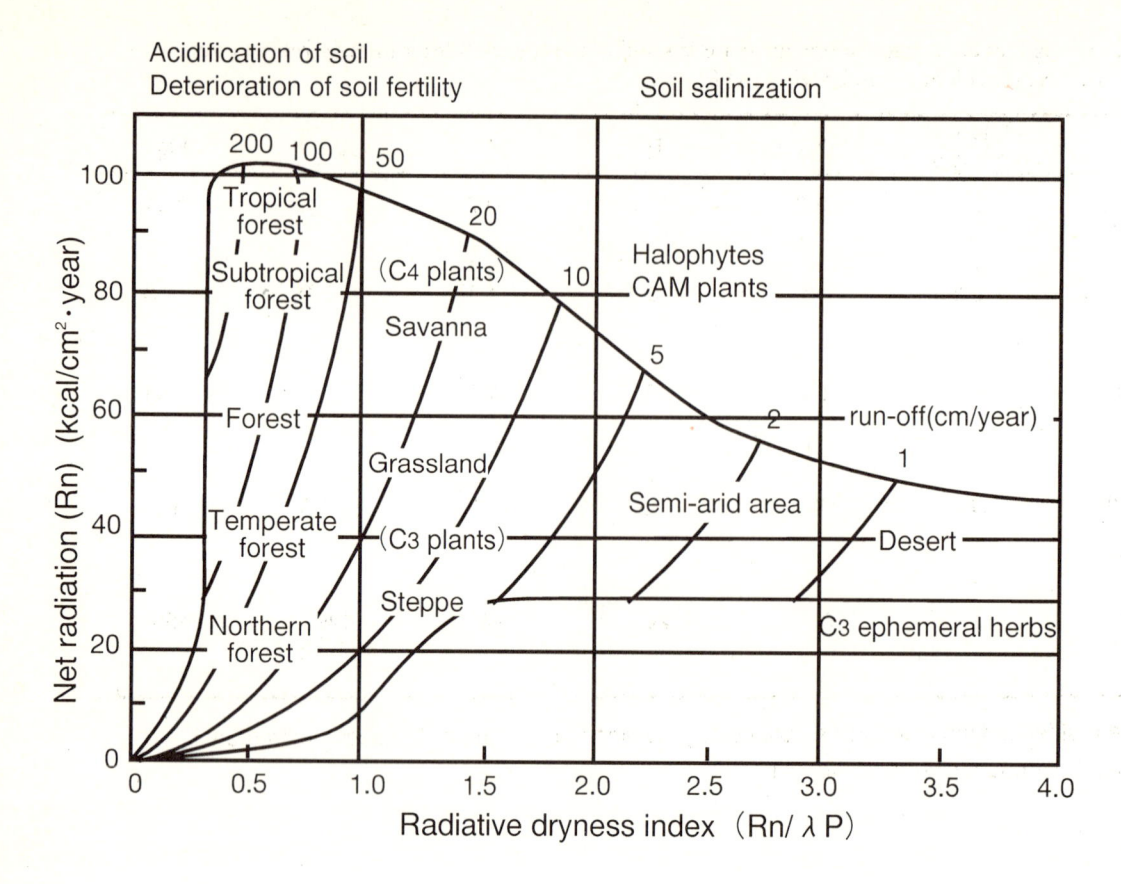

Figure 5.4.
Correspondence between ecosystem types and environmental conditions. Contour lines show the annual amount of run-off water (Oikawa, 1996).

surface, leaving only a small amount of water in the soil and increasing its osmotic pressure. Consequently, absorbing water through plant roots becomes very difficult and excessive Na and Cl tend to harm plants. Under such conditions, the growth of most plants is inhibited. A specific category of plants called halophytes is found in these areas.

Lieth (1975) has pointed out that the reason why the type of vegetation differs depending on the environmental conditions at each location is that the productivity of plants is carried out under specific atmospheric and soil conditions. It has been established that photosynthesis can be carried out using any of three separate carbon fixation methods depending on the humidity and temperature. Plants that utilize each of these three methods of photosynthesis are known as C3 plants, C4 plants and CAM plants, respectively. C4 plants are more drought-resistant than C3 plants, while CAM plants are the most drought-resistant of all. The distribution ranges of each plant type reflects its drought resistance.

Year to year changes in the atmospheric CO_2 concentration

The transfer of carbon between the atmosphere and the oceans as well as between the atmosphere and terrestrial ecosystems determines the CO_2 concentration of the atmosphere. Figure 5.5 shows the CO_2 concentration in the atmosphere as observed at the Mauna Loa observatory in Hawaii (19°32' N, 155°35' W, 3,400 m elevation) between 1958 and 1995 by Keeling et al. (1996).

Two points should be noted from Figure 5.5. First, the CO_2 concentration in the atmosphere has steadily increased each year, and the rate of annual increase in recent years has been nearly 1.5 ppmv (parts per million in terms of the total volume of the atmosphere). The atmospheric CO_2 concentration was 315 ppmv on average in 1958, but had risen above 350 ppmv by 1988 and has continued to increase since that time. This increase is the result of human activity in the form of large-scale combustion of fossil fuels such as oil and coal. Deforestation (D_f) also increases the atmospheric CO_2 concentration.

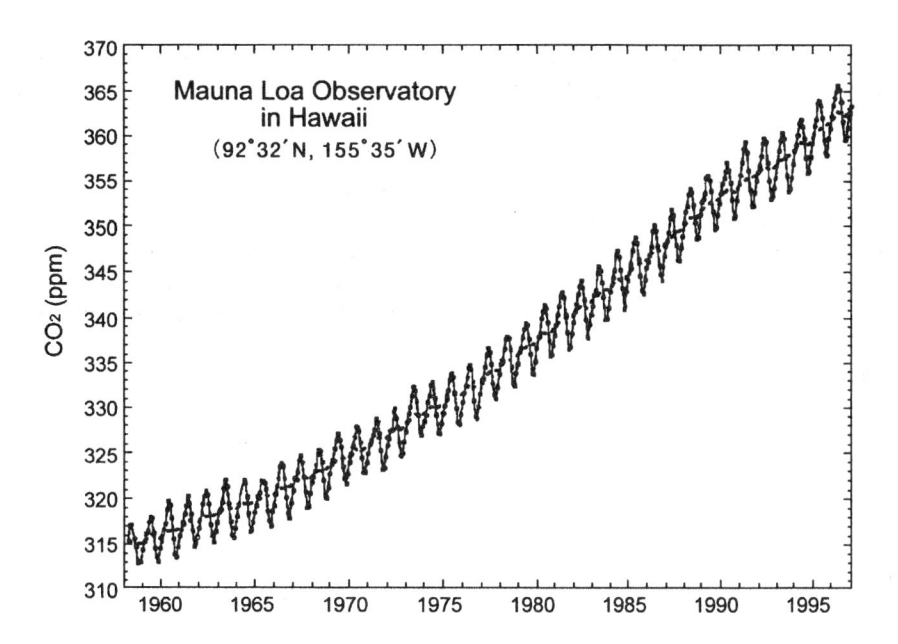

Figure 5.5.
Changes in the atmospheric CO2 concentration observed at Mauna Loa Observatory in Hawaii (Keeling et al., 1996).

Second, the atmospheric CO_2 concentration shows very regular seasonal fluctuation. The maximum concentration during the year is recorded from late April to early May. The concentration rapidly drops and reaches a minimum from late September to early October. The difference between the maximum and the minimum value is approximately 9 ppmv. This seasonal fluctuation is a reflection of photosynthesis by vegetation, especially in the forests of the temperate zone in the Northern Hemisphere. Plants in the temperate zone absorb large amounts of CO_2 in the course of photosynthesis (GPP) from spring to autumn, and in so doing reduce the atmospheric CO_2 concentration. On the contrary, from autumn to spring CO_2 emissions due to respiration (R) and the decay of organic substances in the soil (D) exceed GPP, pushing up the atmospheric CO_2 concentration. The seasonal fluctuation in the atmospheric CO_2 concentration clearly reflects the global exchange of carbon between terrestrial ecosystems and the atmosphere.

The CO_2 concentration in the atmosphere provides us with a mirror for viewing the earth's overall carbon cycle, and as such it will provide important clues to aid research on the roles of the ocean and terrestrial ecosystems in the carbon cycle.

This work benefited from access to the US Department of Energy's (DOE's) Carbon Dioxide Information Analysis Center's data archives, from climatic time series made available by D. R. Cayan of the Scripps Institution of Oceanography (SIO) and J. Eischeid at NOAA's Climate Data Center.

References

Budyko, M. I. 1975. *Climate and Life I & II*. University of Tokyo Press, Tokyo. (in Japanese)

Hattori, A. 1972. Science 42: 20-28.

IPCC. 1990. 1. Greenhouse gases and aerosols. In: (J. T. Houghton, G. J. Jenkins, and J. J. Ephraums, eds.). *Climate Change*. The IPCC Scientific Assessment. Cambridge University Press, New York.

Keeling, C. D., R. B. Bacastow, A. F. Carter, S. C. Piper, T. P. Wholf, M. Heimann, W. G. Mook, and H. Roelofzen. 1996. A three dimensional model of atmospheric CO_2 transport based on observed winds: 1. Analysis of observational data. In: (D. H. Peterson, ed.) *Aspects of Climatic Variability in the Pacific and the Western Americas*. Pp.35-363. Geophysical Monograph 55, AGU, Washington.

Lieth, H. 1975. Some prospects beyond production

measurement. In: (H. Lieth and R. H. Whittaker, eds.) *Primary Productivity of the Biosphere*. Pp.285-304. Springer-Verlag, New York.

Oikawa, T. 1996. Ecology of terrestrial vegetation. In: (N. Handa, ed.) *Global Warming from the Point of View of Atmospheric and Hydrospheric Science*. Pp.241-250. Nagoya University Press, Nagoya. (in Japanese)

Schlesinger, W. H. 1991. *Biogeochemistry*. Academic Press, San Diego, 443pp.

Suzuki, Y. 1997. *Marine Life and Carbon Cycle*. University of Tokyo Press, Tokyo, 193pp. (in Japanese).

Tsutsumi, T. 1989. *Forest Ecology*. Asakura Shoten, Tokyo, 166pp. (in Japanese)

Whittaker, T. H. and G. E. Likens. 1973. Carbon in the biota. In: (G. M. Woodwell and E. V. Pecan. eds.) *Carbon and the Biosphere*. Pp.281-300. US Atomic Energy Commission.

Chapter 6

Influence of Decreased Snowfall due to Warming Climate Trends on the Water Quality of Lake Biwa, Japan

Hiroji Fushimi

Lake Biwa in Shiga Prefecture is located roughly at the center of Japan, and is Japan's largest and most important freshwater resource. Lake Biwa covers 675 km^2, and its catchment area covers 3,174 km^2. This catchment area is surrounded by mountain ranges of slightly more than 1,000m above sea level. During winter, the northern part of this catchment area is covered with snow, which forms a very important water resource for the lake.

Water from melted snow has a high concentration of dissolved oxygen. In years of meager snowfall, the concentration of dissolved oxygen in the deepest layer of the lake, called the hypolimnion, becomes significantly lower. Thus, snowfall plays an important role in sustaining the dissolved oxygen concentration and maintaining the water quality of Lake Biwa. This chapter investigates what will happen to the volume of snowfall in the catchment of Lake Biwa and to the lake's dissolved oxygen concentration in the 21st century due to global warming.

Amount of snowfall

Figure 6.1 shows annual variations in the amount of snowfall and the minimum dissolved oxygen, percent of saturation, and water temperatures of the deep layer of Lake Biwa from 1968 to 1983 (Fushimi, 1983). The amount of snowfall in the Lake Biwa catchment area fluctuated from 0.3 to 1.9 billion tons, with the mean calculated at 1.03 billion tons. When the amount of snowfall is above the mean, a lower water temperature and a higher dissolved oxygen concentration are observed. This is caused by a density-current of melted snow subsiding into the deep layer of Lake Biwa from the mouth of the inflowing river.

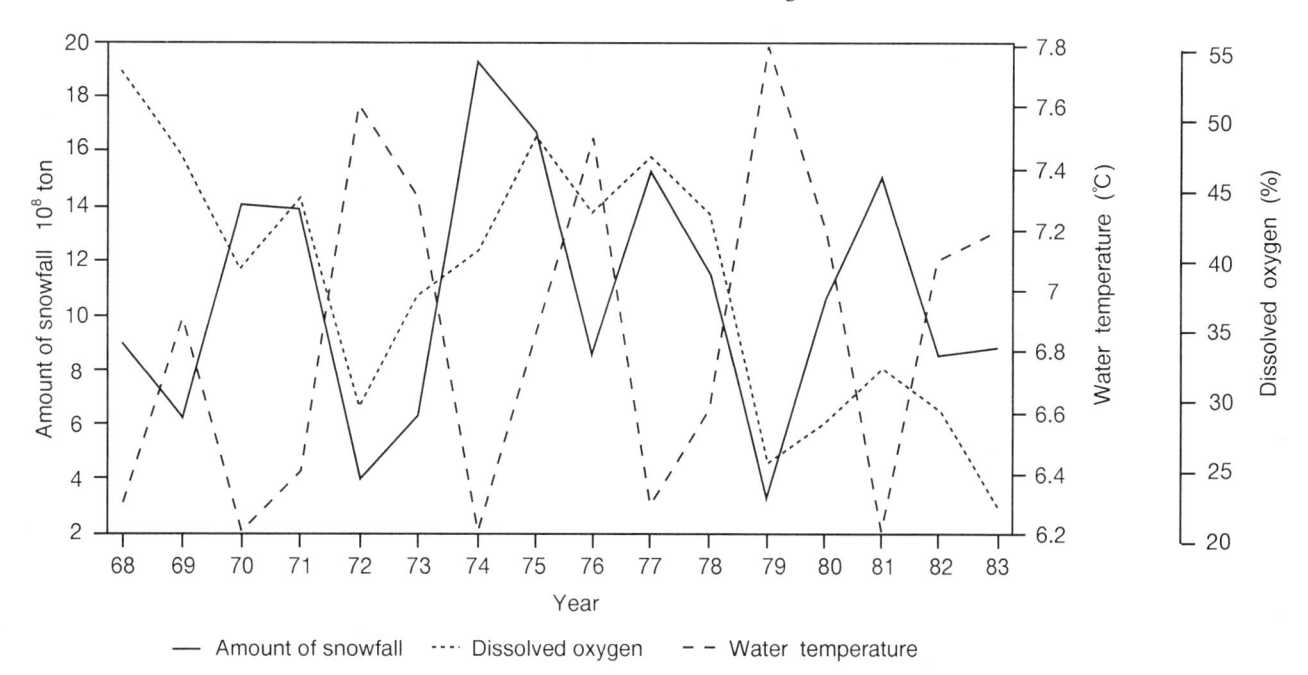

Figure 6.1.
Amount of snowfall in the Lake Biwa catchment area, lowest dissolved oxygen concentration, and minimum water temperature of the deep layer of Lake Biwa.

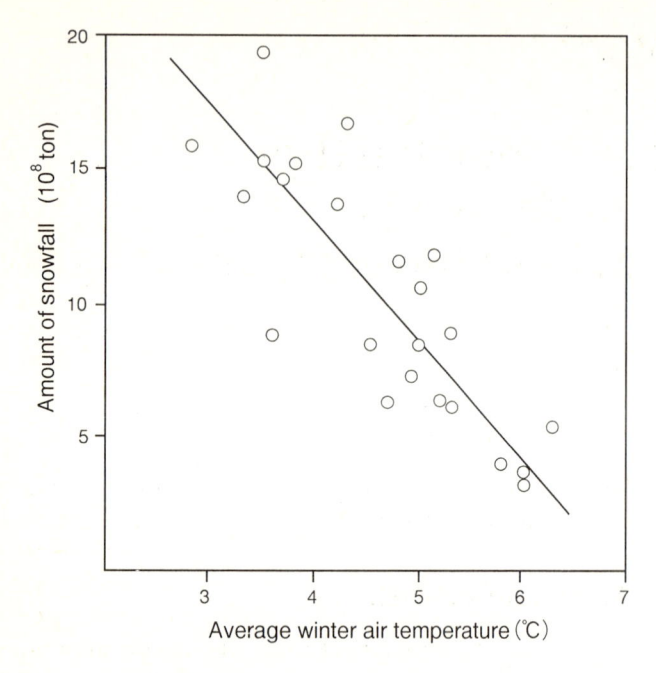

Figure 6.2.
Relationship between amount of snowfall and average winter air temperature.

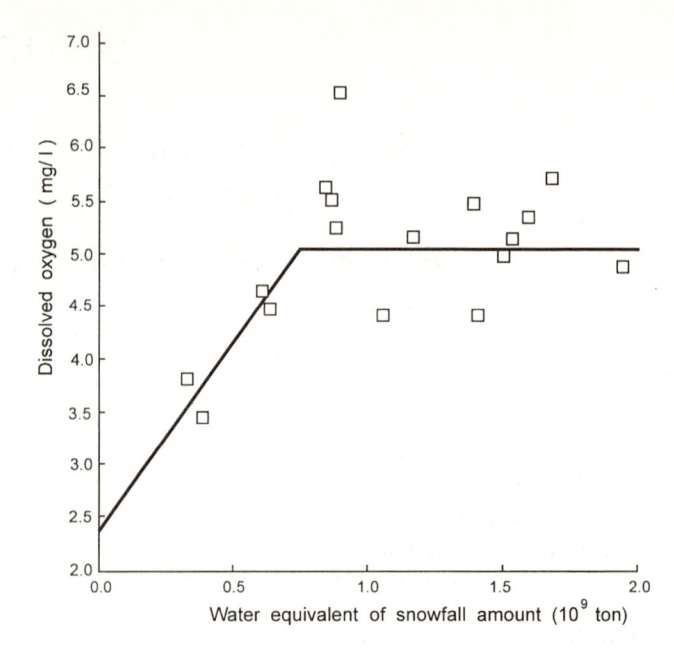

Figure 6.3.
Relationship between amount of snowfall and the minimum dissolved oxygen concentration.

The amount of snowfall affects the dissolved oxygen concentration, the water temperature, and the process of eutrophication in Lake Biwa. Figure 6.2 shows the relationship between the amount of snowfall and the average winter air temperature from December to March at Hikone, in the central part of the Lake Biwa catchment area. Less snow falls in a warmer winter, and more in a colder winter. An increase of 1°C in the average winter air temperature results in a decrease in snowfall of 480 million tons. Therefore, there is a strong possibility that a warming climate will significantly reduce the amount of snowfall. However, a decrease in the amount of snowfall must be considered in relation to an increase in other forms of precipitation, and a rise in the altitude of the snowline that will accompany a warming climate. It is expected that the climate will warm by more than 1.5°C by the 2030s (Tagart et al., 1990).

Dissolved oxygen concentration

Naka (1973) first reported the depletion of dissolved oxygen in the deep layer of Lake Biwa. The minimum was measured in the deep layer (about 80 m deep) in October and November for 30 years from 1958 to 1988. These months were just before the overturning period (the time of year when the layers of lake water turn over, and the upper layers subside to replace the lower layers), when the concentration of dissolved oxygen reaches its lowest point in the deep layer.

Eutrophication in Lake Biwa has been taking place since the 1960s, and the concentration of dissolved oxygen in the deep layer has been gradually decreasing. If this decrease continues, anoxic conditions may prevail in the near future, allowing the release of ammonia and phosphates from lake bottom sediments.

When the amount of snowfall is less than 1 billion tons, the dissolved oxygen concentration in the lake's deep layer rapidly declines, but when the snowfall is more than 1 billion tons, the dissolved oxygen concentration remains above 4.5 mg/l (Figure 6.3). Thus we can consider 1 billion tons of snowfall as the critical amount of average snowfall in the Lake Biwa catchment needed to sustain the dissolved oxygen concentration in the deep layer of the lake.

Discussion and concluding remarks

Due to the topography of the area, the majority of the snowfall is stored at altitudes between 400 m and 800 m above sea level. With climatic warming, precipitation will be more likely to take the form of rain rather than snow, and the altitude of the average snow line will become higher. In other words, the altitude boundary between rain and snow will rise as a result of a warming climate, and this rise in the snow line will cause a decrease in the amount of snowfall. Thus, an estimate of the amount of snowfall in the event of global climatic warming must be based on variations in the amount of total precipitation as well as the altitude of the average snow line.

Figure 6.4 shows the estimated amount of snowfall

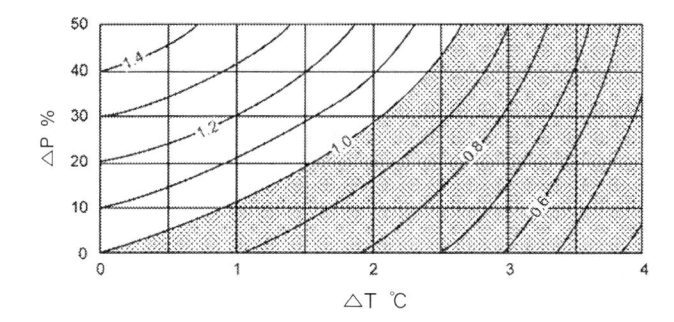

Figure 6.4.
Amount of snowfall estimated from an increase of precipitation (%) and average air temperature (°C). The amount of snowfall is indicated in units of 10^{12} kg. The shaded portion indicates snow fall less than 1 billion tons (the approximate average in recent years) and the unshaded portion an amount greater than 1 billion tons.

in relation to the increase in precipitation and air temperature. The average air temperature is projected to rise 1.5 - 3.5°C by the 2030s (Japan Meteorological Agency, 1989). If the average air temperature does increase by 1.5°C, this would result in snowfall of less than 1 billion tons, unless the total amount of precipitation increases by 20% in excess of present levels. If the average air temperature rises by 3.5°C, the amount of snowfall would decrease significantly, to about 0.6 billion tons, even if the total precipitation increases by 20%.

With declining snowfall and 2°C rise in the air temperature range, the slopes of the snowfall isogram become steeper. This is due to the topography of the area; that is, the areas between 400 m and 800 m above sea level where the greater amount of snowfall is presently stored will come to be below the average snowline under conditions of climatic warming.

Consequently, climatic warming will cause a significant decrease in the amount of snowfall in the Lake Biwa catchment and thus in the dissolved oxygen concentration in the deep layer of the lake, which may further exacerbate the process of eutrophication. If climatic warming progresses as predicted, we will face a difficult time in the 21st century from the viewpoint of both water quantity and quality in Lake Biwa.

Conclusion

1) An increase in the average air temperature by 1.5 - 3.5°C is predicted by the 2030s. If this increase is 1.5°C, the average amount of snowfall will not exceed its present average of 1 billion tons unless total precipitation is 20% in excess of present levels. If the average air temperature rises by 3.5°C, the amount of snowfall will decrease to 0.6 billion tons even if the total precipitation increases by 20% in excess of present levels.

2) When the amount of snowfall is less than 1 billion tons, the minimum dissolved oxygen concentration in the deep layer of Lake Biwa rapidly decreases. However, when the amount of snowfall is more than 1 billion tons, the dissolved oxygen concentration increases. Thus, if climatic warming significantly decreases the amount of snowfall in the Lake Biwa catchment area, the dissolved oxygen concentration in the deep layer of the lake will also decrease, exacerbating the process of eutrophication.

References

Fushimi, H. 1983. Snowfall in the Lake Biwa catchment area . Bulletin of Lake Biwa Research Institute 2: 79-117. (in Japanese)

Japan Meteorological Agency 1989. *Report of Unusual Weather '89*. Japan Meteorological Agency, Tokyo, 433 pp. (in Japanese).

Naka, K. 1973. Secular variation of oxygen change in the deep water of Lake Biwa. Japanese J. of Limnology 34: 41-43. (in Japanese with English abstract)

Tegart, W. J. McG, G. W. Shaeldon, and D. C. Griffiths. 1990. *Climate Change, IPCC Impact Assessment*. Australian Government Publishing Service, Canberra.

Chapter 7

Sudden Global Warming and Sea Level Change in Holocene Japan

Arata Momohara

Since the Middle Pleistocene in about 730,000 BP, glacial epochs and interglacial epochs have been alternating regularly in cycles of about 100,000 years (Ruddiman and Raymo, 1988). During these glacial-interglacial cycles, the expansion of glaciers combined with declines in sea level occurred gradually. On the other hand, the climate warmed quickly until the warmest period of the cycle was reached, so reductions in the volume of glaciers combined with rises in sea level tended to occur rapidly after the cycle reached its coldest point. In the case of the most recent shift from glacial to interglacial stage, which took place at the end of the Pleistocene and into the early Holocene (or Recent), the warming from the point of maximum glaciation until the peak of the hypsithermal stage (when the climate was at its warmest) occurred rapidly - within a period of about 15,000 years.

The sea level at the last glacial maximum was about 120 m lower, and the sea level at the hypsithermal stage was 2 to 3 m higher than today's mean sea level (Kaizuka et al., 1977; Fairbanks, 1989). This means that sea levels rose by more than 120 m over about 15,000 years. During this span of time, there were some periods in which sea levels rose precipitously, and other periods, such as the Younger Dryas in around 10,500 BP, when sea levels either stopped rising or declined. During the period of the most sudden sea level rise, the sea level is thought to have risen by 15 m or more within 1,000 years, a faster rate of sea level rise than is currently expected to accompany global warming in the 21st century.

The rapid warming of the climate and the associated sea level changes resulted in equally rapid changes in the geographic distribution of life forms. Pollen analysis in Europe and North America has provided evidence for the rapid expansion of tree species into areas where icecaps and tundra predominated toward the end of the last glacial (Huntley and Birks, 1983; Delcourt and Delcourt, 1987).

The presence of warm ocean currents flowing northward along the coast of Japan have exerted a strong influence upon both marine and terrestrial life forms. The spatial and temporal distribution of the warm currents flowing northward has been reconstructed using data obtained through analysis of fossil plankton recovered from submarine boring cores. In the Pacific Ocean, the Kuroshio current front had moved as far north as the coast of Shikoku Island by 14,000 BP. A thousand years later it had reached Enshunada on the coast of central Japan, and by 10,000 PB it was flowing as far as the Boso Peninsula (Figure 7.1; Chinzei et al., 1987). Warm currents did not flow into the Sea of Japan during the last glacial. Around 14,000 BP, however, the Tsushima warm current began flowing into the Sea of Japan, and a full-scale inflow began around 8,000 BP. By 6,300 BP or thereabouts, the Tsugaru warm current had developed, passing through the Tsugaru Strait from the Sea of Japan to the Pacific Ocean, then flowing southward (Oba, 1993).

The chronology of warming can also be reconstructed from analysis of the molluscan fauna living in enclosed bay areas around the Japanese coast (Figure 7.1; Matsushima, 1996). *Tegillarca granosa*, a kind of cockle which is limited to areas south of Ise Bay today, migrated north along with the warm current, and its distribution had reached the area around Sendai Bay by sometime around 7,900 to 7,600 BP. Likewise, the distribution of *Standella capillacea*, which is presently found only south of the Ariake Sea of Kyushu Island, and of *Tellinimactra edentula*, which lives south of Taiwan today, also extended further north around 7,500 BP. From the peak of the Holocene transgression (the point of maximum sea level rise in the Holocene), until approximately 6,500 to 5,000 BP, these creatures could be found in the bays of the southern Kanto Region. During this period, giant reef-building coral developed in the present Tateyama City area on the southern Boso Peninsula. This reef-building coral was made up of over 80 coral species and was on a scale that ranks with that of present-day coral fauna found in the area around northern Ryukyu Islands.

Approximately 10,000 years ago, the woodland vegetation in the lowlands south of the Kanto Region

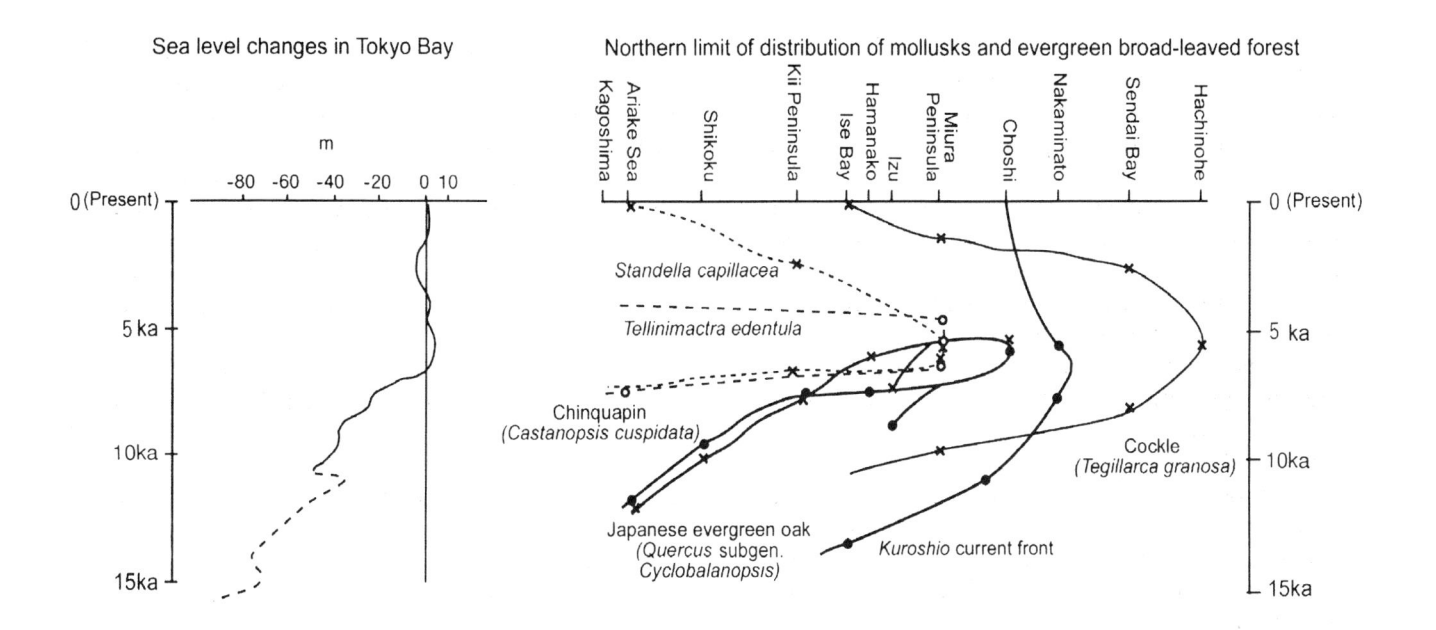

Figure 7.1.
Changes in the sea level of Tokyo Bay (left) and northern limit of distribution of mollusks and evergreen broad-leaved forest (right). Sea level curve (Kaizuka et al., 1977 dotted; Kosugi, 1992), Kuroshio current front (Chinzei et al., 1987), mollusks (Matsushima, 1996), and northern limit of evergreen broad-leaved forest (Matsushita, 1992).

underwent major changes. A coniferous forest in which varieties of spruce (*Picea*), fir (*Abies*) and pine (*Pinus*) were prominent was replaced by a mainly deciduous forest dominated by Japanese Beech *Fagus crenata* and Japanese oak *Quercus* subgen. *Lepidobalanus*. In the process, this forest passed through a transient phase in which species of birch (*Betula*) and alder (*Alnus*) were dominant. Later, the deciduous broad-leaved forests of the Pacific coast were replaced by evergreen broad-leaved forests with Chinquapin *Castanopsis cuspidata* and several kinds of evergreen oak *Quercus* subgen. *Cyclobalanopsis* dominant. Evergreen oak and chinquapin pollen had already been produced south of the Izu Peninsula by 10,000 BP, but it was not until around 7,500 to 6,000 BP that these evergreen broad-leaved trees increased in number and became dominant throughout the lowland forests (Figure 7.1; Matsushita, 1992). The same kind of changes occurred much later in the Kinki Region and in the interior of Kanto. Evergreen broad-leaved forests did not develop until around 3,000 BP in the area surrounding northern Tokyo Bay. On the Sea of Japan side of the country, *F. crenata* and Japanese cedar *Cryptomeria japonica* rapidly expanded their ranges of distribution after 10,000 BP. This is because a climate with heavy snowfall, similar to that of today, had developed along this side of Japan due to the inflow of the Tsushima warm current.

The climate warming that occurred during the period of the Holocene transgression exerted a strong influence upon marine and terrestrial life forms in and around Japan. Since the shoreline during the transgression period was below today's sea level, however, few clues remain as to the direct effects of the rise in sea level on coastal life. Nevertheless, the topographical change of the coastal area must have had a great influence upon life forms in the coastal areas.

During the period of transgression, a topography of rias developed as the advancing shoreline eroded the dissected valleys that had been created during the glacial period. At the peak of the transgression, the sea had penetrated deep into the ravines that dissected the plateaus of the Kanto Region. Shell heaps dating from the Jomon Period of Japanese history (10,000 to 2,200 BP) can be found at the edges of these plateaus. By studying the changes in the shells within these shell heaps, it is possible to learn about the diet of the Jomon people and about the changes occurring in the environment of the inner bay.

Around 5,300 BP the Holocene transgression ended and the sea level began to decline. In the innermost part of Tokyo Bay, the deeper areas were rapidly filled in as river deltas developed. Not only did the shoreline retreat at a rate of 30 m per year, but a sandbar formed at the mouth of the bay, making the water of the bay brackish (Kosugi, 1992). Quahogs, short-necked clams, cockles, and oysters were the main species comprising the shell heaps at the peak of the Holocene transgressions, whereas in 3,500 BP, the shell heaps were mainly composed of corbiculas, and the number of shell heaps themselves began to decrease. The Jomon people became more dependent on plant resources (Kaneyama and Kurata, 1994). As the sea level changed, environmental changes took place in the inner bay which had a strong influence upon their diet and culture.

In the forests of the Kanto Region, since the peak of the Holocene transgression, anthropogenic influences are thought to have been strong in the areas surrounding ruins identified from this period. It is possible that semi-cultivation of trees such as Japanese chestnut had started. However, as far as can be ascertained from examining plant macrofossils found in southern and central Kanto, the species composition of the Jomon-Period forests was rich. For example, in the fossil assemblages at the Tama Hill site, the spruce *Picea* sect. *Picea* and the ash *Fraxinus mandshurica*, both of which were distributed north of the cool temperate zone, coexisted with the Japanese evergreen oak *Quercus acuta* and the Oriental white oak *Q. aliena*, which now grow in the warm temperate zone (Tsuji et al., 1986). Forests containing human settlements in the southern Kanto Region can be thought of as having lost diversity as the destruction of vegetation advanced into early historical times.

Studies of the history of vegetation in various regions of Japan from the peak of the last glacial to the present time provide a good grasp of the rapidity with which different tree species have replaced each other as dominant members of the various forest ecosystems. The same process has occurred in North American and European forests, although the scale and patterns of changes differ from those of Japan. Moreover, the time scales over which certain species of vegetation have actually dominated particular ecosystems represent a mere instant in the course of the environmental changes that have been occurring all through the Quaternary Period (1.6 million BP - present). In fact, during the Quaternary, only in rare cases have the plant species dominating the forests today been found to have repeatedly expanded their ranges during previous interglacials. For example, fossil assemblages where Japanese beech are abundant are rarely found, and there have been only a few interglacials during the Quaternary in which evergreen oak-dominated forests existed as they do today.

On the other hand, it is not unusual to find instances of plants with a limited distribution today that have dominated the vegetation over wide areas at certain times during the past. For example, spruce *Picea* sect. *Picea* is found only rarely in inland Honshu today, but was common throughout the lowlands of Honshu during the most recent glacial.

How, then, are the vegetation and flora of today likely to respond to environmental changes in the future? The genetic diversity of the flora in many regions has already been significantly reduced as a result of progressive destruction of vegetation since prehistoric times. The genetic diversity of the plant species within a given area does not exist simply to help them cope with the environment of today, but is the result of a continuing process of natural selection and repeated adaptation to environmental changes. Even the rarest plants that exist today possess long histories during which they survived environmental changes, including periods in the past when they expanded their distribution, and each hides within itself the potential to expand its distribution again as a result of environmental changes in the future. Today, because the distribution of vegetation throughout Japan is heavily fragmented, it seems that all plants will face difficulties in adjusting their ranges of distribution while maintaining their genetic diversity in the face of environmental changes.

References

Chinzei, K., K. Fujioka, H. Kitazato, I. Koizumi, T. Oba, M. Oda, H. Okada, T. Sakai, and Y. Tanimura. 1987. Postglacial environmental change of the Pacific ocean off central Japan. Marine Micropaleontology 11: 273-291.

Delcourt, P. A. and H. R. Delcourt. 1987. *Long-term Forest Dynamics of the Temperate Zone*. Springer-Verlag, New York. 439 pp.

Fairbanks, R. G., 1989. A 17,000-year glacio-eustatic sea level record: influence of glacial melting rates on the Younger Dryas event and deep-ocean circulation. Nature 342: 637-642.

Huntley, B. and H. J. B. Birks. 1983. *An Atlas of Past and Present Pollen Maps for Europe: 0-13000 BP*. Cambridge University Press, Cambridge. 667 pp.

Kaizuka, S., Y. Naruse, and I. Matsuda. 1977. Recent formation and their basal topography in and around Tokyo Bay, central Japan. Quaternary Research 8: 32-50.

Kaneyama, Y. and E. Kurata. 1994. Human activity in Jomon Period. In: (K. Endo, ed.) *Late Holocene*

Paleoenvironments and Floral Change around Matsudo City, Chiba Prefecture, Central Japan. Pp.127-139. Matsudo Museum, Chiba, Japan. (in Japanese)

Kosugi, M. 1992. History of Tokyo Bay since the last glacial period reconstructed from diatom fossil assemblages. In: (Editorial Board of History of Misato City, History of Misato City, ed.) *Nature*. Vol. 8. Pp.112-193. Misato, Saitama, Japan. (in Japanese)

Matsushima, Y. 1996. Holocene oceanographic change around Japan - the change of Kuroshio current since ca. 7500 BP based on the occurrence of warm temperate fauna. In: (K. Koike and Y. Ota, eds.)*Changing Japanese Coast*. Pp.22-41. Kokin Shoin, Tokyo.

Matsushita, M. 1992. Lucidophyllous forest development along the Pacific Coast of the Japanese Archipelago during the Holocene. Quaternary Research. (Daiyonki Kenkyu) 31: 375-387. (in Japanese)

Oba, T. 1993. Oceanographic changes around Japan since the last glacial. Gakujutu-Geppo 6: 934-938. (in Japanese)

Ruddiman, W. F. and M. E. Raymo. 1988. Northern Hemisphere climate regimes during the past 3 Ma: possible tectonic connections. Philosophical Transaction of the Royal Society of London. Ser. B 318: 411-430.

Tsuji, S., M. Minaki, M. Suzuki, S. Noshiro, and H. Chino. 1986. Tama New Town No.796 Site; stratigraphy and plant fossil assemblages in peat layers of Jomon Periods. Research Report of the Buried Cultural Asset Center of Tokyo Metropolis 7: 72-116. (in Japanese)

Chapter 8

Recent Changes in Glacial Phenomena in the Nepalese Himalayas

Hiroji Fushimi

Heavy precipitation in the Nepalese Himalayas on 9 November 1995 resulted in heavy snowfalls in the Himalayan alpine region at altitudes above 4000m, killing large numbers of livestock and triggering avalanches that claimed the lives of 63 people (Yamada et al., 1996). Other unusual events include the glacier outburst floods (GLOFs) and the related landslide disasters associated with glacial retreat that have occurred recently in the Khumbu district of eastern Nepal. These natural hazards may be closely connected to the warming of the climate.

We have carried out glaciological observations in the Nepalese Himalayas since the 1970s in order to clarify the recent changes in glacial phenomena in the Khumbu district. We have also analysed satellite images taken in the 1980s and 1990s in order to ascertain the regional characteristics of these glacial fluctuations in the Nepalese Himalayas.

From our field surveys and analyses of satellite images, we have concluded that unstable water supplies and shortages of water in reservoirs fed by glaciers in the Nepalese Himalayas are now occurring due to the shrinkage of glacial ice bodies. At the same time, natural disasters such as GLOFs and other related landslide phenomena are taking place as a result of recent fluctuations in glacial termini, expanding glacial lakes and other environmental problems related to climate warming.

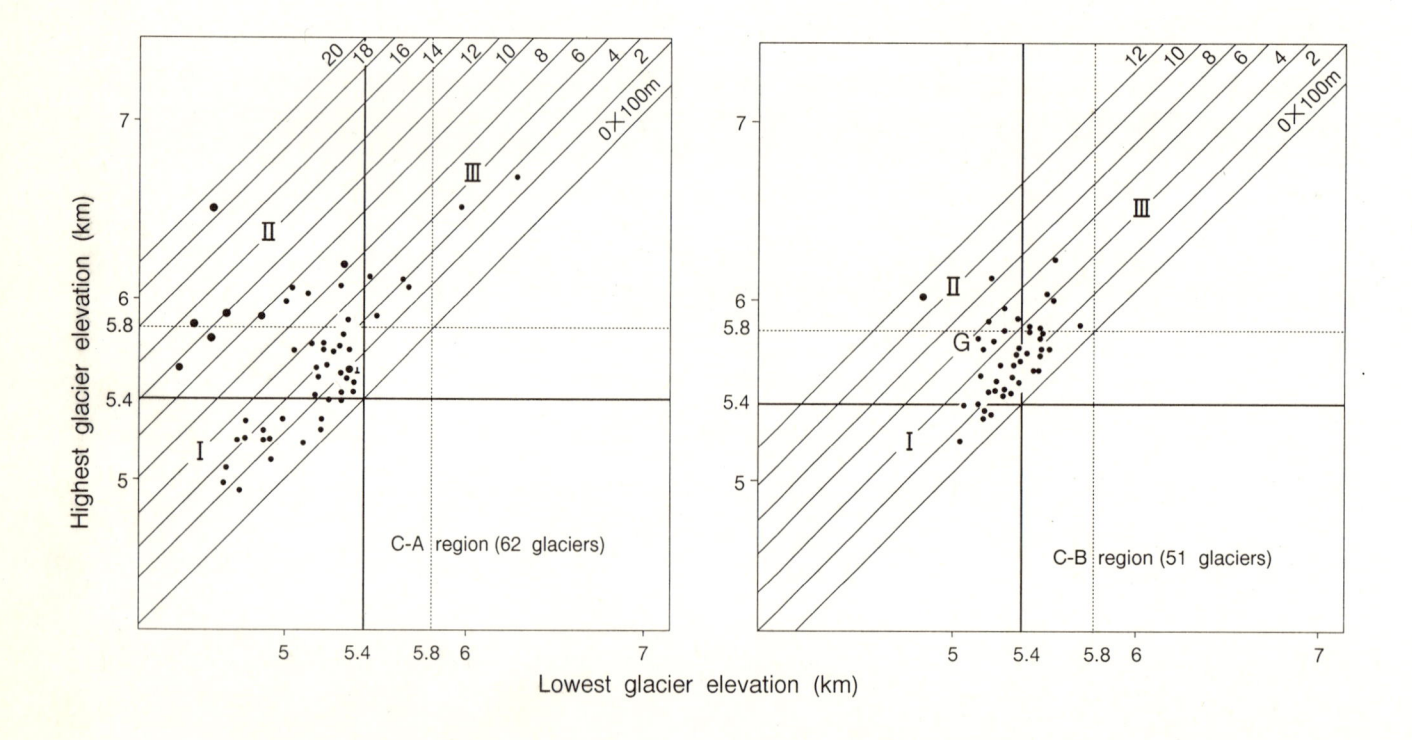

Figure 8.1.
Relationships between the lowest and the highest glacier elevations, the equilibrium line altitude of the 1970s (thick solid line) and 1995 (dotted line) in the Khumbu district, eastern Nepal.

Topographic conditions in the Khumbu district

Frontispiece 12 shows SPOT (Systeme Pour l' Observation de la Terre) images of the Khumbu district taken in 1995. There are two types of glaciers; the debris-covered type which includes relatively larger glaciers such as Khumbu Glacier (K in Frontispiece 12), and the clean type without superficial debris, which includes relatively smaller glaciers such as Gyajo Glacier (G in Frontispiece 12). The latter type are mainly located at lower altitudes below 6000 m.

There are large glacial lakes in the terminal area of the debris-covered type such as the Imja Glacial Lake (I in Frontispiece 12). Some of these large glacial lakes have been sources of the GLOFs that have been observed since the late 1970s in the Mingbo Valley (M in Frontispiece 12).

In order to clarify the terminal fluctuation of glaciers in the Nepalese Himalayas, we must investigate clean type glaciers such as Gyajo Glacier and Kongma Glacier (G and K in Frontispiece 12). This is because the terminal parts of debris-covered type glaciers such as the Khumbu Glacier are inactive (stagnant), indicating the presence of fossil ice bodies formed by glacial advances during the Little Ice Age. Consequently they do not indicate present glacial fluctuations.

Figure 8.1 shows the relationship between the lowest and the highest glacier elevations in relation to the equilibrium line altitude (ELA) in the 1970s and in 1995. There are three domains, divided according to the ELA. Domain I indicates the highest glacier elevation below the ELA, representing unhealthy glaciers in that the entire glacier consists of an ablation area. Domain II consists of the areas in which the ELA is located on a glacier, meaning that the glacier is healthy. Domain III indicates the lowest glacier elevation higher than the ELA where ice bodies are located in accumulation area separated by glaciers of both Domain I and II. Changes in the ELA control the stability of glacial phenomena and climate warming usually makes the ELA higher in cases where ablation dominates over accumulation.

Recent changes in glacial phenomena

Figure 8.2 indicates the differences between the lowest elevations of the clean type glaciers surveyed during the first inventory in 1960 (Müller, 1960) and during our inventory in 1975 (Higuchi et al., 1975). In most cases, the position of lowest elevation of the glacial terminus was higher in 1975 than in 1960. The glaciers in question had retreated by somewhere within the range of 0 to 100 m in terms of terminal height-difference between 1960 and 1975, except for

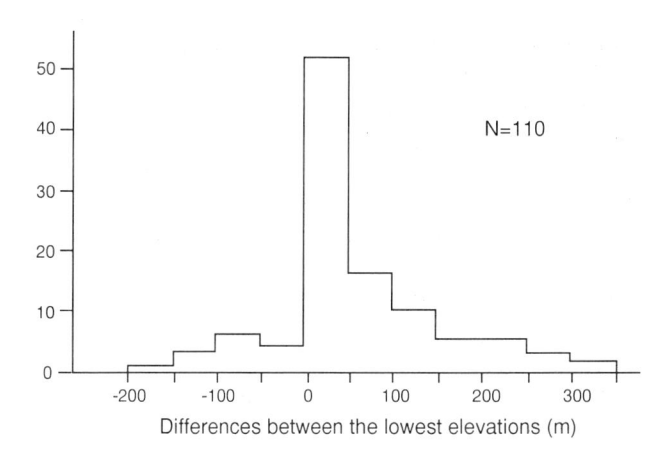

Figure 8.2.
Differences between the lowest elevations of clean type glaciers in inventories of 1960 and 1975.

a few advancing glaciers.

Since 1973, we have set many surveying base points near the glacial termini in order to measure the glacial fluctuations in the Khumbu district. Fifteen glaciers observed to be fluctuating in the 1970s could be divided into four glacial groups: retreating (8 glaciers), stationary (3 glaciers), advancing (3 glaciers) and irregular (1 glacier) according to their fluctuation rates (Fushimi and Ohata, 1980). We were also able to observe the GLOF caused by the collapse of the ice-cored dammed-up moraine in the Mingbo Valley (M in Frontispiece 12) in 1977 (Fushimi et al., 1985).

In the 1980s, almost all the glaciers in the Khumbu district had greatly shrunk, although possible advances were recorded for some glaciers during the first half of the 1980s (Yamada et al., 1992). The rate of retreat of some glaciers accelerated during the 1980s in comparison with the 1970s. In addition to the remarkable glacial retreat in the 1980s, the glacial lakes were expanding and another GLOF was reported to have occurred emanating from Langmoche Glacier in the northwestern part of the Khumbu district in 1985 (La in Frontispiece 12).

Structural changes were found in the Gyajo Glacier (G in Frontispiece 12) located near Mt. Chomolungma (Mt. Everest) between 1972 and 1995. A SPOT image taken in 1995 indicates that the lower part of the glacier had separated from the upper part and that the upper part had become divided into two parts separated by bedrock and ice cliffs (Frontispiece 12). The Gyajo Glacier is no longer a healthy glacier but has changed into a perennial snow patch. The same kind of phenomenon has also been observed in Dzonglha Valley in the central part of this region (Lo in Frontispiece 12) where several glaciers have become separated into distinct ice bodies. These glaciers were once unified as a single glacial ice body, indicating the presence of a healthy glacier in the 1970s.

In the 23 years between 1972 and 1995, remarkable changes have occurred in the Gyajo Glacier. The terminal position has retreated by about 100 m and the lower ice body is becoming separated from the upper one by ice cliffs. Also, bedrock is now visible near the ice cliff and the glacial lakes formed in the terminal area. The equilibrium line altitude (ELA) was 5400 m in the 1970s, but has since risen to about 5800 m which is equal to the highest glacial elevation of the Gyajo Glacier. The entire Gyajo Glacier is now located below the ELA and has become an ablation area, so that the accumulation area of the glacier has totally vanished. This means that the Gyajo Glacier is no longer a healthy glacier as shown in Domain II (Figure 8.1).

Similarly, the great retreat of the terminal part of Kongma Glacier in the Khumbu district was remarkable between 1976 and 1995 (Figure 8.3). Over the 19 years in question, the terminal area retreated more than 100 m and considerable thinning of glacial ice took place. Moreover, we have detected remarkable shrinkage in glacial phenomena such as this all over the Nepalese Himalayas (Yamada et al., 1992).

A GLOF occurred on the south side of Mt. Ama Dablam in the Khumbu district in 1977. At that time, we had an opportunity to conduct the first ever field work on a GLOF in the Nepalese Himalayas (Fushimi et al., 1985). The GLOF occurred on 3 September in the Mingbo Valley (Frontispiece 12) following the collapse of an ice-cored moraine, and formed new terraces along the Mingbo Valley. The volume of the GLOF was estimated to have been 400,000 tons, considering the topography of the former moraine-dammed lake. The flood caused by the GLOF was recorded at the Rabuwa Hydrological Station, 70 km downstream from the Mingbo Valley. The water level at the station, which is on the Dudh Kosi River, abruptly rose by about 1m at that time. Another GLOF, from the Langmoche Glacial Lake, occurred in 1985 in this same region (La in Frontispiece 12). The Langmoche GLOF destroyed the hydroelectric power plant and village facilities near Namche Bazar on the Dudh Kosi River.

The SPOT satellite images show clear lacustrine changes such as the expansion of the Imja Glacial Lake between the 1980s and the 1990s (Frontispiece 12). The Tso Rolpa Glacial Lake will give rise to a GLOF in Rolwaling Himal to the west of this region (Yamada, 1996). Many glacial lakes have been expanding since the 1970s in the Hunku region (H in Frontispiece 12). The glaciers in this region, too, have shown remarkable retreats, and both glacier lakes and rock glaciers now cover larger areas than they did in the 1970s. Thus, the possibility of GLOFs is concluded to be increasing throughout the Nepalese Himalayas.

Figure 8.3.
Fluctuations of the Kongma Glacier in the Khumbu district, eastern Nepal, between 1976 (above) and 1995 (below).

Discussion

The debris-covered type glacier becomes separated along its central section into two ice bodies, and the clean type of glacier also becomes separated into several ice bodies which then become perennial snow patches. A continuous sequence of glacier types has been identified and classified according to the volume of stagnant and dead ice bodies and their structural relationship to the glacial flow. In accordance with glacial retreat, both the GLOF phenomenon and the formation of rock glaciers are intensified.

The equilibrium line altitude (ELA) rose by about 400 m from 5.4 km in 1970 to 5.8 km in 1995 (Figure 8.1), with the result that many glaciers located at lower altitudes now belong to the Domain I glacier type. In this glacier type, the highest glacier elevation is lower than the ELA and the glacier becomes unhealthy and unstable, eventually turning into a collection of perennial snow patches.

Due to recent fluctuations in glacier termini, glacial lakes and related environmental factors, the region under study will face further natural disasters including GLOFs and other related landslide phenomena. There is a need to create a new management system for the rational use of water resources taking into account the recent changes in glacial phenomena in the Nepalese Himalayas.

It is very important to note that the Nepalese Himalayas will face unstable supplies and shortages of glacier-fed water resources due to the shrinkage of glacial ice bodies, and that shortfalls in glacial meltwater will tend to exacerbate drought phenomena, especially during the dry season in areas dependent on water resources from glaciers in the Nepalese Himalayas. Consequently, during the 21st century when the climate is expected to warm further (Shrestha et al., 1999), discharges will need be more carefully utilised during the dry season in the south Asia.

References

Fushimi, H. and T. Ohata. 1980. Fluctuations of glaciers from 1970 to 1978 in the Khumbu Himal, east Nepal. Seppyou 41, Special Issue: 71-81.

Fushimi, H., K. Ikegami, K. Higuchi and K. Shankar. 1985. Nepal case study: catastrophic floods. Techniques for prediction of runoff from glaciated areas. International Association of Hydrological Sciences 149: 125-130.

Higuchi, K., H. Fushimi, T. Ohata, S. Takenaka, S. Iwata, K. Yokoyama, H. Higuchi, A. Nagoshi and T. Iozawa. 1980. Glacier inventory in the Dudh Kosi Region, east Nepal. Proceedings of the Riederalp Workshop, 1978, IAHS-AISH 126: 95-103.

Müller, F. 1970. A pilot study for an inventory of the glaciers in the eastern Himalayas. Perennial Ice and Snow Masses, UNESCO/IAHS, 47-59.

Yamada, T. 1996. Report of the Investigations of Tso Rolpa Glacial Lake, Rolwaling Valley. Water and Energy Commission Secretariat of Nepal/ Japan International Cooperation Agency. 35pp.

Shrestha, A. B., C. P. Wake. P. A. Mayewski, and J. E. Dibb. 1999. Maximum temperature trends in the Himalaya and its vicinity: An analysis based on temperature records from Nepal for the period 1971-94. American Meteorological Society. Journal of Climate 20: 2775-2786.

Yamada, T., H. Shiraiwa, H. Iida, T. Kadota, T. Watanabe, B. Rana, Y. Ageta, and H. Fushimi. 1992. Fluctuations of the glaciers from the 1970s to 1989 in the Khumbu, Shorong and Lantang, Nepalese Himalayas. Japanese Society of Snow and Ice. Bulletin of Glacier Research 10: 11-19.

Yamada, T., H. Fushimi, R. Aryal, T. Kadota, K. Fujita, K. Seko, and T. Yasunari. 1996. Report of the avalanches accident at Pangka, Khumbu Region, Nepal in 1995 . Japanese Society of Snow and Ice 58(2): 145-155. (in Japanese)

Chapter 9

How Will Communities of Alpine Plants be Affected by Global Warming?

Takehiro Masuzawa

Most of the plants growing in mountain regions belong to a group known as the alpine plants. These alpine plants have adjusted themselves to the severe environmental conditions of high altitudes. In Japan, the geographic extent of the environments in which these alpine plants can survive is very limited. Therefore, if the average temperature rises due to global warming, this change will significantly influence these alpine plants, and will also allow lower-altitude plants to expand higher into the mountains.

In this chapter, I will describe the environmental characteristics of Japan's mountains as well as the characteristics and diversity of alpine plants. Next, the influence of global warming on these plants will be examined and experimental research aimed at estimating this influence will be reviewed.

The diversity of alpine plants in Japan

In terms of vertical distribution, alpine plant communities are found at or above the altitude at which the Siberian dwarf pine *Pinus pumila* grows. This species is widely distributed in mountainous regions and defines the landscape in Japan's high mountains. The extent and form of *P. pumila* communities vary widely from one location to another, as they are affected by strong winds or heavy snow. *P. pumila* communities consist of a variety of plant types, including *Rhododendron brachycarpum*, *Vaccinium vitis-idaea*, *Chamaepericlymenum canadense* and *Schizocodon soldanelloides*. At the base of the community can be found *Cladonia stellaris* and bryophytes such as *Polytrichum juniperinum*. Lichens also grow on the trunks of *P. pumila*.

Altitude zones higher than the locations in which *P. pumila* grows are characterized by alpine meadow communities. Strong wind is a characteristic of the high mountains in Japan and significantly influences alpine meadow communities. Although alpine meadow communities are located in very restricted areas, they are typically diverse (Frontispiece 9). Many plant species forming these communities are considered to have migrated from the Arctic zone or other boreal zones by way of several routes (Toyokuni, 1988; Masuzawa, 1997). Other plant species have evolved in Japan's high mountains. These alpine meadows form diverse communities amid the complex geography of the high mountains. Alpine meadow communities can be grouped as follows:

Wind-shaped plant communities. This type of community mainly includes *Kobresia bellardii*, *Carex flavocuspis*, *Oxytropis nigrescens*, *Leontopodium fauriei* and *Gentiana algida*. In terms of plant socio-logy, it belongs to the type of *Oxytropis japonica - K. bellardii* community (Ohba, 1967). Wind-shaped plant communities are located in places where strong winds blow and the height of these plants ranges up to a maximum of 30 cm.

Wind-shaped and prostrated shrub communities. This type of community consists of *Vaccinium uliginosum*, *Empetrum nigrum*, *Diapensia lapponica* and *Arcterica nana*. The major plants are small shrubs of the azalea family. *Acomastylis calthifolia* and *Euphrasia insignis* are also present. This type of community coexists with lichens such as *Cladonia rangiferina*, *Thamnolia vermicularis* and *Cetraria islantica*. Therefore, these communities contain a more diverse flora than wind-shaped plant communities.

Snowbed plant communities. This type of community is seen only in high mountains that experience heavy snow cover. It exists in hollows on mountains or in other places where winter snow is deep. As the accumulated snow melts slowly, plants grow around the edge of the snow, forming concentric circles. The communities are significantly influenced by the state of melting snow over an extended period. Major plants include *Deschampsia flexuosa*, *Arnica unalaschcensis*, *Shizocodon soldanelloides*, *Phyllodoce aleutica* and *Sieversia pentapetala*. *Rhododendron aureum* is also present in some cases.

Rock area plant communities. This type of community forms in areas where *Acomastylis calthifolia*, *Ixeris dentata*, *Carex stenantha*, *Stellaria nipponica* and *Minuartia arctica* are found. These plants grow in gaps between rocks or in small pockets formed by rocks. They tend not to grow densely. This type of community is the most representative in high mountains.

There is another type of community called an alpine meadow, which can be further subdivided into the wet type and dry type. alpine meadows are thick grasslands. In addition, in places formed during the most recent glacial (periglacial) period, land forms, rocky slopes or terraces encompass hexagonal or other unique structures. The low-growing plants that have adapted themselves to this geography are unique among alpine plants communities.

Subtle geographic features in mountains and corresponding plant diversity

Especially in the high mountains and cold areas in Hokkaido, there are many unique relationships between specific geographic features and plant communities.

The areas surrounding former glaciers, which were formed under the strong influence of those glaciers during the most recent glacial period, are very valuable from a research standpoint because glaciers no longer exist in Japan. Topographically, these areas are classed as periglacial landforms, a category that also includes many unique features found in cold regions without glaciers. In areas where the temperature is especially low in Japan, some permafrost still remains. When the temperature drops to an extremely low level in winter, permafrost develops and water in or on the surface of the ground forms crystals. In the process of development, crystallization and melting of permafrost and water/ice, rocks are frozen and progressively broken into small pieces. These pieces of rock tend to move slowly as a result of physical forces, eventually forming a variety of characteristic topographic features. The formation of such features is essentially the result of sudden drops in temperature.

These topographic features include slopes such as terraces, layers of fine and coarse materials and squares. One typical example is called a polygon. Other topographic features found around former glaciers include earth hammocks and solifluctions (Figure 9.1). These periglacial landforms are found in the Japan South Alps in Honshu and in the Taisetsu Mountain Range in Hokkaido.

Moreover, there are examples of the topographic feature known as "sorted steps" on Kiso Komagatake and Kirigamine in Nagano Prefecture in Honshu as well as on Asahidake in the Taisetsu Range. This type of terrace is from 10 cm to 2 m wide and from a few meters to as much as 80 m in length. The layers of such terraces are visible, because not many plants grow on the level parts. On the sides, however, communities of plants of the sedge family and the pulse family as well as *Leontopodium fauriei* are found. There are also "sorted stripes" which are lines of small stones. Communities of plants including *Dicentra peregrina* and other low-growing plants grow between these lines.

Polygons are seen in the Japan South Alps and in one part of Hokkaido. A polygon is an area in which small stones are seen in rows that form hexagons, and alpine plants grow at the sides of the rows. The rows of small stones and the surrounding plants are closely related.

Periglacial landforms have a close interrelationship with alpine plants. Consequently, they are valuable not only in terms of their glacial topography but also on account of the relationships between various alpine

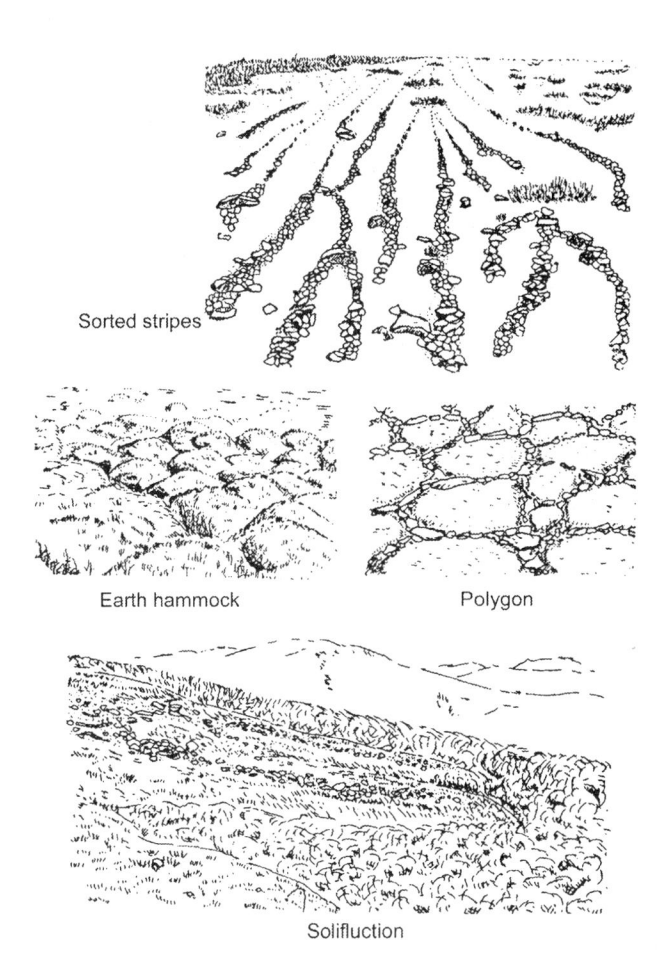

Figure 9.1.
Examples of periglacial landforms that are valued on account of their rarity in present Japan (Koizumi, 1993).

plants and subtly different topographical features. Periglacial landforms are found only in cold locations where small stones are moved gradually. In order for water to freeze and melt repeatedly, the temperature has to drop to a certain level.

If the temperature no longer continues to fall to this level under the influence of global warming, periglacial landforms will no longer be formed nor maintained. In addition, if small stones stop moving and frost heaving does not occur due to warming, certain plants will start growing. These species will occupy new habitats and in the process drive out indigenous species that have unique relationships with the land in question, possibly replacing them totally in the future. If the situation develops in this way, periglacial landforms that were formed about 10,000 years ago and other characteristic topographic features formed under low-temperature conditions will be covered by vegetation and new soil will be generated. In this way, periglacial landforms and alpine topography that have maintained sensitive relationships with these features will rapidly change.

An experiment aimed at forecasting the impact of global warming

Ecosystems in high mountains and northern regions have been attracting widespread attention in relation to global warming for a variety of reasons. First, it is predicted that the influence of global warming will be most significant in the high latitude areas of the Northern Hemisphere. Forecasts of the extent of warming vary depending on the details of the calculation model employed. Nevertheless, the year-round average global temperature in or around the year 2100 is estimated to be about 2°C higher than the present level. However, the average temperature is projected to rise much more than this in high-latitude and high-altitude areas.

Second, the ambient conditions that characterize ecosystems in Polar Regions and in high mountains are extreme; plants are almost constantly exposed to low temperatures and strong winds, and their annual growing period is short. Therefore, even a slight change in temperature can significantly influence their chances of survival.

In this context, a series of experiments was planned in an effort to study how the expected rise in temperature is likely to influence living organisms on a global scale. These experiments are being conducted under the International Tundra Experiment Plan (ITEX Plan). Under this plan, temperature change and its influence on living organisms are being examined using an experimental device called an open top chamber (OTC) mainly in Arctic regions and on high mountains in the temperate zones (Figure 9.2). An OTC is essentially a set of acrylic boards without a ceiling that surround a plant. The lighting conditions for a plant are considered to be almost the same inside and outside an OTC. The temperature, however, differs markedly. The influence of wind is less significant inside an OTC and this factor means that the temperature of the ground surface and of the plant itself inside the OTC differs from that outside. Indeed, the interior temperature can rise by anything from 2°C to 10°C depending on the location (slope, direction and geographic features) and the time. The aim of the device is to raise the temperature of selected plants to approximately 2°C to 3°C above the ambient temperature. Experiments using OTCs have been conducted on Mt. Fuji, Tateyama in Toyama Prefecture, the Central Alps in Nagano Prefecture, and the Taisetsu Range in Hokkaido. The National Institute of Polar Research has set up the OTCs and

Figure 9.2.
Open Top Chamber (OTC) installations in alpine areas of Mt. Fuji.

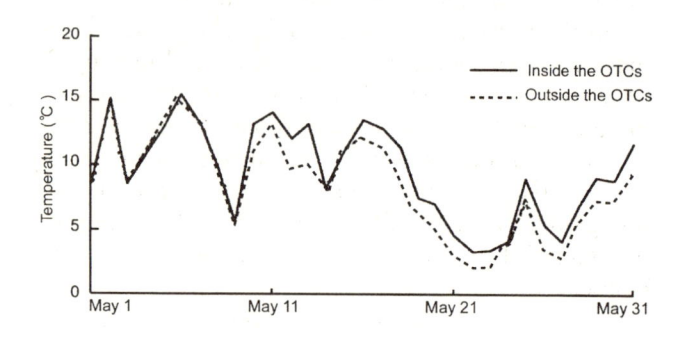

Figure 9.3.
A data logger was used to continuously measure the temperature 10 cm above the ground. The average temperature in May was approximately 9.5°C inside and 8.4°C outside the OTCs, respectively. The temperature inside the OTCs was approximately 1.1°C higher. The difference in the temperatures inside and outside the OTCs was approximately 2.1°C during the day and 0.1°C at night.

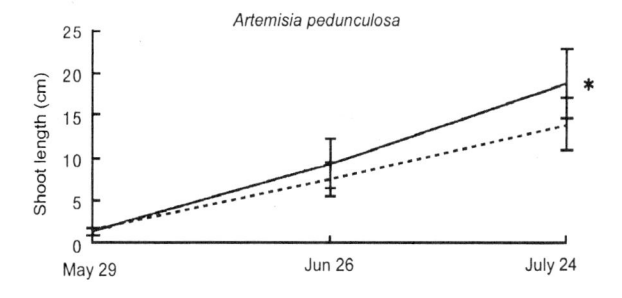

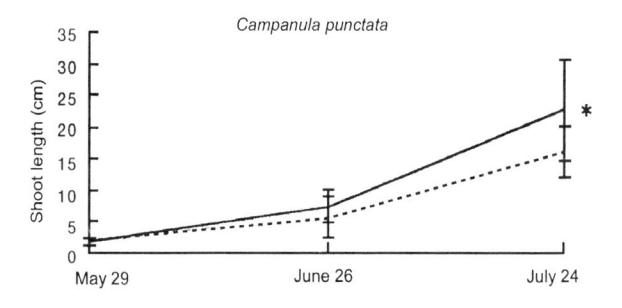

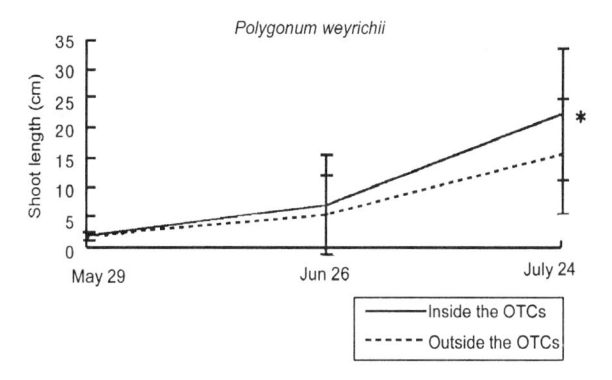

Figure 9.4.
The length of the shoots of three plants. All of them grew taller inside the OTCs. (* denotes that measurement inside and outside the OTCs was statistically significant).

has been monitoring the situation over an extended period.

On Mt. Fuji, for example, OTCs were set up on the mountain at elevations of approximately 2,500 m. We recorded changes in temperature inside and outside the OTCs as well as the corresponding growth of plants (Figures 9.3 and 9.4). The average temperature inside and outside the OTCs from May to early June, when plants start growing, was 9.5°C inside and 8.4°C outside the OTCs (Figure 9.3). The difference in temperature between the inside and outside was approximately 2.1°C during the day and 0.1°C during the night. The temperature difference became even larger during the day from June to July, reaching as high as 2 - 3°C

The growth of three typical alpine species (*Artemisia pedunculosa, Campanula punctata,* and *Polygonum weyrichii*) were examined (Figure 9.4). All of these plants grew taller inside the OTCs, and the difference in the shoot length in July was several centimeters. This results indicates clearly that the plants will grow taller if the ambient temperature is 2 - 3°C higher. Monitoring of these plants is continuing with respect to different phenologies, changes in productivity, the invasion of new species, the reduction of alpine plant species and a number of other factors.

The results of the experiments of the Japan ITEX Plan can be summarized as follows:
(1) All changes in phenology occur earlier except for autumnal colors.
(2) Regarding reproduction, the number of flowers and seeds are increasing.
(3) The number of shoots is increasing, and the number of plants per unit is also increasing.
(4) The invasion of other plant species has been observed.

Increases in the variety of plants and in the amount of primary production have been found to be in direct proportion to rises in temperature. Productivity has significantly increased, but species diversity has decreased in some locations. Annual and seasonal changes in climate also influence plants, so long-term observations are necessary before firm conclusions can be reached.

The reactions of tree species were not as obvious as those of grasses. True grasses were the most reactive plants, followed in order by broad-leaved grasses, deciduous trees and evergreen trees.

The results of these experiments indicate that both the species diversity and the number of individual plants are likely to increase. Moreover, it has been established that increases in temperature have impacts on living organisms in the soil, activate visiting insects such as defoliators and influence their reproduction rates. Plants in OTCs that had not previously been damaged by defoliators were severely damaged in 1997 on Mt. Fuji. Research has just begun on this issue in Japan and in other countries, and research methods need to be improved. The use of data to comprehensively analyze the research results also has to be discussed.

In our experiments on Mt. Fuji, the rise in the temperature inside the OTCs obviously increased the biomass. Inside the OTCs plants growing at lower elevations became established. It is highly likely, therefore, that plants that have previously been unable to survive in alpine plant communities will be able to establish themselves there due to global warming. Consequent-ly, alpine plants that are at a disadvantage in terms of their light and nutrient absorption capabilities will have to move to higher elevations. Where high mountain areas are large enough, they should be able to spread from lower to higher elevations. In Japan, however, the alpine zone is so narrow that alpine plant communities may disappear even as the result of a slight increase in temperature.

Warming and mountain plant communities

In 1996, a global warming assessment group working under the Research Committee on Global Warming of the Japan Environment Agency published a report entitled "Influence of Global Warming on Japan, 1996". According to a forecast in the report based on a climate change model, the global average temperature in 2100 will be 2°C higher than it was in 1990. The situation of places that appear to have already been influenced by increases in temperature will be described below.

It has been projected that the total area suitable for alpine plants in Japan's high mountains will shrink as the climate warms. The scale of the change can be described with reference to Mt. Apoi, located to the south of the Hidaka Mountains in Hokkaido. An extremely wide variety of alpine plants grow near the summit of Mt. Apoi (alt. 810m). These include endemic species of *Erigeron thunbergii* and *Veronica achmidtiana*. Moreover, alpine plants that have significantly declined elsewhere in terms of numbers can still be seen on Mt. Apoi.

Over the past 30 years, however, the area of suitable habitat at higher elevations has shrunk, and the variety of alpine plants that grow there has been rapidly reduced. Watanabe (1997) observed that most of the alpine plant communities that existed 30 years ago have been replaced by communities of trees. The process began when Nutcrackers *Nucifraga caryocatactes* hoarded seeds of *Pinus parviflora* in alpine meadows on the southern slopes. Fifteen years later, the height of these pines was approximately 2.5 m, and the Japanese bush clover and *Miscanthus sinensis* also invaded the area. These alpine meadows are expected to almost completely change into forests in the near future. Although this change cannot be said to have been exclusively due to global warming, the speed of the transformation of vegetation on Mt. Apoi will certainly accelerate if global warming escalates. There is concern that the loss of the grasslands on Mt. Apoi will mean the disappearance of *Hypochoeris crepidioides*, endemic to this mountain, and *Crepis gymnopus, Veronica achmidtiana* and other indigenous species from the mountain.

Grabherr et al. (1994) warned of the loss of alpine plants due to warming based on empirical data. They examined changes in vegetation over time on 26 mountains with peaks higher than 3,000 m in the central part of the European Alps. The diversity of species has greatly increased during the past 10 to 20 years, and plants are tending to migrate to higher

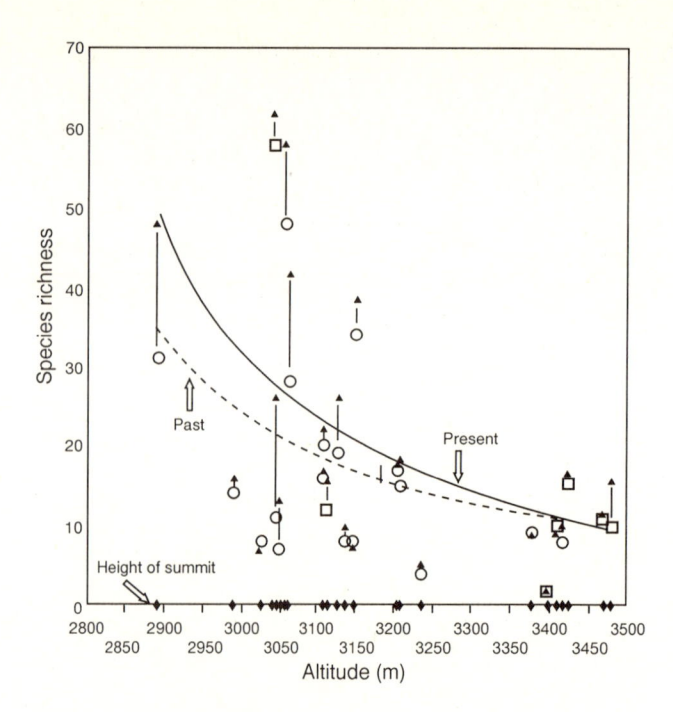

Figure 9.5.
Species diversity in the central part of the European Alps in the past and at present. The species diversity of vascular plants at different altitudes on 26 mountains higher than 3,000 m are shown. ○ : 1895 - 1918, □ : 1947 - 1953, ▲ : present (Grabherr et al., 1994).

elevations. Most species were found to be moving upwards by approximately 1 m over ten years, while the fastest moving species observed moved 4 m over ten years (Figure 9.5). Their conclusion was that plants are migrating due to global warming and that the speed of this migration has undoubtedly already accelerated. They also warned that alpine plants that are currently restricted to locations close to summits are certain to disappear in the near future.

The influence of the rise in temperature due to global warming can be expected to reveal itself in the following ways:
(1) Photosynthesis and other physiological activities will be stimulated.
(2) Biomass will increase.
(3) The formation of flowers and the production of seeds will be stimulated.
(4) The parts of plants located above the ground will live longer.
(5) Competition for resources between indigenous and invading plant species will intensify.

The influence of warming is not necessarily negative for alpine plants. Nevertheless, plants that are currently prevented from growing in high mountains due to temperature restraints will expand into higher areas and enter into severe competition over resources with alpine plants. When they initially invade the areas of alpine plant communities, species diversity will increase over the short term. However, the unique diversity that alpine plants have established as a result of their long-term presence in the alpine environment will be lost. Consequently, alpine plants will be forced to migrate to even higher elevations. Those plants with distributions confined to ridges or around summits have no other place to go, and seem destined to disappear over the longer term.

The areas in Japan where alpine plants are distributed at present are periglacial landforms that were previously influenced by glaciers. If highly fecund species from lower areas invade these areas, they will flourish there and the subtle geographic features unique to the high mountains will not be maintained. If global warming escalates at its present pace, the unique topography as well as the alpine flora of the high mountain regions will be lost in the near future.

References

Grabherr G. et al. 1994. Climate effects on mountain plants. Nature 369: 448.

Environment Agency 1997. Implications of climate change for Japan -produced in 1996. Working group on implications of climate change, Tokyo. (in Japanese)

Koizumi, T. 1993. *Why is the Japanese Mountain Beautiful?* Kokin-Syoin, Tokyo. (in Japanese)

Masuzawa, T. 1997. *The Ecology of Alpine Plants.* University of Tokyo Press, Tokyo. (in Japanese)

Ohba T. 1967. *Alpine and Subalpine.* Gensyoku Gendaikagaku Daijiten 3 Syokubutsu. Gakken Publishing Co., Tokyo. (in Japanese)

Toyokuni, H. 1988. *Alpine Plants in Japan.* Yama to Keikoku-sya, Tokyo.(in Japanese)

Watanabe, T. 1997. *Relationship with the Forest.* Iwanami Syoten, Tokyo. (in Japanese)

Chapter 10

Aquatic Plants at Risk

Yasuro Kadono

Many lakes, ponds, reservoirs, marshes, swamps and other wetlands in Japan have been wiped out by drainage and reclamation or degraded through civil engineering projects and water pollution. Many aquatic plants have been deprived of their habitats and are facing extinction. The Red List of plants in Japan (Environment Agency 1997) lists 79 freshwater aquatic plants, accounting for more than one third of all species of this type in the country. When other wetland-dependent species are added, this number doubles.

The main reasons for the rapid extinction of aquatic plants are water pollution and the loss and degradation of plant habitats through human activity, such as drainage and reclamation of ponds and other wetlands, river channelisation, and other civil engineering works. Such activities can be seen as regional issues, and efforts are now beginning at the regional level to save endangered species. However, it is becoming clear that influences arising from human activity, such as acid rain, are changing the global environment and, as a result, the Earth's biota may be subject to irreversible effects.

It is rather difficult to anticipate what influence global warming will have on aquatic plants. Aquatic habitats experience a smaller range of thermal differences than do terrestrial habitats, and some people even assume that there are fewer differences between tropical and temperate aquatic habitats than there are between tropical and temperate terrestrial habitats. The existence of cosmopolitan aquatic plants contributes to this assumption. However, there is no doubt that thermal factors limit the distribution of many aquatic species. Tropical aquatic plants introduced into Japan have become naturalized, serving as an example of what would happen as a result of global warming.

Naturalized exotic species and biodiversity

Washitani and Morimoto (1993) have divided the environmental problems we face into three broad categories, 1) inappropriate use of natural resources, 2) pollution, and 3) biological invasion. The ecological influences arising from biological invasion, or the disturbance caused to the composition and biodiversity of native communities by the introduction of exotic species, are the subject of much research and discussion. There are about 200 species of aquatic plants in Japan. Among these, 20 are of exotic origin, such as the water hyacinth *Eichhornia crassipes,* the Brazilian elodea *Egeria densa*, and the fanwort *Cabomba caroliniana*. Two of the best-known naturalized aquatic plants in Japan are *Elodea nuttallii* from North America, and *Egeria densa* from South America. *Elodea nuttallii* was first observed in Lake Biwa, Japan's largest lake, in the early 1960s. Its explosive growth became an issue in the late 1960s and early 1970s. It seems to have been introduced along with young hatchery "ayu" (sweetfish), which had been transferred to stock rivers and lakes in other areas. Since then, its distribution has expanded throughout western Honshu, and to Shikoku and Kyushu. Established patches of the plant were recently found in Hokkaido.

Naturalized aquatic plants spread very rapidly in an appropriate climate when a means of transportation is available. *Egeria densa* was first observed in nature back in the 1940s, but it started to spread through Lake Biwa in the late 1970s. It came to dominate over *Elodea nuttalli*, and spread throughout the lake. Ecologists were concerned about the competitive exclusion of the native submerged plant community by the rapid expansion and growth of these exotics, as the biomass of native species declined dramatically with the invasion of these two species (Figure 10.1). Monoculture communities of *Elodea nuttallii* and *Egeria densa* began replacing the species-rich native submerged plant community of Lake Biwa, and *Hydrilla verticillata*, a plant of similar growth form, was particularly seriously affected.

The reasons have not yet been determined, but recently *Egeria densa* growths have receded dramatically, and *Elodea nuttallii* has decreased and stabilized enough to be able to co-exist with native species. Many aquatic plant species, however, have been

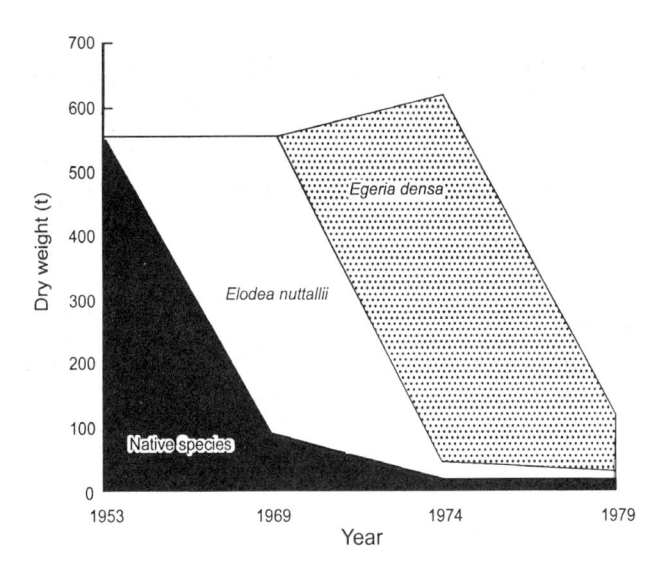

Figure 10.1.
Change in biomass of *Elodea nuttallii*, *Egeria densa*, and native species in southern Lake Biwa (drawn from Ikusima, 1991).

eliminated from Lake Biwa in recent decades. This seems to be due to the eutrophication of lake waters and the construction of shore protection dikes, and not to the invasion of both plants. However, the above incident clearly shows how seriously native species can be damaged by the invasion and establishment of foreign species (Kadono, 1996a).

The explosive growth of both exotic plants must be the result of dynamic ecological interactions, including those with non-plant components of the ecosystem such as fungi and invertebrates. The sudden explosive growth and resulting annoyance created by plants of Asian origin, such as *Hydrilla verticillata* and *Myriophyllum spicatum*, in the United States also supports this theory.

However, an additional factor - global warming - may bring about a different kind of situation. The naturalization of tropical aquatic plants may serve as an example of what could happen.

Threat of tropical aquatic plant naturalization

The most widely known naturalized tropical aquatic plant in Japan is the water hyacinth (Kadono 1996b), which originated in Brazil and Argentina. It has become naturalized in warm climates outside its region of origin and has come to clog up lakes and waterways. The water hyacinth reproduces vegetatively by creeping stolons or runners, from which new plants develop. This type of vegetative reproduction can be repeated very rapidly; in Japan the number of these plants can double within just six or seven days. A few water hyacinths in early spring may cover the entire surface of a body of water by autumn (Figure 10.2). In this situation, sunlight does not reach the water and the result is oxygen depletion such that submerged plants and most fish are unable to survive. In winter, the dead plants degrade the water quality.

Until about the late 1920s, naturalized water hyacinth was limited to Kyushu. By the 1960s, it had spread to Shikoku, and to the Chugoku and Kinki districts of Honshu. At present, the northern limit to which water hyacinth can survive the winter is said to be the southern Tohoku district, but if the average temperature rises by 1 or 2°C due to global warming, this limit will shift northward.

There is another issue that may have a bearing on the future extension of the water hyacinth. Its flower does not often succeed in producing fruit. The water hyacinth has normally spread through vegetative

Figure 10.2.
Eichhornia crassipes covers the surface over a short time period from August (above) to September (below) (Tarumi Ward in Kobe City, Hyogo Prefecture).

reproduction, thought to be the result of a lack of pollinating insects. In the near future, however, a pollinator may appear from among native insects or insects that may migrate to Japan from southern regions. If the rate at which the water hyacinth produces fruit increases and the plant can grow from seedlings, a new situation will develop. When it can survive the winter in the form of seeds, it will be able to expand its distribution further north. Also, sexual reproduction may allow the development of new genotypes that better fit Japan's environment.

So far water hyacinth has grown mainly in polluted water where most native aquatic plants cannot survive, but in the future it will probably spread to areas of cleaner water where the native community is still established. Global warming is sure to enhance the adaptability of the water hyacinth and accelerate the extension of its distribution.

The aquarium boom and tropical aquatic plants

Aquariums with many species of exotic plants and fish are popular for interior decoration purposes, and the market for them is expanding. Rare new plant species are highly prized and aquatic plants are being collected from all over the world to be imported and sold. A similar situation prevails with regard to aquatic plants grown in garden ponds and greenhouses.

Water lettuce *Pistia stratiotes* is a floating aquatic plant widely distributed in tropical and sub-tropical regions (Figure. 10.3). I first saw it in southern Kagoshima Prefecture about 20 years ago. Recently, however, water lettuce is sold not only in aquarium shops but also in discount stores. In many areas west of the Kinki district, water lettuce has come to cover water surfaces. Its ability to become naturalized depends on how well it can survive the winter. Some plants survive at sites well protected from the cold, but it has been reported recently that some survive in the form of seeds. Sexual reproduction creates more genetic diversity than vegetative reproduction, increasing the possibility that the plant will adapt to its new environment. In this way, tropical aquatic plants are poised to expand their distribution as soon as conditions for growth are fulfilled.

The banana plant *Nymphoides aquatica* has recently established a community from an abandoned plant in a reservoir in Hyogo Prefecture and is expanding its area of coverage (Figures 10.4 and 10.5). In winter this plant dies back, but it forms winter buds. These winter buds do survive the winter and every year the plant continues to expand its coverage. This reservoir had maintained a high-quality natural environment with clean water and native aquatic plants *Brasenia schreberi* and *Nymphaea tetragona*, but the latter are being pushed out by the banana plant. In reservoirs where the structure of the water basin is relatively simple, native species may be completely driven out by exotics.

Salvinia mollesta (Figure 10.6), and alligator weed *Alternanthera philoxeroides* have also become naturalized in Japan. *Vallisneria gigantea* is reported to be establishing large communities in Kyushu.

The influence of global warming on aquatic plants needs to be understood in the context of a 50 or 100 year time frame. However, the extensive growth of tropical aquatic plants in Japan may be an early example of what could happen on a larger scale in the future. In addition to species that will naturally shift their distribution northward as the Earth warms, there are many species that may become naturalized when transported by humans. All such species could threaten native aquatic plants.

Figure 10.4.
Nymphoides aquatica (origin: Florida, USA).

Figure 10.3.
Pistia stratiotes spreads in a pond in Nishi Ward, Kobe City.

Figure 10.5.
Growth of *Nymphoides aquatica* in a reservoir in Yokawa Town, Hyogo Prefecture. Top: June 1990, *Brasenia schreberi* and *Nymphaea tetragona* seen on water surface. Middle: August 1993, *Nymphoides aquatica* starting to grow from the far end of the reservoir. Bottom: September 1994, most of the surface is covered by *Nymphoides aquatica* and native species are almost eliminated.

Figure 10.6.
Above: *Salvinia mollesta*. Below: *Salvinia mollesta* covering the water surface (Suma Ward in Kobe City).

Most aquatic habitats on land are normally isolated from one another. Ponds and lakes exist like independent islands, and rivers and other waterways are separated into their own watersheds. It is difficult for aquatic plants to move from one ecosystem to another in the state of nature. With enough time, they may be able to migrate to a new environment, but environments suitable for aquatic plants are diminishing rapidly. The pressure of exotic plant invasions is added to this. In short, we must take measures to stop global warming, but we must also be aware of the threats inherent in the careless introduction and naturalization of exotic plants.

Some predict that the effects of global warming will not be limited to mere temperature rises, but that other climatic changes will take place. A decline in precipitation will cause lowered water tables and decreases in spring water sources, affecting an even wider range of aquatic plants. We can also expect that there are many more aspects to the problem that lie beyond our current powers of anticipation. We should be alert to what is happening now, and be ready to see how climate change is affecting biological diversity.

References

Ikusima, I. 1991. Changes and present status of aquatic macrophytes in Lake Biwa. In: *Changes and Present Status of Biota of Lake Biwa. Proceedings of 9th Lake Biwa Symposium*. Pp.70-84. Shiga Prefectural Lake Biwa Institute, Ohtsu. (in Japanese)

Kadono, Y. 1996a. Influence of exotic plants on the native flora, with special reference to naturalized aquatic macrophytes. Bulletin of Kansai Organization for Nature Conzervation 18: 115-120. (in Japanese)

Kadono, Y. 1996b. Water hyacinth - a million dollar weed. In: (K. Inoue, ed.) *Survival Strategy of Plants*. Pp.168-178. Heibonsha, Tokyo. (in Japanese)

Washitani, I. and N. Morimoto. 1993. *Alien Plants and Animals Naturalized in Japan*. Hoikusha, Osaka, 191pp. (in Japanese)

Chapter 11

Warming and Japanese Seagrasses

Keiko Aioi and Yuji Omori

Characteristics of seagrasses in Japan

In Japan, seven temperate seagrasses of the Family Zosteraceae inhabit the coastal waters of Hokkaido, Honshu, and Kyushu (Figure 11.1). With the exception of the cosmopolitan eel grass *Zostera marina*, all are endemic to the northwestern Pacific and are distributed only in a limited number of localities (Aioi, 1998). Ocean currents surrounding the Japanese Archipelago are the Oyashio Cold Current, and Kuroshio and Tsushima Warm Currents. These currents have made possible the species diversity of the Family Zosteraceae off northern Honshu. Their endemism is thought to be an evolutionary result of the paleogeological process in which the main Japanese islands were connected to the Asian Continent and then separated from the Chinese and Korean coasts (Hamada, 1995). The morphological diversity of their flowering shoots is caused by the complicated topography of the coasts (Table 11.1).

Global warming and the possibility of changes in the marine flora of Japan

If the atmosphere warms by between 2 and 5°C due to global warming, global oceanic circulation patterns will change, with recognizable effects on the habitats of marine organisms in coastal waters throughout the Japanese Archipelago. This will occur because the rich biodiversity of the seas around Japan results from a unique combination of geological and atmospheric conditions.

The distribution of tropical seagrasses is limited by the average seawater temperature in February, the coldest month. In the case of *Halophila ovalis*, the northern limit is Tokyo Bay on the Pacific Coast and the Noto Peninsula on the Japan Sea Coast. The average temperature in February varies from 10°C to 15°C. In other tropical grasses such as *Enhalus acoroides*, the northern limit of distribution is Miyako Island, and the lowest temperature around 20°C. On the contrary, the southern limit of distribution of temperate seagrasses is determined by seawater temperature in August, the warmest month. This is from 28°C to 29°C on the coast of Kyushu region (Miki, 1933).

Although bays along the coast are strongly influenced by the oceanic climate in summer, the seawater temperature in these locations is also affected by the terrestrial climate. Water temperature in bays is usually colder than the water in the open ocean in winter. Global warming will influence the distribution of seagrasses, because the increase in the seawater temperature will affect the locations of the vegetation zones, and unpredictable changes in ocean currents may have an effect on species dispersion.

As a general rule, the actual habitats of marine macrophytes are cooler than their optimal temperature for photosynthesis (Aruga, 1965a, 1965b; Yokohama, 1973; Davison, 1991). Optimal photosynthesis conditions for *Z. marina* and *Z. caulescens* in Otsuchi Bay on the northern Pacific coast occur at a temperature of 28°C (Aioi et al., unpublished). Photosynthesis increases linearly until the temperature reaches 28°C, but in the higher temperature activity begins to decline markedly. The highest biomass of natural seagrass vegetation in Otsuchi Bay is obtainable in July, at seawater temperatures between 15 and 18°C.

In terms of horizontal distribution, two temperate alga species (Laminariales) have different northern limits along the Pacific coast, that of *Eisenia bicyclis* (Phaeophyta) being in Miyagi Prefecture, and that of *Ecklonia cava* (Phaeophyta) being further south in Ibaragi Prefecture. The vertical distribution of *E. bicyclis* usually involves zonation in areas shallower than 5 m, whereas *E. cava* occurs at depths below 5 m in Shimoda Bay in the south of the Izu Peninsula. *E. bicyclis* selects an environment with a 1°C higher year-round average seawater temperature than that selected by *E. cava*.

The optimal temperature for photosynthesis in both species is 25°C under saturated light conditions. In comparing the photosynthesis performance of the two species, *E. bicyclis* exhibits higher activity than *E.*

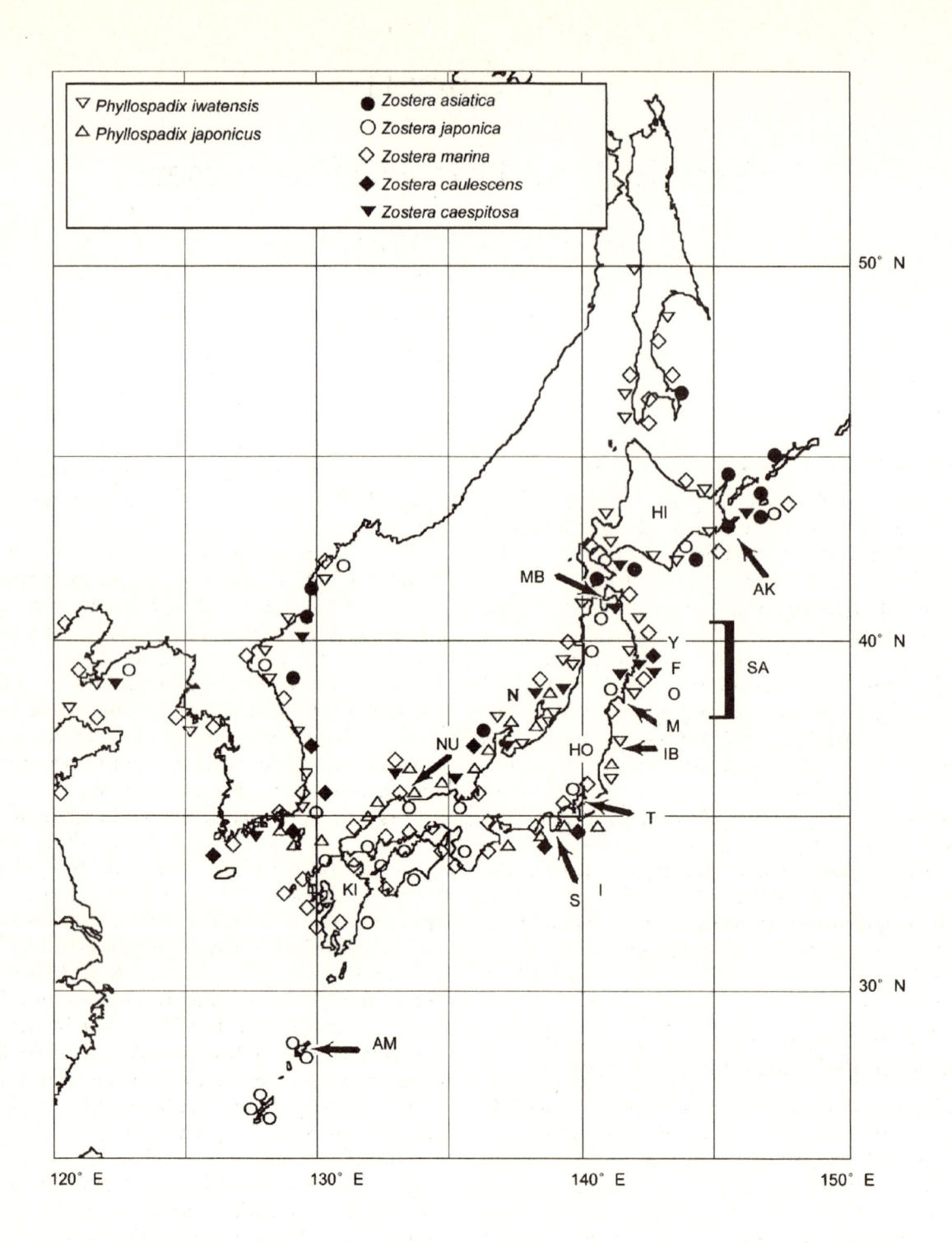

Figure 11.1.
Distribution map of seven temperate seagrass species (*Zostera* and *Phyllospadix*) around Japan, Korea, and China. AK: Akkeshi, AM: Amami Island, F: Funakoshi Bay, HI: Hokkaido Island, HO: Honshu Island, I: Izu Peninsula, IB: Ibaragi Prefecture, KI: Kyushu Island, M: Miyagi Prefecture, MB: Mutsu Bay, N: Niigata Prefecture, NU: Nakaumi, O: Otsuchi Bay, S: Shimoda, SA: Sanriku, T: Tokyo Bay, and Y: Yamada Bay.

Table 11.1. List of Japanese seagrass species and their distribution areas.

Family / Genus	Species	Species number	Area
Hydrocharitaceae			
Enhalus		1	
	E. acoroides		TR
Thalassia		1	
	T. hemprichii		TR
Halophila		2	
	H. ovalis		TR, TE
	H. decipiens		TR
Zosteraceae			
Zostera		5	
	Z. marina		TE
	Z. asiatica		TE, AR
	Z. caulescens		TE
	Z. caespitosa		TE, AR
	Z. japonica		TR, TE, AR
Phyllospadix		2	
	P. iwatensis		TE, AR
	P. japonicus		TE
Cymodoceaceae			
Cymodocea		2	
	C. rotundata		TR
	C. serrulata		TR
Halodule		2	
	H. uninervis		TR
	H. pinifolia		TR
Syringodium		1	
	S. isoetifolium		TR
Total		16	

TR: from sub-tropic to tropic; TE: temperate; AR: from sub-arctic to arctic.

cava at a seawater temperature of 25°C. However, daily compensation light quantity-temperature curves suggest that *E. cava* adapts to higher temperatures and darker seabed conditions than *E. bicyclis* does (Kurashima, 1996).

Only *E. cava* occurs in habitats along the western coast of the Izu Peninsula where the year-round average seawater temperature is 1.5°C higher than the optimal temperature (Kurashima, 1996). In the south of the peninsula, the blades of *E. cava* died back and only the stalks of the plant remained among the shallow vegetation in August 1994, and again in August 1996, when the average water temperature of 22.6°C rose to 27.0°C (Ueda et al., unpublished).

The same phenomenon has been observed in Nakaumi, Tottori Prefecture, where the leaves of *Z. marina* were shed at the upper level of the thermocline in summer and the plants all died in the autumn (Nakatani, pers. comm.). Therefore, global warming can be predicted to affect the photosynthetic activities of marine plants, and a warming of 2 or 3°C in the seawater temperature may prove fatal to shallow bottom-dwelling vegetation in areas less than 10 m deep. Besides this, changes of tidal ranges will influence the zonation of rocky flora as well as fauna dwelling on the seabed in shallow areas.

Porphyra onoi (Rhodophyta) and *Dasya sessilis* (Rhodophyta) have both disappeared from Tokyo Bay since 1950 (Tanaka and Omori, 1998) and *Z. marina* and *Z. caulescens* have also disappeared from the bayhead of Tokyo Bay (Aioi, 1989). The disappearances and changes in the marine plants there have mainly been caused by the construction of ports, land reclamation and pollution (Numata and Furota, 1997). In the past, these organisms have been able to recover from damage to their habitats through storms and other natural disturbances experienced during their evolutionary history (Aioi et al., 1996). However, reclamation and pollution are not reversible disturbances over the short term. Climate warming, too, will cause lethal damage to temperate and arctic species like *Z. marina* which live in shallow water habitats.

In Odawa Bay near Tokyo, the distribution of subtidal seagrasses has changed. As compared with the data in 1977, a remarkable decline and disappearance of *Z. marina* has been observed and *Z. caulescens* has increased in a limited area (Kudo, 1999). The noticeable decline of *Z. marina* was likely caused by changes in the coastal environment. Eutrophication accelerated in the bayhead area, leading to a decline in light conditions. The replacement of the dominant species *Z. marina* by *Z. caulescens* might occur in the subtidal deeper bottom, and *Z. marina* might be damaged in the shallow bottom as a result of seawater warming.

Most of the endemic seagrass species in Japanese waters have been listed as Data Deficient species (DD) in the Red List of Japanese plants by the Environment Agency (Aioi, 1998). Moreover, many species of shallow water flora such as seagrasses and algae along the coasts of Japan are at risk of declining rapidly toward extinction as a result of global warming.

Seagrass beds provide nursery grounds and habitats for fish and small animal communities. The disappearance of seagrasses may well prove disastrous for many fisheries as well as for the cultural identity of countless communities throughout Japan.

References

Aioi, K. 1989. Ecology of Japanese sea-grasses with comments on their conservation. Collecting and Breeding 51(8): 352-356. (in Japanese with English summary)

Aioi, K. 1998. On the red list species of Japanese seagrasses. Aquabiology 114, 20 - (1): 7-12. (in Japanese)

Aruga, Y. 1965a. Ecological studies on photosynthesis and matter production of phytoplankton. I. Seasonal changes in photosynthesis of natural phytoplankton. The Botanical Magazine, Tokyo 78: 280-288.

Aruga, Y. 1965b. Ecological studies on photosynthesis and matter production of phytoplankton. II. Photosynthesis of algae in relation to light intensity and temperature. The Botanical Magazine, Tokyo 78: 360-365.

Davison, I. R. 1991. Environmental effects on algal photosynthesis: Temperature. J. of Phycology 27: 2-8.

Hamada, T. 1995. *Earth Science of the Japanese Archipelago*. Society for the Promotion of Education, University of the Air, 175 pp. (in Japanese)

Kudo, T. 1999. Distribution of seagrasses in Odawa Bay, central Japan. Reports of Kanagawa Fishery Research Institute 4: 51-60. (in Japanese with English summary)

Kurashima, A. 1996. Study on physiology and ecology concerning photosynthesis and growth of *Eisenia bicyclis* and *Ecklonia cava*. Ph.D. thesis. Faculty of Fishery Science, Tokyo University of Fisheries, 132 pp. (in Japanese)

Miki, S. 1933. On the seagrasses of Japan. I. *Zostera* and *Phyllospadix*, with special reference to morphological and ecological characters. Botanical Magazine, Tokyo 47: 842-862.

Numata, M. and T. Furota. 1997. *Biohistory of Tokyo Bay*. Tsukiji Shokan, Tokyo. 411pp. (in Japanese)

Tanaka, J. and Y. Omori. 1998. Marine algae collected from Honmoku, Yokohama in Tokyo Bay in 1945 - 54. Data on the Natural History of Kanagawa 19: 105-189. (in Japanese)

Yokohama, Y. 1973. A comparative study on photosynthesis-temperature relationships and their seasonal changes in marine benthic algae. Internationale Revue der gesamten Hydrobiology 58: 463-472.

Chapter 12

The Impact of Global Warming on Insects

Hidenori Ubukata

More then 800,000 species of insects have been recorded on Earth (Gaston, 1991), and this class contains the largest number of differentiated species among all classes of animals and plants. According to one estimate, about 30 million species of insects remain to be described on Earth, especially in the tropical forests (Erwin, 1982). Consequently, insects can be said to account for the largest single portion of the Earth's biodiversity. At present, a considerable number of insect species are becoming extinct, especially in the tropics, as a result of environmental destruction. Against this background, what kind of impact will global warming have on insect diversity?

Global warming — What is happening to insects now?

The Earth has already experienced a warming of 0.5°C during the course of the 20th century. Due to increased emissions of "greenhouse gases" such as carbon dioxide, which result from growth in economic activities, many scientists have forecast that more rapid global warming will occur in the 21st century. In drawing up a scenario of the changes in insect diversity in the 21st century, it is important to understand how global warming has affected insects in the 20th century, especially during the last two decades. In this chapter I discuss what kinds of changes have occurred during these periods by focusing on butterflies and dragonflies, which have been relatively well investigated. A significant amount of research has been done on the effects of global warming on insects (Kiritani, 1991; Tracy, 1992; Harrison, 1993; Hassell et al., 1993; Imura et al., 1993).

What is happening to butterflies? Northward expansion of southern butterflies

Recently, expansion in the distribution range of southern butterflies has become a common topic of conversation among insect lovers. Since ancient times, butterflies of the subtropical zone or the warm temperate zone have occasionally been captured here and there in Honshu, Japan's largest island. Recently, however, some of these species have established colonies in Honshu and are also expanding their distribution northward.

Nakasuji (1988) writes that ten species of southern butterflies are expanding their ranges northward in Japan: *Papilio memnon*, *Papilio helenus*, *Precis almana*, *Cyrestis thyodamas*, *Melanitis phedima*, *Udara albocaerulea*, and *Notocrypta curvifascia*, all of which inhabit the main Japanese islands; and *Appias paulina*, *Idea leuconoe* and *Megisba malaya* in the Nansei Islands. Many other species of southern butterflies seem to be expanding their ranges northward, too.

The great Mormon *P. memnon* is distributed mostly in the subtropical zone, and its larva feeds on the leaves of the Family Rutaceae, such as the mandarin orange. In Japan the northern limit of this butterfly's range was formerly Kyushu and southern Shikoku. However, its presence was confirmed in Yamaguchi Prefecture in the 1930s, in Hiroshima Prefecture in the 1950s and in Okayama Prefecture in the 1970s. In Shikoku its range expanded to cover the entire island by 1950, and then continued on into Wakayama, Osaka and Hyogo Prefectures by 1980 (Figure 12.1). More recently, the range of this butterfly is reported to have reached Mie Prefecture (Environmental Agency, 1996).

The Common map *C. thyodamas* is distributed from Afghanistan through Indochina, southwestern China and Taiwan and into southwestern Japan. The northern limit of this species' range in Japan is along a line connecting Mie and Shimane Prefectures (Fukuda et al., 1983). Yodoe (1994) reported that this species has been expanding its range eastward as well as into higher altitudes, and has increased its population in the Chugoku Region during the past two decades. He suggested the effect of global warming as a contributing factor, and cited an alternative hypothesis by Kazuo Watanabe of Hiroshima University that environmental changes near places of human habitation caused by lifestyle changes have fueled this population expansion.

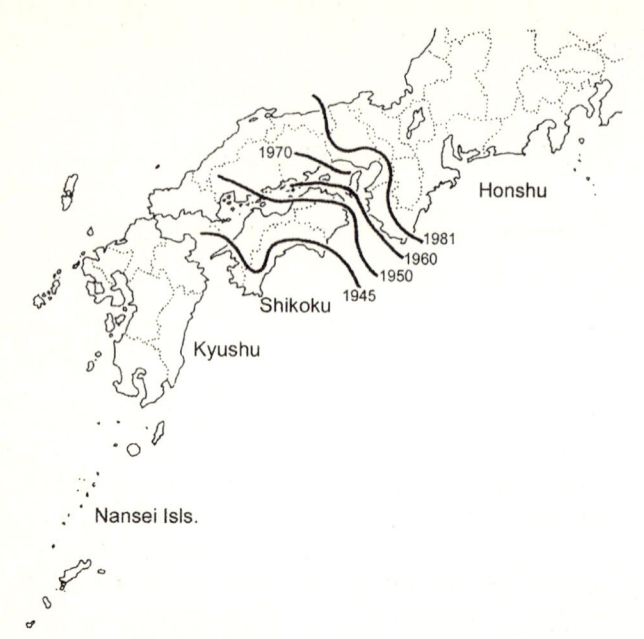

Figure 12.1.
Changes in the northern limit of *Papilio memnon* (Fukuda et al., 1983).

Figure 12.2.
Edith's checkerspot *Euphydryas editha* (photo by Dexter Sear).

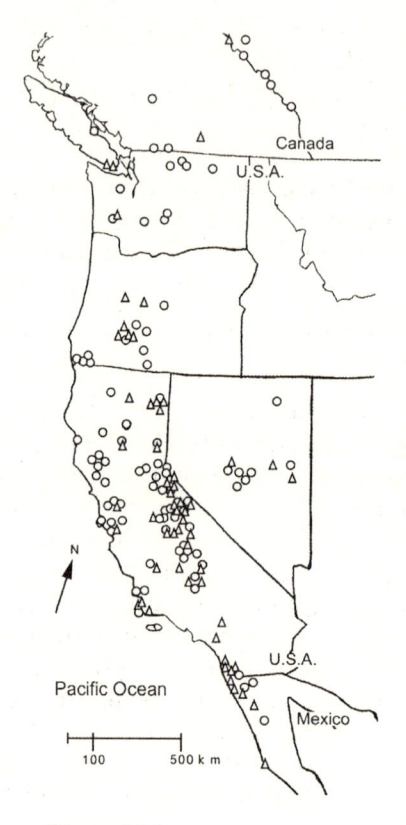

Figure 12.3.
Distributions of present populations and extinct populations of *Euphydryas editha* (from Parmesan, 1996). △ Extinct, ○ Present.

Besides this species, in the Sanin Region *Parnassius glacialis, Papilio memnon, Libythea celtis, Argyreus hyperbius* and *Narathura japonica* are said to have expanded their ranges. With the exception of *P. glacialis*, these are of southern origin and distributed across southwestern Japan. Ford (1982) noted that *Ladoga camilla* and *Polygonia c-album* had expanded their ranges widely during the past 100 years in the British Isles and put forward the pioneering explanation that these expansions were prompted by a climate warming of about 0.5°C.

Butterflies expanding northward and becoming extinct toward the south of their ranges

Whether or not northern butterflies in the cool-temperate or subarctic zones are retreating from the southern limits of their ranges is not an easy problem to investigate. While the presence of a butterfly can be easily proved, its disappearance is difficult to verify.

Edith's checkerspot *Euphydryas editha* (Figure 12.2), is distributed from northern Mexico to southern Canada. This butterfly is univoltine and was confined to serpentine outcrops where its host plant, *Plantago erecta*, grows (Ehrlich, 1961). Consequently, the habitats of *E. editha* are patchy and isolated from each other, and the populations at different patches have been observed as becoming extinct relatively frequently (Ehrlich et al., 1980). Through extinction and re-establishment in vacant space, the meta-population (a set of populations that are independent over ecological time) maintains a kind of balance (Singer and Ehrlich, 1979; Harrison et al., 1988). Ehrlich et al. (1980) reported that innumerable populations of this butterfly were exterminated in California and in neighboring regions by the severe drought that struck from 1975 to 1977. The drought accelerated host plant senescence, so that the larvae became unable to feed on them (Murphy

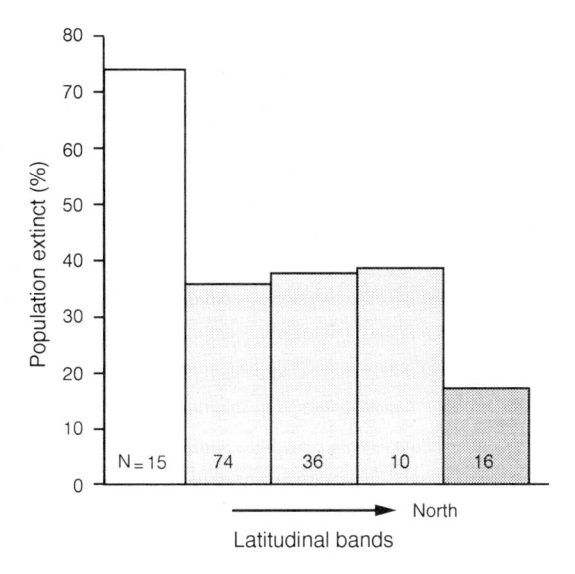

Figure 12.4.
Proportions of extinct population of *Euphydryas editha* in five latitudinal bands (from Parmesan, 1996). The differences were significant ($P<0.05$) among the bands of different shades (post-hoc subdivided analysis).

and Weiss, 1992). Climate warming enhances the extinction frequency of *E. editha* by increasing both the frequency and the degree of drought.

Parmesan (1996) compiled historical population records of this butterfly and surveyed 115 sites to confirm whether this butterfly still inhabited historically recorded sites. The butterfly had indeed become extinct at many sites (Figure 12.3). The more southerly distributed populations are becoming extinct at a higher rate. The extinction rate showed a statistically significant geographic cline according to latitude with the south being the higher end (Figure 12.4). Also, sites at lower elevations showed higher extinction rates, although this trend was less evident. Thus, global warming was suggested as the cause of the observed range shift. On the west coast of North America the average temperature increased by about 2°C during the 94 years between 1900 and 1994.

What has happened in dragonflies?
Northward expansion of dragonflies in Japan

Among the dragonflies of Japan there are a considerable number of species that have powerful flying capabilities. It is known that *Pantala flavescens*, *Tramea virginia* and *Anax guttatus* travel over the ocean reaching far north to Hokkaido, as well as across the other three of Japan's main islands (Ishida et al., 1988). *P. flavescens* eventually reaches Kamchatka and Alaska after performing repeated copulation, oviposition and emergence on the way. However, the larvae, being unable to tolerate low temperatures, cannot overwinter at high latitudes (Eda, 1976). In such cases the species cannot be regarded as having established colonies.

Recently, dragonflies have expanded their ranges and established colonies in new territories. Watanabe (1989) reported that five libellulid dragonflies, *Brachydiplax chalybea*, *Brachythemis contaminata*, *Trithemis aurora*, *Pseudothemis zonata* and *Hydrobasileus croceus*, have established colonies and successive generations have expanded the species' range from south to north, crossing the ocean in the process.

A large dragonfly, *Ictinogomphus pertinax*, is famous for expanding its range in Japan's main islands. This species is distributed from southern and central China through Taiwan to southwestern Japan. Its northern limit in Japan prior to 1985 lay along a line connecting northern Fukuoka Prefecture, southern Yamaguchi Prefecture, southern Okayama Prefecture, the northern part of Awajishima Island and southern Mie Prefecture (Hamada and Inoue, 1985). The fact that this species is gradually expanding northward had already been pointed out by Ishida (1969) and Hamada and Inoue (1985). Aoki (1997) meticulously examined the literature and investigated the state of expansion of this species' range from Shikoku into the Kinki Region from prior to the 1950s until the early 1990s (Figure 12.5). *I. pertinax* crossed the Seto Inland Sea from Shikoku to

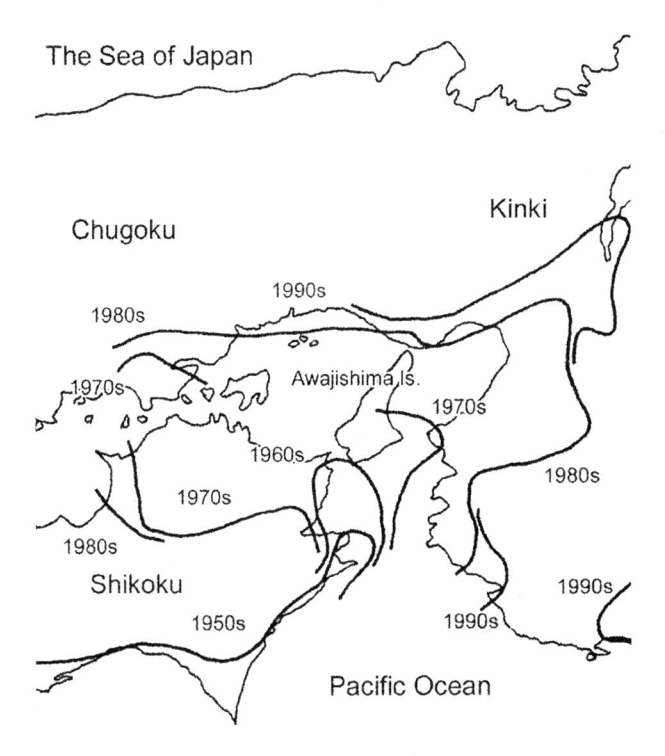

Figure 12.5.
Changes in the northern limits of *Ictinogomphus pertinax* in the Shikoku and Kinki Regions (from Aoki, 1997).

Okayama Prefecture and the western end of the Kii Peninsula in the 1970s, and reached Lake Biwa via the Osaka Plain in the early 1990s. The northward shift of the isothermal line coincides well with that of the northern reach of *I. pertinax*. The year-round mean air temperature rose by 1°C between 1900 and 1994 (Aoki, 1997).

Northward expansion of dragonflies in America and in Europe

In North America, several dragonflies are expanding their ranges northward (Sidney Dunkle, pers. comm.). *Anax longipes* has invaded the states of Indiana and Wisconsin since the 1930s, and has recently appeared in Michigan. *Orthemis ferruginea* was known only in the Florida Keys in the US prior to 1930, but is now common throughout the southern United States. An increase in the number of artificial ponds seems to have contributed to the expansion. *Archilestes grandis* has been spreading northward from Ohio to Wiscon-sin during the 50 years prior to 1987, partly as a result of forest clearance.

D. Paulson performed an extensive survey of the dragonfly fauna of southern Florida in the 1960s (Paulson, 1999). *Erythemis plebeja*, *Micra-thyria aequalis* and *M. didyma* all appeared there between 1971 and 1985. *E. plebeja* has now reached central Florida (S. Dunkle, pers. comm.). More recently, populations of *Tholymis citrina* and *Tramea calverti* have become established, and *Chrysobasis lucifer* and *Nehalennia minuta* have appeared (Dennis Paulson, pers. comm.). These dragonflies could have been carried to Florida from Cuba by hurricanes (S. Dunkle, pers. comm.), although some of the species are known long-distance dispersers and could have made the crossing with their own flight capabilities (D. Paulson, pers. comm.).

The Scarlet darter *Crocothemis erythraea* is distributed widely in the Mediterranean region (Askew, 1988). In Germany, however, it has been regarded as a strayer from southern Europe since it was first recorded there in the early 20th century. Strayers are species which cannot establish a population in a region because their larvae cannot survive there, though adults are occasionally seen. Ott (1996) marked the habitats (the spots where the larvae grow and emerge) of *C. erythraea* (Figure 12.6), and found that its distribution extended as far north as latitude from 49°30' in 1976 to 49°45' in 1984 and 50°25' in 1996. Thus, the details of the northward shift of the northern reach of this species between the late 1970s and the early 1990s have been clarified. The northward expansion of *C. erythraea* is also in progress in central Europe (Ott, in press). Ott (1996) also identified global warming as a cause of this northward expansion, because the mean air temperature in Europe has risen by 0.5 to 1.5°C over the past 100 years, or even during the past two or three decades.

Twelve Mediterranean dragonflies (two coenagrionids, one lestid, four aeshnids, and five libellulids) are also expanding their ranges, some in Spain and France, and others into the Scandinavian countries by crossing Germany and Poland (Ott, in press).

Ott (in press) reported that two northern species, *Aeshna juncea* and *Coenagrion hastulatum*, had disappeared from Kaiserslautern in Germany, while Mediterranean species like *C. erythraea* and *Sympetrum fonscolombii* had become newly established there. This case indicates that northern dragonflies have declined near their southern limits due to the influence of climate warming.

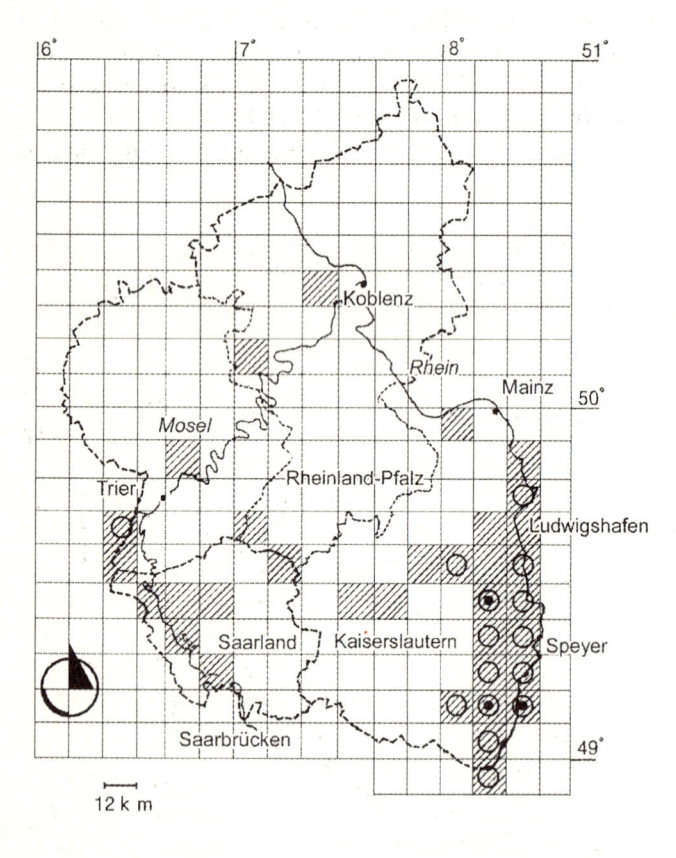

Figure 12.6.
Changes in the northern limits of *Crocothemis erythraea* in Rheinland-Pfalz and Saarland, Germany (Ott, 1996). ●: before 1970s, ○: 1980s, shaded areas: as of 1996.

Impact of global warming...What will happen to insects due to further warming?

How far north can butterflies and dragonflies reach?

As insects are poikilothermic, their geographic ranges are limited by temperature in many cases. The minimum accumulated effective temperature which is necessary for completion of the life cycle can be roughly defined for each species. This, together with the endurable lower temperature limit for wintering, determines the northern limit of insects in most cases. On the other hand, when it is too warm, the life cycle of some insects is disturbed by the acceleration of larval growth or by awakening from diapause (Masaki, 1986). As a result, the southern limits are also determined to some extent by the effect of temperature. To expand its range beyond these limits, evolutionary changes in the mechanisms regulating an insect species' life history are required. Besides climatic factors, there are many cases in which a species' distribution range is indirectly influenced by temperature through biological factors such as food, hosts, natural enemies, competitors or vegetation structure. As a result of these processes, the northern and southern limits of many insects coincide fairly well with isotherms or accumulated effective isothermal lines.

In the case of a 2.5°C rise in temperature in Japan, isotherms are predicted to shift northward by 400 km latitudinally, and to rise by 400 m in altitude. Assuming that insects shift northward in accordance with the northward shift of isotherms, what will happen in Japan? Using the range data by Fukuda et al. (1982, 1983, 1984a, 1984b) and Hamada and Inoue (1985), tropical or sub-tropical butterflies and dragonflies which now have their northern reaches in central Kyushu, southern Shikoku and the southern part of the Kii Peninsula - approximately on the 16°C isotherm - will be able to reach Hokuriku, Tokai, and the southern Kanto region (*Graphium doson, Everes lacturnus, Acytolepis puspa, Agriocnemis femina, Ceriagrion latericium, Hemicordulia mindana, Lyriothemis elegantissima, Orthetrum sabina,* and *Tholymis tillarga.*)

In Hokkaido, butterflies and dragonflies of the warm temperate or temperate zones, which currently have their northern reaches at the Oshima Peninsula or Hidaka region, will be able to reach Cape Soya or Cape Nosappu by crossing through Hokkaido (*Quercusia fujisana, Strymonidia mera, Polygonia c-aureum, Neptis alwina, Mycalesis gotama, Daimio tethys, Mortonagrion selenion, Indolestes peregrinus, Gynacantha japonica, Lyriothemis pachygastra,* and *Crocothemis servilia*).

'Green deserts' and 'concrete jungles' that obstruct northward shifts in range

Japan's plains have been transformed into concrete cities surrounded by patchworks of farmlands and residential areas. These environments are 'concrete jungles' and 'green deserts' for most insects, and as such form almost impenetrable barriers for them. Relatively few species of insects that have become adapted to urban areas and farmlands can live there. The lowlands of Japan have also been transformed by developments such as residential areas, golf courses and resorts. It is some consolation that natural vegetation remains in a continuous form along the backbone mountain ridges of Honshu. This is the montane 'green corridor', a narrow path for migration that remains for animals living in the mountains. Continuous paths for the animals of the lowlands or plains are almost non-existent, however, making it very difficult for such creatures to retreat to the north or to the highlands to escape warming.

Apart from some highly migratory insects, and even in the case of butterflies and dragonflies, certain species which are weak with respect to their flying or reproductive capabilities will have their migration routes closed off almost completely by the 'green deserts' and 'concrete jungles'. Walking beetles, such as carabid beetles, or ground beetles, and soil insects such as springtails, lack an effective means of migration.

The problem of migration is a complex one. Insects occupy certain parts of ecosystems. Without synchronous shifts in the ranges of prey animals and host plants, as well as of the vegetation structure they use for shelter, migrating insects cannot adapt to life in new regions. Leaving aside for the moment carnivorous or omnivorous insects such as dragonflies and ants, butterflies, moths and sawflies that depend upon specific plant species cannot expand their ranges unless a northward shift of their food or host plants occurs either at the same time or in advance of their migration. But the horizontal migration of plants is very slow in comparison with the northward shift in the climate precipitated by global warming. To keep pace with global warming, plants would need to migrate at a speed of about 4 km per year, but their maximum speed is only 0.05 to 2.0 km annually (Kiritani, 1991; Davis and Zabinski, 1992). To take an extreme example, *Asarum kooyanum*, the food plant of *Luehdorfia japonica*, can shift its range by only a few kilometres in 10,000 years (Moriyama, 1988). Furthermore, topographical barriers and areas developed by humans obstruct the migration of plants (Myers, 1992). For example, in North America, the northward shift of the trees *Tsuga* and *Fagus* in the post-glacial period was prevented by the Great Lakes for about 1,000 years (Davis et al., 1986).

The life forms that can actually move north are, in the case of plants, mostly weeds or naturalized plants with high seed dispersal ability that grow in wastelands, and in the case of insects, opportunistic strategists in terms of life-cycle which possess high migratory or dispersal ability and can multiply rapidly even in an unstable environment. Kiritani (1983) listed the traits of successful insect colonizers as follows: high migratory capability (undormancy); short generation (multivoltine); high reproduction rate (parthenogenesis); omnivorous (polyphagy); tolerant of climate change (adaptability); and not influenced by or avoiding inbreeding. Unfortunately, the creatures exhibiting these traits are not rare species, but common agricultural pests like locusts, leafhoppers, plant lice, and army worms.

Will a 3°C warming exterminate a quarter of the butterflies in highland areas?

Murphy and Weiss (1992) estimated to what extent the number of species of animals (mammals, birds, and butterflies) inhabiting boreal habitats would decline under the influence of global warming based upon the species-area curve, a theory of biogeography. For example, the species number of sedentary butterflies (S) lacking dispersal capabilities in the Great Basin of North America is shown by the following regression equation:

$$S = 2.01 A^{0.27}, r^2 = 0.43,$$
where A is the size of the habitat area.

The lower boundary of boreal habitats will move upward from 2,300 m to 2,800 m above sea level in the case of a 3°C rise in year-round mean temperature. Consequently, the area occupied by such habitats will be reduced to between one third and one tenth of their present area. As a result, the 7 to 21 species of sedentary butterflies with low dispersal capabilities that are now limited to boreal habitats were predicted to be reduced to between 6 and 10 species, with the mean rate of decrease being 32%. In particular, the larger a highland area is, the larger the number of species it will contain, and consequently we should expect to find larger decreases in the number of species inhabiting larger areas under the influence of a given degree of warming. We cannot predict which particular species of butterfly will become extinct, but a decrease in the number of species will occur. With respect to the number of plant species in the same areas, 17% were predicted to become extinct under the same estimation procedure.

The fate of northern insects

In response to an increase of 2 to 3°C in the year-round mean temperature, most northern species will retreat northward or into the highlands as a result of the collapse of their life-cycle regulation through loss of prey or host species or by an inability to outwit natural enemies or competitors of more southern origin in the southern parts of their ranges (Peters and Lovejoy, 1992; Kareiva et al., 1993). Populations left behind on hilltops, remote islands or in habitats that are isolated by 'green deserts' can survive only if they are able to endure interspecific competition with southern species and able to adapt to a warmer climate. In order to do so, the population must possess sufficient genetic variation related to ecological traits in advance. In the case of isolated populations, however, particularly populations that indulge in asexual reproduction or inbreeding, genetic variation is impoverished to the extent that it will be difficult for them to respond to rapid environmental change (Travis and Futuyma, 1993).

In the highlands of Hokkaido and Honshu as well as in the coastal area of eastern Hokkaido, insects of the arctic or sub-arctic zones are found as relic populations from the most recent glacial. Members of the same species are also found in Siberia, Kamchatka, Alaska, and other boreal regions. These relic populations inhabited the plains of northern Japan during the last glacial about 18,000 years ago, when the air temperature was about 6 to 7°C lower than at present (Hatori and Shibazaki, 1971) and alpine glaciers covered the Japan Alps in Honshu and the Hidaka Mountains in Hokkaido. In those days, northern Hokkaido consisted of grassland where the dwarf Siberian pine *Pinus pumila* and the larch *Larix gmelini* grew sparsely on the discontinuous permafrost, and the regions from southern Hokkaido to the inland of central Honshu were covered with subarctic coniferous forests or taiga (Ono and Igarashi, 1991).

In the course of subsequent climate warming, butterflies such as *Parnassius eversmanni*, *Oeneis melissa*, *Clossiana freija*, *Vaccinina optilete*, moths such as *Anarta melanopa*, *A. cordigera*, *Sympistis funebris*, and dragonflies such as *Somatochlora alpestris* and *Aeshna subarctica*, all of which had been inhabiting the tundra or taiga, retreated toward Siberia via Sakhalin. Some populations became relic populations after retreating into highland areas such as the Taisetsu Mountains or the Hidaka Mountains, or into wetlands on the Pacific side of eastern Hokkaido where the air temperature in summer remains relatively low. Among these populations, the populations of genuine alpine insects (Hiura, 1980) that inhabit the alpine zone exclusively will lose their current habitats completely in several mountain areas and face the threat of extinction in the event of further warming, unless they possess sufficient flying capability or latent adaptability to climate change. As

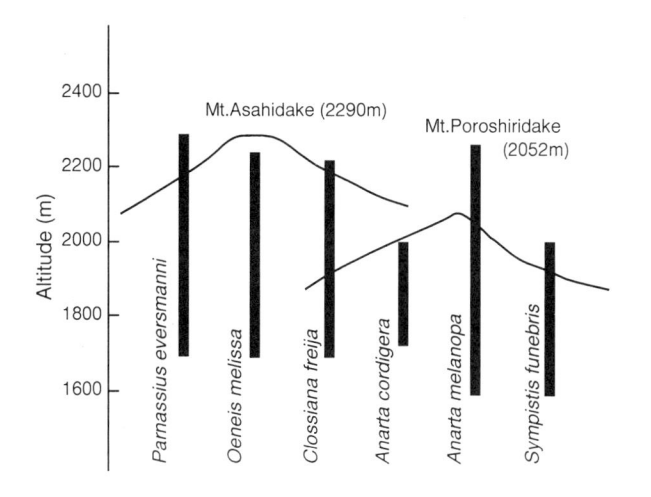

Figure 12.7.
Vertical distribution of alpine butterflies and moths in the Taisetsu Mountains and in the Hidaka Mountains in Hokkaido (from Jimbo, 1984; Watanabe, 1986).

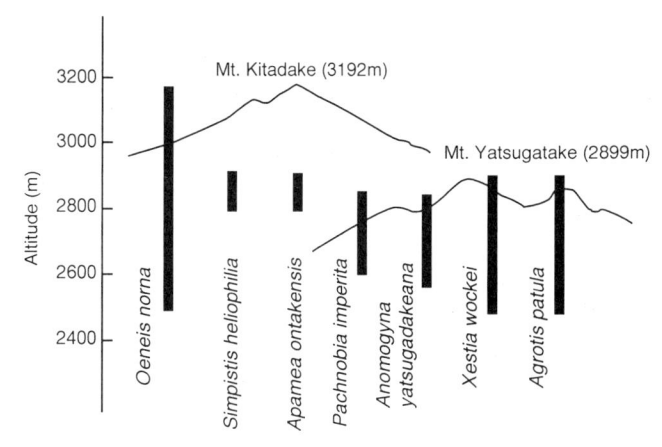

Figure 12.8.
Vertical distributions of alpine butterflies and moths in the central mountains of Honshu (from Jimbo, 1984; Watanabe, 1986).

the alpine zone in central Hokkaido starts from about 1,600 m above sea level, the populations of genuine alpine insects inhabiting between 1,700 and 2,000 m face extinction in the event of a 2 to 3°C rise in the year-round mean temperature.

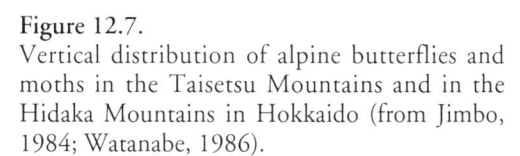

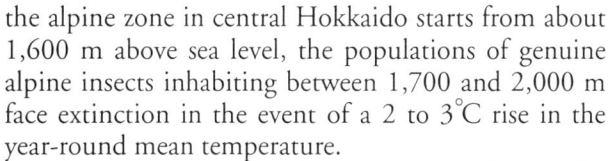

The Japanese Archipelago experienced a similar degree of climate change during the period between 8,000 and 5,000 years ago when the sea level was about 2 to 3 m higher than at present (Ono and Igarashi, 1991; Hatori and Shibazaki, 1971). In those days, southern insects such as *Oncotympana maculaticollis* and *Verarifictorus mikado* were widely distributed in the lowlands of eastern Hokkaido, and have continued to survive at some volcanic geothermal spots such as in Akan National Park. On the other hand, many species of alpine insects that have survived on the Taisetsu Mountains died out in the Hidaka Mountains or the Akan Mountains during the Hypsithermal Period (8,000 - 5,000 years ago) (Yasuda, 1993), a fact that is proved by the numbers of species of alpine moths now found in each area: 39 species in the Taisetsu Mountains, 13 species in the Hidaka Mountains and 8 species in the Akan Mountains (Kosugi et al., 1994). This is because several peaks of the 2,100 m class in the Taisetsu Mountains are connected in a group by ridges, whereas in other mountain areas the peaks are lower and more isolated. The extinction rates of fragmented populations driven to near the latter summits, therefore, must have been correspondingly higher.

At present, genuine alpine butterflies in Hokkaido, such as *Parnassius eversmanni* (Frontispiece 10), *C. freija* and *O. melissa* inhabit the Taisetsu Mountains at heights of above 1,700 m (Figure 12.7) (Watanabe, 1986), but if warming of 2 to 3°C occurs, these butterflies will be threatened with extinction at heights below 2,000 m. *Oeneis melissa* in the Hidaka Mountains, where 1,900 m-class peaks connect to the highest peak of Mt. Poroshiri-dake (alt. 2,052 m), may also be threatened. In Honshu *Oeneis norna*, inhabiting altitudes above 2,400 m in the Hida Mountains and Mt. Yatsugatake (Figure 12.8), may be forced to retreat to higher elevations, and there is an increased probability of its extinction on Mt. Yatsugatake, which rises to a peak of 2,899 m.

Similar scenarios could be written for genuine alpine beetles such as *Nebria daisetsuzana* and *Pterostichus subrugosus* in Hokkaido (Yasuda, 1978), and for genuine alpine moths like *A. cordigera* (Figure 12.7), *Sympistis heliophila*, *Pachnobia imperita*, *Anomogyna yatsugadakeana*, *Agrotis patula*, *Xestia wockei*, and *Apamea ontakensia* (Figure 12.8) (Jimbo, 1984).

Among the dragonflies of Japan, *Somatochlora alpestris*, which has survived in the central highland of Hokkaido, is the species that most prefers cold regions. Its larvae inhabit shallow ponds with peat moss at elevations between 1,310 and 1,680m in the Taisetsu Mountains and on Mt. Ashibetsudake, from the upper sub-alpine to the lower alpine zones (Environment Agency, 1980; Ubukata and Itou, 1990). If it were to shift its range upward by 400 m under the impact of climate change, *S. alpestris* may be forced to abandon large ponds at elevations between 1,400 and 1,500 m in the Taisetsu Mountains.

In the far south of the Japanese Archipelago, Asahina's skipper *Ochlodes asahinai* lives near the summits of the highest peak of Mt. Omotodake (525 m) on Ishigaki Island, and Mt. Gozadake (420m) on Iriomote Island. The genus *Ochlodes*, which is one of the groups ranging from the warm temperate to cool temperate zone, expanded its range into the Ryukyu Islands during the most recent glacial when these islands were linked to each other by land bridges, and then remained on the summits following the warming during the current interglacial (Fukuda, 1984b). *O. asahinai* may be endangered by the upward shifting of its range toward the summits under the impact of further warming.

The above mentioned predictions with respect to insects living in highland areas or near summits have been discussed under the assumption that other factors constituting insect habitats such as plants, soil and level of snowfall would shift in parallel with the upward shift of the isotherms. However, plant migration and soil formation proceed much more slowly than insect migration. Provided that suitable food and shelter are available, some of these insect species may survive by keeping pace with changes in vegetation and enduring higher temperatures. There may be a way for them to adapt to higher temperatures, but it is difficult to imagine that such small populations have sufficient genetic variation to do so.

Will endemic dragonflies disappear from brackish water habitats?

The Hinuma damselfly *Mortonagrion hirosei*, an endangered species in the Japanese Red Data Book, is endemic to Japan. About 25 habitat locations - including lagoons, large rivers estuaries, and coastal wetlands along the Pacific coast - have been recorded, but the destruction of these habitats is now in process (Asahina, 1989; Hirose, 1993). Similarly, *Orthetrum poecilops miyajimaensis*, an endemic subspecies, is distributed only near the seashore of the island of Miyajima in Hiroshima Prefecture, and inhabits small bogs adjacent to places which are nearly submerged at high tide (Sawano, 1993).

These rare species which are confined near seashores are not only threatened by the deterioration of their habitats due to land development, but are also endangered by loss of habitat due to a rise in sea level. Should the sea level rise by 95 cm due to further climate change, the remaining small populations of these species will face extinction.

What should we do?

Populations or species of insects often face extinction as a result of the synergistic effects of climate change and habitat fragmentation, and this will lead to a significant reduction in biodiversity. Among insect groups besides butterflies and dragonflies, a variety of changes are most likely occurring even if they are not yet documented, and these changes will progress more rapidly in the future. My discussion is based on the assumption that a rise in temperature of 2 to 3°C will occur within the next one or two centuries.

As for the influence of climate warming, shifts in the ranges of northern and southern species tend to attract attention, but there are also innumerable species that exist marginally under special habitat conditions here and there in Japan as well as elsewhere in the world, such as *Luehdorfia japonica* and *Orthetrum poecilops*. These species are weak in terms of their dispersal ability and fecundity. Moreover, the vegetation and habitat conditions on which they depend do not tend to shift easily in response to climate change. To prevent the total extinction of many species such as these, that is to say, to protect biodiversity which is the Earth's greatest natural treasure, it is necessary to eliminate the factors contributing to global warming. At the same time, of course, it is necessary to stop the destruction of the environment through development, and to maintain and preserve the environment in as close to a natural state as is practically possible.

Here I would like to offer one proposal. The construction of 'green highways' that run through the plains and lowlands of the Japanese main islands should be undertaken. To put this proposal into concrete terms, continuous belts of broad-leaved forests some 100 to 200 m wide should be created running along both the Pacific Ocean and the Sea of Japan sides of the country from northern Hokkaido to southern Kyushu and connected with the existing rural forests in each locality. These belts will not only serve as corridors for the migration and dispersal of wildlife that would otherwise be obstructed by the 'green deserts', but can also be used for hiking and nature education. If we are serious about protecting biodiversity, we are going to have to act practically and quickly.

References

Aoki, T. 1997. Northward expansion of *Ictinogomphus pertinax* (Selys) in eastern Shikoku and western Kinki Regions, Japan (Anisoptera: Gomphidae). Odonatologica 26: 121-133.

Asahina, S. 1989. Candidate species of the Odonata to be listed in the red data book of Japan. Tombo 32: 45-46. (in Japanese).

Askew, W. W. 1988. *The Dragonflies of Europe*. B. H. and A. Harley, Martins, Essex.

Davis, M. B., K. D. Woods, S. L. Webb, and R. P. Futuyma. 1986. Dispersal versus climate: Expansion of *Tsuga* in the upper Great Lakes Region. Vegetation 67: 93-103. (Requoted from Davis and Zabinski, 1992.)

Davis, M. B. and C. Zabinski. 1992. Changes in geographical range resulting from greenhouse warming: effects on biological diversity in forests. In: (R. L. Peters and T. E. Lovejoy, eds.) *Global Warming and Biological Diversity*. Pp. 297-308. Yale University Press, New Haven and London.

Eda, S. 1976. *A Guide to the Collection and Observation of Dragonflies*. New Science Co. Ltd., Tokyo, 100pp. (in Japanese)

Ehrlich, P. R. 1961. Intrinsic barriers to dispersal in Checkerspot butterfly. Science 134: 108-109.

Ehrlich, P. R., D. D. Murphy, M. C. Singer, C. B. Sherwood, R. R. White, and I. L. Brown. 1980. Extinction, reduction, stability and increase: the responses of Checkerspot butterfly (*Euphydryas*) populations to the California drought. Oecologia 46: 101-105.

Environment Agency. 1980. *Important Insects of Japan*. Hokkaido edition, 76pp. (in Japanese)

Environment Agency. 1996. *The Report of the Fourth Fundamental Investigation for the Conservation of Natural Environment: The Result of the Survey on the Distribution of Animals and Plants. Insects (Butterflies)*. 357pp. (in Japanese)

Erwin, T. L. 1982. Tropical forest: their richness in Coleoptera and other arthropod species. Coleoptersits Bulletin 36: 74-75.

Ford, M. J. 1982. *The Changing Climate: Responses of the Natural Fauna and Flora*. George Allen & Unwin, London, 190pp. (Requoted from Peters, 1992)

Fukuda, H., E. Hama, T. Kuzutani, A. Takahashi, M. Takahashi, B. Tanaka, H. Tanaka, M. Wakabayashi, and Y. Watanabe. 1982. *The Life Histories of Butterflies in Japan*. Vol. 1. Hoikusha Publishing Co. Ltd., Osaka, 277pp. (in Japanese)

Fukuda, H., E. Hama, T. Kuzutani, A. Takahashi, M. Takahashi, B. Tanaka, H. Tanaka, M. Wakabayashi, and Y. Watanabe. 1983. *The Life Histories of Butterflies in Japan*. Vol. 2. Hoikusha Publishing Co. Ltd., Osaka, 325pp. (in Japanese)

Fukuda, H., E. Hama, T. Kuzutani, A. Takahashi, M. Takahashi, B. Tanaka, H. Tanaka, M. Wakabayashi, and Y. Watanabe. 1984a. *The Life Histories of Butterflies in Japan*. Vol. 3. Hoikusha Publishing Co. Ltd., Osaka. 373pp. (in Japanese)

Fukuda, H., E. Hama, T. Kuzutani, A. Takahashi, M. Takahashi, B. Tanaka, H. Tanaka, M. Wakabayashi, and Y. Watanabe. 1984b. *The Life Histories of Butterflies in Japan*. Vol. 4. Hoikusha Publishing Co. Ltd., Osaka. 373pp. (in Japanese)

Gaston, K. 1991. The magnitude of global insect species richness. Conservation Biology 5: 183-186.

Hamada, K. and K. Inoue. 1985. *The Dragonflies of Japan in Color*. Kodansha, Tokyo, 370pp. (in Japanese)

Harrison, S. 1993. Species diversity, spatial scale, and global change. In: (P. M. Kareiva et al., eds.) *Biotic Interactions and Global Change*. Pp.388-401. Sinauer, Sunderland, Massachusetts.

Harrison, S., D. D. Murphy, and P. R. ehrlich. 1988. Distribution of the Bay Checkerspot butterfly, *Euphydryas editha bayenses*: evidence for a metapopulation model. American Naturalist 132: 360-382.

Hassel, M. P., H. C. Godfray, and H. N. Comins. 1993. Effects of global change on the dynamics of insect hostparasitoid interactions. In: (P. M. Kareiva et al., eds.) *Biotic Interactions and Global Change*. Pp.402-423. Sinauer, Sunderland, Massachusetts.

Hatori, K. and T. Shibazaki (eds.) 1971. *The Quaternary Period*. Kyoritsu Shuppan, Tokyo, 348pp. (in Japanese)

Hirose, M. 1993. *Mortonagrion hirosei*. In: (S. Asahina, ed.) *Fifty Insect Species Endangered in Japan*. Pp.21-23. Tsukiji-shokan, Tokyo. (in Japanese)

Hiura, I. 1980. Notes on Japanese alpine fauna and flora. Nature and Insects 15(9): 2-11. (in Japanese)

Imura, O., N. Morimoto, and T. Niura. 1993. Potential effect of global warming on the distribution of insects in Japan. Proceedings of the International Symposium on Insect Diversity Research in Korea, Chucheon. Pp.44-57.

Ishida, S. 1969. *Insect's Life in Japan: Vol. 2. Dragonflies*. Hoikusha Publishing Co. Ltd., Osaka, 261pp. (in Japanese)

Ishida, S., K. Ishida, K. Kojima, and M. Sugimura. 1988. *Illustrated Guide for Identification of the Japanese Odonata*. Tokai University Press, Tokyo, 140pp. (in Japanese)

Jimbo, K. 1984. *Alpine Moths: Moths Flying around in the Highlands*. Tsukiji-Shokan, Tokyo, 191pp. (in

Japanese)

Kareiva, P. M., J. G. Kingsolver, and R. B. Huey (eds.) 1993. *Biotic Interactions and Global Change*. Sinauer, Sunderland, Massachusetts. 559pp.

Kiritani, K. 1983. Colonising insects 3: What makes a successful colonizer? Insectarium 20: 310-317. (in Japanese)

Kiritani, K. 1991. Potential impacts of global warming on insects. Insectarium 28: 212-223. (in Japanese)

Kosugi, T., M. Nakatani, and Y. Hirama. 1994. Alpine moths of Mt. Oakandake and Mt. Meakandake. In: *The Nature of Akan National Park, 1993*. Pp.1068-1074. Maeda Ippoen Zaidan, Akan, Hokkaido. (in Japanese)

Masaki, S. 1986. Crickets: their range expansion through climatic adaptation. In: (K. Kiritani) *The Insects of Japan: Ecology of Invasion and Turbulence*. Pp.149-156. Tokai University Press, Tokyo. (in Japanese)

Moriyama, H. 1988. *What is it to Protect Nature?* Nosangyoson Bunka Kyokai, Tokyo, 260pp. (in Japanese)

Murphy, D. D. and S. B. Weiss. 1992. Effect of climate change on biological diversity in western North America: species losses and mechanisms. In: (R. L. Peter and T. E. Lovejoy, eds.) *Global Warming and Biological Diversity*. Pp.355-368. Yale University Press, New Haven and London.

Myers, N. 1992. Synergisms: Joint effects of climate change and other forms of habitat destruction. In: (R. L. Peters and T. E. Lovejoy, eds.) *Global Warming and Biological Diversity*. Pp.344-354. Yale University Press, New Haven and London.

Nakasuji, F. 1988. Migration of butterflies and their evolutionary adaptation. In: *Recent Progress in Lepidopterology, Special Reports of the Lepidopterological Society of Japan 6*. Pp.211-249. (Requoted from Kiritani, 1991) (in Japanese)

Ono, Y. and Y. Igarashi. 1991. Travel in the forests in the glacier age. In: *Natural History of Hokkaido*. Hokkaido University Press, Sapporo, 219pp. (in Japanese)

Ott, J. 1996. Zeigt die Ausbreitung der Feuerlibelle *Crocothemis erythraea* Brullé in Deutschland eine Klimaveränderung an? Naturschutz und Landschaftsplanung 28(2): 53-61.

Ott, J. (in press) *Die Ausbreitung mediterraner Libellenarten in Deutschland und Europa - die Folge einer Klimaveränderung?* Norddeutsche Naturschutzakademie Berichte, Schneverdingen, Germany. (in Germany)

Parmesan, C. 1996. Climate and species range. Nature 382: 765-766.

Paulson, D. R. 1999. Dragonflies (Odonata: Anisoptera) of south Florida. Slater Museum of Natural His-tory, Occasional Paper No. 57: 1-139.

Peters, R. L. and T. E. Lovejoy (eds.). 1992. *Global Warming and Biological Diversity*. Yale University Press, New Haven and London, 386pp.

Sawano, J. 1993. *Orthetrum poecilops*. In: (S. Asahina, ed.) *Fifty Insect Species Endangered in Japan*. Tsukiji-Shokan, Tokyo. (in Japanese)

Singer, M. C. and P. R. Ehrlich. 1979. Population dynamics of the Checkerspot butterfly *Euphydryas editha*. Fortschritte der Zoologie 25: 53-60.

Tracy, C. R. 1992. Ecological responses of animals to climate. In: (R. L. Peters and T. E. Lovejoy, eds.) *Global Warming and Biological Diversity*. Pp.171-179. Yale University Press, New Haven and London.

Travis, J. and D. J. Futuyma. 1993. Global changes: lessons from and for evolutionary biology. In: (P. M. Kareva et al., eds.) *Biotic Interactions and Global Change*. Pp.251-263. Sinauer, Sunderland, Massachusetts.

Ubukata, H. and M. Itou. 1990. The Odonata collected at Mt. Taisetsu in July, 1987, and July and September, 1989. Sylvicola 8: 71-74. (in Japanese)

Watanabe, K. 1989. Some dragonfly species expanding their range in the Ryukyus. Tombo 32: 54-56 (in Japanese).

Watanabe, Y. 1986. *Alpine Butterflies: Highlands, Butterflies and I*. Tsukiji-Shokan, Tokyo, 209pp. (in Japanese)

Yasuda, N. 1978. Notes on the beetles on Mt. Taisetsu. Jezoensis 5: 35-39. (in Japanese)

Yasuda, N. 1993. *Parnassius eversmanni*. In: (S. Asahina, ed.) *Fifty Insect Species Endangered in Japan*. Pp.126-128. Tsukiji-Shokan, Tokyo. (in Japanese)

Yodoe, K. 1994. Range expansion of *Cyrestis thyodama mabella*. In: (Sanin Society of Entomologists, ed.) *Butterflies of the Sanin Region*. Pp.184-185. Sanin Chuo Shimposha, Matsue. (in Japanese)

Chapter 13

Global Warming and Alpine Moths in Raised Bogs in Eastern Hokkaido

Masahiko Nakatani

The Pacific Coast of eastern Hokkaido is rich in wetlands. There are several well known marshes such as Kushiro Marsh, the largest marsh in Japan, and Kiritappu Marsh, as well as many other large and small marshes. Marshes are categorized into three groups – fens, intermediate moors, and raised bogs – according to their stage of development. In the cold climate of eastern Hokkaido, raised bogs that have developed hammocks of *Sphagnum* are recognized as one type of climax vegetation. A group of moths known as alpine moths, relic species from the most recent glacial age, still exist and form part of the unique raised bog ecosystems.

Raised bogs in eastern Hokkaido

Kushiro Marsh used to cover an area of approximately 30,000 ha, but had been reduced to 18,290 ha by 1985 due to agricultural and urban development. Approximately 70% of the total area is fen consisting of reeds and sedges. Raised bog accounts for less than 2% (Nature Conservation Society of Japan, 1990). Kiritappu Marsh covers 3,168 ha and its central area consists of a raised bog. There are a number of other small (a few hectares) raised bogs in eastern Hokkaido (Figures 13.1 and 13.2).

The vegetation common to all raised bogs includes thick alpine and northern plants such as *Empetrum nigrum*, *Vaccinium oxycoccus*, *Vaccinium vitis-idaea*, *Ledum palustre*, *Andromeda polifolia* and *Chamaedaphne calyculata*, all of which are found on developed hammocks of *Sphagnum*.

Alpine moths

Alpine moths are species which breed more frequently in alpine zones in high mountains than in sub-alpine and lower zones (Jinbo, 1984). In Hokkaido,

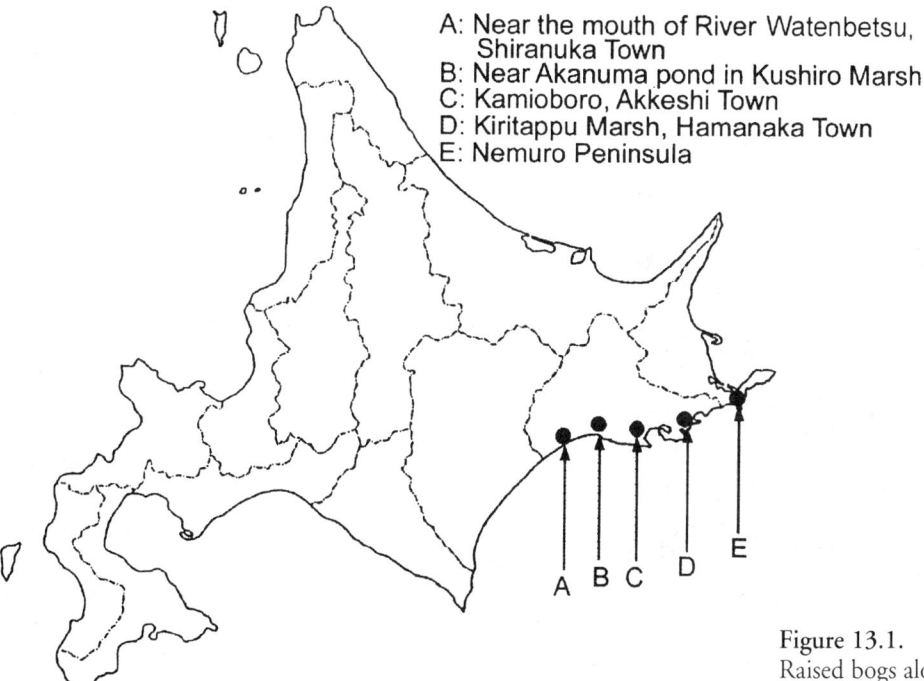

Figure 13.1.
Raised bogs along the Pacific Ocean coast of eastern Hokkaido (A - E: survey locations).

A: Near the mouth of River Watenbetsu, Shiranuka Town
B: Near Akanuma pond in Kushiro Marsh
C: Kamioboro, Akkeshi Town
D: Kiritappu Marsh, Hamanaka Town
E: Nemuro Peninsula

Figure 13.2.
Raised bog surrounded by homogenous forest of *Pinus glehnii* on the Nemuro Peninsula.

moths living at elevations of 1,500 m or higher are called alpine moths and are categorized into six families and 38 species (Kusunoki and Yasuda, 1997). Since the smaller species have not been well studied taxonomically, the number of known alpine moth species may increase in the future.

Most of the alpine moths in Japan are also found in other boreal zones, such as in Scandinavia, Siberia, Amur, Kamchatka and Alaska. In these places, their distribution ranges extend to lower mountain elevations and even into plains below the tree line. In Japan, one of the southernmost countries at which these creatures are found, they were long thought to live only in the high mountains.

Some species of alpine moths, however, have been spotted recently in raised bogs in the lowlands of northern and eastern Hokkaido (Table 13.1). Out of ten species of alpine moths found in lowland areas in eastern Hokkaido, nine (the exception being *Heterothera taigana sounkeana*) are found in raised bogs and the surrounding areas (Table 13.2). *Selenodes lediana* was found in the raised bog in Shiranuka Town; *S. lediana* and *Phiaris hokkaidana* (Figure 13.3) were found in Kushiro Marsh; *Lozotaenia forsterana*, *S. lediana*, and *Olethreutes bipunctana yama* were found in Kamioboro, Akkeshi Town; *Aphelia septentrionalis*, *S. lediana*, and *P. hokkaidana* were found in Kiritappu Marsh; and all nine species were found in raised bogs on the Nemuro Peninsula (Nakatani, 1995).

Of these nine alpine moths, seven (the exceptions being *Eriopsela quadrana* and *Agrotis ruta*) feed on *L. palustre*, *E. nigrum* and *V. viti-idaea*, all of which grow on raised bogs. Consequently, there is a close relationship between alpine moths and raised bogs.

Influence of global warming

A number of raised bogs that are home to alpine moths exist in small patches on the Nemuro Peninsula. The most notable characteristic of these raised bogs is that most are located on tablelands and so are not supplied with water from inflowing rivers. Their water is provided exclusively from precipitation and from sea fog. Unlike other raised bogs such as those in Kushiro Marsh, which have been formed within fens, those on the Nemuro Peninsula are pure raised bogs, not part of any larger marshland area but surrounded mainly by homogenous forests of *P.*

Figure 13.3.
Phiaris hokkaidana which feeds on *Empetrum nigrum*.

Table 13.1. Distribution of alpine moths in Hokkaido (Kusunoki and Yasuda, 1997)

FAMILY, Species	Mt. Rishiri	Mt. Shokanbetsu	Mt. Yotei	Mt. Muine	Mt. Yubari	Hidaka Mtns.	Teshio Mtns.	Taisetsu Mtns. A	B	C	D	E	F	Akan Mtns.	Shiretoko Mtns.	East lowlands	North lowlands	Others
TORTRICIDAE																		
Aphelia septentrionalis	●															●		
Aphelia christophi					●						●							
Lozotaenia kumatai			●		●	●	●	●	●	●	●	●	●		●			
Lozotaenia forsterana								●						●		●		
Clepsis insignata					●	●		●	●	●	●		●					
Clepsis aliana							●	●	●	●	●							
Daemilus mutuurai											●							
Apotomis kusunokii						●	●	●	●	●			●		●			
Cymolomia jinboi									●	●		●	●					
Selenodes lediana						●		●						●	●	●		
Olethreutes sohulziana			●			●		●	●	●	●	●			●			
Olethreutes bipunctana yama				●			●	●	●	●				●		●		
Phiaris hokkaidana							●		●	●			●	●		●		
Ancylis unguicella												●		●				
Epinotia pinicola	●				●	●	●	●	●	●	●				●			
Gypsonoma erubesoa						●		●	●	●	●							
Eriopsela quadrana								●	●	●						●	●	
Rhopobota ustomaculana		●	●		●	●	●	●	●	●	●	●	●	●	●	●	●	
COCHYLIDAE																		
Hysterosia vulneratana						●	●		●	●	●	●						
Hysterosia inopiana						●	●	●	●	●			●					
Aethes deutschiana								●		●	●							
Smaller moths: subtotal	2	1	3	1	7	10	7	14	14	17	10	6	7	6	7	7	2	0
GEOMETRIDAE																		
Xanthorhoe fluctuata									●	●								
Xanthorhoe sajanaria						●		●	●	●	●	●	●					
Entephria amplicosta								●	●	●	●	●						
Heterothera taigana sounkeana	●	●	●		●	●	●	●	●	●		●	●	●	●	●		
Eupitheoia perpaupera										●								
Psodos coracina								●	●	●	●	●	●					
Yezognophos sordaria										●		●						
LYMANTRIIDAE																		
Gynaephora rossii								●		●		●						
ARCTIIDAE																		
Grammia quenseli								●	●	●								
NOCTUIDAE																		
Agrotis ruta	●							●	●	●	●		●			●		
Anomogyna speciosa	●		●		●	●		●	●	●		●	●	●	●			
Pachnobia imperita						●	●	●	●	●		●	●		●			
Anarta melanopa								●	●	●		●	●					
Anarta cordigera						●				●	●	●						
Hada skraelingia									●	●	●							
Sympistis funebris									●	●	●							
Syngrapha ottolenguii	●	●	●	●	●	●	●	●	●	●	●	●	●	●	●	●		
Larger moths: subtotal	4	2	3	1	3	6	3	11	13	17	8	15	10	3	4	3	0	0
Smaller and larger moths: total	6	3	6	2	10	16	10	25	27	34	18	21	17	9	11	10	2	0

A: Tokachidake Mtns.; B: central Taisetsu; C: northern Taisetsu; D: Mt. Niseikaushuppe; E: eastern Taisetsu (Mt. Ishikari); F: eastern Taisetsu (Mt. Nipesotsu); East lowlands: eastern Hokkaido; North lowlands: northern Hokkaido.

Table 13.2. Distribution of alpine moths in raised bogs of eastern Hokkaido

Species name	Shiranuka	Kushiro	Akkeshi	Hamanaka	Nemuro	Main diet
A. septentrionalis				●	●	L. palustre, E. nigrum, etc
L. forsterana			●		●	L. palustre
S. lediana	●	●	●	●	●	L. palustre
O. bipunctana yama			●		●	L. palustre, E. nigrum,
P. hokkaidana		●		●	●	E. nigrum
E. quadrana					●	Unknown
R. ustomaculana					●	V. vitis-idaea
A. ruta					●	Dicentra peregina. In Nemuro, unknown
S. ottolenguii					●	E. nigrum, V. vitis-idaea
Total	1	2	3	3	9	

See locations of areas surveyed in Fig. 13.1.

glehnii.

Why alpine moths, which have survived as relic species since the most recent glacial, inhabit such completely different environments as high mountains and raised bogs in lowlands is not well understood. It is likely, however, that species from the sub-polar zone and other northern regions moved south relatively late in the glacial and continued to survive as the climate warmed by migrating to high mountain areas and raised bogs (peat beds) where suitable climatic conditions prevailed (Kusunoki, 1991). Even in summer, areas along the Pacific coast of eastern Hokkaido have a number of foggy days, relatively few hours of sunshine and often low temperatures. In this severe climate, which resembles that on high mountains, alpine moths as well as alpine plants are able to survive. The distribution of alpine moths on the Nemuro Peninsula correlates exactly with the distribution of raised bogs and both distribution ranges are completely isolated.

In this situation, alpine moths can hardly migrate in response to the direct or indirect influence of global warming, and their continued survival is completely dependent on the extent of global warming and the resilience of the raised bog ecosystem, including the moths themselves. It is thought that most of the hammocks of *Sphagnum* that form raised bogs in Hokkaido will be able to grow under a relatively wider range of temperatures and so will not be greatly affected by moderate changes in temperature. However, if the amount of precipitation and the number of foggy days are reduced as a consequence of global warming, there will be significant changes in the growth of hammocks of *Sphagnum* (Environment Agency, 1997).

It is unlikely that most alpine moths will be greatly affected by a small change in temperature, because most of the species living in raised bogs at present are also distributed throughout several high mountain areas as well as in relatively large areas of the low altitude zone. These species should be able to adapt well to the anticipated environmental changes. On Mt. Atosanupuri, an active volcano in Kawayu, Teshikaga Town, where the temperature in summer rarely rises above 30°C, volcanic ash zones in the foothills at elevations of about 200 m are covered by colonies of alpine plants such as *Pinus pumila, L. palustre,* and *E. nigrum*. Four alpine moth species that also live on the Nemuro Peninsula (*Lozotaenia forsterana, Selenodes lediana, Olethreutes bipunctana yama,* and *Phiaris hokkaidana*) have been found there (Kumata et al., 1994). This also indicates that these moths are highly adaptable to changes in temperature.

The high adaptability of individual species in raised bogs to climate change does not necessarily mean that the raised bog ecosystems as a whole are also highly adaptable, however. Changes in the composition of the species that form the ecosystem may have a negative effect on the entire ecosystem. Moreover, if global warming results in a sudden and significant change in climate, the situation will undoubtedly worsen.

The Nemuro Peninsula is the coldest area in the lowland plains of Hokkaido according to the warmth index. The average annual temperature in Japan is expected to increase by between 1°C and 2.5°C from its present level due to global warming over the next about 100 years. Calculating from this figure without taking into account seasonal fluctuations, the warmth index of the Nemuro Peninsula is projected to increase by between 6 and 15 points to between 51 and 60.

The distribution of butterflies from Hokkaido to the southern Kuril Islands and Sakhalin is closely related to the warmth index. The boundary between the distributions of temperate and subarctic butterflies is found in the regions where the warmth index is between 45 and 55. This is also very close to the boundary between the temperate zone (warmth index 55 to 88) and the subarctic zone (warmth index 15 to 55) (Biology Teachers' Association of Hokkaido, 1983). Consequently, if the annual average temperature suddenly rises, not only the alpine moths but also other species inhabiting raised bogs that have maintained these subarctic ecosystems in isolation may be lost.

References

Hokkaido Seibutsu Kyouiku Kai (Biology Teachers' Association of Hokkaido). 1983. *A Guidebook to the Wildlife of Hokkaido.* 85pp. (in Japanese)

Jinbo, K. 1984. *Alpine Moths.* Tsukiji-Shokan, Tokyo, 191pp. (in Japanese)

Environment Agency (Working Group on Implications of Climate Change). 1997. *Implications of Climate Change for Japan-produced in 1996.* Environment Agency. (in Japanese)

Kumata, T., K. Ijima, Y. Suma, M. Nakatani, Y. Hirama, H. Ubukata, T. Kosugi, K. Haga, and N. Ichijo. 1994. Insects of Akan. In: (Y. Katsui, J. Samejima, H. Abe, T. Suda, and H. Kataoka, eds.) *The Nature of Akan National Park.* Pp.991-1189. Maeda Ippoen Foundation, Akan, Hokkaido. (in Japanese)

Kusunoki, Y. 1991. Moths associated with the alpine region and the peatlands in Hokkaido: a preliminary report. Yugato (Journal of Research on Moths) 124: 77-83.

Kusunoki, Y. and N. Yasuda. 1997. Distribution of alpine moths in Hokkaido. Kamikawa-cho no Shizen (The nature of Kamikawa Town), 19: 59-60. (in Japanese)

Nakatani, M. 1995. Alpine moths of raised bogs in the Pacific coastal area of eastern Hokkaido II. Sylvicola (Journal of Kushiro Insect Lovers' Society) 13: 1-8. (in Japanese)

Nature Conservation Society of Japan. 1990. *Nature Watching at Kushiro Marsh.* 46pp. (in Japanese)

Chapter 14

Global Warming and Forest Insect Pests
An Example from Hokkaido

Kenji Fukuyama

As the global climate warms, will forest damage increase as a result of more frequent insect outbreaks? This question cannot be answered easily because unlike most cases involving single species, outbreaks of forest insect pests occur only when the following four factors are all present: insects capable of harming trees, trees that can be harmed, a favorable biological environment, and a favorable abiotic environment (Figure 14.1). How these factors interact is still unclear.

Global warming changes the abiotic environmental factor, which in turn influences other factors. This is why outbreaks of forest insect pests cannot easily be forecasted. In addition, certain insects are considered harmful because they have a negative influence on human life or activities. However, when the damage caused by insect pests is not very significant economically, they are not considered harmful. To take an extreme example, if in the future trees and forests were to be considered of no value, there would be no forest insect pests whatsoever. On the other hand, should the existence of forests become more precious in the future, not only for the value of their timber but in their own right, then outbreaks of defoliating insects on more than a certain scale would be regarded as harmful.

In Hokkaido, Japan's northernmost main island, there are a variety of different types of forest. Within these forests, outbreaks of many kinds of insect pest occur at frequent intervals and information related to these outbreaks has been accumulated over more than 40 years. In this chapter we attempt to examine what kind of influence global warming will have on forest damage due to insect pests in Hokkaido.

Outbreaks of forest insect pests and the influence of warming
Physiology of insects

A major factor in outbreaks of insect pests is an increase in the "pest" species' intrinsic rate of natural increase. This means that the species in question has boosted its reproductive success by increasing the number of eggs laid, the size of the eggs, and/or the rate of incubation, as well as by decreasing its mortality rate. If the temperature rises, insects tend to grow faster and the rate at which their larvae survive after incubation may increase. Moreover, at higher temperatures a single generation requires less time to reach maturity, allowing more generations per year and increasing the species' rate of reproduction.

On the other hand, insects whose physiology, for example dormancy, is controlled by photoperiodism may experience a reduction in their survival rate; they may become dormant despite the high temperature or due to overly rapid growth. Insects that damage plant buds and make galls may fail to reproduce because their phenological characteristics and those of their host plants no longer complement each other.

Forest insect pests whose distribution ranges are currently limited by temperature factors are likely to be able expand their ranges northward. For example, the fall webworm *Hyphantria cunea* is presently unable survive in Aomori Prefecture and areas further

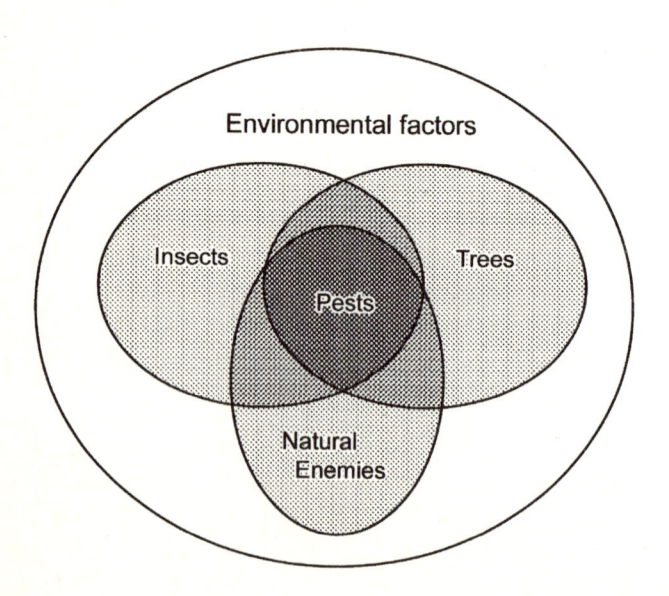

Figure 14.1.
Correlation among factors contributing to outbreaks of forest insect pests.

north, because these areas are not warm enough for either the photoperiodism-induced dormancy or the growth of this species (Ito, 1972). However, the progress of global warming may make it possible for them to survive in these areas.

Physiology of trees

In comparison to insects, trees are much less capable of rapidly shifting their distribution ranges, and consequently such changes in response to global warming will be very slow. As global warming intensifies, trees in many locations will be placed under increasing stress over a long period due to changes in temperature and water availability. In such circumstances, their physiological resistance against insect pests may weaken and their germination period may also change. Trees that have resisted insect damage up to the present may no longer be able to continue doing so under such conditions. Moreover, trees may not have resistance to newly appearing insects which migrate north in response to climate warming, with the result that they could be damaged significantly.

Biological environment surrounding forest insect pests

The number of defoliators is thought to be limited to a low level due to the presence of natural enemies such as predators, parasites and microorganisms. The influence which global warming will have on these natural enemies is very difficult to predict. Nevertheless, natural enemies will not initially display their abilities to the full at times when forest insect pests rapidly expand their distribution ranges and adapt themselves to feeding on and thereby damaging new kinds of trees. This prediction is endorsed by the fact that newly appearing insect pests can suddenly bring about damage to trees. In Hokkaido, a number of insect species harmful to larches, many of which are not indigenous to Hokkaido, have recently made an appearance.

The reason why larches in Hokkaido have been seriously damaged seems to be that the trees themselves are not native to Hokkaido. For some time after larches were planted during the post World War II period, they were damaged by the gypsy moth *Lymantria disper* and other insects that are known to be harmful to broadleaf trees. Subsequently, insects harmful to larches that are native to Honshu, such as larch sawflies, *Pristiphora erichsoni* and *P. wesmaeli*, began to appear in Hokkaido. More recently, new kinds of insect pests have been establishing themselves in Hokkaido and causing repeated outbreaks of tree damage, but this phenomenon does not seem to be directly related to climate warming.

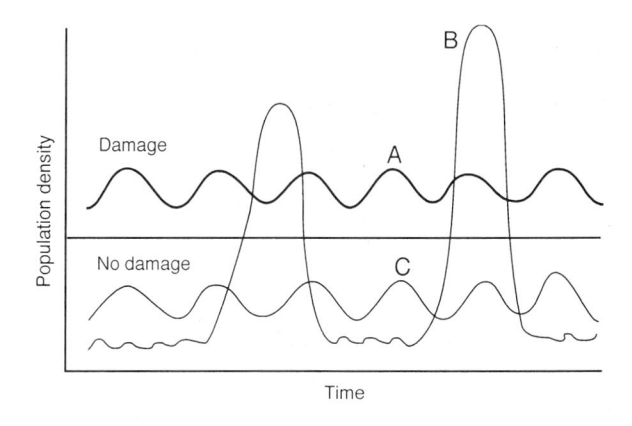

Figure 14.2.
Types of outbreak of forest insect pests and fluctuations in their population density. A: Continuous outbreak, B: Sudden outbreak, and C: Ordinary forest insects (Yamaguchi, 1989).

Types of forest insect pest outbreak and climate warming

Many species of insects harmful to forests are known, and more than 180 kinds have been recorded as forests insect pests in Hokkaido. Most can be grouped into three types: defoliating insects such as moths, sawflies, and leaf beetles; sapsucking insects such as aphids; and wood boring insects such as bark beetles, longicorns, and weevils.

There are three types of outbreak: sudden outbreaks, continuous outbreaks and specific outbreaks (Figure 14.2). Although the causes of these types are more or less the same, the influence of climate warming on each type would be different.

Damage by sapsucking insects (continuous outbreaks)

The number of forest insect pest species does not increase to plague proportions very frequently. Like agricultural pest insects, however, these species reproduce continuously as long as certain conditions are fulfilled. Once an outbreak occurs, it can continue to cause damage for a long period. Insect pests of this type include the todo-fir aphid *Cinara todocola*, the Yezo-spruce gall aphid *Adelges japonicus* and other aphid species. These insects formerly lived on naturally growing young trees, and their populations remained small. However, their populations rapidly increase when large areas are planted in massive forestry development plans.

C. todocola damages the todo fir *Abies sachalinensis* and the young trees of other fir species. The rapid expansion of *A. sachalinensis* plantations during the postwar period was accompanied by an increase in cases of damage caused by the todo-fir aphid

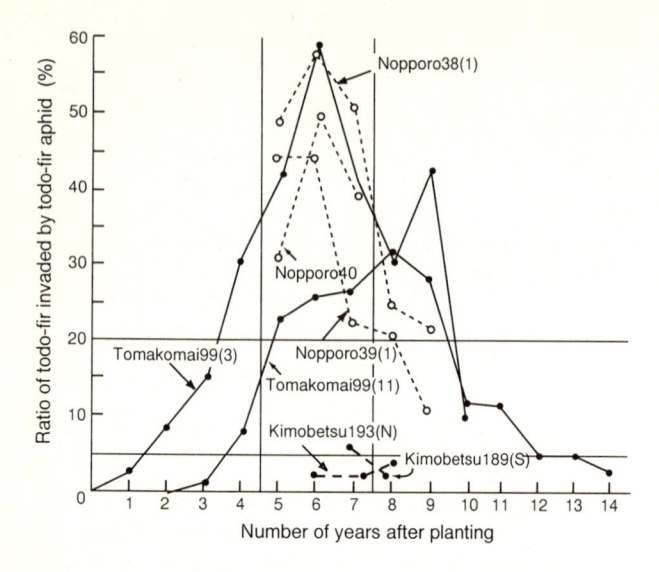

Figure 14.3.
Fluctuations of *Cinara todocola* hosting *Abis sachalinensis* (Yamaguchi, 1976).

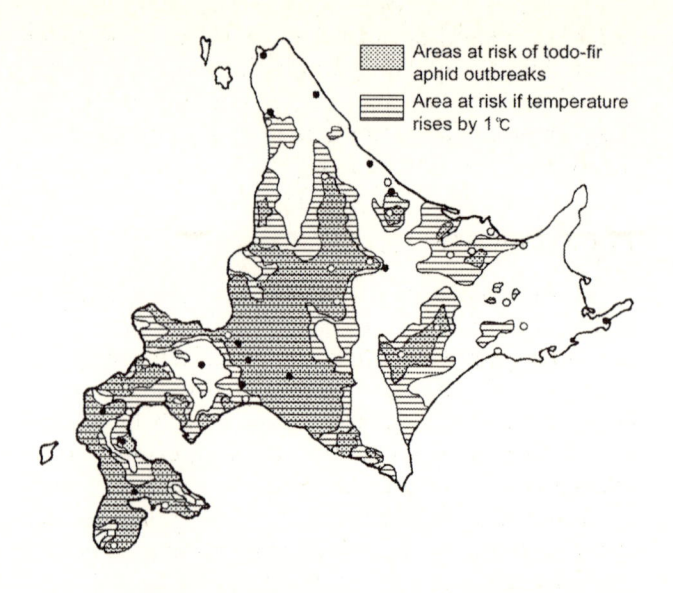

Figure 14.4.
Areas subject to potential *Cinara todocola* outbreaks at present and in the case of a 1°C rise in air temperature.

(Yamaguchi, 1976). Initially, it was thought that the trees would not die due to aphid damage. In the case of serious damage, however, trees were found to have died, and this prompted large-scale aphid control measures.

Aphid damage of this type affects only younger trees up to approximately age ten. The rate of increase in the population density of the todo-fir aphid is more or less stable. This means that the later the insects enter an area after tree planting, the lower their population density will be and the less damage they will cause (Figure 14.3). Moreover, the rate of increase in their population density is influenced by temperature. Consequently, in low-temperature areas, even the highest population densities of this aphid have been found to not approach a level that causes economic damage.

A survey of fluctuations in the aphid population density at several locations in Hokkaido also found that the population density does not reach a level that results in unacceptable tree damage in cold areas. It has been established that population density is closely related to the accumulated temperature during the period between April and August. When the average temperatures for each month from April through August minus 5°C are added together, if the total obtained is 45°C or more, the population density at the surveyed places can reach a level that causes significant tree damage.

In the todo-fir aphid potential damage area map (Yamaguchi, 1976), the occurrence of damage by the aphids is determined by three factors: the existence of newly planted areas, the timing of invasion into these areas, and the average temperature.

The shaded areas in Figure 14.4 represent the potential damage areas at the present temperature level. A rise of 1°C in the average temperature from April through August above the present level is equivalent to an increase of 5 in accumulated temperature. In the case of a 1°C rise, areas where the accumulated temperature from April through August is 40°C at present will be under threat of damage by the todo-fir aphid (Figure 14.4). On the basis of current trends in forestry in Hokkaido, however, new plantings in areas susceptible to significant aphid damage seem unlikely to be developed.

Damage by wood-boring insects (specific outbreaks)

Wood borers do not essentially damage and kill healthy trees. When host trees exist under abnormal physiological conditions or the insects themselves act abnormally, however, the trees can be damaged by boring. A typical example is that of the eight-spined ips *Ips typographus japonicus*. The population of this species, which reproduces in dead wood, can greatly increase after a large number of trees are felled by a typhoon. In such cases, outbreaks spread and cause damage to healthy trees in surrounding areas. In Hokkaido, a large number of trees in the Taisetsu Mountains were felled by a typhoon in 1954, and the subsequent damage led to an outbreak of *I. typographus japonicus*. In 1981, similar damage was caused by *I. typographus japonicus* after a typhoon. In northern Europe, a storm and subsequent dry weather resulted in damage by *I. typographus* which blighted significant numbers of Norway spruce (Christiansen and Bakke, 1988). In North America, large numbers of pine trees have been killed by bark beetles (Stark, 1982).

The imagoes of *I. typographus japonicus* spend the winter beneath tree bark, and emerge in the spring to make holes in weak or recently blighted trees for the purpose of reproduction. The male imagoes emit aggregative pheromones to attract females to the holes for mating. The larvae grow by eating the wood under the bark and become pupae and imagoes there. In cold locations, they spend the winter under tree bark, but in warm locations they sometimes reproduce again. Imagoes attracted to blighted or weak trees by aggregative pheromones, however, may move to nearby healthy trees to make holes. In such cases, most of the boring insects are killed by the tree's resin. Healthy trees invaded by a large number of imagoes can be weakened by microorganisms that are brought along by *I. typographus*, and this can lead to blight. This has been established through studies of instances of damage by *I. typographus* (Horntvedt et al., 1983).

The damage caused by *I. typographus japonicus* occurs mainly in trees subject to physiological stress or in conditions of large-scale blighting, so that the influence of climate warming is likely to become apparent through changes in tree physiology. If a region is subject to reduced precipitation or greater frequency of typhoons in addition to an increase in temperature, damage by bark beetles will increase.

Damage by defoliators (sudden outbreaks)

Defoliators such as moths, sawflies and leaf beetles can cause sudden outbreaks of tree damage by rapidly increasing their population density and stripping their host trees of leaves. Such damage comes to an end several years later.

There is normally an inexhaustible amount of foliage compared to the population of defoliating insects. Consequently, it is believed that the restricting factors on the population of such insects are external causes of death, such as predators and climate, rather than the availability of host trees.

Similarities can be identified between the circumstances under which forests in Hokkaido are damaged by defoliators. For example, a number of similar species tend to appear in plague proportions at the same time across a large geographical area. It can be deduced that some factor with a homogeneous influence over a large area is playing an important role in the outbreak, and the most probable factor is climate.

Individuals of the hemlock caterpillar *Dendrolimus superans* spend the winter in larval form in the soil and emerge in April or May. They ascend into trees at this time and become imagoes from June to August. *D. superans* can survive winter at any stage of its growth except for the first stage (Yamaguchi, 1977). In Hokkaido, the time between successive generations of this species is more than a year, so imagoes appear at different periods of the year (Figure 14.5). This reduces possibilities for mating and lowers the reproduction rate. If, however, the accumulated temperature is pushed up due to climate warming, one generation could reach adulthood within a year, allowing the appearance of imagoes to be concentrated at a certain time of the year, resulting in a rise in the reproduction rate.

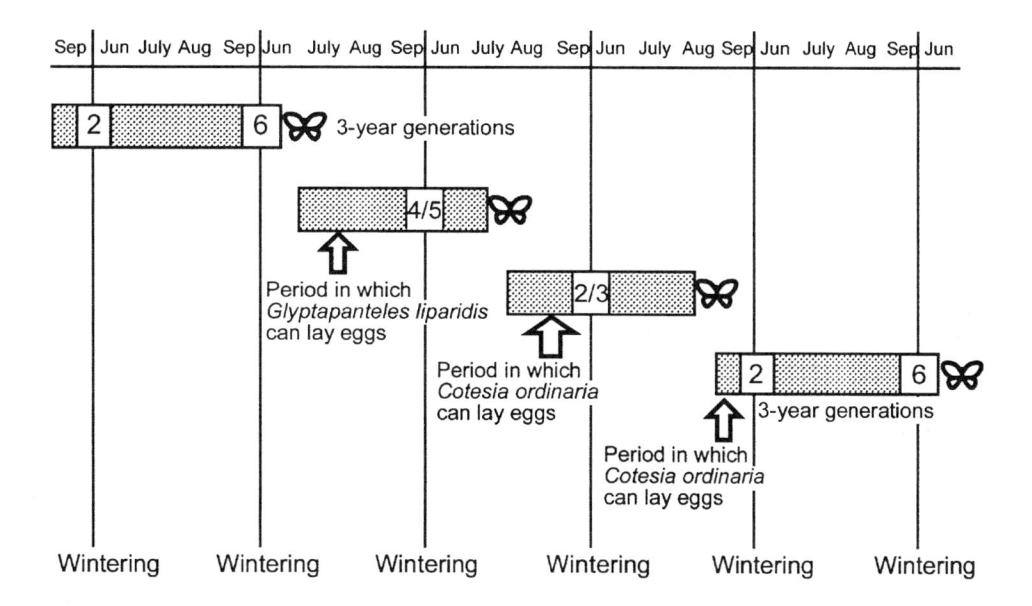

Figure 14.5.
Life cycle of *Dendrolimus superans* and periods in which parasitic wasps can lay eggs (Fukuyama, 1981).

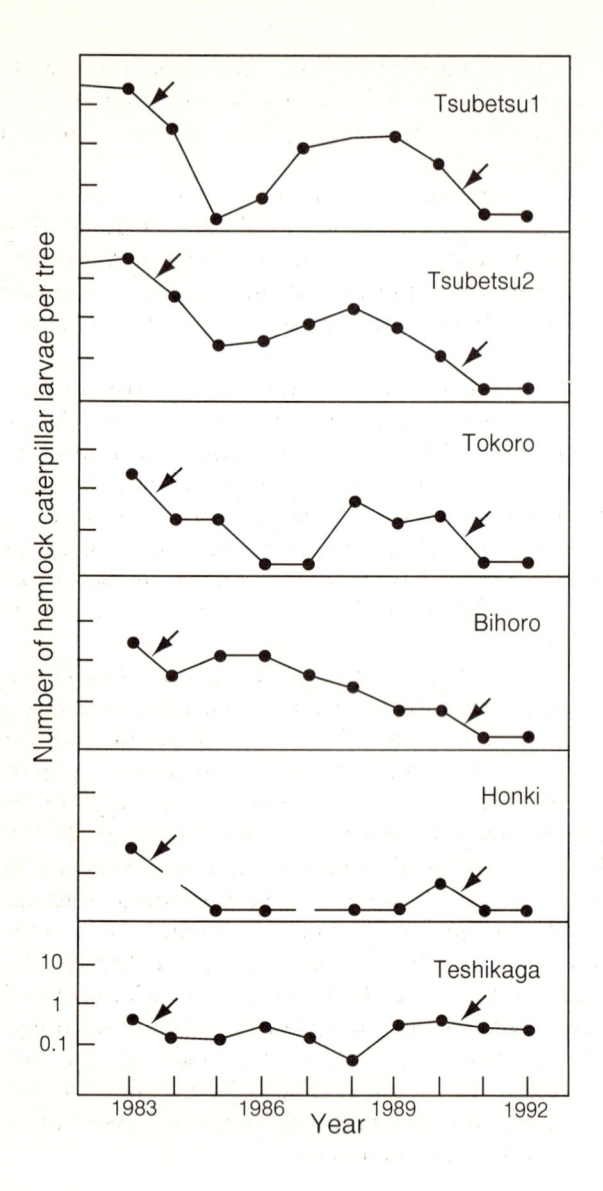

Figure 14.6.
Annual fluctuations in population of *Dendrolimus superans* larvae at locations in eastern Hokkaido (Maeto and Fukuyama, 1994; Tsubetsu 1 and 2 are from unpublished data).

The hemlock caterpillar damages the todo-fir. In the years 1919 to 1923, the outbreak of these insects consumed the foliage of 230,000 ha of natural Yezo spruce forests in Sakhalin (Aizawa, 1924). In Hokkaido, especially in the Kitami Region, large-scale outbreaks of the hemlock caterpillar were observed approximately every ten years until about 20 years ago. The last such outbreak was in Tsubetsu Town near Kitami in 1976, when about 400 ha of trees in plantation forests were damaged.

The population density of the hemlock caterpillar is usually very low, making it difficult to study its long-term fluctuations. Measuring fluctuations in adult populations has been made possible, however, by effective catches of larvae passing the winter (Fukuyama, 1977). Long-term fluctuations in the hemlock caterpillar population since the outbreak at Tsubetsu have been observed using this method. My research revealed that the population of the hemlock caterpillar larvae passing the winter fluctuates greatly from one year to another; the same tendency is observed at locations several kilometres apart. Fluctuations of populations in more distant areas that have similar climatic conditions have also exhibited the same tendency (Figure 14.6). Analysis of the timing of outbreaks and variations in climate have also shown that outbreaks tend to occur after two consecutive years in which the temperature in August and September is high (Maeto, 1991).

Outbreaks of the hemlock caterpillar in Hokkaido have so far been limited to the Kitami Region. In this region, the climate is cold in winter and hot in summer, and precipitation is low in summer and winter. The low temperatures, combined with little snow cover, allow the soil to freeze for long periods, limiting the winter activities of voles and other predators. In addition, the high summer temperatures with relatively little rain appear suitable for the growth of larvae, but not for disease outbreaks. Therefore, climatic conditions are the most important factor governing outbreaks of *D. superans*. Its outbreaks formerly occurred about every ten years, but have not occurred in recent years, probably because the average August and September temperatures have not been high enough (Figure 14.7).

If global warming results simply in an increase in the average temperature, then outbreaks of the hemlock caterpillar will occur more often due to the increased frequency of warmer summers. On the other hand, if global warming results in warmer winters and cooler summers, outbreaks will occur more rarely. In any case, if the periodic variation in

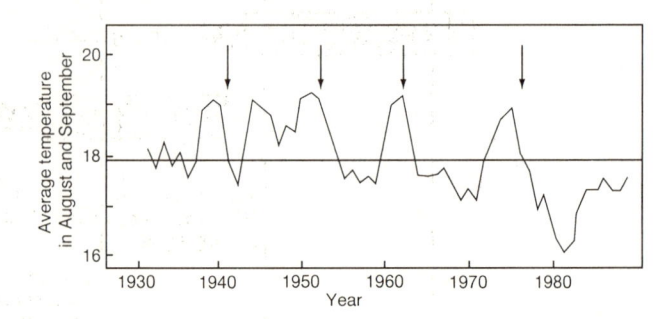

Figure 14.7.
Relation between outbreaks of *Dendrolimus superans* in the Kitami Region (indicated by arrows) and the average temperature in August and September during the three years immediately prior to the outbreak. The horizontal line shows the average temperature of the entire period (Maeto and Fukuyama, 1994).

climate that produces warmer summers at intervals of about ten years is disturbed, the pattern of outbreaks of forest insect pests is likely to change.

The gypsy moth is a relatively large moth and is a typical defoliator in Hokkaido, with outbreaks occurring approximately every ten years. The gypsy moth passes the winter in the egg stage. The eggs are usually laid in tree trunks close to the ground. After hatching in early May, the larvae move to the leaves and start eating them. In order to move about more efficiently, they send out threads which are blown in the wind. Outbreaks of the gypsy moth often occur synchronously with those of the hemlock caterpillar in Hokkaido. The numbers of other moths of Family Lymantriidae also tend to increase greatly at the same time. These synchronized outbreaks indicate that they are largely governed by common climatic factors. When an outbreak of the gypsy moth occurred during 1986 - 1988, however, there was no significant increase in the hemlock caterpillar population. Therefore, the factors involved in generating outbreaks of these two species may not be identical. Although high temperatures in August and September seem to be a major factor for the hemlock caterpillar, it is unlikely to be very important for the gypsy moth already in the adult or egg phase.

Gypsy moths lay eggs some distance from leaves of host plants, so the larvae may die if the temperature is too low for them to move after hatching (Yogo, 1962). Furthermore, the gypsy moth population is high in years when the temperature in May is high (Higashiura, unpublished). Therefore, it can be assumed that outbreaks of the gypsy moth will occur more frequently if the temperature in May rises due to global warming. If global warming leads to lower snowfall in winter, this may result in a smaller gypsy moth population as snow cover protects the eggs from predators (Higashiura, 1989).

Characteristics of recent trends in outbreaks of forest insect pests

In recent decades, the number of insect species causing serious damage to trees in a given year has increased in Hokkaido (Figure 14.8). This trend is especially prominent in natural forests although, on

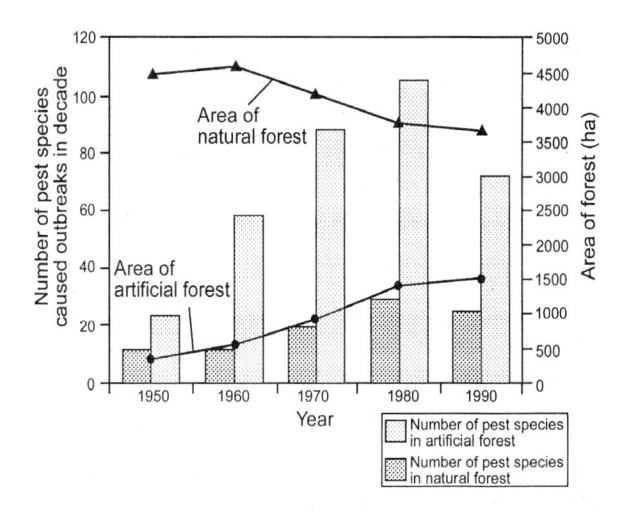

Figure 14.8.
Number of pest species causing outbreaks causing damage in successive decades in Hokkaido.

the whole, outbreaks in plantation forests are much more frequent. The overall area of plantation forest rapidly expanded in the postwar period, which may account for the increase in the number of pest insect species. On the other hand, despite a reduction in the overall area of natural forests, the variety of insect pests has been increasing. Indeed, the number of pest insect species per unit area is declining in plantation forests, but increasing in natural forests.

Moreover, outbreaks of pest-induced damage used to be confined mainly to broadleaf trees. Recently, however, a number of coniferous trees, such as the dwarf Siberian pine *Pinus pumila* and the Japanese white pine *Pinus pentaphylla*, have begun to be affected by outbreaks of insect pests. It is unclear whether this change is directly related to climate warming or not.

Although it is difficult to clarify the relationship between outbreaks of forest insect pests and climate warming, an intensification of global warming will certainly place forest trees under significant stress. The ecological balance among insects, their host trees, and their predators is likely to be unstable and abnormal outbreaks of pests are highly likely to occur.

References

Aizawa, T. 1924. Report of outbreak of pine caterpillar in the Kuril Islands. Report of Forest Experiment Station 10: 99-147. (in Japanese)

Christiansen, E. and A. Bakke. 1988. The spruce bark beetle of Eurasia. In: (A. A. Berryman ed.) *Dynamics of Forest Insect Populations. Patterns, Causes, Implications.* Pp.479-503. Plenum Press, New York and London.

Fukuyama, K. 1978. The population estimation of *Dendrolimus superans* Butler in the low density population. Japanese J. of Applied Entomology and Zoology 22: 122-123. (in Japanese)

Fukuyama, K. 1981. Life of *Dendrolimus superans* Butler. Hopporingyo (Northern Forestry, Japan) 33(9): 1-5. (in Japanese)

Higashiura, Y. 1989. Survival of eggs in the gypsy moth *Lymantria disper* II. Oviposition sites selection changing environments. J. of Animal Ecology 58: 413-426.

Horntvedt, R., E. Christiansen, H. Solheim, and S. Wang. 1983. Artificial inoculation with *Ips typographus* associated blue-stain fungi and kill healthy Norway spruce trees. Medd. Nor. Inst. Skogforsk 38: 1-20.

Ito, Y. (ed.) 1972. *History of the Fall Webworm*, Hyphantria qunea. Chukoshinnsho, Tokyo, 185pp. (in Japanese)

Maeto, K. 1991. Outbreak of *Dendrolimus superans* (Butler) (Lepidoptera: Lasiocampidae) related to weather in Hokkaido. Applied Entomology and Zoology 26: 275-277.

Maeto, K. and K. Fukuyama. 1994. Will an outbreak of *Dendrolimus superans* not occur in the future? Shinrinhogo (Forest Protection) 239: 2-4. (in Japanese)

Stark, R. W. 1982. Generalized ecology and life cycle of bark beetles. In: (B. Mitton and K. B. Sturgen, eds.) *Bark Beetles in North America Conifers. A System for the Study of Evolutionary Biology*. Pp.21-45. University of Texas Press, Austin.

Yamaguchi, H. 1976. Biological studies on the todo-fir aphid *Cinara todocola* Inouye, with special reference to its population dynamics and morph determination. Bulletin of the Government Forest Experiment Station 283: 1-102. (in Japanese with English summary)

Yamaguchi, H. 1977. Relationship between temperature, day length and growth rate of *Dendrolimus superans* Butler. Forest Pests 26: 9-12.(in Japanese)

Yamaguchi, H. 1989. *Life Cycle of Forest Insects*. Soubun, Tokyo, 185pp. (in Japanese)

Yogo, S. 1962. A procedure in the forecast to the forest damage by the gypsy moth (*Lymantria disper* L.) feeding on larch leaves. Annual Report of the Hokkaido Branch Forest Experiment Station 1963: 125-134. (in Japanese with English summary)

Chapter 15

What Will Happen to Marine Organisms in the Future?

Masayuki M. Takahashi

This chapter looks at how marine organisms and ecosystems will be affected by global warming, and is based on the assumption that the concentration of CO_2 and other greenhouse gases will double within 70 years. The oceans cover a total area of 361 million km^2, or more than 70% of the Earth's surface, and hold 1.5 billion km^3 of water. Water is the most abundant substance on the Earth's surface, and 98% of it is in the form of seawater. The oceans, which contain this vast amount of water, have an average depth worldwide of about 3,800 m. Whereas terrestrial organisms live mainly on the Earth's surface, numerous marine species are scattered throughout the oceans, living at a range of depths from the surface to the sea bed. Most marine biomass, however, is concentrated in coastal sea regions ranging out to the edges of continental shelves, and in the surface ocean layers at depths of less than 200 m.

Our knowledge and understanding of current marine conditions is extremely poor. For example, the existence of hydrothermal vents or submarine hot springs was not discovered until 1977. That said, we must utilize the limited knowledge we do have to urgently consider the effects of global warming on marine organisms.

Expected global warming and its effect on the marine environment

With global warming, atmospheric temperature will increase, leading to a rise in seawater temperature. This temperature rise will be largest near the surface of the ocean. Significant changes in seawater temperature will probably be limited to within a few tens of meters of the surface. According to model estimates, the rise in atmospheric temperature is expected to be larger at higher latitudes than at lower latitudes. The rise in seawater temperature is also predicted to be larger at higher latitudes than at lower latitudes (IPCC, 1990). The year-round global mean surface seawater temperature increase will be on the order of $0.5 - 2.5 °C$ assuming a doubling in atmospheric CO_2 concentration. The rise in surface seawater temperature at high latitudes will reduce the area of the Arctic and Antarctic zones while the sub-arctic and sub-Antarctic zones and the temperate zones will extend into higher latitudes.

The seawater temperature increase will produce a variety of effects, one of which will be a rise in the sea level resulting from an expansion in the volume of the surface seawater layer. The sea level rise due to water volume expansion has been estimated using several models, but the extent of the predicted rise given by these models differs considerably, ranging from 7 to 28 cm taken as a global average (IPCC, 1990). The sea level will also rise as a result of increased melting of ice and snow in the polar regions caused by the higher atmospheric temperature. This effect will be especially great in the case of Antarctica where huge amounts of snow and ice are accumulated on land in the ice cap. In the Arctic, where the polar ice cap floats on the ocean, even a total melting of the ice would have only a negligible influence on the sea level. Overall the global rise in sea level is estimated to be 18 - 50 cm with a doubling in atmospheric CO_2 concentration.

The rise in the surface water temperature enlarges the vertical difference in seawater temperature, making it more difficult for the different layers of water to mix vertically. As the vertical mixing of seawater is also influenced by atmospheric and ocean currents, it is difficult to judge the extent to which temperature changes affect this phenomenon. However, the vertical mixing of seawater will inevitably be affected by global warming to some extent, and it follows that the speed of upward nutrient supply in the oceans will also change. Climate models suggest that the decreased temperature difference between high and low latitudes caused by the increased temperature in high latitudes will reduce the trade winds, which will in turn weaken the surface layer ocean currents and restrain the equatorial upwelling in the eastern tropical ocean areas (IPCC, 1996). But actual long-term observation in the tropical Atlantic Ocean has shown that global warming causes the atmospheric temperature above

Table 15.1. Biological groups of plants and animals on the Earth and their principal distribution areas

	Plant				Animal		
	Marine	Fresh water	Terrestrial		Marine	Fresh water	Terrestrial
Bacteriophyta	◎	◎	◎	Protozoa	O	O	O
Cyanophyta	◎	◎	O	Mesozoa	O		
Pyrrhophyta	◎	O		Porifera	O	O	
Chrysophyta	◎	O		Coelenterata	O		
Phaeophyta	◎			Platyhelminths	O	O	O
Phycomyceta	O	O	O	Nemertea	O	O	
Archaea			◎	Entoprocta	O		
Myxomycota			◎	Nematoda			O
Eumycota			◎	Rotifera	O	O	
Lichenobion			◎	Annelida	O	O	O
Rhodophyta	◎	O		Mollusca	O	O	O
Euglenophyta	O	O		Arthropoda	O	O	O
Chlorophyta	◎	O		Mulluscoidea	O	O	
Charophyta		◎		Chaetognata	O		
Bryophyta			◎	Echinodermata	O		
Pteridophyta			◎	Urochordata	O		
Spermatophyta	O	O	◎	Vertebrata	O	O	O

land to increase. This widens the temperature difference between land and sea, creating stronger winds which will in turn drive more intense mixing of seawater. Although it is not yet clear exactly how global warming will influence seawater mixing, global warming will certainly change the pattern and strength of the wind and this will inevitably have repercussions for the mixing of seawater in the surface layers.

Because ice and snow in the polar regions will progressively melt and more of the sea surface will be exposed, sunlight which is currently reflected will penetrate into the seawater, brightening the water immediately below the surface and raising its temperature.

It is predicted that global warming will also change precipitation patterns. When the water temperature in high latitudes rises, evaporation from the sea will be enhanced, leading to increased precipitation. Changes in the intensity and pattern of precipitation will be particularly strong in coastal regions. Changes in precipitation naturally entail changes in the amount of cloud cover and hence in the amount of sunlight reaching the sea surface. It is possible that such changes may fundamentally alter the flow patterns of water in the sea such as global ocean circulation. Global ocean circulation, in particular, is expected to weaken, and as a result differences between high and low latitudes with respect to thermal and other conditions will widen (IPCC, 1996).

Global warming is also expected to promote further desertification on land. When desertification occurs and the patterns or strength of the seasonal winds change, the amount and dispersal patterns of the materials swept up and carried from land into the sea by winds will also change. At the same time, the rise in sea level will accelerate the erosion of coastal areas, speeding up the accumulation of sediments along the coastlines. New problems may possibly be identified in the future, some of which may have more serious effects on living organisms than those stated here.

The range of temperature rise due to global warming is not unusually large in comparison with previous changes that the Earth has undergone during its long geological history. The problem is the extremely rapid pace of the change. During the current period of anthropogenic global warming, the rise in temperature is estimated to be occurring at a rate approximately 100 times that of similar, albeit natural, episodes in the past. Many species and ecosystems will have difficulty surviving the rapid and continuous pace of change and its various direct and indirect effects.

Living organisms in mud flats and sea grass/seaweed beds

Coastal areas containing mud flats and sea grass and seaweed beds are the richest environments on Earth in terms of biodiversity. Of each of the 17 divisions of animals and plants, 16 divisions of animals and 10 divisions of plants are found to inhabit marine ecosystems (Table 15.1), and most of these are found in coastal areas (May, 1988). Many species live on land, especially in tropical rain forests, but these belong to a very limited number of broader biological divisions. In other words, terrestrial animals and plants exhibit rich species diversity within limited biological division diversity. On the other hand, the species diversity of coastal areas is not as broad as that of tropical rain forests, but the species that inhabit coastal areas belong to a much more varied range of biological divisions. That is to say, the environment in coastal areas is a suitable habitat for organisms of radically different natures.

Coastal areas inhabited by various kinds of organisms are not only important for taxonomical and ecological reasons, but also helpful in supporting human life in a variety of ways. The most significant and direct effects of global warming are projected to be a rise in the sea level and changes in the climate. Furthermore, global warming may possibly produce indirect effects such as increased erosion of coastal areas due to wave action and storms; increased salinity in estuaries and subterranean water layers; changes in mud flats, rivers and gulfs; altered transport of sediments and nutrients; differing chemical and microbiological pollution patterns in coastal zones; and increased flooding in coastal areas.

At present, very little is known about what kind of effects the environmental changes due to global warming will have on organisms living in coastal areas. As the environmental changes that coastal areas undergo will be extremely diverse, the number of species and broader biological divisions which are able to overcome these changes may be limited. Organisms dwelling in coastal areas have already been significantly disturbed by various human activities. For these organisms, global warming will come as a powerful additional blow. In particular, those organisms whose living conditions have already deteriorated due to recent environmental changes are likely to be at greater risk from the severe effects of global warming.

Coral reef organisms

The coral reefs in tropical and subtropical oceans are estimated to cover a total area of 600,000 km^2, or about 0.1% of the entire global surface. Up to the present, about 91,000 species have been recorded as living in these coral reefs (IPCC, 1996), a figure equal to between 4 - 5% of all known living species.

Coral reefs are said to be exceptionally susceptible to temperature changes (IPCC, 1996). If seawater temperatures rise by between 3 and 4°C, the sea water in tropical regions will become warmer than the upper limit for coral growth, and coral reefs will generate symbiont algae and exhibit discoloration known as chlorosis. If this condition continues for more than about six months, the coral reef will not recover. If the period is shorter, recovery is possible. Even in such a case, however, complete recovery takes a long time. In Indonesia, coral reefs exhibited chlorosis in response to the temporary rise in seawater temperature caused by the 1983 El Ninõ phenomenon. In 1988, the first signs of recovery were seen, but this has not progressed very far. As the degree of global warming is expected to be small at low latitudes, the damage caused by higher seawater temperatures may not be so serious. On the other hand, coral growth may become more active due to the higher seawater temperatures in the northern or southern limits of current coral reef ranges.

Global warming-induced sea level rise is expected to be approximately 0.5 cm (0.2 - 0.9 cm) per year on average (IPCC, 1996). The growth of coral by

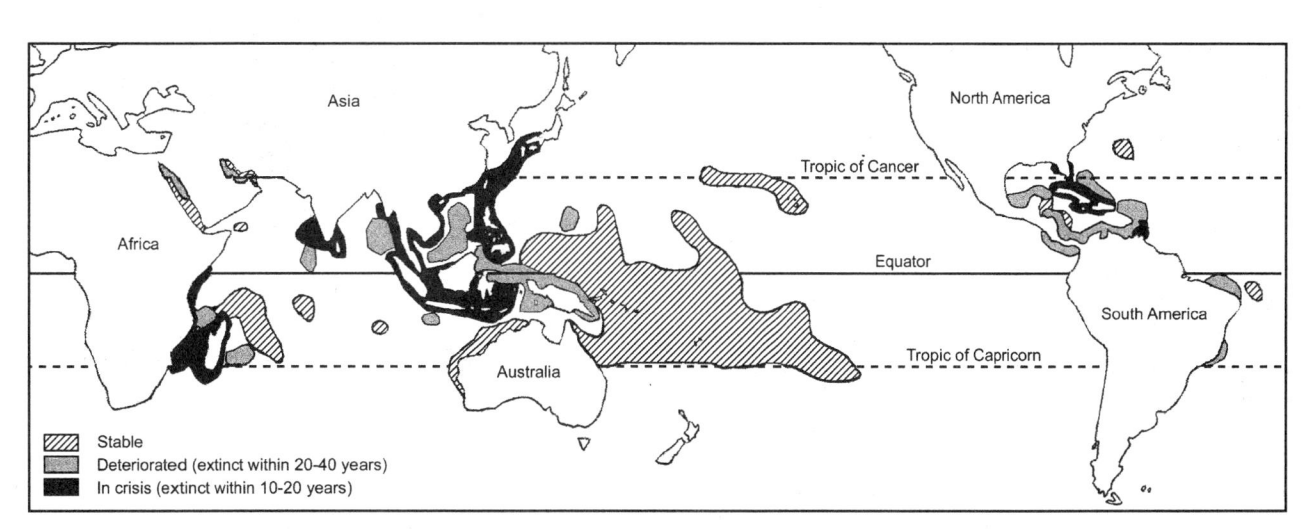

Figure 15.1.
Deterioration of coral reefs (after RITE, 1996).

calcification is estimated to be about 1 cm per year. Therefore, coral reefs can easily survive at such a pace of sea level rise. However, it is important to stress that in many places today, coral reefs are unable to maintain their vitality owing to human activity-induced damage including eutrophication of surrounding waters, large amounts of sediment flowing into the sea as a result of deforestation, the effects of dynamite fishing, etc. (Figure 15.1). Under such conditions, it is doubtful whether coral reefs can maintain their recuperative ability when exposed to simultaneous rises in seawater temperature and sea level. Coral reefs sited near densely populated areas or off the coasts of continents, in particular, will be affected by various factors, and there is a significant risk that the effects of global warming will be far greater than they are capable of coping with.

Organisms in the pelagic ocean

Marine ecosystems are centred on plankton. As plankton also play a major role in most continental shelf ecosystems, with the exception of areas very near the coast, nearly 70% of the Earth's surface is occupied by plankton-based ecosystems. Therefore, any changes that occur equally throughout the plankton ecosystems are very likely to have significant global effects.

The initial effect of global warming on plankton ecosystems is a rise in the seawater temperature. When the seawater temperature rises or falls by 10°C, marine organism activity is observed to double or halve, respectively. At present, the seawater temperature fluctuates by around 20 to 30°C depending on the place, time of day and season; temperature fluctuations of this order of magnitude can change the level of marine organism activity by a factor of ten. In the ocean at high latitudes, the seawater temperature is as low as 2 to 3°C and its normal range of fluctuation is small, so that even a small temperature change can be expected to have a great influence on the marine organisms of these regions. Since the degree of global warming is expected to be larger at the high latitudes, its influence on the activity of marine organisms should be strongest in these regions.

In general, higher temperatures stimulate the activity of organisms and, accordingly, biological production is promoted and the total biomass increases. At the same time, as the impact of temperature change differs from species to species, it is possible for a change of ambient temperature alone to alter the species composition of the ecosystem. Moreover, when the biomass of organisms is increased or the composition of living species in the ocean changes, the light absorption characteristics of the water are altered and this can be expected to further raise the water temperature.

The influence of temperature rise is expected to be particularly strong on marine organisms inhabiting the layer several tens of meters below the surface. Most organisms are concentrated within the ocean at depths of less than 200 m, but even at depths of several thousand meters the impact of the temperature rise which is centred on the surface layers of the ocean cannot be ignored. An increase in temperature will have a strong effect on the world's plankton ecosystems, particularly at high latitudes.

When seawater flow patterns change under the influence of global warming, the vertical mixing of water and the speed of the nutrient supply from the lower layer to the surface layer will also change accordingly. This phenomenon will influence the output of primary production and creates a strong

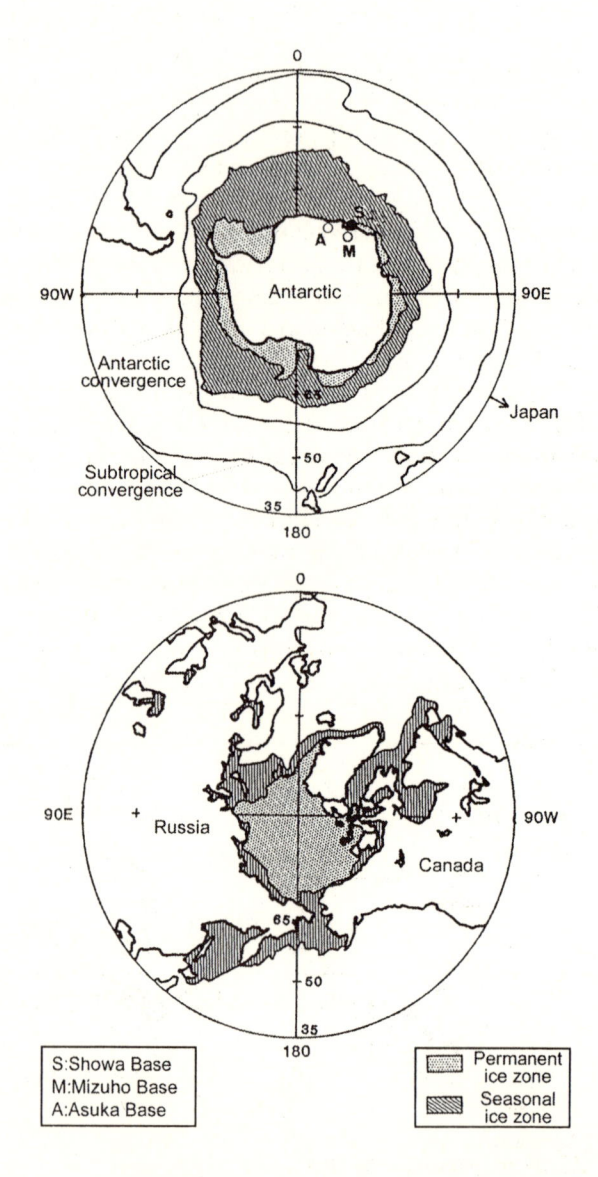

Figure 15.2.
Distribution of permanent sea ice zone and seasonal sea ice zone around the Antarctic (above) and the Arctic (below).

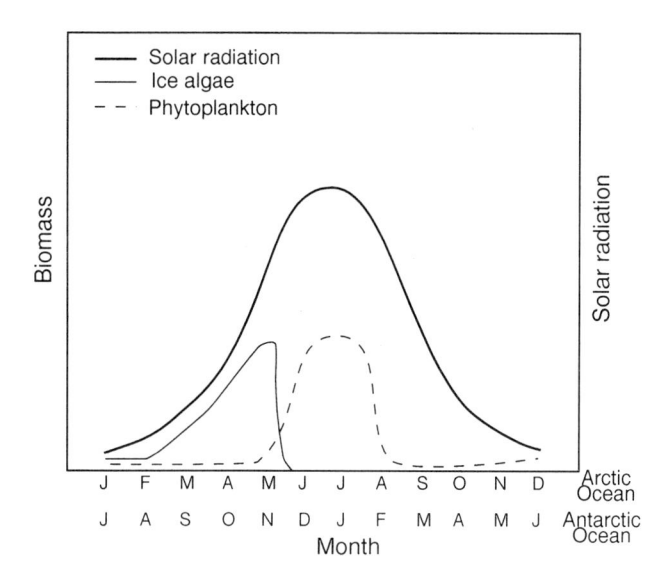

Figure 15.3.
Strength of sunlight in the seasonal sea ice zones in the Arctic and Antarctic Oceans and seasonal changes of the biomass of ice algae and other phytoplankton. Months in Arctic Ocean are from January to December, and those in Antarctic Ocean from July to June.

possibility that major changes will occur in the population structure of primary producers. These changes will naturally affect other biological divisions in the ecosystem and lead not only to changes in living biomass but also to the alteration of species. When vertical stratification becomes stronger, the speed of the nutrient supply from the lower layer to the surface layer slows down and oligotrophy in the surface layer is promoted. According to the results of observations off northern Hawaii, during the period of the 1991/92 ENSO (El Niño and Southern Oscillation) phenomenon an initially phosphorus-deficient environment was transformed into a nitrogen deficient environment and the major phytoplankton were replaced by *Trichodesmium*, a form of blue green algae capable of fixing nitrogen (IPCC, 1996).

With a rise in water temperature at high latitudes, the area of the icebound zones in the polar regions will decline, and the freezing period will be shortened. These changes will extend the active period of organisms in these regions and raise their productivity, while the biological divisions which are adapted to frigid zones will be restricted to smaller habitats.

The seas surrounding the North Pole and the South Pole can be divided into three zones: permanent sea ice zones covered with ice all the year round, seasonal sea ice zones covered with ice in winter but ice-free in summer, and permanent thaw

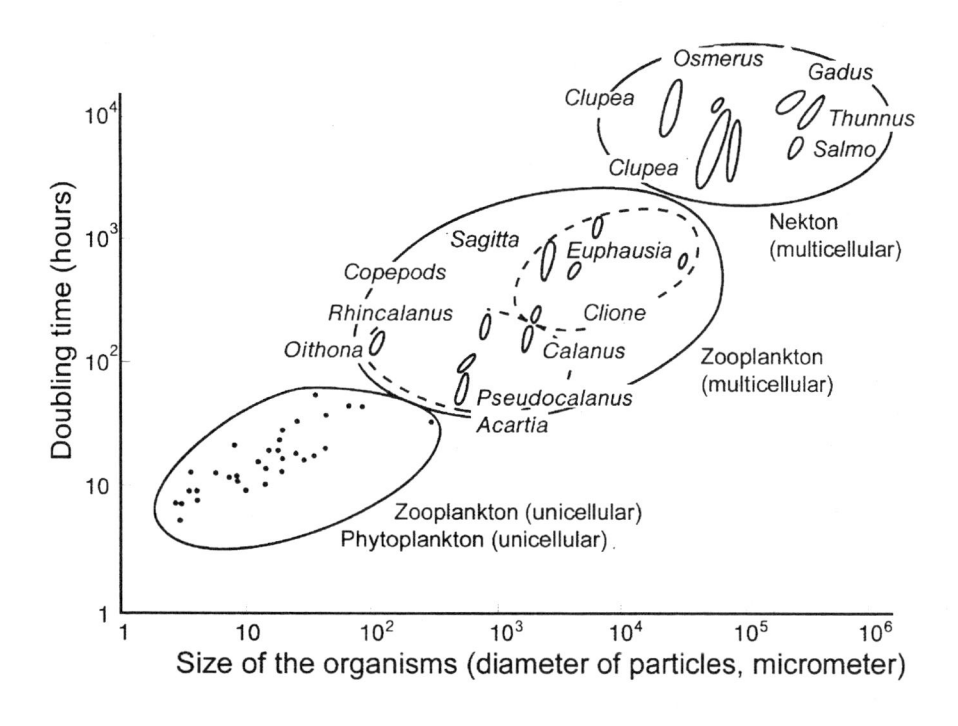

Figure 15.4. Relationship between generation time and size of organisms.

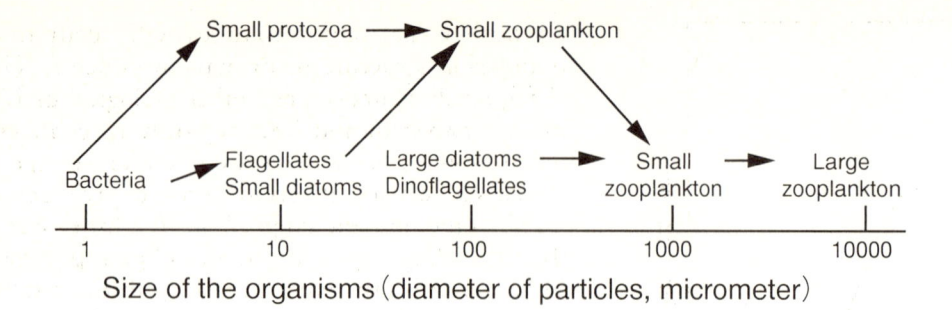

```
Small protozoa ──▶ Small zooplankton
      ▲                ▲
      │                │
Bacteria ──▶ Flagellates   Large diatoms  ──▶ Small      ──▶ Large
             Small diatoms  Dinoflagellates    zooplankton      zooplankton
   │            │               │               │               │
───┼────────────┼───────────────┼───────────────┼───────────────┼───
   1           10              100            1000           10000
```

Size of the organisms (diameter of particles, micrometer)

Figure 15.5.
Relationships between predator-prey interaction and organism size in marine plankton ecosystems.

zones free of ice cover throughout the year (Figure 15.2). In the ice of the seasonal sea ice zone, a form of phytoplankton known as ice algae propagates on the undersurface of, as well as inside, the ice as the amount of incoming solar radiation increases after the winter solstice. This ice algae propagates to the extent that the ice appears brown, and supplies valuable organic products that sustain the ecosystem in the early spring when other food sources are in short supply. When the water temperature rises and the seasonal sea ice melts, the meltwater mixes with the surrounding surface seawater and reduces its salinity, thereby promoting water stratification in the surface seawater. The surface seawater has also been made nutrient-rich as a result of active vertical mixing, and phytoplankton propagate there in large quantities by consuming the available nutrients once the water stratification process is completed. Phytoplankton are observed at the edge of ice sheets and move with the edge as the ice melts. In the seasonal sea ice zone, the reproduction of ice algal type phytoplankton at the edge of ice is commonly observed to occur earlier than the propagation of other phytoplankton in late spring or early summer, and this phenomenon has the effect of supplying the ecosystem with organisms of high trophic value on two occasions, first in spring and again in summer (Figure 15.3). In this way, a high level of biological productivity is maintained in the seasonal sea ice zone (Smith and Sakshaug, 1990).

When the seasonal sea ice zone is reduced due to temperature rise, the ice algae will become extinct and the propagation of other phytoplankton at the ice sheet edges will also cease. This will result in a comparable reduction in the biomass of related species.

In terms of size, the organisms that comprise the plankton ecosystem are very diverse (Ishizaka et al., 1998): from bacteria as small as 1 micrometre or less in length to tuna measuring several meters or whales several tens of meters in length (Figure 15.4). As a rough rule, the smaller an animal's size, the faster its metabolism and the shorter its life span. Moreover, larger animals tend to live by consuming smaller animals (Figure 15.5). In the ocean, there are tens of thousands of species at a single location (primary production) belonging solely to a phytoplankton group which produces organic matter, and their sizes vary greatly from less than 1 micrometre to several millimetres in length. The animals that exploit the phytoplankton are extremely diversified and make up a complex food web. When the organisms which compose the plankton ecosystem on the ocean surface are classified into groups, their total biomass differs significantly according to location and season, but their composition ratios are known to be very similar regardless of location or season (Figure 15.6). It is still unclear what kind of changes the constituent organisms of the ecosystem undergo and where in the ecosystem they eventually settle themselves.

Very little is known about the type and life cycles of organisms which dwell in the intermediate and deep sea layers at depths below 200 m. Since global warming-induced change in water temperature will be small at such depths, these organisms will not be influenced directly by temperature rise. However, they will be affected by changes in water movement and on the ocean surface upon which they depend either directly or indirectly for their food.

Compared with the coastal sea areas, the ocean is less influenced by human activities, and in this sense ocean-dwelling organisms are in a better position to cope with the effects of global warming. However, it is not possible at this stage to make accurate quantitative predictions regarding the extent to which this will occur.

Coastal areas, where a great variety of organisms are concentrated, are especially vulnerable to the influence of human activities. There is concern about the ability of these organisms, which are already threatened by a range of other factors, to adapt to the effects of global warming.

The start button for global warming has already

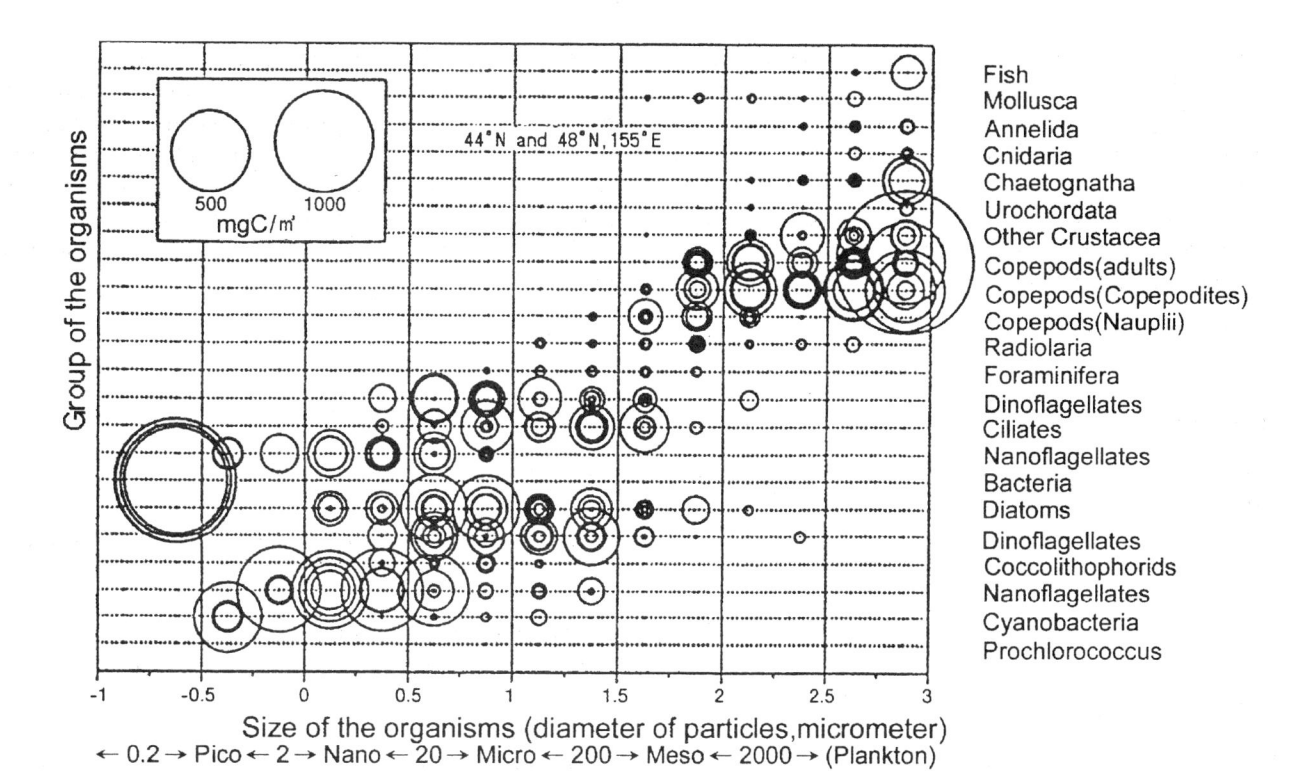

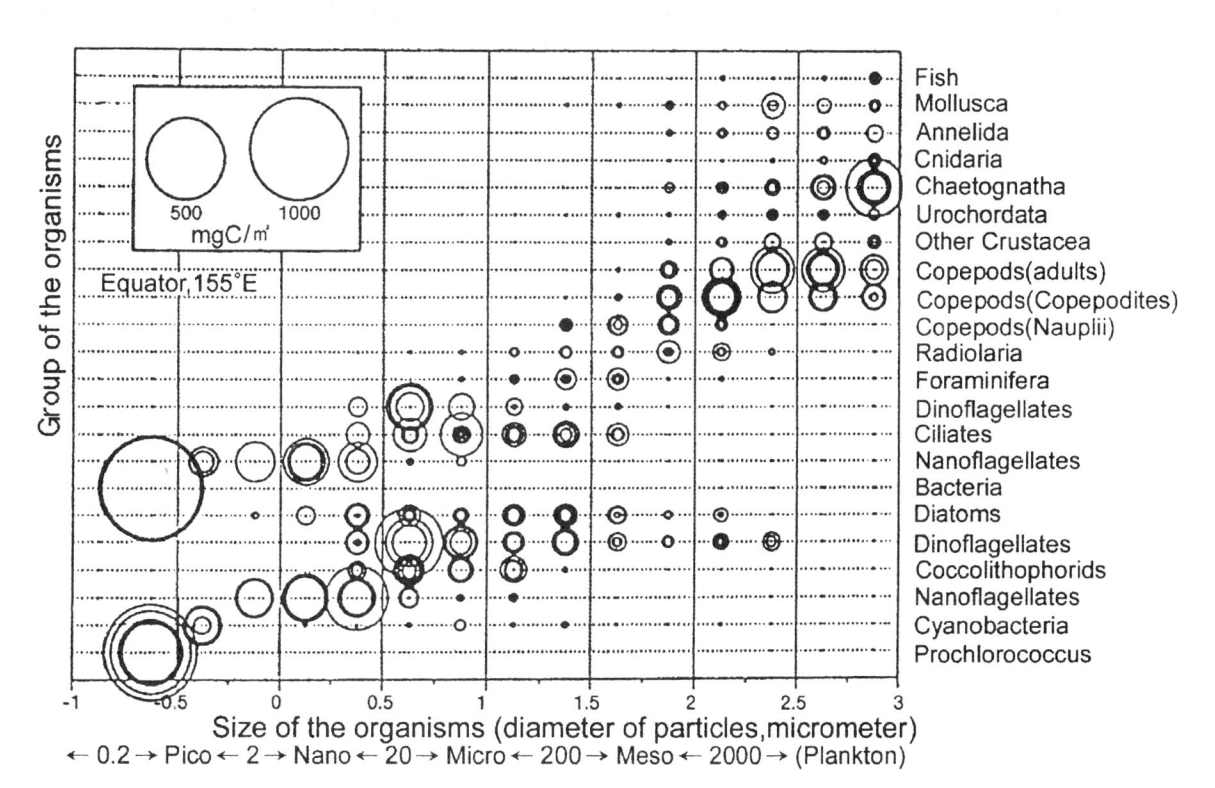

Figure 15.6.
The biomass of organisms constituting the plankton ecosystem by individual size (total amount from the surface to 200 m depth). Circle graphs show results over four years from 1991 to 1994 by biological groupings at 44°N and 155°E (above), and at the equator (below).

been pushed and more and more precise predictions are now being made concerning its speed and extent. The indirect influences of warming have also been clarified. A major question is how global warming will influence marine organisms. At present, we do not have enough information on the organisms that live in the sea. Our knowledge of the oceans beyond the continental shelves and of the intermediate and deep layers below 200 m in depth is particularly poor. Under these circumstances it is very difficult to predict the effect of global warming on ocean-dwelling organisms and ecosystems. However, despite this unfavourable situation we cannot afford to delay action, because even in the ocean regions that are unknown to us, the effect of anthropogenic global warming is steadily progressing.

References

IPCC 1990. *Climate Change: The IPCC Scientific Assessment.* Cambridge University Press, Cambridge.

IPCC. 1996. *Climate Change 1995: The Science of Climate Change.* Cambridge University Press, Cambridge.

Ishizaka, J., K. Harada, K. Ishikawa, H. Kiyosawa, H. Furusawa, Y. Watanabe, H. Ishida, K. Suzuki. N. Honda, and M. Takahashi 1998. Size and taxonomic plankton community structure and carbon flow at the equator, 175°E during 1990 - 1994. Deep-Sea Res. 44: 1927-1949.

May, R. M. 1988. How many species are there on Earth? Science 241: 1441-1449.

Research Institute of Innovative Technology for the Earth. 1996. RITE Now . No. 18. 21pp. (in Japanese)

Smith, W. O. Jr. and E. Sakshaug. 1990. Polar phytoplankton. In: *Polar Oceanography, Part B: Chemistry, Biology and Geology.* Pp.477-525. Academic Press, London.

Box 1

How Will the Expansion of Deserts Affect the Sea?

Masayuki M. Takahashi

The phytoplankton and seaweeds that perform photosynthesis in the oceans utilise the energy from sunlight to absorb various substances from seawater. These substances are then converted into organic compounds, which are passed through various ecosystems along food chains. The energy driving these processes comes from outside the ecosystems and leaves the ecosystems after being utilised. Most of the substances in seawater, such as nutrients, circulate and are reused repeatedly within the ecosystems.

In general, because the sea is a poor source of nutrients, substances are available in insufficient quantities to use up the available energy from sunlight that is absorbed by the phytoplankton. Most of the organic matter is utilised and then returned to the nutrient pool in the surface layer of the sea down to a depth of 100 m. A portion of the organic matter, however, is continually lost from the surface layer when it is excreted by marine animals in the form of fecal pellets and sinks into intermediate and deep ocean layers at depths below 100 m.

Consequently, the sea is particularly lacking in the nutrients nitrogen and phosphorus. In addition, it has been pointed out recently that the supply of iron is also insufficient. Nutrients that are lost from the surface layer are replenished by upwelling (the upward movement of water from lower layers of the ocean to the surface) and are also supplied from the atmosphere. Nitrogen and phosphorus are supplied by both upwelling and the atmosphere, but this is not the case with iron. Iron released into the surface ocean waters through the decomposition of organic substances is bivalent, but when it sinks into the intermediate and deep layers it is oxidised by oxygen in the water and becomes trivalent. Trivalent iron, or iron oxide, is difficult for organisms to utilise and easily sinks to the sea bed.

Consequently, the iron concentration in the ocean's surface layer is mainly supplemented via the atmosphere. The terrestrial regions where the largest amounts of iron originate are the deserts. Iron and grains of sand are swept up from the desert surface by the wind and carried over long distances. It appears that the prevailing westerlies carry most of the iron, much of which eventually falls onto the surface of the ocean with sand or rainfall. The amount of iron supplied in this way is larger in the western than eastern parts of the ocean on account of the prevailing westerlies. It has been pointed out that there are no suitable continental regions to supply the Eastern and Southern Pacific with sufficient iron, and the reproduction of phytoplankton in these waters may be suppressed as a result.

Nevertheless, these same ocean areas have substantial amounts of nitrogen and phosphorus. International collaborative research projects have been conducted twice recently in the Eastern Pacific where the surface is rich in nitrogen and phosphorus to ascertain the extent to which a shortage of iron suppresses the productivity of marine ecosystems. When the results of this research are examined, the extent of the influence of iron on the productivity of the sea will be clarified. However, if the desert areas on the continents expand under the influence of climate warming, the supply of iron to the sea will change. The situation is further complicated because the strength of wind is also a factor in determining the iron supply.

Box 2

How Will Ice Algae be Affected by Rapid Changes Induced by Global Warming?

Masayuki M. Takahashi

Ice algae are literally "algae which inhabit ice." A variety of phytoplankton species, most of which are diatoms, live both inside and on the undersurface of sea ice. As phytoplankton are on the order of several hundred micrometres long or less, individual ice algae are invisible to the naked eye. However, in seas such as the Sea of Okhotsk, where large numbers of ice algae can exist packed close together, sea ice covered with these algae feels slimy and appears stained with brown and yellow when pulled up from the water. The existence of ice algae has been known since ancient times, but little attention was paid to the phenomenon until 1950s.

Ice algae drift in the seas in cold regions, performing photosynthesis by utilising solar radiation as energy and absorbing nutrients from the surrounding water to produce organic materials. Unlike other phytoplankton, however, when the sea is covered with sea ice, the ice algae adhere to the inside and undersurface of the ice where they continue to actively photosynthesise and propagate in large quantities, growing into colonies large enough to be visible to the human eye. As the amount of incoming solar radiation increases following the winter solstice, the biomass of ice algae increases steadily. Generally, the higher the latitude, the later the time at which ice algae appear. In the case of the Sea of Okhotsk, because of its low latitude, ice algae become visible on the undersurface of the sea ice in February and develop to form dense populations by mid-March when the seasonal sea ice begins to melt. As food availability drops drastically during winter, the ice algae that propagate in the early spring become an important food source for organisms at higher trophic levels in the marine ecosystem. As a result, ocean regions with seasonal sea ice zones can provide richer food sources for various organisms than regions without sea ice where food sources are in short supply until the propagation of other phytoplankton begins in late spring or early summer.

In regions where seasonal sea ice zones retreat or disappear due to global warming, ice algae will no longer be able to propagate on the sea ice and will barely exist as free-floating phytoplankton. Consequently, a number of species that are currently dependent on the ice algae as a food source will face starvation. The impact of the retreat or disappearance of sea ice zones on both ice algae and related species will be significant as the seasonal sea ice zones in the Arctic and Antarctic regions together cover approximately 24 million km^2, equivalent to 4% of the total surface area of the planet.

Box 3

The Blessings of Floating Ice

Nobuo Gouchi

The amount of floating ice in the Sea of Okhotsk in winter has been steadily shrinking during recent years and the pile-ups of ice that were regularly observed from Hokkaido during the 1970s can no longer be seen. Instead, the sea surface remains visible throughout the winter. In 1989, floating ice did not reach the Hokkaido coast at all (Figure 1).

When floating ice reaches the coast of Hokkaido, the Sea of Okhotsk becomes a vast ice floe. This creates a continental climate in the coastal region of Hokkaido along the Sea of Okhotsk during winter. The temperature can drop suddenly in such a climate, bringing extremely cold weather. For example, a temperature of -33°C was recorded in the region along the Sea of Okhotsk on 15 February 1977. In recent years, however, the surface of the sea has remained visible at all times, and a maritime climate has continued throughout the winter.

What kinds of changes will the scarcity of floating ice bring? The milder winter climate obviously makes it easier for people to live and lowers their heating costs. Nevertheless, in the case of northern Hokkaido serious negative influences are also beginning to become apparent.

The major industry of Shari Town on the Shiretoko Peninsula is salmon fishing (mainly white salmon). The annual catch is between 5,000 and 10,000 tons, and an interesting relationship between floating ice and the salmon catch has been identified. When we look at the extent of the floating ice recorded at Abashiri City between 1965 and 1988 and compare the period during which floating ice is seen (the number of days between the first day and final day) with the size of the salmon catch using fixed nets at Shari Town (Figure 2), we find that the longer the period in which floating ice is seen, the higher the catch of salmon. The extent of the floating ice appears to influence the size of the salmon catch.

The water beneath the floating ice in the Sea of Okhotsk is rich in plankton because of the nutrients carried by the ice. Salmon and other large fish gather there in search of plankton. Salmon migrate in a three-year cycle and eventually return to the river where they hatched. Consequently, bumper catches of salmon should theoretically repeat every three years. According to Figure 2, however, the catch fluctuates in a cycle spanning two to four years, which matches that of the variations in the extent of floating ice.

The Meteorological Agency has forecast that floating ice will disappear from the seas near Japan within the next one hundred years due to global warming. This development will certainly affect the salmon fishery that is currently the major industry in the regions bordering the Sea of Okhotsk.

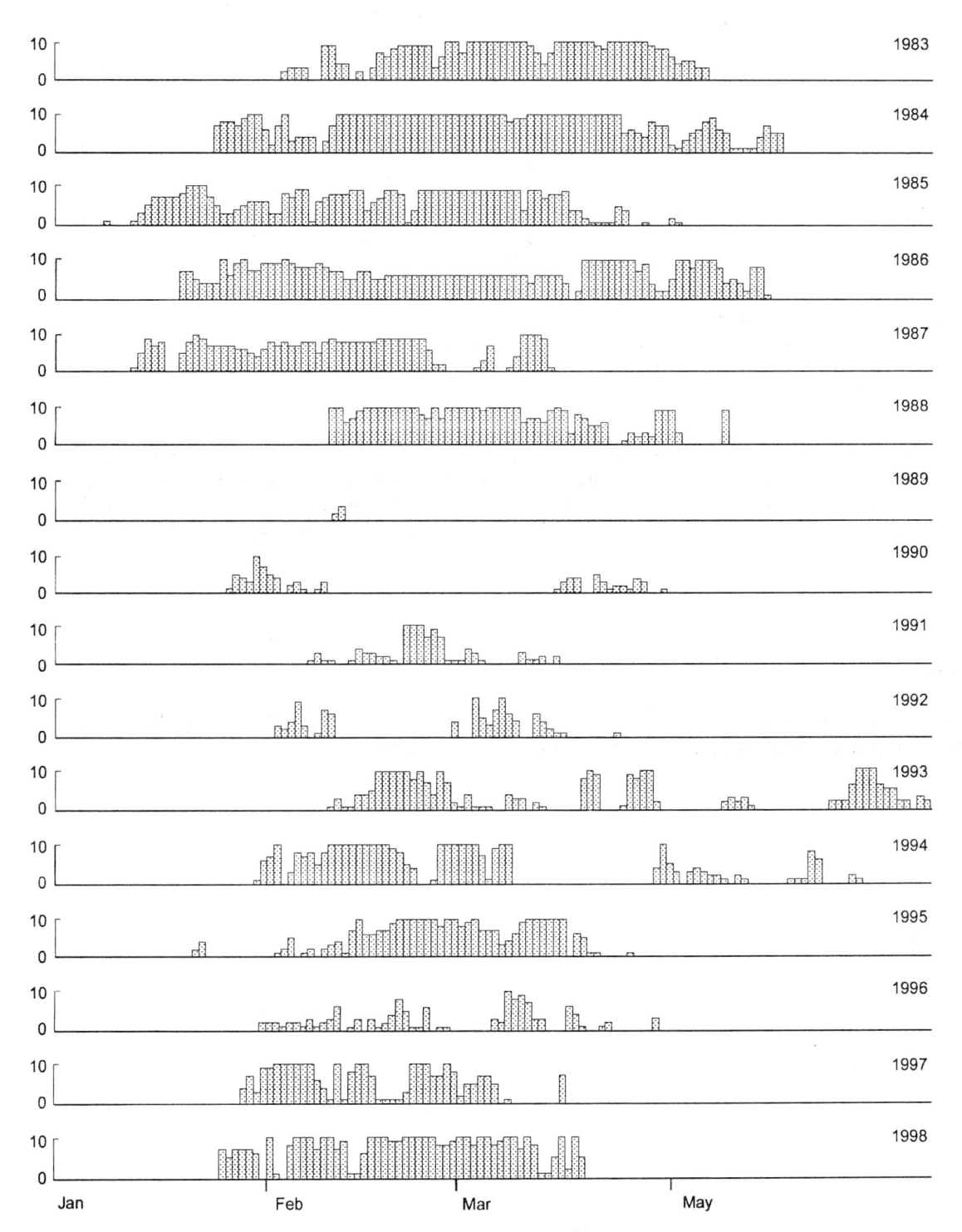

Figure 1.
Fluctuations in the amount of floating ice and the period during which floating ice is observed at Abashiri, eastern Hokkaido

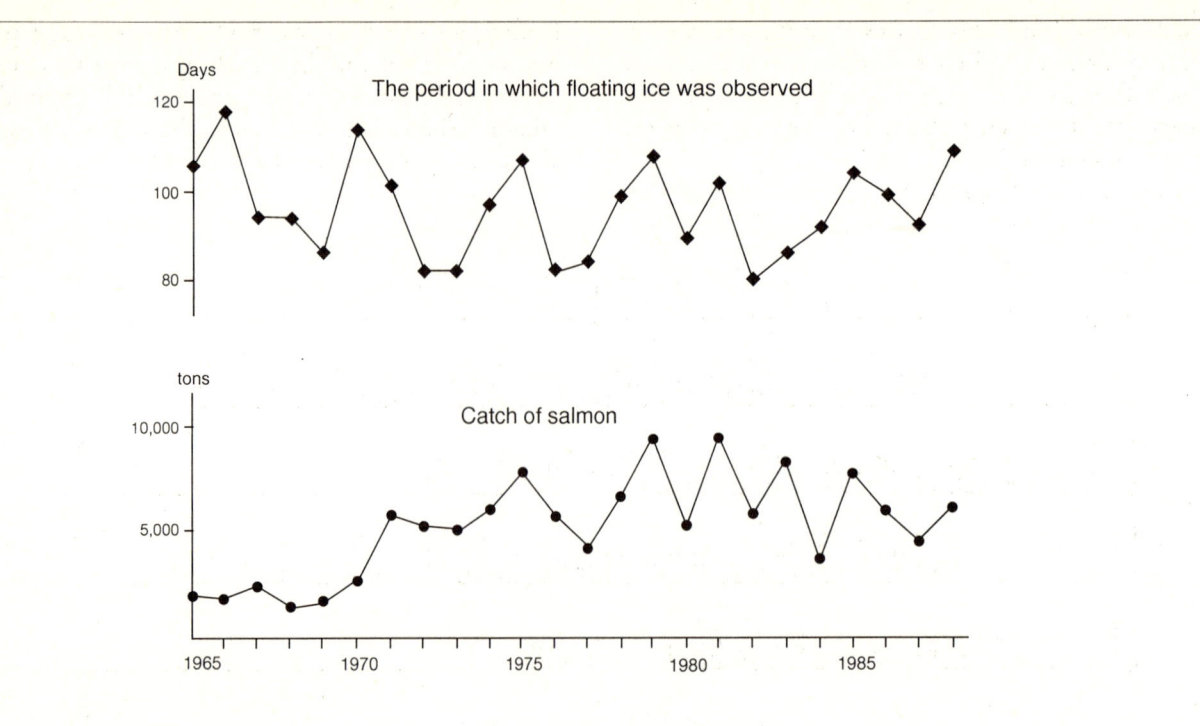

Figure 2.
Fluctuations in the length of the period during which floating ice was observed and in catches of salmon in autumn. In 1965, fishing techniques stabilized as a result of improvements in fishing boats and fishing gear. 1988 was the year before the salmon hatchery industry developed and fry began to be released artificially (Sapporo District Meteorological Observatory, 1982; Shari Town Marine Industry Report, No. 24, 1997).

Reference

Sapporo District Meteorological Observator. 1982. Climate of Hokkaido. Incorporated Foundation Japan Weather Association Hokkaido Regional Head Office. (in Japanese)

Chapter 16

Global Warming and Coral Reefs

Kiyoshi Yamazato

Coral reef scientists believe that global warming has already started. Since the 1970s, bleaching has been observed on reef-building corals both in the Indo-West-Pacific and the Atlantic coral reef systems. Bleaching is a phenomenon in which corals lose their microscopic endo-symbiotic algae, known as zooxanthella, due to abnormal environmental factors such as abnormally high or low sea water temperature, high or low salinity, heavy deposition of sediments over the coral body, etc.

In the tropics, the surface seawater temperature normally remains constant at about 29°C throughout the year, while in subtropical regions it reaches 28 or 29°C only in the summer. During the summer of 1980 the surface water temperature over the reef at Sesoko Island in Okinawa Prefecture reached 30 to 31°C during the daytime at low tide. This high water temperature resulted in the bleaching of many species of corals and some of them eventually died without recovering their algae populations (Frontispiece 5; Yamazato, 1981). After this, corals elsewhere also began to exhibit frequent bleaching during summer, suggesting that the surface sea water temperature is rising due to global warming.

In the summer of 1998, unusually high water temperatures prevailed and unusually extensive bleaching was recorded throughout south-western Japan. This bleaching was a global phenomenon (Descamp et al., 1998; Obura and White, 1998; Teleki et al., 1998).

Bleaching is only the most obvious of many ways in which corals are likely to react to global warming. Since corals are animals, many aspects of their metabolism are dependent upon temperature. While most of the metabolic reactions of coral to temperature change are similar to those of other marine animals, there are also some aspects unique to corals. One characteristic of corals is that calcification, or skeletogenesis, appears to be controlled separately from tissue growth. Because corals are dependent on photosynthesis performed by zooxanthella, the effect of global warming on photosynthesis is also important. Additionally, corals are unique in terms of their method of reproduction. Most corals experience a reproductive period once a year, probably in response to seasonal temperature changes. Consequently, the reproductive cycle of corals is also likely to be sensitive to global warming.

Global warming will cause some degree of melting of polar ice and this in turn will lead to a rise in sea level. Various coral organisms are adapted to living at different depths, principally in response to the degree of light penetration and the water temperature. As the sea level rises, corals will be forced to adapt to changes in factors such as depth, illumination and temperature.

Global warming and coral bleaching

The first incidence of coral bleaching in Okinawa took place in the summer of 1980 (Yamazato, 1981). Corals which grew on or near a 43 m sea water pipe which stretched perpendicular to a reef margin were observed on four separate occasions - 10 August, 22 September and 2 November 1980, and 1 January 1981. Altogether, 14 coral species or species groups were observed (Table 16.1). Among these corals, the most susceptible to bleaching was the Pocilloporid species, followed by *Montipora*, *Acropora*, and *Porites*, and the least susceptible were *Favia*, *Favites*, and *Goniastrea*. In only *Psammocora contigua* was bleaching never observed to occur. In short, approximately half of the corals remained normal, while about half were observed to be either partially or completely bleached in August and September. About half of the bleached corals were found to be partially or completely dead in November and January (Figure 16.1).

As to the cause of the bleaching, Yamazato (1981) suggested high seawater temperatures, which in turn were caused by a prolonged period of high solar radiation and unusually low precipitation. Temperatures monitored on the reef flat from June to August 1980 were 29 to 30°C at high tide, and 31 to 32°C during the daytime at low tide, indicating that water temperature over the reef drops due to mixing

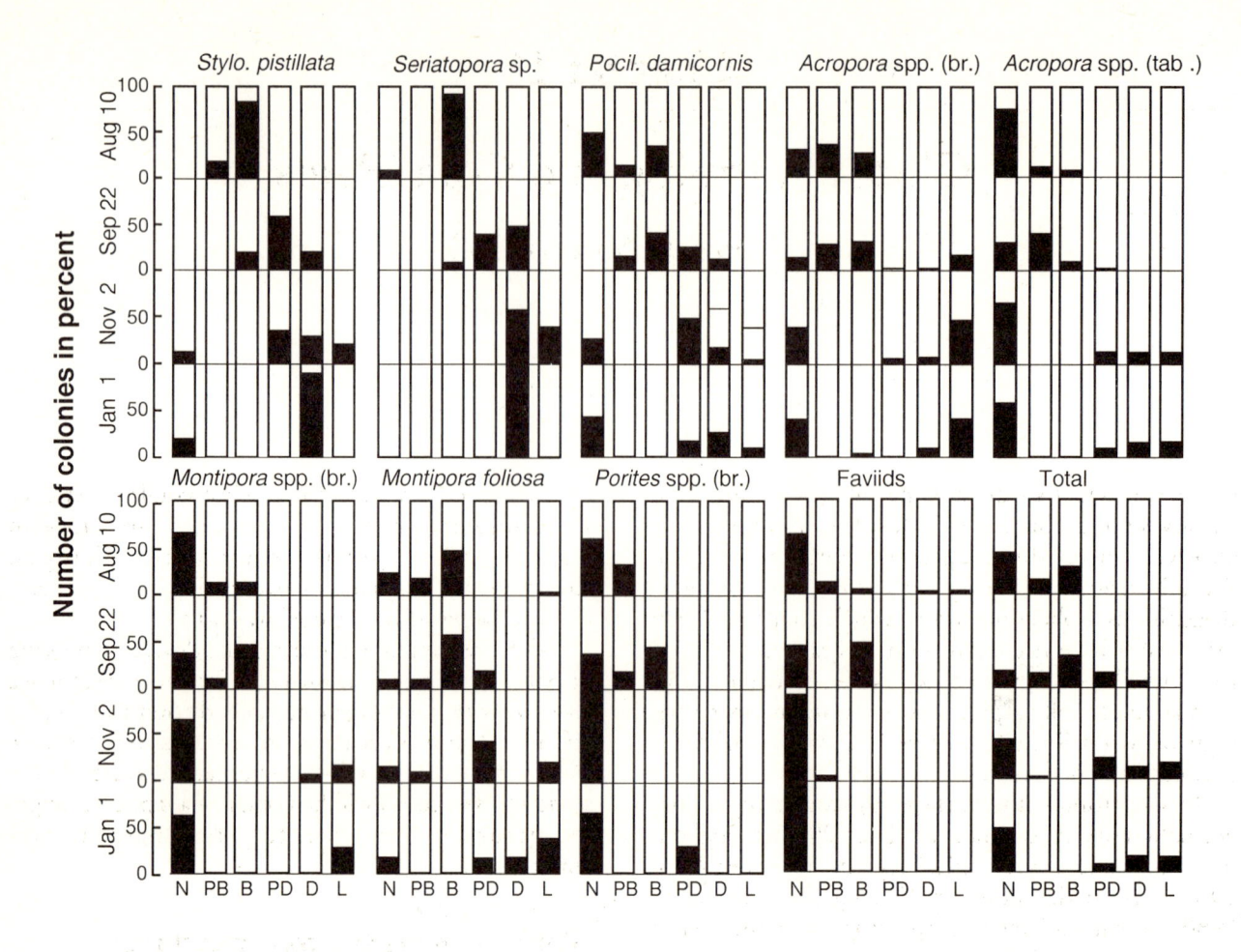

Figure 16.1.
Histograms showing the changes in the relative composition of coral colonies according to living conditions from August to January. N: Normal, PB: partially bleached, B: bleached, PD: partially dead, D: dead, and L: lost (Yamazato, 1980).

with cooler water from the open ocean at high tide. It is reasonable to conclude that the critical temperature for coral bleaching is about 30 to 31°C.

Kamezaki and Ui (1984) observed a coral-bleaching event in the Yaeyama Islands in 1983. They suggested that a prolonged period of high seawater temperatures above 31°C may have been the cause. In Indonesia, the sea water temperature rose to above 33°C and about 80 - 90% of corals died on some reef flats in 1983 (Brown and Suharsono, 1990; Brown and Ogden, 1993).

Coral bleaching was again observed in 1986 on reefs off the southern part of Okinawa Island (Tsuchiya et al., 1987). Coral bleaching was also observed in 1993 in reefs off Iriomote Island, the other main island in the Yaeyama Islands, and also off the Miyako Islands (Okinawa Prefecture Environmental Science Center, 1994). At this time the recorded sea water temperature was 30°C off the coast of Miyako Island.

In 1998, the most extensive bleaching events took place in southern Japan and even the non-reef coral communities of Amakusa in the Kyushu region were affected (Nojima, pers. comm.). Also, a brief observation of the coral reef off Sesoko Island, Okinawa Prefecture, revealed that many more species of corals were affected in 1998 than in the 1980 event on the same reef. All species of coral were affected with the singular exception of *P. contigua*, the same species reported as being the most tolerant coral in 1980 (Yamazato, 1981).

Prolonged fine weather may be one of the factors contributing to the high seawater temperatures. These weather conditions may be increasing the exposure of coral to UV radiation, and this may also be a factor contributing to coral bleaching either independently of or in association with high seawater temperatures. Glynn et al. (1992) showed experimentally that the bleaching of *Pocillopora damicornis* and *Acropora valida* is enhanced synergistically by a combination of high temperature and high UV irradiation. There are an increasing number of reports indicating that coral bleaching is being caused by UV radiation (Brown, 1997).

Table 16.1. Results of four successive censuses on the extent of summer stress to the corals on the reef flat of Sesoko Island, Okinawa Prefecture in 1980

Corals	Date	Number of colonies						
		Normal	Partially bleached	Bleached	Partially dead	Dead	Lost	Total
Psammocora contigua	Aug 10	5	0	0	0	0	0	5
	Sep 22	5	0	0	0	0	0	5
	Nov 2	4	0	0	0	0	0	4
	Jan 1	1	0	0	0	0	0	1
Stylophora pistillata	Aug 10	0	4	20	0	0	0	24
	Sep 22	0	0	5	14	5	0	24
	Nov 2	2	0	0	5	4	3	14
	Jan 1	1	0	0	0	4	0	5
Seriatopora spp.	Aug 10	1	0	9	0	0	0	10
	Sep 22	0	0	1	4	5	0	10
	Nov 2	0	0	0	0	3	2	5
	Jan 1	0	0	0	0	3	0	3
Pocillopora damicornis	Aug 10	37	10	25	0	0	0	72
	Sep 22	0	10	25	16	8	0	59
	Nov 2	16	0	0	30	11	3	60
	Jan 1	12	0	0	5	7	3	27
Acropora spp. (branching)	Aug 10	11	13	10	0	0	0	34
	Sep 22	5	10	11	1	1	6	34
	Nov 2	11	0	0	1	2	13	27
	Jan 1	8	0	1	0	2	8	19
Acropora spp. (tabular)	Aug 10	16	3	2	0	0	0	21
	Sep 22	11	14	7	1	0	0	33
	Nov 2	17	0	0	3	3	3	26
	Jan 1	11	0	0	2	3	3	19
Monitipora spp. (branching)	Aug 10	17	4	4	0	0	0	25
	Sep 22	9	3	11	0	0	0	23
	Nov 2	15	0	0	0	2	5	22
	Jan 1	6	0	0	0	0	3	9
Montipora spp. (encrusting)	Aug 10	5	0	0	0	0	0	5
	Sep 22	3	0	2	0	0	0	5
	Nov 2	3	0	0	1	0	0	4
	Jan 1	0	0	0	2	0	0	2
Montipora foliosa	Aug 10	5	4	10	0	0	1	20
	Sep 22	2	2	12	4	0	0	20
	Nov 2	2	1	0	4	0	2	9
	Jan 1	1	0	0	1	1	2	5
Porites spp.	Aug 10	8	4	1	0	0	0	13
	Sep 22	5	2	5	0	1	0	13
	Nov 2	7	0	0	0	0	0	7
	Jan 1	2	0	0	1	0	0	3
Favia spp.	Aug 10	3	2	1	0	1	1	8
	Sep 22	0	0	6	0	0	0	6
	Nov 2	5	1	0	0	0	0	6
	Jan 1	2	0	0	0	0	0	2
Favites spp.	Aug 10	5	0	0	0	0	0	5
	Sep 22	4	0	1	0	0	0	5
	Nov 2	4	0	0	0	0	0	4
	Jan 1	2	0	0	0	0	0	2
Goniastrea spp.	Aug 10	5	1	0	0	0	0	6
	Sep 22	4	0	2	0	0	0	6
	Nov 2	6	0	0	0	0	0	6
	Jan 1	5	0	0	0	0	0	5
Millepora spp.	Aug 10	2	0	4	0	0	0	6
	Sep 22	0	0	2	3	0	1	6
	Nov 2	1	0	0	1	0	0	2
	Jan 1	0	0	0	0	0	0	0
Other corals	Aug 10	2	0	0	0	0	0	2
	Sep 22	2	0	0	0	0	0	2
	Nov 2	0	0	0	0	1	0	1
	Jan 1	0	0	0	0	0	0	0

Table 16.2. Monthly total number of observed and planulated colonies, and the percentage of planulated colonies together with monthly average of water temperature for outdoor colonies. Water temperature for indoor colonies were kept at 26°C. The cells marked by two asterisks are shown in an inset table (Yamazato et al., in preparation).

Coral spp.	Year	1993				1994											1995				
	Month	Sep	Oct	Nov	Dec	Jan	Feb	Mar	Apr	May	Jun	Jul	Aug	Sep	Oct	Nov	Dec	Jan	Feb	Mar	Apr	May
	WT (°C)	26	25.1	23.1	21.4	20.4	19.3	19.9	21.8	23.1	25.8	28.2	28	26.8	24.6	23.1	22.1	18.9	18.2	18.9	21.3	23.2
P. dam. Outdoor	Observed	300	82	20	97	48	12	40	42	135	119	134	132	84	108	135	112	76	45	50	55	20
	Planulated	133	4	0	14	0	0	0	2	10	38	26	17	13	2	13	7	2	0	0	0	7
	%	44.3	4.9	0	14.4	0	0	0	4.8	7.4	31.9	19.4	12.9	15.5	1.8	9.6	6.2	2.6	0	0	0	40
P. dam. Indoor	Observed	-	39	25	75	37	10	17	50	56	30	-	7	**	**	**	78	85	27	50	51	16
	Planulated	-	3	2	16	0	1	3	7	14	12	-	5	**	**	**	14	21	0	0	15	11
	%	-	7.7	8	21.3	0	10	17.6	14	25	40	-	76.4	**	**	**	17.9	25.3	0	0	29.4	68.8
S. hyst. Outdoor	Observed	99	202	52	60	32	-	18	49	65	60	191	281	182	234	231	208	168	108	120	132	48
	Planulated	6	2	0	0	0	-	0	0	3	2	40	5	0	0	0	0	0	0	0	0	0
	%	6.1	1	0	0	0	-	0	0	4.6	3.3	20.9	1.8	0	0	0	0	0	0	0	0	0
S. pist. Indoor	Observed	92	134	36	33	16	-	8	46	71	141	267	330	204	234	231	144	117	36	40	44	16
	Planulated	3	0	0	0	0	-	0	0	10	50	56	4	0	0	0	0	0	0	0	0	0
	%	3.3	0	0	0	0	-	0	0	14.1	35.5	21	1.2	0	0	0	0	0	0	0	0	0

Coral spp.	Year	1995									1996					
	Month	Apr	May	Jun	Jul	Aug	Sep	Oct	Nov	Dec	Jan	Feb	Mar	Apr	May	Jun
	WT (°C)	21.3	23.2	26.1	29.6	30.2	30.1	28.4	24.5	21.8	20.7	19.8	22.7	24	24.1	28.1
S. pist. Outdoor	Observed	40	96	112	80	80	80	64	72	70	72	64	80	24	30	35
	Planulated	0	0	6	14	12	0	0	0	0	0	0	0	0	0	18
	%	0	0	5.4	17.5	15	0	0	0	0	0	0	0	0	0	51.4
S. pist. Indoor	Observed	40	88	112	72	88	56	64	56	66	41	40	40	20	20	32
	Planulated	0	0	38	45	22	2	0	0	3	0	5	36	0	3	24
	%	0	0	33.9	62.5	25	3.6	0	0	4.5	0	5.6	90	0	15	80

Monthly percentage of planulating colonies of *P. damicornis* in 1994.

	Aug	Sep	Oct	Nov
WT (°C)	24	22	20	-
	35.5	63.2	75	50
	15.4	3.8	0	0

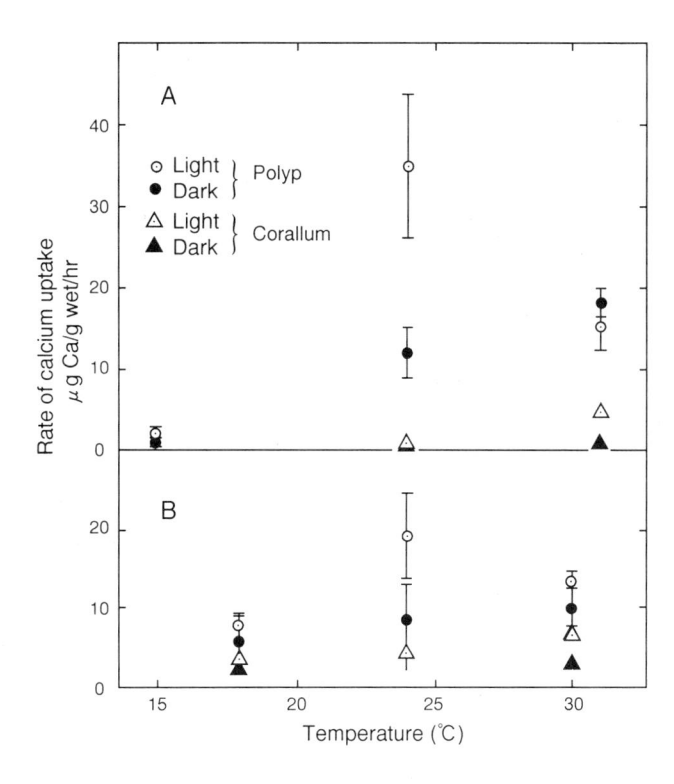

Figure 16.2.
Rate of calcium uptake as a function of temperature by living polyps of *Fungia scutaria* in bright light (3000 lux) and in the dark, during a 26-hour incubation in sea water containing 11.45 μg-at. P/l (A) and 2.70 μg-at. P/l (B) of dissolved inorganic phosphate. Vertical lines drawn through the points represent standard deviations from the mean. Rates of exchange of calcium by dead coral are also included (Yamazato, 1970).

The extent to which coral reef communities will be lost as a result of future global warming is difficult to forecast, however. Even if corals inhabiting shallower waters in tropical and subtropical regions become extinct, those in deeper waters may release propagules that will colonise new locations in the tropical, subtropical, and temperate regions which become suitable habitats as a result of the warmer climate. In addition, there is some evidence to indicate that corals may be able to adapt to global warming, indicating that a complete loss of coral species can be avoided (Buddmeier, 1992). Although species diversity may decrease due to the disappearance of those corals which are most sensitive to high temperature and high UV irradiation, coral reef communities may be able to survive global warming by adapting their community structures and functions to changing conditions.

Global warming and reproduction

Most corals reproduce once a year, spawning during late spring to early summer, probably in response to seasonal temperature changes. During the spawning season, the release of gametes is regulated according to the lunar cycle and the time of day. However, the reproductive behavior of corals varies according to the latitude at which they live. Typical annual cycles are found among subtropical corals, with the tendency shifting toward more dispersed timing of spawning toward the tropics where the water temperature remains constant throughout the year at about 29°C. Although it has been suggested that the influence of global warming will be stronger in subtropical than in tropical regions, it is not known whether the annual temperature patterns of the subtropics will simply become more like those that currently prevail in the tropics as the climate warms. If this happens, the reproductive patterns of present-day subtropical corals may change to match those of tropical corals.

Some corals, including *Pocillopora damicornis*, *Stylophora pistillata* and *Seriatpora hystrix*, reproduce by releasing planula larvae once every lunar month throughout the year. Interestingly, reproduction in these species is typically an annual event in the tropics, but at higher latitudes reproduction does not take place during the cooler winter months (Stoddart and Black, 1985; Yamazato et al., in preparation). For example, *P. damicornis* does not produce planula during the four coldest months, while *S. pistillata* and *S. hystrix* planulate only during a three-month period in spring (April to June or May to July) in Okinawa. It was previously assumed that the latter two species cease planulating not only during the winter but also during the summer months due to temperature conditions. Hariott (1983) reported that planula production of *P. damicornis* in the Great Barrier Reef is reduced during the summer months when temperatures exceed the thermal optimum (Jokiel and Coles, 1990).

The reproductive patterns of these corals suggest that they may planulate even during their current non-reproducing periods in the winter and summer months if the temperature is suitable. To test this hypothesis, two species of corals, *P. damicornis* and *S. pistillata*, were kept at a constant year-round temperature of 26°C and observed to planulate throughout the year (Table 16.2) (Yamazato et al., in preparation). From this experiment it was concluded that these corals were originally inhabitants of the tropics, where they exhibit a characteristic monthly cycle of planulation, and that they later expanded their range of distribution to higher latitudes, where they ceased reproduction during those periods when conditions were either too cold or too hot. This conclusion leads to the conjecture that as global warming progresses, the temperature conditions of coral habitats at higher latitudes may approach those in the tropics where the ancestors of these corals may have originated, with the result that their reproduction patterns may revert to those typical of tropical corals.

We do not know, however, that year-round temperature conditions in the subtropical regions will approach those of the tropics in the future. In addition, if the sea water temperature rises so high that the bleaching and eventual death of entire coral communities occur, then obviously further reproduction will not take place.

Global warming, calcification, and photosynthesis

When pieces of the coral species *Fungia scutaria* were subjected to different water temperatures during the course of short-term calcium-45 labelling experiments, the maximum calcification rate occurred at 24°C (Figure 16.2; Yamazato, 1966, 1970), which is close to the summer temperature of the seawater near Hawaii, where this study was made. Similarly, Clausen and Roth (1975) also found that the optimal growth temperatures of a number of coral species were close to the summer temperature maximum of the regions which they inhabit. According to Jokiel and Coles (1990), many authors have reported finding the same growth patterns in their long-term experiments.

In coral calcification, the Ca^{2+} is thought to be supplied from seawater through diffusion and the CO_3^{2-} from sea water as well as from metabolic CO_2. Although there are dissenting views, the consensus is that coral calcification releases CO_2 from the ocean into the atmosphere. Consequently, a rise in the atmospheric CO_2 concentration should, in principle, inhibit calcification. If this is the case, both the rise in temperature and the increasing atmospheric CO_2 concentration can be expected to inhibit coral growth.

Moreover, although there have been some dissenting reports, it is generally accepted that coral calcification is enhanced by photosynthesis performed by endo-symbiotic zooxanthella, with calcification rates dependent on photosynthesis rates. According to Coles and Jokiel (1977), coral photosynthesis decreases when the ambient temperature rises above the standard summer temperature. The decreases in calcification rates observed at higher temperatures may be the result of reduced photosynthesis. Coles and Jokiel (1977) also found that tropical corals generally exhibit higher rates of photosynthesis at high temperatures than do subtropical varieties of the same species. This indicates that corals may be temperature adaptive, which would make them better able to cope with climatic changes.

References

Brown, B. E. 1997. Coral bleaching: causes and consequences. Proceedings of the 8th International Coral Reef Symposium (Panama) 1: 65-74.

Brown, B. E. and Suharsono. 1990. Damage and recovery of coral reefs affected by El Ninõ related to sea water warming in the Thousand Islands, Indonesia. Coral Reefs 8:163-170.

Brown, B. E. and J. C. Ogden. 1993. Coral bleaching. Scientific American January 1993: 44-50.

Buddmeier, R. W. 1992. Corals, climate and conservation. Proceedings of the 7th International Coral Reef Symposium (Guam)1: 3-10.

Clausen, C. D. and A. A. Roth. 1975. Effect of temperature adaptation on calcification rate in the hermatypic coral *Pocillopora damicornis*. Marine Biology 33: 93-100.

Coles, S. L. and P. L. Jokiel. 1977. Effects of temperature on photosynthesis and respiration in hermatypic corals. Marine Biology 43: 209-216 (cited from Jokiel and Coles, 1990).

Descamp, P., D. Fray, B. A. Thomassin, S. Castellani, and J. Layssac. 1998. Massive mortality following a huge bleaching of reef corals at Mayotte I. (SW Indian Ocean) at the end of the 1998 austral summer (Abstract). Programme and Abstracts, International Society for Reef Studies (ISRS) European Meeting, 1st to 4th 1998 (Perpignan): 62.

Glynn, P. W., R. Imai, K. Sakai, Y. Nakano, and K. Yamazato. 1992. Experimental responses of Okinawan (Ryukyu Islands, Japan) reef corals to high sea temperature and UV radiation. Proceedings of the 7th International Coral Reef Symposium (Guam) 1: 27-37.

Harriot, V. J. 1983. Reproductive ecology of four scleractinian species at Lizard Island, Great Barrier Reef. Coral Reefs 2: 9-18.

Jokiel, P. L. and S. L. Coles. 1990. Response of Hawaiian and other Indo-Pacific reef corals to elevated temperature. Coral Reefs 8: 155-162.

Kamezaki, N. and S. Ui. 1984. Bleaching of hermatypic corals in Yaeyama Islands. Marine Parks

Journal 61: 10-13. (in Japanese)

Obura, D. O. and K. V. White. 1998. El-Nino related coral bleaching in eastern Africa, March to May 1998. Programme and Abstracts, International Society for Reef Studies (ISRS) European Meeting, 1st to 4th September (Perpignan):13.

Okinawa Prefectural Environmental Science Centre. 1994. *Coastal Survey of Miyako, Ishigaki, and Iriomote Islands and their Neighboring Islands*. Okinawa Prefectural Planning and Development Department, 327pp. (in Japanese)

Stoddart, J. A. and R. Black. 1985. Cycles of gametogenesis and planulation in the coral *Pocillopora damicornis*. Marine Ecology Progress Series 23: 153-164.

Teleki, K. A., T. Spencer, C. Bradshaw, and M. D. Spalding. 1998. Coral bleaching in the western Indian Ocean - A sign of the times? Programme and Abstracts, International Society for Reef Studies (ISRS) European Meeting, 1st to 4th September (Perpignan): 176.

Tsuchiya, M., K. Yanagiya, and M. Nishihira. 1987. Mass mortality of the sea urchin *Echinometra mathaei* (Blainville) caused by high water temperature on the reef flats in Okinawa, Japan. Galaxea 6: 375-385.

Yamazato, K. 1966. Calcification in a Solitary Coral, *Fungia scutaria* Lamarck, in Relation to Environmental Factors. Ph.D. Dissertation, University of Hawaii, 130 pp.

Yamazato, K. 1970. Calcification in a solitary coral, Fungia scutaria Lamarck, in relation to environmental factors. Bulletin of Science & Engineering Division, University of the Ryukyus, Mathematics & Natural Science No.13: 57-122.

Yamazato, K., 1981. A note on the expulsion of zooxanthellae during summer, 1980 by the Okinawan reef-building corals. Sesoko Marine Science Laboratory Technical Report No. 8: 9-18.

Yamazato, K., M. Sai, E. Suwardi, and S. Sultana. Coral response to global warming in marginal environments: effects on reproduction.(in preparation)

Chapter 17

Potential Impacts of Global Warming on Freshwater Ecosystems in Japan

Hiromi Kobori

Rivers, lakes, and other freshwater ecosystems in Japan are highly diversified in terms of plant and animal species. These freshwater ecosystems have been placed under stress by environmental burdens, exploitation of natural resources, transformation of land, and recreational activities that have been carried out by humans over a long period of time. Many scientists have expressed concern that global warming may further damage species living in these freshwater ecosystems.

According to the IPCC (IPCC, 1995), the rapid warming that has taken place in the 1990s is caused by human activities. Even a moderate scenario of future global warming predicts that the CO_2 concentration in the atmosphere will double, causing the average temperature on Earth to increase by $2°C$ and the sea level to rise by 50 cm. Can species in rivers, lakes, and other typical wetlands in Japan survive global warming and maintain healthy ecosystems?

It is difficult to specify scientifically the extent to which global warming will influence species and ecosystems. For example, it is not easy to distinguish the influence of warming itself from the complex influences of other factors. The long-term ecological data needed to estimate the impact of regional warming and other aspects of climate change are insufficient; however, there is evidence that lakes, marshes, and rivers that have already deteriorated due to various human activities will be further damaged by warming.

Few studies have been undertaken to date on the influence of warming on Japanese rivers and lakes. It is likely, however, that freshwater ecosystems will be affected by warming because they are closed systems that contain a much smaller volume of water compared to most saltwater ecosystems, such as oceans. The discussion that follows will explain characteristics of Japanese freshwater ecosystems and their present conditions. In addition, the influence of warming on species and ecosystems will be predicted based on the available data.

Physical effects on Japanese lakes and marshes

Freshwater ecosystems such as lakes and marshes are not evenly distributed in the long, narrow Japanese Archipelago. Approximately 89% of the 98 natural lakes and marshes that are at least 1 km^2 in area are located in the northern half of the country (Figure 17.1). At present, 282 lakes and marshes in Japan - 59% of the total - freeze over during winter.

Many of the species that live in these northern lakes and marshes are cold-water species that probably will be significantly influenced by warming. Temperature changes that seem small- as little as $5°C$- may inhibit or even completely halt the growth and reproduction of many species. Species that could be affected by global warming range from common microscopic zooplankton to fish, including species belonging to the Family Salmonidae that are adapted to cold waters and cannot survive if the water temperature exceeds $20°C$.

Moreover, temperature changes may affect the physical structure of freshwater ecosystems. Field data from Lake Biwa (Figure 17.1, site D), the largest lake in Japan at 673.8 km^2 in area, shows that the decreased snowfall expected under conditions of global warming increases the water temperature and consequently increases the standing crops of algae in the epilimnion - the water column above the thermocline - while decreasing the dissolved oxygen concentration in the hypolimnion (Fushimi, 1990). Effectively, decreased snowfall contributes to eutrophication.

Eutrophication of lakes and marshes

Eutrophication has occurred in a number of lakes and marshes in Japan, primarily as a result of human activities. Increasing amounts of nutrients such as nitrogen and phosphorus are flowing into lakes and marshes. Consequently, algae-bloom has increased and the quality of water has deteriorated. Blue-green algae (cyanobacteria) that breed in eutrophic

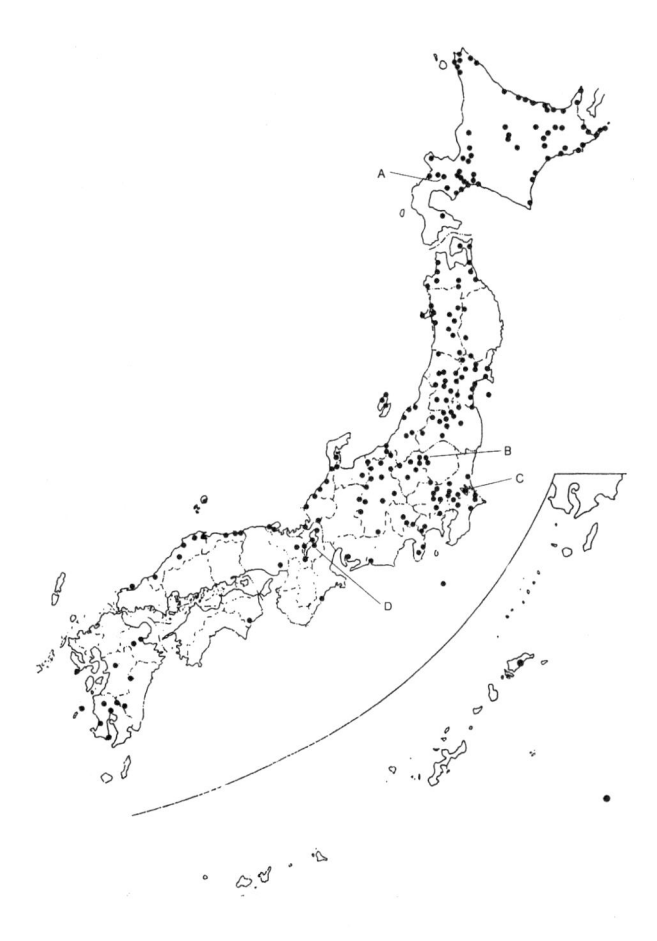

Figure 17.1.
Location of major lakes in Japan. See text for A-D. A: the Makkari Stream, B: Lake Yunoko, C: Lake Kasumigaura, D: Lake Biwa.

conditions can adjust to increases in temperature.

Fujimoto et al. (1995) analyzed data from 211 lakes and marshes throughout Japan and found that the ratio of blue-green algae to other types of algae increases along with an increase in the N/P ratio and water temperature in eutrophic lakes (total phosphor ≥ 0.035 mg l^{-1}). Blue-green algae occupied more than 80% of lakes with temperatures of 30°C or higher (Figure 17.2A). Moreover, among blue-green algae, the ratio of *Microsystis* was found to be in close direct proportion to water temperature. When the water temperature exceeded 30°C, *Microsystis* occupied more than 80% of the biomass among four genera of blue-green algae: *Microsystis, Anabaena, Oscillatoria,* and *Phormidium* (Figure 17.2B). Because the suitable temperature for *Microsystis* is 30 to 35°C (Iwamura, 1981), warming will further stimulate the dominance of blue-green algae, particularly *Microsystis*.

Hosomi et al. (1996) developed a combined water temperature - ecological model that is employed to simulate the effects of global warming on lake ecosystems. When the model was benchmarked against Lake Yunoko (Figure 17.1, site B), a dimictic or stratified lake, fairly good correlation was obtained with the effects of water temperature on the lake's dynamics, e.g. composition of phytoplankton species, their respective concentrations, and nutrient concentrations over a four-year period.

Influence of expansion of oligoaerobic layers on benthos

In a number of eutrophic lakes and marshes in Japan, the bottom layer tends to lack oxygen. When water temperature in the surface layer rises due to warming, blue-green algae grow rapidly, and other species also undergo blooms. Consequently, organic substances increase in the water column and the amount of dissolved oxygen content decreases (Blumberg and Di Toro, 1990). Increases in temperature in summer keep the stratification of water stable for a long period of time, reducing the supply of oxygen from the surface to the deep layer (McCormick, 1990). This phenomenon will tend to harm shellfish and other animals in the lower levels of lakes.

Effects on microorganisms and aquatic insects

Although temperature increases can promote damaging blooms of algae, increases in water temperature in summer can cause declines in a number of species that are not resistant to high temperatures. The cladoceran *Daphnia* is a dominant zooplankton in many Japanese lakes; many species of this genus cannot survive in water at temperatures of 25°C or higher (Moor et al., 1996). The species *Daphnia logispina* is found in deep layers where the water temperature is around 12°C in the alpine eutrophic Lake Yunoko (Figure 17.1, site B). In laboratory experiments using *D. logispina*, the organisms grew well between 10°C and 25°C, but all individuals died without maturing when the water temperature was increased to 30°C (Hanazato and Yasuno, 1985). Laboratory evidence shows that the number of days required for an embryo of *D. logispina* to grow and the number of days up to first parturition become shorter as the temperature increases. The relationship between time and temperature can be expressed by the following formula established by Bottrell (1975):

$$\ln D = \ln a + b (\ln T)^2$$

where D = the duration of egg development or age at the first parturition in days, T = temperature measured (°C), a = the intercept of the regression line, and b = the slope of the regression line. This equation demonstrates that water temperature strongly influences the growth and life cycle of *D. logispina*. Furthermore, the body size of many kinds of

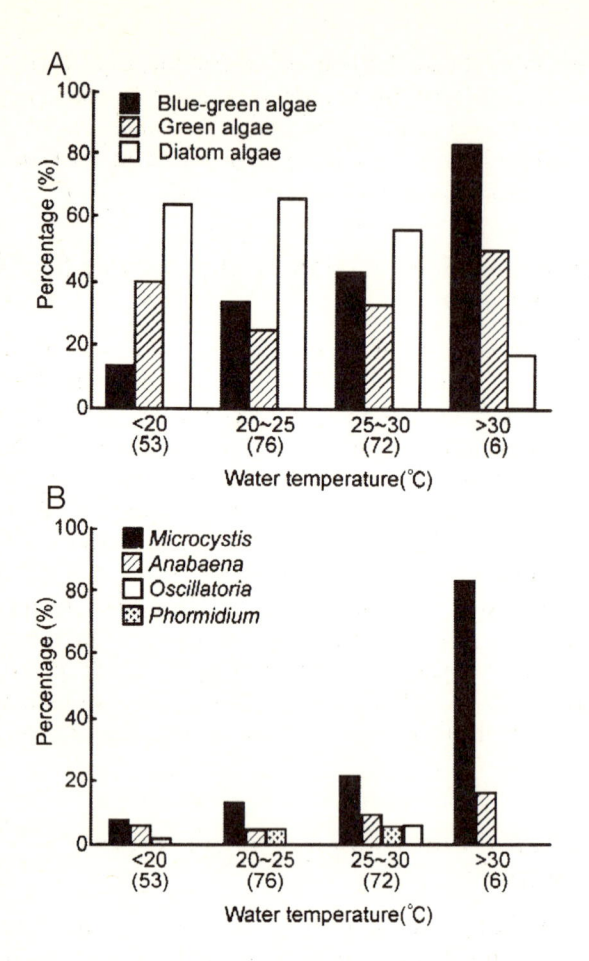

Figure 17.2.
Effect of water temperature on dominance of three types of algae in 207 Japanese lakes.
A: Percentage of lakes which are dominated by blue-green algae, green algae, and diatom algae.
B: Percentage of lakes which are dominated by four genera of blue-green algae (Fujimo et al., 1995). Note: Percentage exceeds 100% because dominance was evaluated independently according to dominance ratio.

zooplankton and aquatic insects is reduced as water temperature increases (Moor et al., 1996; Hayashi 1990); for instance, mature *D. logispina* are an average of 25% smaller when the water temperature is 25°C than at more normal temperatures of around 15°C (Hanazato and Yasuno, 1985).

Another genus of zooplankton, *Neomyces*, contains many species that also are not resistant to high temperatures. *Neomyces intermedia* inhabits the brackish waters in hyper-eutrophic Lake Kasumigaura - the second largest lake in Japan (Figure 17.1, site C) - and does not grow at all during the high temperatures of summer (Toda et al., 1983). The rate of growth of young *N. intermedia* is maximized during periods when the water temperature drops to 20°C; growth completely halts at 29°C (Toda et al, 1984). From these observations, it is estimated that the number of *N. intermedia* will decline if the high temperature period in summer is prolonged due to global warming conditions.

Other microorganisms, such as the amphipoda family Anisogammaridae, respond poorly to increased temperatures. Seven *Jesogammarus*, species are known to live in lakes, marshes, rivers, and springs on the Pacific side of Japan. Growth of young *Jesogammarus spinopulps* is deterred for three months from May to August. Laboratory experiments have shown that such suppression of growth is caused by exposure of this species to temperatures of 25°C or higher (Kusano et al., 1987). Unlike many kinds of Anisogammaridae, which reproduce semi-annually in rivers and in seawater where changes in water temperature are relatively moderate, *J. spinopulps* reproduces annually. This distinction is considered to be a product of temperature-related growth sup-pression, and could potentially lead to population declines in the event that global warming increases temperatures beyond this species' tolerance level.

Microorganisms are not the only living creatures with sensitivity to temperature. Among insects, larvae of *Chaoborus flavicans* (Diptera) have poor resistance to high temperatures. Individuals captured in marshes and brought to laboratories showed an increased death rate at certain stages of growth when exposed to temperatures of 25°C or higher, and all individuals died without reaching the pupa stage at 30°C (Hanazato and Yasuno, 1989). Moreover, emergence of some species of Diptera is known to be temperature-dependent. *Tokunagayusurika akamushi*, a species that resides in eutrophic marshes and lakes in Japan, emerge all at once in autumn. This emergence begins when water temperatures in deep layers of lakes and marshes reach 10 - 18°C (Iwakuma et al., 1989).

Effects on macrobiota
Psychrophilic fish species

Temperature changes affect larger organisms as well. For example, psychrophilic (cold-loving) fish populations will decline because increased water temperatures will limit the amount of available habitat (Hills and Magnuson, 1990). Suitable temperatures for the rainbow trout *Onconhynchus mykiss*, which was released in many lakes in Japan, are 10 to 20°C, so it is likely that these fish could also be adversely affected by global warming. Psychrophilic fish living at the southern limit of their distribution will be the first to be affected. For instance, growth of dolly vardens *Salvelinus malma*, a river-dwelling psychrophilic fish, is inhibited when water temperatures exceed 16°C. Its southernmost habitat, a river in southern Hokkaido called the Makkari Stream (Figure 17.1, site A), extends over 20 km and is colder at the source than in

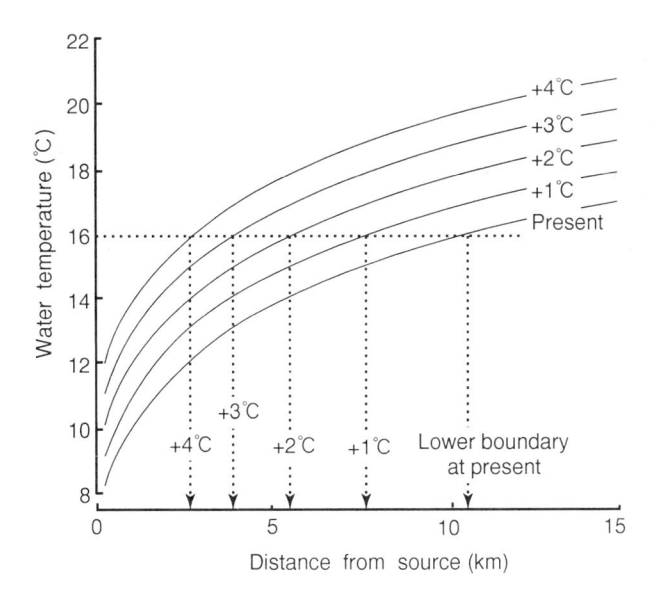

Figure 17.3.
Simulation of stream-temperature elevation (solid line) and the movement of the thermal habitat barrier of 16°C for *Salvelinus malama* (arrow) due to increases of 1 - 4°C mean air temperature in the Makkari Stream. The longitudinal temperature profiles corresponding to the increase of air temperature from the simple regression analysis for mean maximum temperature in the high temperature period (Kitano et al., 1995).

the lower reaches. Kitano et al. (1995) predicted that an increase of 1 - 4°C in the average atmospheric temperature would reduce the existing habitat of the *S. malma* by 25 - 74% in this river (Figure 17.3). This prediction is based on an understanding of the relationship between atmospheric temperature and water temperatures, established by examining records for 30 years (1928 - 1957) and measuring source water temperatures in 36 other rivers. The relationship can be expressed by the following formula:

$$Ts = 1.083 + 0.939(Ta)$$

where Ts is the water temperature (°C) and Ta is the annual average atmospheric temperature. At present, the water temperature at the source is stable at 8°C. According to the above formula, water temperature at the source increases by 0.9, 1.9, 2.8, and 3.8°C when the annual average atmospheric temperature increases by 1.0, 2.0, 3.0, and 4.0°C, respectively. When water temperature at the source increases, the temperature in the lower reaches increase further. Atmospheric temperature increases of even 1°C increase the water temperature in the river's lower reaches to above 16°C in a 2.6 km stretch of the river, making this area uninhabitable for *S. malma*. Successive incremental increases in temperature eliminate 4.8, 6.6, and 7.7 km of habitat for this species - roughly 25%, 46%, 62%, and 74%, respectively, of the total river habitat (Figure 17.3). However, this forecast does not count the influence of the ground temperature along with warming and sudden increases in temperature in summer that are not reflected in the average temperature. Therefore, this forecast of reduction in habitat of *S. malma* due to global warming should be considered the minimum level of what could actually occur.

Nakano et al. (1996) also examined the relationship between water temperature and habitat size in the case of *Salvelinus leucomanaenis*, a species in the same genus that competes with *S. malma*. This study forecasted that the same incremental increases in average atmospheric temperature described above could reduce the present area of habitat for *S. leucomanaenis* by approximately 4%, 20%, 34%, and 46%, respectively. These estimates indicate that global warming could rapidly narrow the available habitats for psychrophilic freshwater fish, reducing the number of populations and population sizes. Reduction of the population size will be accelerated because of losses of genetic variability; loss of demographic variation, environmental variability, and catastrophes could also contribute to population declines (Primack, 1998; Primack and Kobori, 1997). With such potential pressures, it is likely that the reduced populations or extinction of one or more species of psychrophilic fish will alter the species composition and structure of ecosystems.

Effects of temperature changes may most strongly impact one aspect of a species' life cycle. For example, psychrophilic fish such as the chum salmon *Onconhynchus keta* hatch in the southernmost area of their range in Honshu, but must migrate northward when spring and summer temperatures increase beyond the 10 - 13°C suitable for salmon fry (Irie, 1990). Thus, any increase in water temperature will greatly reduce the survival rate of salmon fry.

Changes in species interactions and food chain

It is important to note that increases in atmospheric and water temperature, while having a direct influence on the survival rate, life cycle, and breeding rate of organisms such as zooplankton and fish that have low resistance to high temperatures in lakes and marshes, will also indirectly effect entire ecosystems. For example, *Daphnia* is a keystone species in marsh and lake ecosystems; if increased temperatures cause *Daphnia* numbers to decline, this reduction will influence phytoplankton that they eat, as well as other species higher in the food chain. Because of such linkages, even species that are not directly affected by increases in temperature will nevertheless come under wider stress due to global warming.

A
- 3%
- 9%
- 8%
- 80%

▨ River crossing works exist, which enables fish to move upstream

■ River crossing works exist, which enables 90% of fish to move upstream

▦ River crossing works which prevent fish from moving upstream

☐ River without any crossing work

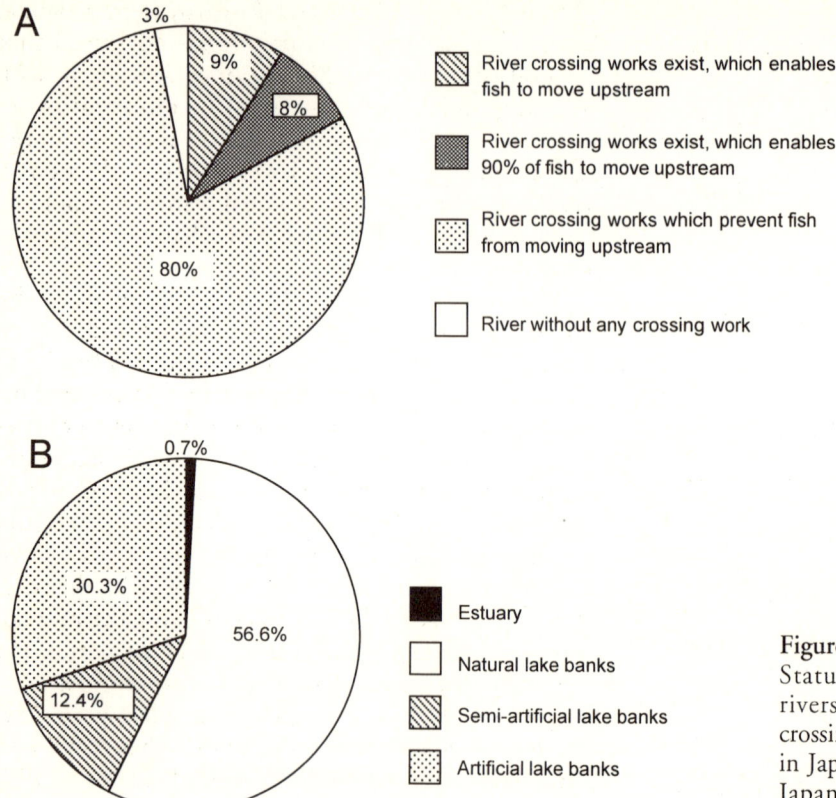

B
- 0.7%
- 30.3%
- 12.4%
- 56.6%

■ Estuary
☐ Natural lake banks
▨ Semi-artificial lake banks
▦ Artificial lake banks

Figure 17.4.
Status of man-made structure in the major rivers and lakes in Japan. A: Status of river crossing works nationwide in 113 major streams in Japan. B: Status of lake banks nationwide in Japan (the National Survey on the National Environment Survey, 1993, Environment Agency).

It has been reported that increases in water temperature influence the dominance of *Microsystis* in eutrophic lakes and marshes along with other species. Dominance of *Microsystis* is known to deter the reproduction of *Daphnia* (Hanazato, 1989) and change the competing relationship between two species of *Bosmina* (Okino and Arakawa, 1994). Similarly, the decreased size of zooplankton and aquatic insects associated with increases in temperature alters the predator-prey relationship. Many kinds of Diptera, which reproduce annually in high latitude areas of Europe and North America, produce five generations or more in a year in eutrophic marshes in Japan where water temperatures exceed 30°C (Iwakuma et al., 1989). As water temperatures increase due to global warming, populations of Diptera in Japan - and possibly in Europe and North America - may also grow rapidly, as more lakes and marshes become warm enough to promote repeated episodes of reproduction in these species. Growth in Diptera species would undoubtedly alter the species composition of their habitat, as competition for prey becomes fiercer, and as predators that eat Diptera increase in numbers. These phenomena show that global warming will change the interaction of species in lakes and marshes as well as the structure and energy efficiency of food chains.

Also, effects of warming may produce subtle, yet no less damaging, changes. Aside from episodes of extreme heat in summer, global warming will cause winters to be less cold. If, for example, the lakes that normally freeze over in the winter stop freezing because of warmer winter temperatures, there may be changes in the habits of freshwater species that migrate seasonally, including birds and mammals. The effects of such changes on species and ecosystems cannot be predicted.

Direct effects of human activities
Toxic chemicals

Organisms usually are more easily affected by toxic chemicals when the temperature is high (Moor and Folt, 1993). Organochlorine compounds and heavy metals accumulate more in organisms as temperatures increase. For example, accumulation of DDT in *Daphnia* was seen to increase as water temperatures rose (Nawaz and Kirk, 1995). Moreover, pesticide use is likely to increase as temperatures rise because harmful insects become more abundant in warmer conditions. Increased concentrations of harmful substances added to warmer conditions will only enhance the effects of these substances on zooplanktons (Hanazato, 1995), particularly large zooplankton species. Havens and Hanazato (1993) showed that large zooplankton are more sensitive to these chemicals, a sensitivity influenced by the stress-induced changes caused by temperature.

Artificial structures in rivers and lakes

Because warming will reduce habitat availability in lower, warmer reaches of rivers, animals and plants in rivers will be forced to change their habitat from the lower to the upper rivers. In all except three of Japanese 110 major rivers, however, there are obstacles such as dams and sluices that make upriver migrations difficult (Figure 17.4A). Only 9% of all rivers have routes to allow fish to move upstream (Environment Agency, Government of Japan, 1993). Therefore, even the aquatic species that are capable of migrating are prevented from moving upstream, causing them to be increasingly isolated from suitable habitats. Consequently, a number of species will not be able to overcome the influence of warming and will probably go extinct. Furthermore, although river banks are an important habitat for many aquatic plants and animals, 21% of river banks and 43% of lake banks in Japan have been built upon in some way (Fig. 17.4B). The decrease in natural river banks makes rivers more vulnerable to fluctuations in temperature, thus increasing the potential for stress on aquatic species.

Conclusion

An increase in water temperatures associated with global climate change will be a significant factor affecting the balance of freshwater ecosystems. A possible scenario of changes in freshwater ecosystems in Japan due to global warming can be summarised as follows: 1) In lakes, high water temperature will expand the thermal stratification period and deepen the thermocline such that the dissolved oxygen concentration in the hypolimnion will decline. 2) The growth rate and standing crops of algae will increase with rising temperatures. Particularly, massive growth of blue-green algae such as *Microsystis* and *Anabaena* will be accelerated and prolonged. Such blooms further deplete oxygen levels and contribute to eutrophication. 3) Psychrophilic organisms such as zooplankton, including *Daphnia* and *Mysina*, and fish in the salmon family will decline because of habitat loss. 4) Reduction in size of many kinds of zooplankton and aquatic insects, which occurs in higher temperatures, will decrease their efficiency at feeding on algae, further contributing to the increased abundance of phytoplankton, especially blue-green algae. This will change the energy efficiency of the food chain in the ecosystem. 5) Keystone species such as *Daphnia* will decline as higher temperatures reduce their available food supplies in the hypolimnion, lowering their reproductive rates. 6) Greater susceptibility to pollution at higher temperatures will also decrease the *Daphnia* population. As a result, species that depend upon *Daphnia* may be affected, resulting in changes in the composition of the ecosystem. 7) For many psychrophilic fish, habitat will become restricted to upper streams and rivers. 8) A shortened life cycle and a decrease in the mature size of aquatic insects will affect the relationship and interaction between species, resulting in changes of structure and function of the river ecosystem.

The empirical data used in this paper can provide valuable qualitative information on the effects of increased temperature on aquatic species and ecosystems, and they are helpful in predicting future changes. Quantitative analyses and models that can simulate changes in ecological responses corresponding to long-term effects of global warming, however, are not available at the moment.

It is important to take comprehensive protective measures immediately. We should not delay preventative measures until the influence of warming is completely scientifically clarified. Marshes, lakes, and rivers are closed environments and are easily influenced by warming. Therefore, the later preventative measures are taken, the more significant the influence of warming will be. The impact on the environment and the social costs will also increase. Among global environmental problems, the problem of global warming is the most significant in terms of space and time, and its cause is deeply rooted within human society. The existence of our modern energy-intensive industrial society is the cause of warming. All of human civilization, all species, and every wetland ecosystem on Earth will be influenced by warming. Consequently, competition between human beings and other species for land and wetlands will intensify, and ecosystems and the composition of biological communities will change. Concrete preventative measures are needed before the situation becomes irreversible.

References

Blumberg, A. F. and D. M. Di Toro. 1990. Effects of climate warming on dissolved oxygen concentration in Lake Erie. Transactions of the American Fisheries Society 119: 210-233.

Bottrell, H. H. 1975. The relationship between

temperature and duration of egg development in some epiphytic *Cladocera* and *Copepoda* from the River Thames, reading with a discussion of temperature functions. Oecologia 18: 63-84.

Environment Agency Government of Japan. 1993. *Quality of the Environment in Japan*. Tokyo. (in Japanese)

Fujimoto, N., T. Fukushima, Y. Inamori, and R. Sudo. 1995. Analytical evaluation of relationship between dominance of cyanobacteria and aquatic environmental factors in Japanese lakes. Water Environment (J. of Japan Society on Water Environment) 18: 901-908. (in Japanese)

Fushimi, K. 1990. Effects of snowfall on water supply in Lake Biwa. Annual Research Report of Lake Biwa Research Institute, Shiga Prefecture, 1990: 58-74. (in Japanese)

Hanazato, T. 1989. Relationship of cyanobacteria and zooplankton in eutrophicated lakes. Japanese J. of Limnology 50: 53-67. (in Japanese)

Hanazato, T. 1995. Influence of temperature on the effects of an insecticide on recovery patterns of a zooplankton community in experimental ponds. Proceedings of the 6th International Conference on Conservation Management, Lake Kasumigaura '95, pp.1083-1086.

Hanazato, T. and M. Yasuno. 1985. Effect of temperature in the laboratory studies on growth, egg development and first parturition of five species of *Cladocera*. Japanese J. of Limnology. 46: 185-191.

Hanazato, T. and M. Yasuno. 1989. Effect of temperature in the laboratory studies on growth of *Chaoborus flavicans* (Deptera: Chaoboridae). Archiv für Hydrobiologie 114: 497-504.

Havens, K. E. and H. Hanazato. 1993. Zooplankton community responses to chemical stressors: A comparison of results from acidification and pesticide contamination research. Environmental Pollution 82: 277-288.

Hayashi, F. 1990. Variation of mature size of aquatic insects and related environmental factors. Japanese J. of Limnology 51: 199-215. (in Japanese)

Hill, D. K. and J. J. Magnuson. 1990. Potential effects of global warming on the growth and prey consumption of Great Lake fish. Transactions of the American Fisheries Society 19: 165-275.

Hosomi, M., T. Saigusa, T. Okubo, and A. Murakami. 1996. Use of a water temperature-ecological model to simulate global warming effects on a lake ecosystem. In: *Climate Change* and *Plants in East Asia*. Pp.109-136. Springler.

IPCC. 1995. The IPCC second assessment synthesis of scientific-technical information relevant to interpreting article 2 of the UN framework convention on climate change.

Irie, T. 1990. Ecological studies on the migration of juvenile chum salmon (*Onconhynchus keta*), during early ocean life. Bull. Seika National Fishery Research Institute 68: 1-142.

Iwakuma, T., Y. Sugaya, and M. Yasuno. 1989. Dependence of the autumn emergence of *Tokunaga-yusurika akamushi* (Diptera: Chironomidae) on water temperature. Japanese J. of Limnology 50: 281-288.

Iwamura, N. 1981. Studies on the water blooms in Lake Kasumigaura. 1981. Verhandlungen der Internationalen Vereinigung für Theoretishe und Angewandte Limnologie 21: 652-658.

Kitano, F., S. Nakano, K. Maekawa, and Y. Ono. 1995. Effect of stream temperatures on longitudinal distribution of fluvial Dolly Varden and potential habitat loss due to global warming . Wildlife Protection 1 (1): 1-11. (in Japanese)

Kusano, H., T. Kusano, and Y. Watanabe. 1987. Life history and reproduction of *Jesogammarus spinopulps* (Anisogrammaridae: Amphipoda) inhabiting a lowland pond in Tokyo. Japanese J. of Limnology 48: 117-126.

McCormick, M. J. 1990. Potential changes in thermal structure and cycle of Lake Michigan due to global warming. Transactions of the American Fisheries Society 119: 183-184.

Moore, M. and C. L Folt. 1993. Zooplankton body size and community structure: Effects of thermal and toxicant stress. Trends in Ecology & Evolution 8: 178-183.

Moor, M. V., C. L. Folt, and R. S. Stemberger. 1996. Consequences of elevated temperatures for zooplankton assemblages in temperate lakes. Archiv für Hydrogiologie 135: 289-319.

Nakano, S., F. Kitano and K. Maekawa. 1996. Potential fragmentation and loss of the thermal habitats for charrs in the Japanese Archipelago due to climate warming. Freshwater Biology 36: 711-722.

Nawaz, S. and K. Krick. 1995, Temperature effects on bioconcentration of DDE by Daphnia. Freshwater Biology 34: 173-178.

Okino, T. and H. Arakawa. 1994. Effects of changes of water quality on zooplankton in Lake Suwa. Annual reports on Grant of the Ministry of Education, 1994, pp.5-13. (in Japanese)

Primack, R. B. 1998. *Essentials of Conservation Biology*. 2nd ed. Sinauer Associates Inc., Sunderland, MA.

Primack, R. B. and H. Kobori. 1997. *Introduction to Conservation Biology*. Bunichi-sougou-shuppan, Tokyo. (in Japanese)

Toda, H., S. Nishizawa, M. Takahashi, and S. Ichimura. 1983. Temperature control on the post-embryonic growth of *Neomysis intermedia* Czerniawsky in a hypereutropic temperate lake. J. of Plankton Research 5: 377-392.

Toda, H., M. Takahashi, and S. Ichimura. 1984. The effect of temperature on the post-embryonic growth of *Neomysis intermedia* Czerniawsky (Crustacea, Mysidacea) under laboratory conditions. J. of Plankton Research 6: 647-662.

Chapter 18

The Influence of Global Warming on Fish

Seiichi Mori

Global warming will do more than simply increase the temperature and change the environment. The increase in temperature will not be uniform; some areas of land and sea will warm more than others. This will result in increased local differentiation in climate, as well as major changes in the amount and distribution of precipitation. In some locations, localized torrential downpours will occur on a scale that has not been previously recorded. Such extraordinarily heavy rain is expected to trigger erosion, thereby washing large amounts of earth and sand into rivers and lakes. On a local scale, this will dramatically alter the environment in which fresh water fish live.

Moreover, global warming will change the area of the sea. To take a drastic scenario, if the snow and ice which currently cover 2% of the Earth's surface were to melt, the sea level would rise by about 10 - 45 m. Consequently, the area of the sea would expand while that of freshwater would shrink significantly. This would substantially decrease the area in which freshwater fish could survive. Thus, global warming is predicted to reduce the area of fresh water and to increase the amount of erosion, thereby increasing the clouding and silting of freshwater.

Such drastic changes in the environment due to global warming would significantly affect fish. Abnormal water temperatures have been recorded in the past, although on a less significant scale than the changes forecast based on scenarios of future global warming, and are considered to have precipitated rapid changes in the distribution and population size of many species (Murawski, 1993). Therefore, some species may become extinct or suffer steep population declines. On the other hand, certain conditions favorable to the feeding and growth of fish may also be created.

Fish physiology and changes in temperature

The physiological characteristics of species are often related to the activities carried out under certain temperature conditions. A number of experiments have been conducted on how increases in temperature affect the survival, physiology, growth and sexual maturity of fish. In most of these experiments, fish placed in water at temperatures differing by 5 to 10°C are observed over a short period. In such experiments, it is difficult to forecast the long-term influence of the predicted global warming of 2 to 4°C.

Muscle function and temperature

Stress produced by extremely high or low water temperatures can be fatal for fish. In general, however, the temperature itself is not the direct cause of death. Increases in temperature within a certain range suitable for fish can affect their growth rate, primarily as a result of changes in digestive function and metabolism.

Generally, fish that can survive only a narrow range of temperature variations are more sensitive to changes in water temperature than those that can tolerate a wider temperature range. The muscle function of the former is less adaptable to changes in

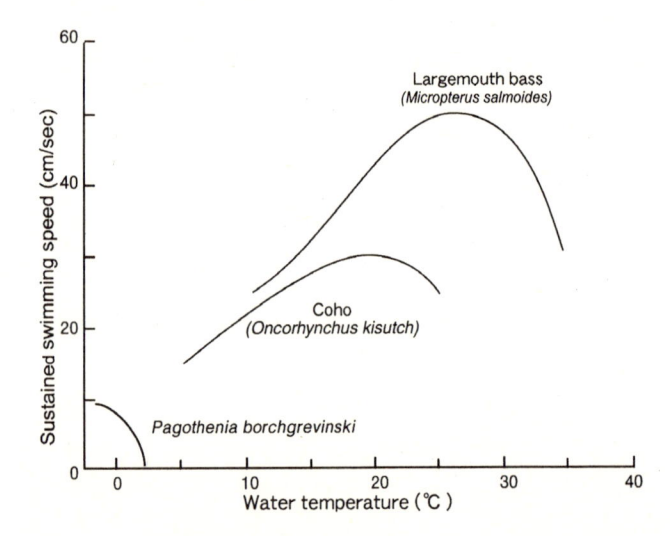

Figure 18.1.
Influence of temperature on the maximum sustainable swimming speed of fish (from Beamish, 1978).

temperature. For example, an increase of a few degrees will have a significant impact on the swimming ability of *Pagothenia borchgrevinski*, which tolerates only a very narrow temperature range of between -1.86 to 0°C. This can be compared to the largemouth bass *Micropterus salmoides*, which experiences temperatures between 4 and 30°C during the course of a year (Figure 18.1; Beamish, 1978). Reduced swimming ability due to higher temperatures will affect a fish's survival and reproduction rate by reducing its feeding ability and increasing its vulnerability to predators.

The influence of temperature on muscle function may affect fitness (the criterion of benefit over cost bestowed by natural selection on individuals) over the long term. In other words, swimming ability, which is vital for the survival of fish, is largely influenced by temperature and consequently, a fish's swimming ability is closely related to its lifestyle.

Consumption of oxygen and temperature

The metabolic cost to a fish is directly correlated with water temperature and oxygen consumption varies significantly in line with changes in temperature. Generally, oxygen consumption is lower in cold water zones. For example, the brown trout *Salmo trutta* can maintain its swimming ability even if the water temperature rises from 5°C to 15°C. In order to achieve this, however, the species' routine rate of oxygen consumption doubles. The oxygen consumption of tilapia fish increases when the water temperature rises from 12 to 34°C. These fish consume more oxygen when recovering from exhaustion than during their normal state (McKenzie et al., 1996). The sockeye *Oncorhynchus nerka* doubles its oxygen intake when water temperature rises from 5°C to 15°C (Brett, 1964). This means that the duration over which the individuals of this species can perform anaerobic burst swimming is shortened, which in turn restricts their potential for feeding and escaping predators.

The poisonous properties of heavy metals such as copper are typically correlated with temperature as they are significantly more reactive at higher temperatures. When fish are exposed to high concentrations of copper in high temperature, the cells on their gill epithelia are seriously damaged (Kirk and Lewis, 1993), and their activity is depressed.

Reproduction and temperature

Water temperature significantly influences reproduction and mating as well as gametogenesis and gamete maturation. Generally, most fish in temperate and tropical zones have a certain adaptive temperature somewhere within the range of 0°C to 30°C and spawn at slightly higher or lower temperatures. This phenomenon is related to the fact that the tolerable

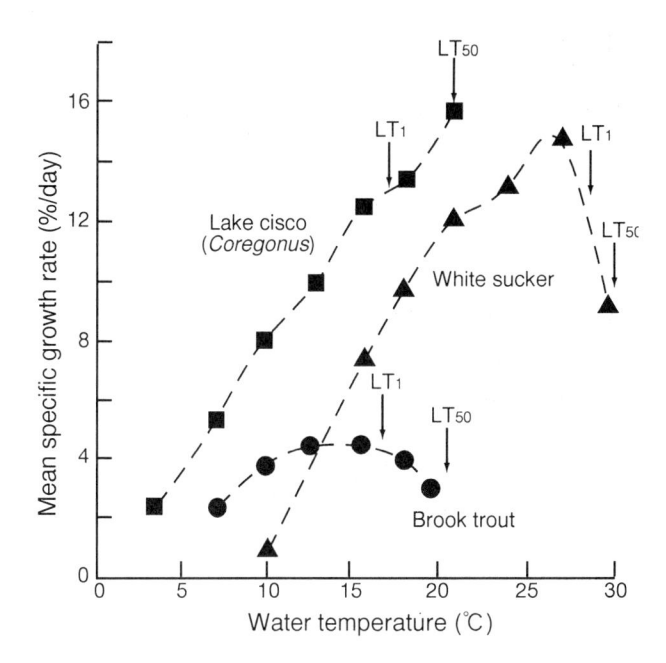

Figure 18.2.
Relationship between the average growth rate and temperature.
LT1: upper lethal threshold, LT50: temperature at which the fatality rate is 50% (from Rombough, 1997).

temperature range for eggs is approximately +/- 5°C wider than that for fish.

Increased temperature due to global warming will push up the survival rate of fish in temperate zones in winter, while it will reduce the reproduction rate of fish that require a cold period for normal gonad development. Our understanding of physiological reactions of fish to temperature that have an impact on the entire species or on populations is still limited. Furthermore, long-term surveys on the influence of changes in temperature on the reproduction and growth of fish have not yet been conducted.

Growth and temperature

Temperature has a considerable impact on the metabolic rate of fish embryos and larvae. Unlike in juveniles and adult fish, high water temperatures do not constrain the growth of larvae (Brett, 1970). Around the middle of the tolerable range is the most suitable temperature for growth of both juveniles and adult fish, and this temperature differs from one species to another. In the brook trout and the white sucker *Catostomus commersoni*, the growth rate does not begin to decline until near the upper lethal threshold, whereas the growth rate of the lake cisco *Coregonus* continues rising up to a temperature corresponding to 50% mortality (Figure 18.2;

McCormick et al., 1977).

Although growth is facilitated as the temperature rises, the growth rate peaks and starts to decline at a certain temperature. However, the factors affecting growth also include food resources, so the growth of fish cannot be discussed in terms of temperature alone.

Temperature tolerance

Most research so far carried out on the tolerance of fish to temperature has been conducted using adult fish. Natural selection, however, occurs at all stages of the life cycle, and a key to understanding the reaction of fish to the increases in temperature due to global warming may lie in research focused on the early stages of the life cycle.

Embryos and larvae are more sensitive to changes in temperature than juvenile and adult fish. Water temperature affects the metabolism of respiration, and the influence is more notable during embryo formation and the early larval periods. On average, the temperature coefficient ($Q10$) of late-stage embryos and yolk-sac larvae was 3.0, while that of juveniles and adult fish was only about 2.0 (Rombough, 1988).

The tolerable temperature range (upper lethal temperature minus lower lethal temperature) of fish in temperate zones is much narrower when embryos are formed (about 11.6°C) than during the later stages of their lives (20 to 25°C) (Figure 18.3). Embryos of temperate species are most sensitive to temperature change early in development, during cleavage and gastrulation. The capacity to tolerate temperature extremes is built up progressively as growth proceeds.

The tolerable temperature range of most species in the temperate zone changes along with their growth, and the medium temperature of the range normally shifts upwards. This is because the reproductive period of most species is in the spring when the water is warming up.

The range of tolerable temperature for tropical fish does not vary greatly. For example, in the Mozambique tilapia *Oreochromis mossambica*, the upper lethal temperature varies within a range of only about 2°C at all stages from embryo to adult. The tolerable range is almost the same at all stages of growth. This is understandable, because seasonal change in temperature is relatively small in the tropical zone.

Fisheries: the influence of climate change on cod

It is important to understand the extent to which the annual change in the volume of fish is influenced by the size of the fisheries catch and to what extent it is influenced by global warming and other environmental factors.

Cod (Family Gadidae) has been a major resource for the North Atlantic Ocean fisheries for over 500 years, and more research has been carried out on cod than on any other marine fish (Cushing, 1982). Fisheries records going back over several centuries make cod a suitable species for studying the influence of environmental changes. The total annual catch of cod in the North Atlantic Ocean started to increase in the early 20th century, reaching a peak of 460,000 tons in 1962 and steadily declining since that time. The reason for the steep reduction of cod in recent years is generally considered to be over-catching. However, if climate change accelerates, the influence of climate change is likely to become larger than that of over-catching in the decades ahead. In the event that cod has simply shifted its distribution, the catch would have been affected over the short term, but there would have been no change in the present volume.

Cod was rarely found off the western coast of Greenland during the first decade of the 20th century. After 1917, however, its distribution gradually expanded northwards. The northward expansion of cod and its increased abundance coincided with the

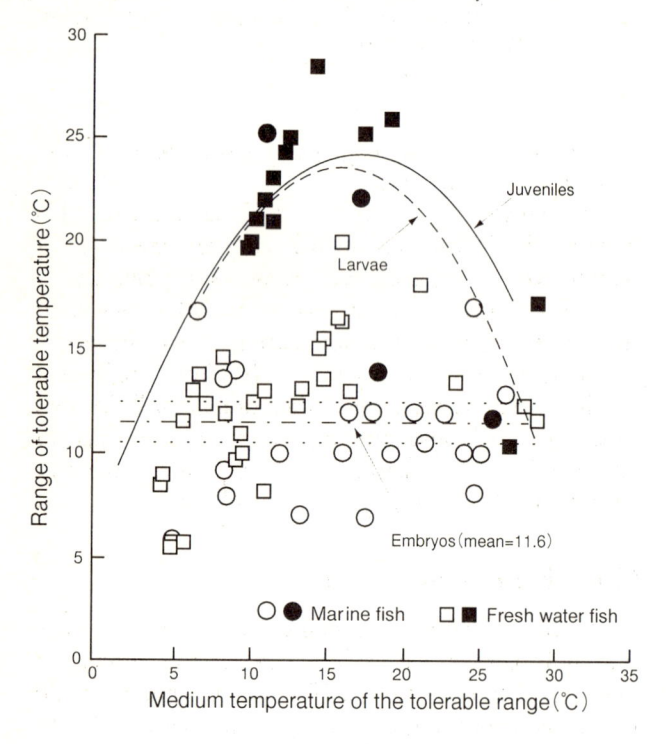

Figure 18.3.
The range of tolerable temperature (highest to lowest) of embryos (open symbols) and larvae (closed symbols), and the relationship between the range and the medium temperature of the range. Symbols for juveniles are not plotted. The range of tolerable temperature of embryos is narrow (from Rombough, 1997).

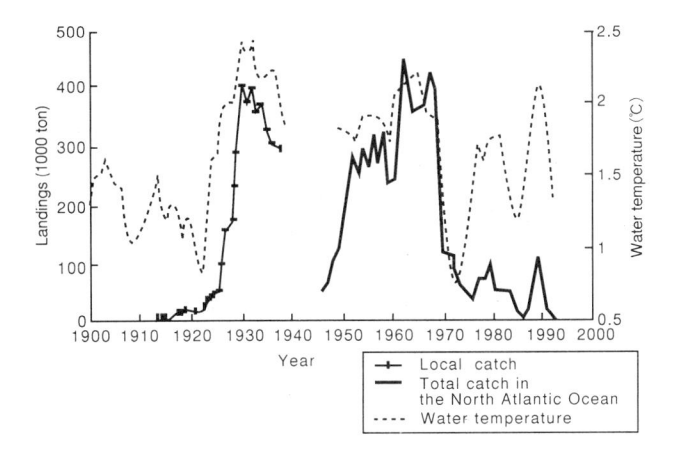

Figure 18.4.
Relationship between the West Greenland cod catch and temperature. The temperature is the five-year average temperature of the surface layer (from Brander, 1997). The catch and temperature were in direct proportion for 22 years from 1950 to 1972 ($r^2 = 0.92$). The catch volume in the region is 1/20 of the total catch in the North Atlantic Ocean.

movement of many other marine fish toward the arctic zone in the 1920s and 30s. This phenomenon occurred during a warm period that lasted until the 1960s (Figure 18.4). That is, the 45-year period in the 20th century during which cod was abundant around Greenland was a time in which the climate in the Northern Hemisphere was remarkably warm (Brander, 1997). Changes in the present volume of marine fish may be fundamentally related to changes in the deep circulation of the oceans, which is governed by density contrasts caused by temperature and salinity differences and is therefore known as a thermohaline circulation. At present, sea water in the surface layer of the ocean sinks deep below the surface in the northeastern Atlantic around Greenland. Changes in this circulation are thought to play a crucial role in global climate change.

Evolutionary time and warming

The temperature of the oceans and of freshwater on Earth has changed greatly on several occasions since their formation. In the early Cenozoic Era (65 million years ago - present time), the cod and salmon families, which are widely distributed throughout the oceans at present, first became common. At the same time, benthic fishes diversified. They have undergone a striking adaptive radiation to fill a number of ecological niches (or ecological status). Their radiation occurred because they were able to occupy a variety of habitats during the interglacials. Lack of competition due to the extinction of other species also contributed to their spread. Historically, climate change has played an important role in the evolution of fish.

During the periods of rapid cooling and warming that occurred in the past, the pace of temperature change was between one tenth and one 100th the expected rate of global warming during the 21st century. Changes in temperature in the past took place over generations and were of long enough duration to clearly affect evolution. The time required for a fish to mature is from several weeks in the case of the killifish (a freshwater fish) to between five and eight years in the case of marine fish living in cold areas. A key to the continued survival of a fish species lies in the speed of its evolution in response to temperature change. If warming takes place over a long period in medium to high latitude areas, species inhabiting these areas may become more diversified than at present. Adaptability to temperature change is the most important issue to be considered in the context of how global warming will influence fish.

The preferred temperature differs among individuals within the same species as well as between species (Coutant, 1987). Individuals of a given age that have experienced a given temperature tend to prefer a similar temperature. In species distributed widely from high to low latitudes, some populations are subject to different environments in terms of average temperature and timing of growth. In such cases, individuals living at low latitudes tend to grow more rapidly than those at high latitudes. Some species at high latitudes display growth rate compensation and grow faster than their counterparts at low latitudes. In general, however, the growth rate of freshwater fish in the temperate zone in the Northern Hemisphere is lower than that of similar individuals living further south.

Little attention has been paid so far to individual differences in temperature preferences. Individual variations were considered exceptional and the possibility that individual variations may reflect diversification through inheritance has tended to be neglected (Bennett, 1987). According to an experiment related to temperature change using three channel catfish of the same age that were raised under the same conditions, all three exhibited normal behavior but each preferred a completely different temperature (Figure 18.5). It cannot be easily determined whether this was a result of a hereditary factor or of an environmental factor. However, individual variation in terms of preferred temperature must be at least partially due to genetic variability in response to selection pressure generated by changes in temperature.

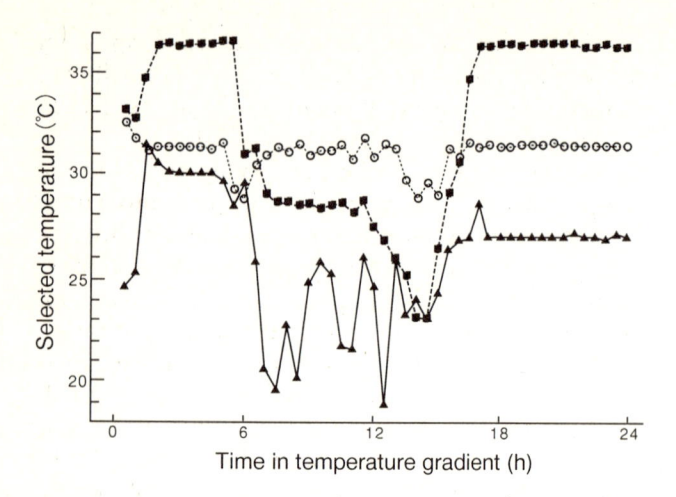

Figure 18.5.
Temperature preferred by three channel catfish of the same age raised under the same conditions (Crawshaw and O'onner, 1997).

Distribution shifts of species

Global warming models forecast that increases in water temperature will be more significant toward the polar regions (Matthews and Zimmerman, 1990). If so, species will become either locally or totally extinct around the low latitude limits of their distributions. At the same time, areas of distribution at high latitudes will shift toward polar regions. In general, the influence of global warming is predicted to be more significant in closed freshwater systems than in the oceans.

If freshwater fish living at high latitudes can migrate to new habitats, they will be able to move toward the polar regions in response to warming. It is estimated that an increase of 4°C in the water temperature will shift the distribution ranges of the smallmouth bass *Micropterus dolomieu* and the yellow perch (a species of sea bass) northward by 5° latitude, approximately 500 km (Shuter and Post, 1990). Global warming is also expected to limit the number of spawning grounds for fish of the salmon family, as well as to shift northward the northern limits of the ranges of Atlantic salmon *Salmo salar* and rainbow trout in Europe. Populations living in rivers near the northern limits of their distribution in northern Norway will increase their rates of feeding and growth, while those living near the southern limits around northern Spain and southwestern France will be threatened with extinction.

It is estimated that most freshwater fish spend two thirds of their lives within the range of +/- 4°C of their optimal temperature, and that the range of temperature over their entire life span is approximately 10°C. In order to do this, fish in lakes and rivers where water of various temperatures is available search for a temperature suitable for survival. For example, fish in rivers move upstream in summer in search of springs and cold water areas, or dive to deeper and cooler layers if these are available.

Will global warming cause extinctions?

Each species has a temperature range in which it can grow to a certain size while achieving sufficient swimming and feeding ability to maximize the hatching rate of its eggs and the survival rate of its larvae. Freshwater fish in North America are largely categorized into cold water fish, cool water fish and warm water fish according to the temperature they prefer (Hokanson, 1977). It has been estimated that the habitats available for fish in the rivers of North America will shrink by 47% in cold water areas, by 50% in cool water areas, and by 14% in warm water areas due to global warming (Figure 18.6). On the contrary, warm water fish such as bluegill *Lepomis macrochirus* and largemouth bass *Micropteris salmoides* will increase their populations as the climate warms. The populations of cold water fish and cool water fish inhabiting shallows that lack layers of different water temperature will decline. On the other hand, deep lakes will continue to be stratified and have various layers of water at differing temperatures, such that a greater variety of species can exist there including cold, cool, and warm water fish.

Cool water fish living in rivers in the mountains of

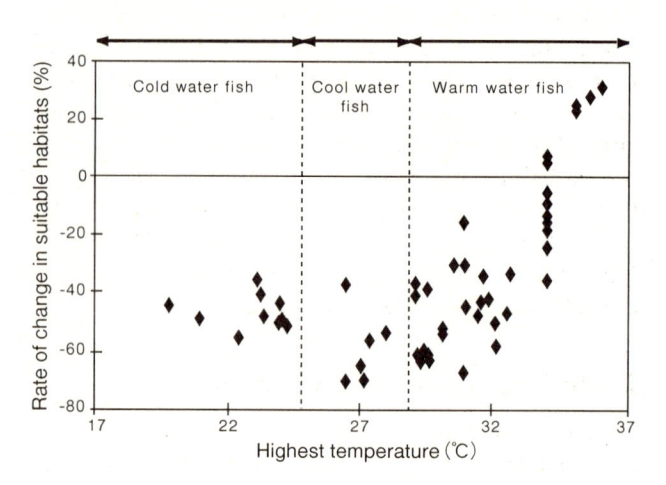

Figure 18.6.
Changes in habitats suitable for river fish in North America in response to expected warming. On average, habitat is expected to be reduced by 47% in cold water zones, by 50% in cool water zones, and by 14% in warm water zones (IPCC, 1996).

Wyoming in the United States are predicted to lose habitat due to a slight increase in water temperature. Seven to 16% of their habitats will be lost in the event of a temperature rise of 1°C, 15 - 26% with a 2°C rise, 24 - 39% with a 3°C rise, 42 - 54% with a 4°C rise, and 64 - 79% with a rise of 5°C (IPCC, 1996). Nakano et al. (1996) estimated the degree of decrease in distribution of dolly varden *Salvelinus malma* in Hokkaido and char in other parts of Japan in the case of a 1 - 4°C increase in annual average temperature. According to their research, the degree of decrease is significant not only in the southern part of their distribution but also in low altitude areas. Populations that survive in the remaining habitats will be subject to the specific conditions of each location. In any case, there will be a higher probability of extinction due to disturbances in the ecosystem.

Fish living in water that undergoes large temperature changes on a daily or seasonal basis in the temperate zone or near the seashore usually experience temperature changes of several degrees within a short period. For example, fish in the open sea stay in a cool water layer during the day and rise vertically to a warmer layer in the evening. Moreover, the killifish *Fundulus* living in salty swamps in North America experiences from 12°C at high tide to approximately 30°C at low tide on a hot early summer day (Sidell et al., 1983). Some species in small ponds also live in an environment in which the temperature changes by more than 20°C on a daily or seasonal basis.

Some fish hibernate when the temperature is low, and many kinds of fish can adjust to wider temperature ranges in order to survive. The relatively small changes in temperature expected to occur due to global warming will not have a significant impact on the swimming ability or other aspects of the lives of such fish.

Global warming may neither bring about the worst case scenario, the extinction or drastic reduction of entire populations, nor have significant impacts on fish. On the contrary, the higher temperatures may actually be favorable for fish. If there is enough food, the distribution ranges of fish may not shift toward the polar regions but rather expand as a result of global warming. It has been pointed out that at least in the initial phase of global warming, populations of relic species such as those of lake cisco, whose larvae grow faster at higher temperatures, may increase (Trippel et al., 1991). Increased winter temperatures will probably increase the survival rate of fish in temperate zones in winter. According to climate change scenarios where warming will be more significant in winter than in summer, this is expected to have a very significant impact on the survival rates of fish both at high and low latitudes.

Case study: Fish in spring-fed waterbodies

In spring-fed waterbodies in which the temperature and other environmental factors are stable throughout the year, fish have a unique ecology. They can adapt only to very small changes in temperature. Therefore, changes in temperature, however small, will have a disproportionately large effect. One of those is the *leiurus* form (low-plated morph) of the threespine stickleback *Gasterosteus aculeatus* found mainly in spring-fed waterbodies in Japan.

The *leiurus* form of the threespine stickleback occurs naturally only in northeast Shiga Prefecture and southwest Gifu Prefecture. It is designated as critically endangered by the Environment Agency. Fish of the Family Gasterosteidae are originally from the north and are found widely at high latitudes in the Northern Hemisphere. The distribution range in Japan forms one of the southernmost habitats (35° north latitude) of the distribution of the family (Mori, 1997). The distribution range of this species used to include the largest spring-fed waterbodies in Japan and still is largely confined to "spring-fed ecosystems" Its distribution range corresponds almost totally to the locations of spring-fed waterbodies at elevations of from several meters to 20 m above sea level around the northwest Nobi Plain. (Figure 18.7).

For the threespine stickleback to survive in these areas, it is crucial that the water temperature in spring-fed waterbodies not exceed 20°C in summer (Mori, 1994). Because the water temperature around the mid-reaches of the main streams in this region usually approaches 30°C in summer, the threespine stickleback cannot survive there. Water temperature in summer is, therefore, a problem for this species. In addition, males of the species build nests for reproduction, so conditions at the nesting ground also greatly affect the reproductive success of this species (Mori, 1993, 1995).

Generally, the temperature of spring-fed waterbodies is almost the same as the annual average temperature of the area. The water temperature of the springs in which the threespine stickleback live is about 15°C. Its reproduction can be observed throughout the year, although it peaks around late April to early May. In springs with stable water temperatures, year-round reproduction of this fish is observed (Mori, 1985). Eighty percent of the nests built by this species are located in water within the temperature range of 14 to 18°C.

If the atmospheric temperature rises by 2°C due to global warming, leading to a similar rise in the water temperature of the springs within a short period, the number of nests built by the threespine stickleback will drastically decline. Consequently, its population will decline and its distribution range will be further fragmented. If the temperature rises by 5°C, the water

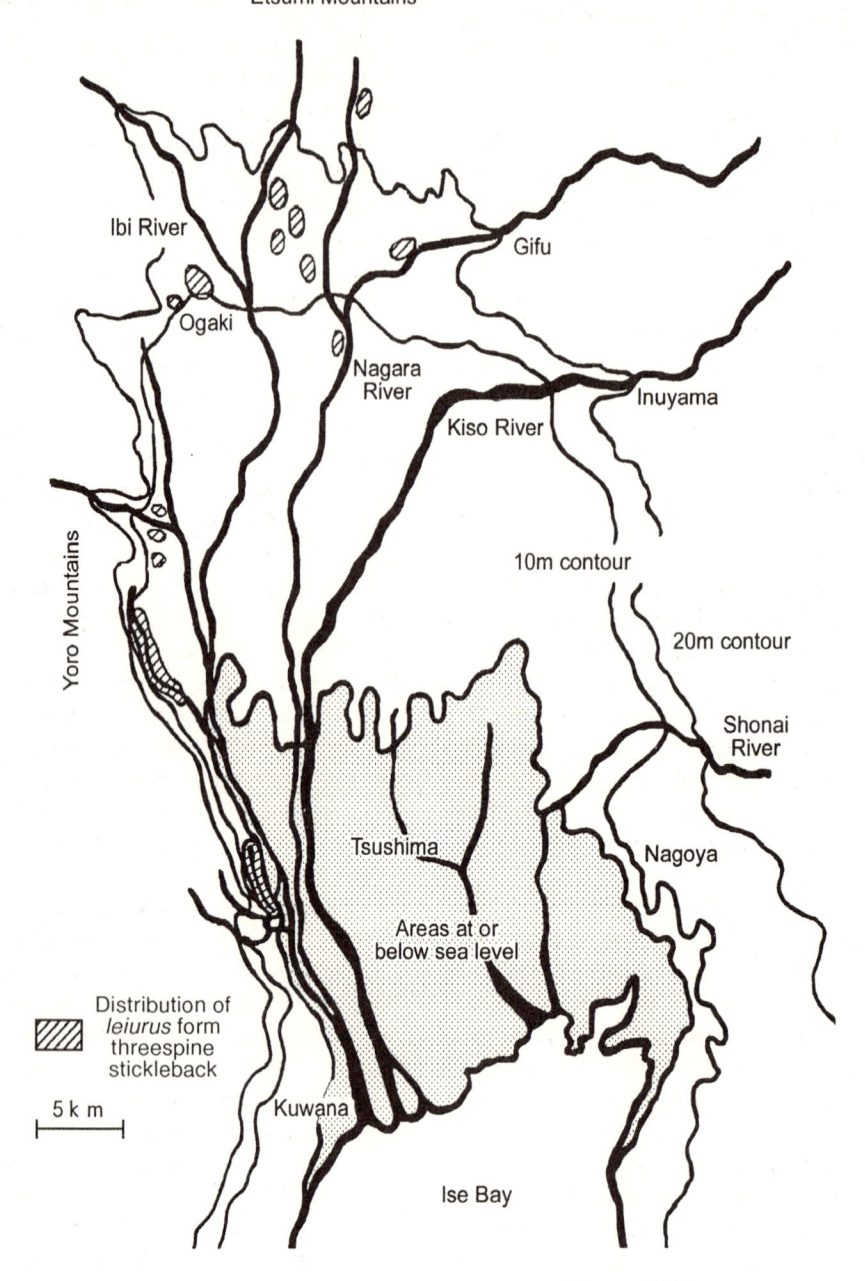

Figure 18.7.
Distribution of the *leiurus* form of threespine stickleback in the Nobi Plain during the 1970s. The shaded area is at or below sea level.

temperature in the springs will exceed the range for nest building. The threespine stickleback will not be able to find a suitable temperature for reproduction and will cease year-round reproduction (Figure 18.8). Calculating from these assumptions, the number of annual nest buildings will decline by three quarters, leading to a rapid decline in the population. The possibility of extinction of the threespine stickleback will then arise.

Influence of transgressions on freshwater fish distribution

The transgression of the sea which occurred several thousand years ago is known in Japan as the Jomon transgression as it took place during the Jomon Period of Japanese prehistory (about 6,000 BC to 300 BC). By some accounts, the sea level rose to a maximum of about 8 m above its present level. As a result, most of Japan's lowland plains were submerged. What was the

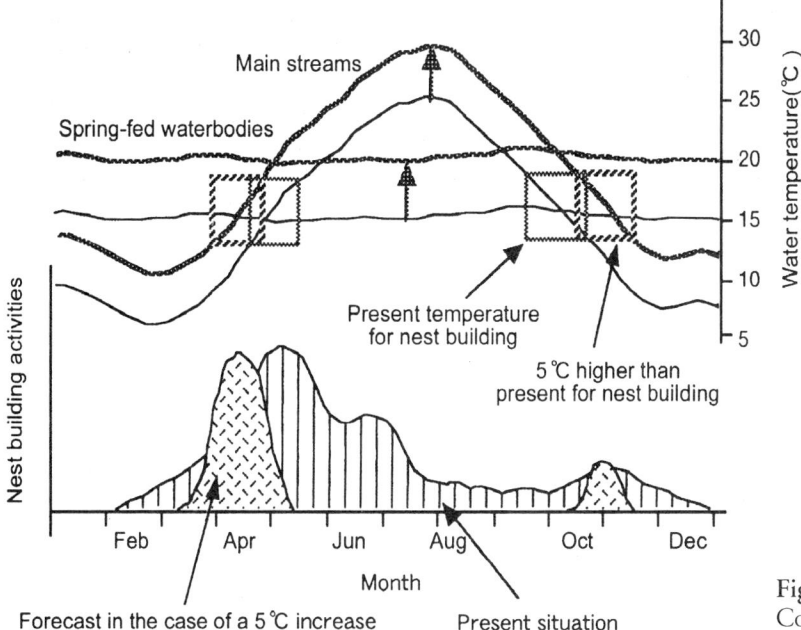

Figure 18.8.
Comparison of annual nest building activities at present water temperature and at 5°C higher in spring-fed waterbodies and main streams.

distribution of freshwater fish in those days?

The Nobi Plain is an alluvial plain formed by three large rivers, the Kiso River, the Nagara River, and the Ibi River. Of the entire area of the plain lying at an elevation of 10 m or less above sea level, approximately 30% consists of riverside areas at or below sea level (Figure 18.7). Fish of the temperate zone such as those of the Family Cyprinidae, including species of carp and loach, are abundant in this area. Migratory fish such as the red-spot masu salmon *Salmo masou macrostomus*, sweetfish (ayu fish) *Plecoglossus altivelis*, and eel *Anguilla japonica* are also found here. If the existing banks did not exist and the sea level rose by about 70 cm above its current level due to global warming, the habitats of these fish would be submerged beneath the sea. Even if there were no dams or weirs, it would be difficult for these fish to migrate upstream. Fresh water would mix with sea water even in the upper reaches of the rivers and the area of brackish water would expand, reducing the habitats of fish stricken fresh water. However, red-spot masu salmon, which lives only in the upper reaches, the Chinese minnow and other species of the Family Cyprinidae that live in cool water, and species of the Family Gobiidae would not be significantly affected by a 70 cm transgression.

Global warming is expected to result in increased evaporation and precipitation. This may lead to unusually large-scale flooding of rivers in this area. Consequently, large amounts of earth and sand may be washed away, significantly altering the living environment of freshwater fish. This will be clearly observable in Japan, a mountainous country with a number of rivers with steep gradients. Sediment produced from earth and sand is expected to fill the spaces on river banks and between stones, drastically reducing the number of sites available for fish to live and reproduce. Benthic fishes such as species of the Families Gobiidae and Cottidae, as well as eels and the bullhead which hide under stones, will be especially disadvantaged. Moreover, the flooding of rivers will lead to buildups of sediment around the mouths of rivers and along coasts. As a result, the ecosystems of these areas will be altered with repercussions for the fish living there.

Perspectives: Diversification and global warming

Species are usually more diversified at lower latitudes than at higher latitudes. This tendency is related to temperature change with latitude. In North America, the diversity of fish in areas between two lines of latitude and two lines of longitude has been found to be more closely related to climatic factors than to latitude and longitude. The level of diversity increases in line with temperature and drops as the climate becomes dryer. Taken together, however, temperature and precipitation explain only 38% of the distribution patterns of species (IPCC, 1996). A broad perspective does not yield enough information or knowledge concerning the long-term influence of global warming on the biological diversity in specific waterbodies. If qualitative research on the influence of climate warming on living things is to be conducted, the ecology of local species and shoals should be examined so that useful information can be obtained.

There is a considerable body of work regarding whether certain species or individuals in certain locations will become extinct, but research is rarely conducted on how relationships between different species in a certain place would be affected by the extinction of one or more local species. Ecological analysis of the dynamic relationships among species within local ecosystems, for example, relationships between predator and prey species, will be important in the context of global warming (Blaxter, 1992). We must stop limiting our discussions to generalities and start summarizing specifics so that we will be better able to produce and propose concrete principles and measures.

References

Beamish, F. W. H. 1978. Swimming capacity. In: (W. S. Hoar and D. J. Randall, eds.) *Fish Physiology*. Pp.101-187. Academic Press, New York.

Bennett, A. F. 1987. Interindividual variability: an underutilised resource. In: (M. D. Feder, A. F. Bennett, W. W. Burggren, and R. B. Huey, eds.) *New Directions in Ecological Physiology*. Pp.147-169. Cambridge University Press, Cambridge.

Blaxter, J. H. S. 1992. The effect of temperature on larval fishes. Netherlands J. of Zoology 42: 336-357.

Brander, K. M. 1997. Effect of climate change on cod (*Gadus morhua*) stocks. In: (C. M. Wood and D. G. McDonald, eds.) *Global Warming: Implications for Freshwater and Marine Fish*. Pp.225-253. Cambridge University Press, Cambridge.

Brett, J. R. 1964. The respiratory metabolism and swimming performance of young sockeye salmon. J. Fish. Res. Bd. Canada 21: 1183-1226.

Brett, J. R. 1970. Temperature - fishes. In: (O. Kinne, ed.) *Marine Ecology. Vol. I. Environmental Factors*, Part I. Pp.515-560. Willey-Interscience, London.

Coutant, C. C. 1987. Poor reproductive success of striped bass form a reservoir with reduced summer habitat. Transactions of the American Fisheries Society 116: 154-160.

Crawshaw, L. I. and C. S. O'donnor. 1997. Behavioural compensation for long-term thermal change. In: (C. M. Wood and D. G. McDonald, eds.) *Global Warming: Implications for Freshwater and Marine Fish*. Pp. 351-376. Cambridge Univ. Press.

Cushing, D. H. 1982. *Climate and Fisheries*. Academic Press, London.

Hokanson, K. E. F. 1977. Temperature requirements of some percids and adaptations to the seasonal temperature cycle. J. Fish. Res. Bd. Canada 34: 1524-1550.

IPCC 1996. *Climate Change 1995*. Cambridge University Press, Cambridge.

Kirk, R. S. and J. W. Lewis. 1993. An evaluation of pollutant induced changes in the gills of rainbow trout using scanning electron microscopy. Environmental Technology 14: 577-585.

Matthews, W. J. and E. G. Zimmerman. 1990. Potential effects of global warming on native fishes of the southern Great Plains and the southwest. Fisheries 15: 26-32.

McKenzie, D. J., G. Serrini, G. Piraccini, P. Bronzi, and C. L. Bolis. 1996. Effects of diet on response to exhaustive exercise in Nile tilapia (*Oreochromis nilotica*) acclimated to three different temperatures. Comparative Biochemistry & Physiology 114A: 43-50.

McCormick, J. H., B. R. Jones and K. E. F. Hokanson. 1977. White sucker (*Catostomus commersoni*) embryo development, early growth and survival at different temperatures. J. Fish. Res. Bd. Canada 34: 1019-1025.

Meissner, J. K. 1990. Potential loss of thermal habitat for brook trout, due to climatic warming, in two southern Ontario streams. Transactions of the American Fisheries Society 119: 282-291.

Mori, S. 1985. Reproductive behaviour of the landlocked three-spined stickleback in Japan. Behaviour 93: 21-35.

Mori, S. 1993. The breeding system of the three-spined stickleback with reference to spatial and temporal patterns of nesting activity. Behaviour 126: 97-124.

Mori, S. 1994. Nest site choice by the freshwater three-spined stickleback. J. Fish Biology 45: 279-289.

Mori, S. 1995. Spatial and temporal variations in nesting success and the causes of nest losses of the freshwater three-spined stickleback. Environmental Biology of Fishes 43: 323-328.

Mori, S. 1997. *The Streams of Sticklebacks: Conservation of the Freshwater Environment.* Chuko Shinsho, Chuo Koronsha, Tokyo. (in Japanese)

Murawski, S. A. 1993. Climate change and marine fish distributions: forecasting from historical analogy. Transactions of the American Fisheries Society 122: 647-658.

Nakano, S., F. Kitano, and K. Maekawa. 1996. Potential fragmentation and loss of thermal habitats for charrs in the Japanese archipelago due to climate warming. Freshwater Biology 36: 711-722.

Rombough, P. J. 1997. The effects of temperature on embryonic and larval development. In: (C. M. Wood and D. G. McDonald, eds.) *Global Warming: Implications for Freshwater and Marine Fish.* Pp.177-223. Cambridge Univ. Press.

Rombough, P. J. 1988. Respiratory gas change, aerobic metabolism, and effects of hypoxia during early life. In: (W. S. Hoar and D. J. Randall, eds.) *Fish Physiology, Vol. XIA.* Pp.59-161. Academic Press.

Shuter, B. J. and J. R. Post. 1990. Climate, population viability and the zoogeography of temperate fishes. Transactions of the American Fisheries Society 119: 316-336.

Sidell, B. D., I. A. Johnston, T. S. Moerland, and G. Goldspink. 1983. The eurythermal myofibrillar complex of the mummichog (*Fundulus heteroclitus*): adaptations to a fluctuating thermal environment. J. of Comparative Physiology B 153: 167-173.

Trippel, E. A., R. Eckmann, and J. Hartmann. 1991. Potential effects of global warming on whitefish in Lake Constance, Germany. Ambio. 20: 226-231.

Chapter 19

The Impact of Global Warming on Sea Turtles

Naoki Kamezaki

Sea turtles in Japanese waters

According to fossil records, the ancestors of today's sea turtles became adapted to different environments during the Cretaceous Period (146 to 65 million years ago) and in so doing branched out into a large number of different species. The majority of those species are now extinct; only two families containing seven species remain. Fossils of turtles from the still existing genera *Caretta* and *Chelonia* have been found in Cretaceous Period strata in North America and Europe, indicating the extraordinary length of these animals' history.

A hundred million years of climatic change and continental drift-induced topographical change no doubt helped bring about both the appearance of new species and the extinction of established ones that were no longer able to adapt. It is also thought that along with shifts in climate and topography came competition between turtle species and between turtles and other animals over food and habitat. This competition altered interrelationships within ecosystems and eventually led to the extinction of some species.

Excluding Kemp's ridley *Lepidochelys kempii* and the Flatback turtle *Natator depressus* whose distributions are limited to the Caribbean Sea and the coastal waters of northern Australia respectively, the remaining five species of turtle are widely distributed throughout the Indian and Pacific Oceans, the Atlantic Ocean, and the Mediterranean Sea. These five species differ in terms of both habitat and preferred diet, thereby avoiding competition with each other. For instance, while both the Green turtle *Chelonia mydas* and the Hawksbill turtle *Eretmochelys imbricata* inhabit tropical waters, the former is herbivorous while the latter feeds on sponges. This seems to indicate that these highly migratory species, which were able to spread quickly throughout tropical and temperate waters, overwhelmed and drove competitor species to extinction. As such, it can be argued that the remaining five species - which, as indicated above, have different habitats and diets and are therefore relatively mutually uncompetitive - are stable in evolutionary terms.

Present day sea turtles appear to have strong adaptive capabilities and would not seem to be threatened by extinction. However, as a result of recent human activities, the populations of all sea turtle species are declining. According to the IUCN Red List (1996) *E. imbricata* and *L. kempii* are listed as critically endangered, the Loggerhead turtle *Caretta caretta* as well as *C. mydas*, the Olive ridley *L. olivacea*, and *Dermochelys coriacea* are endangered, and *N. depressus* is vulnerable. In other words, all of these sea turtles are in danger of extinction.

The distribution of sea turtles in Japanese waters

Because the Kuroshio Current brings a constant stream of warm water past the Pacific Coast of Japan, all five species can be seen in Japanese waters. In particular, *C. caretta*, *C. mydas* and *E. imbricata* use the Japanese coast as mesting sites (Figures 19.1, 19.2). Furthermore, the southern coastal areas of Japan, particularly the shallow seas around the Nansei Islands, are known to serve as habitats of young *C. mydas* and *E. imbricata* individuals. The following section briefly discusses the habitat of each turtle species.

The loggerhead turtle *Caretta caretta*. *C. caretta* is the most representative of Japan's sea turtles. The diet of *C. caretta* is comprised of molluscs, hermit crabs and other benthos. The breeding areas of this species include the coastal areas of southern Japan, northeastern Australia, Oman, the eastern coast of South Africa, Brazil, and the southeastern coastline of the United States. As Japan and Australia are *C. caretta*'s only Pacific breeding areas, Japan is of particular importance to this species. It was recently found that the populations of *C. caretta* that breed in Japan and Australia are genetically distinct, a discovery that reinforces the importance of Japan for this species (Bowen et al., 1994).

The green sea turtle *Chelonia mydas*. The principle breeding grounds of *C. mydas* are in the Indian and Pacific Oceans, as well as in the tropical waters of the Atlantic. In Japan, *C. mydas* nests on the Ogasawara Islands and the Nansei Islands. The meat of this herbivorous turtle has historically been used for food in many parts of the world, including the Ogasawara Islands.

The hawksbill turtle *Eretmochelys imbricata*. The primary habitats of *Eretmochelys imbricata* are in areas of well-developed coral reefs, and its breeding areas are on the islands scattered among these coral seas. In Japan, *E. imbricata* only breeds south of Ryukyu Islands. In addition, the coral reefs of the Nansei Islands provide an important environment for its young to grow to adulthood. The shells of *E. imbricata* are used for tortoise-shell craftwork in Japan. This is one of the primary reasons for the decline in *E. imbricata* populations.

Olive ridley and leatherback turtles. None of these *L. olivacea* and *Dermochelys coriacea* breed in Japan. The closest breeding areas are Malaysia for the former and Malaysia and Papua New Guinea for the latter. On rare occasions, there are reports of individual turtles from these species being caught in fishermen's nets near Japanese waters.

Population changes

One of the methods used for studying changes in sea turtle populations is to count the number of turtles that nest on particular beaches. Relative changes in turtle populations are ascertained by counting either the number of nesting or emerging turtles. In Japan, local volunteers living near nesting beaches have been doing these counts, some since 1950 (Kamezaki and Matsui, 1997). Counts of *C. caretta* populations have been carried out over extended periods in the following areas: Inakahama Beach (Yakushima Island), Miyazaki Beach, Ohama and Kamouda Beaches (Tokushima), Senri Beach (Wakayama), and Omaezaki Beach (Shizuoka).

Sea turtles nest several times per season; thus, it is estimated that the actual number of female sea turtles is between a third and half the number of nests per season. Sea turtles frequently come ashore and then return to the sea without nesting, so the nesting number is smaller than the emergence number. Whether or not a turtle will succeed in nesting depends on several factors, including the ease with which a nest hole can be dug in the sand and the quietness of the beach. It is difficult to estimate the nesting number from the emergence number, but the latter is still a good indicator of population changes.

The records kept of *C. caretta* nesting on Ohama

Figure 19.1.
The three species of turtle that breed in Japan (top: *Caretta caretta*, middle: *Chelonia mydas*, bottom: *Eretmochelys imbricata*).

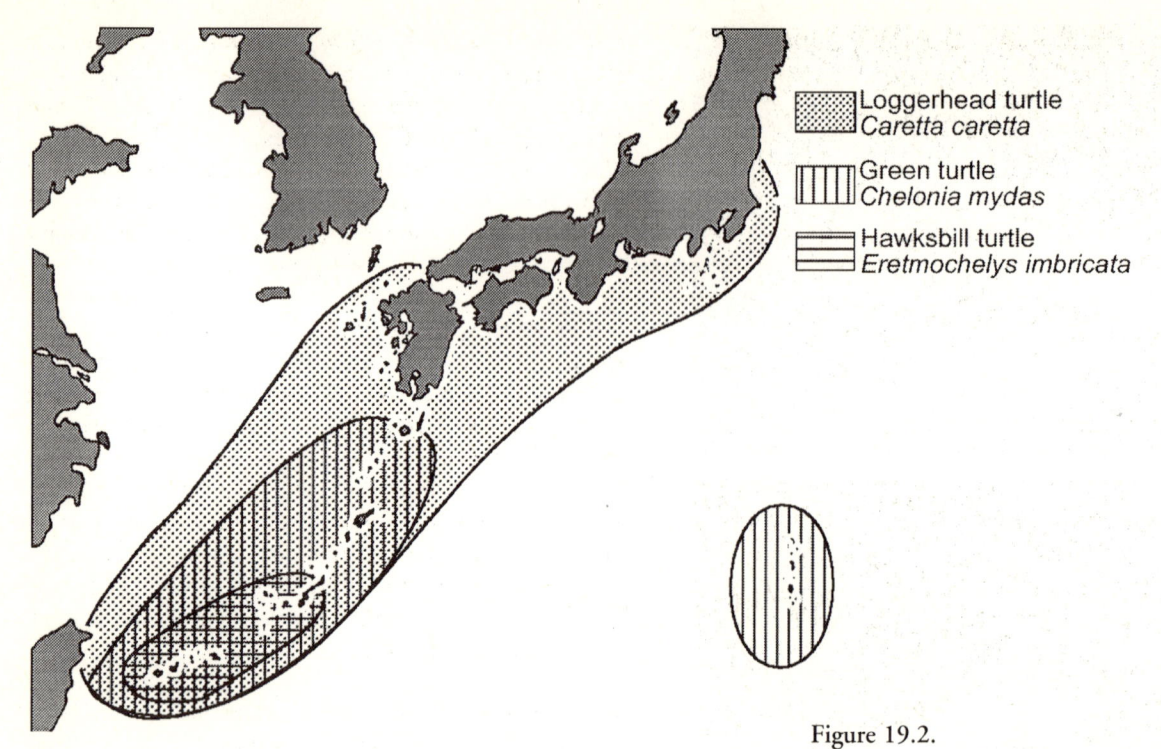

Figure 19.2.
Distribution of nesting beaches in three sea turtle species.

and Kamouda Beaches (Tokushima Prefecture) are the world's longest. Season-to-season fluctuations have been significant for both areas since the 1970s, with the emergence numbers fluctuating between 20 and 300. However, records from the late 1950s to 1970 for Kamouda Beach show that the number of turtles emerging was far higher than at present; during some seasons more than 600 sightings were recorded (Figure 19.3). These precious records show that many more *C. caretta* individuals visited this beach in the past than do now. On the other hand, there is no significant difference in the number of sightings now and the numbers recorded in the 1950s for Ohama Beach.

Since the 1970s, records have been kept along the coast of Miyazaki and at Omaezaki Beach in Shizuoka. Records for Inakahama Beach on Yakushima Island and Senri Beach in Wakayama have been kept since the 1980s. In Figure 19.4, which plots the data for these four locations, it is not possible to detect a downward trend for the 1970s and 1980s. However, since 1990 the number of turtle emergences and nestings have decreased at all locations. Moreover, the 1997 season witnessed the lowest numbers of turtles at most nesting sites in the country since records began. The Japan Sea Turtle Conference reported that in 1996, a total of 2,329 nests were counted in Japan. If we assume that the average female nested 2.5 times in a season, this means that only 932 *C. caretta* females nested in Japan in 1996.

The *C. caretta* population which breeds in Japan is in critical condition.

The effects of global warming

This section will look at the effects that global warming is projected to have on sea turtles. The

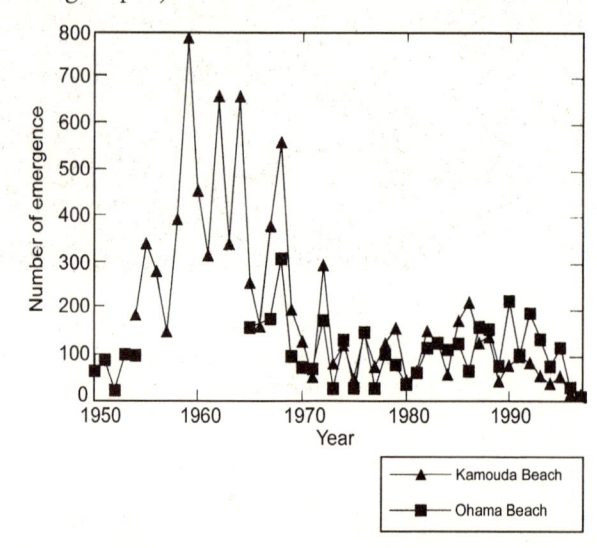

Figure 19.3.
Changes in the number of emergences of *Caretta caretta* females at Ohama Beach and Kamouda Beach, Tokushima Prefecture, Shikoku.

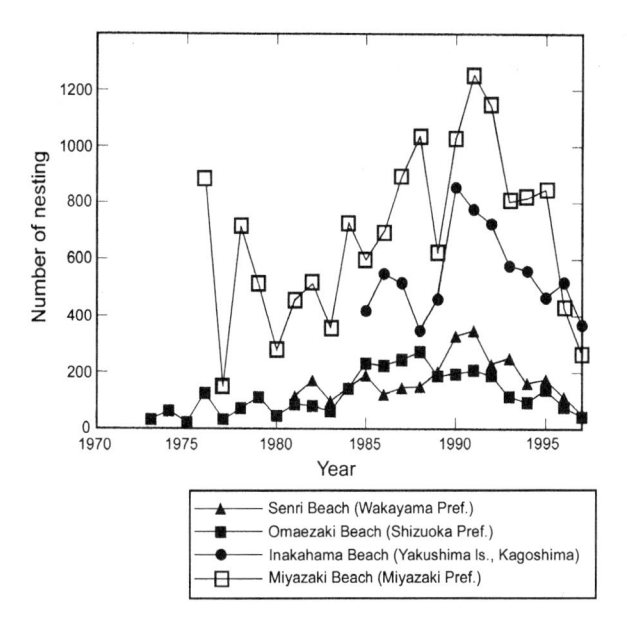

Figure 19.4.
Changes in number of nests at four beaches. The figure for Miyazaki Beach is an estimate based on the density of nests. Data were obtained from the Yakushima Sea Turtle Research Group, Miyazaki Wild Animal Research Society, Hiwasa Sea Turtle Museum, Kamouda Elementary School, Minabe Sea Turtle Research Group, and Omaezaki-Town Education Committee.

following are anticipated to be the most important effects:
1) Changes in the sex ratio of hatching turtles caused by increasing sand temperatures.
2) Decreasing beach areas for breeding due to rising sea level.
3) Changes in turtle life cycles caused by changes in climate and ocean currents due to higher temperatures.

It is very difficult to predict what effect global warming will have on turtles given what we now know about climate change and turtle ecology. However, bearing in mind the endangered status of turtles in recent years, the following section presents a worst case scenario.

Changing sex ratios

The sex of many turtles, including the Leatherback (Family Dermochelydae) and the six species of sea turtle (Family Cheloniidae), is determined by the temperature during embryonic development. The TSD (Thermal Dependence of Sex Determination) in sea turtles was only established in the 1980s (see Mrosovsky 1994 as review).

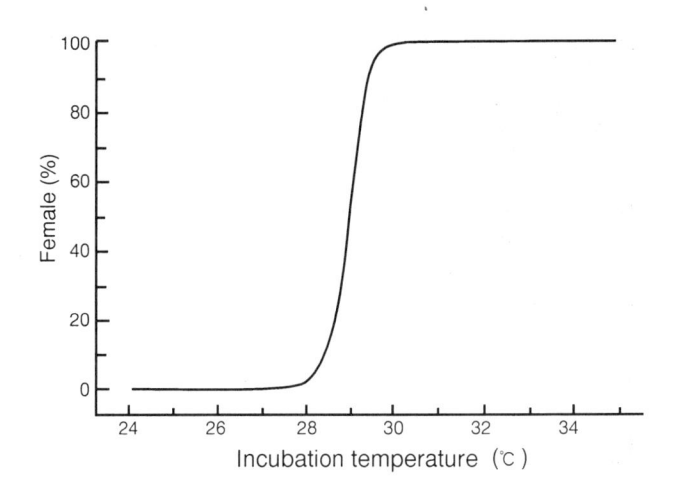

Figure 19.5.
Relationship between temperature during development and female percentage of *Caretta caretta* hatchlings (Kamezaki and Kuroyanagi, 1991).

For sea turtles, the pivotal temperature is approximately 29°C. At temperatures above 29°C, females tend to predominate. The opposite is true at temperatures below 29°C (Figure 19.5). This phenomenon has been experimentally documented in Japan for both *C. caretta* and *C. mydas*. The fact that temperature affects the sex ratio of hatchlings has also been found to hold true under natural conditions. In a study by Kuroyanagi and Kamezaki (unpubl. data), turtles that hatched during the relatively cool summer of 1993 on the beaches of the Atsumi Peninsula in Aichi were all found to be male, while hatchlings from the same place during the hot summer of 1994 were all female. Furthermore, due to temperature changes in the sand during the 1991 season, turtles that emerged from eggs deposited earlier in the season were all male, while eggs laid late in the season (in July) produced mostly females.

These findings indicate that changes in sand temperatures significantly affect the sex ratio of hatchlings in natural populations. Thus, it appears that global warming will affect the sex ratios of sea turtles and lead to a higher proportion of females in the population.

Decreasing beach area due to sea level rise

C. caretta comes ashore, digs a 40 - 60 cm deep nest chamber, and deposits its eggs. *C. mydas* excavates an even deeper nest chamber. Because the development of the embryo stops if the egg comes into contact with sea water, sea turtles require beaches where areas of sand at least 60 cm in depth exist above the high tide level. In recent years, the narrowing of

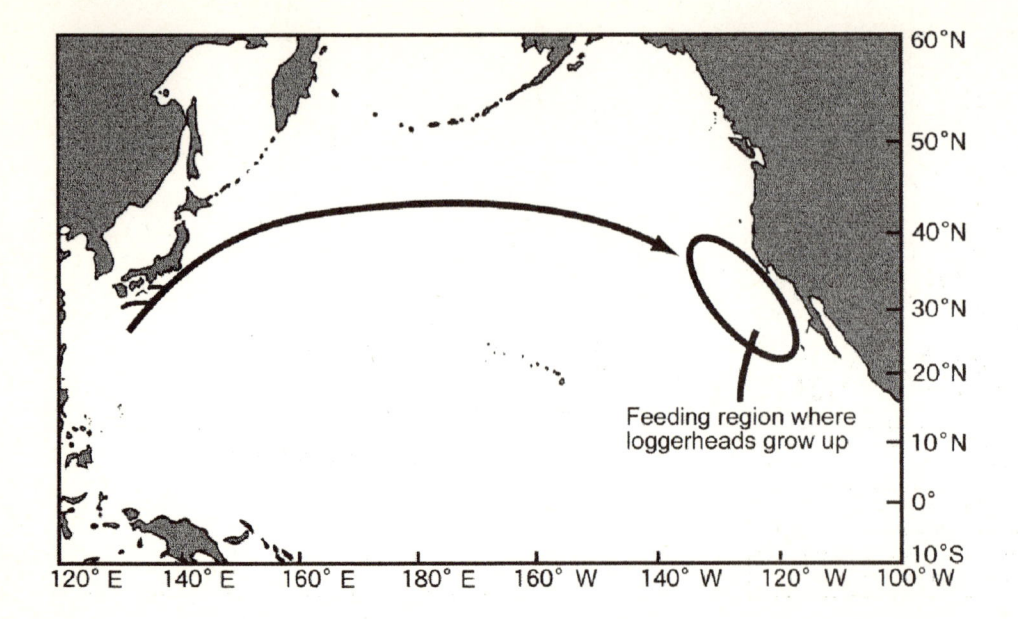

Figure 19.6.
Estimated migration route of *Caretta caretta* born in Japan.

beaches due to sand loss has become a serious problem for nesting on the beaches of Yakushima Island, Miyazaki, Wakayama, and Shizuoka. A number of factors have contributed to this problem, including a reduction in the sand supplied to beaches due to dams on rivers that feed into the sea, the removal of sand from shallows or river estuaries for construction purposes, and increasing construction around harbors and jetties that inhibits the natural flow of currents. The resulting sand reduction is leading to a decrease in the area of beaches suitable for nesting by sea turtles. At the same time, it is also encouraging the building of shore protection works on the inland side of beaches. As a consequence of the anticipated global warming-induced sea level rise, beaches already narrowed by sand loss and inshore coastal protection works will be narrowed still further.

Undoubtedly, increased losses of beach sand will lead to coastal protection plans. These will include the construction of sea walls designed to control currents and bring about the accumulation of more sand on beaches. Using this method, some beaches will see greater sand accumulation. However, for those sandy beaches used by sea turtles for breeding purposes, this solution is too simplistic. First, coastal protection works erected in shallow waters off the coast could become an obstacle for turtles trying to reach the beaches upon which they nest. Furthermore, it is likely that the artificial beaches created will not be suitable for turtles to use.

If you were to dig a hole similar to a turtle's nest chamber at a beach frequented by turtles, you would notice the ease with which this task can be accomplished. Beaches used by turtles for nesting usually face the open sea and are characterized by thick deposits of loose sand. Furthermore, the sand usually contains little clay or organic material and is very beautiful. This type of sand accumulation is suggestive of a beach that is being continuously destroyed and rebuilt. If one observes a sandy beach for a year, one will see that its shape changes profoundly as typhoons sweep away huge quantities of sand. However, over time the wind and the waves will usually return it to its former shape. In other words, the types of beaches suitable for turtles are not those that are perpetually stable but those that are dynamic, where the sand is washed away and then re-accumulated over and over again. It is a tragic mistake to think that by simply protecting beaches we are also protecting turtle breeding areas.

If global warming continues, the number of beaches where sea turtles can breed will decline. No simple solution to this problem exists.

The effect of changes in climate and currents

Global warming will precipitate changes in both the climate and in the flow of ocean currents. In particular, changes in the latter will greatly influence the life cycle of sea turtles. It is expected that global warming will alter the flow of the Kuroshio and Kuril Currents, which will in turn affect the living creatures that depend on these currents. Exactly how will changes in ocean currents affect sea turtles?

Figure 19.7.
Nesting beaches of sea turtles. The upper beach (Iriomote Island) is backed by vegetation. Note the tracks of sea turtles into the vegetation. The lower beach (Atsumi Peninsula) is backed by concrete blocks.

As soon as hatchlings emerge from the sand on a beach, they head towards the sea and disperse. As their ability to swim is limited, much of their time is spent floating on the surface of the ocean. Therefore, the movement of young turtles is largely dependent on ocean currents. The Kuroshio Current flows past the Japanese breeding grounds of *C. caretta*. Any changes in this current are likely to have a significant impact on *C. caretta* individuals. To examine this problem more deeply, it is important to understand where the young of *C. caretta* go after they hatch. Fortunately, recent research has shed much light on the life cycle of Japan's *C. caretta* population.

Although adults can be seen in Japan's coastal waters at certain times of the year, in the winter they completely disappear. In other words, Japan is a breeding area for the northern Pacific population of *C. caretta*, but outside of the breeding season the turtles live elsewhere. *C. caretta* individuals with carapaces measuring 20 - 50 cm are occasionally caught in nets and long lines off the southern end of the Aleutian Archipelago and northern Hawaii. It is also known that many juvenile *C. caretta* individuals live in the waters off Baja California in Mexico. Mitochondrial DNA testing has shown that most of these turtles were born in Japan (Bowen et al., 1995). In short, young *C. caretta* individuals are carried by the Kuroshio and later the North Pacific Current and in the process are dispersed widely throughout the Pacific. Some of these turtles travel over 10,000 km, cross the Pacific and grow to maturity in the rich waters off the coast of Mexico where food is abundant (Figure 19.6). Although the details of the migration of the Northern Pacific *C. caretta* population are unknown, it is clear that whether or not they end up in hospitable environments depends on the currents. Given that we do not know the details of this species' movements or their development into adulthood, and that we also do not know what the precise effect of global warming will be on the ocean currents, predicting the effect of climate change on these animals is impossible. Nevertheless, there can be no doubt that changes in ocean currents will have a profound effect on the early stages of the turtles' life cycles.

The future of sea turtles

So far this chapter has discussed the anticipated influence of global warming on turtles in terms of the disruption of sex ratios, the loss of beaches used for breeding, and the changes in the ocean currents that control the destiny of these animals. On the basis of these three factors alone, the future of sea turtles appears a tragic one. However, global warming by itself will not bring about the extinction of any species of turtle. If one or more species do become extinct, this will be due not to global warming but to specific human activities. This is because all the existing species of turtles have survived over an immensely long period of geological history during which time they have experienced numerous climatic changes. In other words, turtles can adapt to a certain degree of climate change. However, if human activities inhibit the adaptation of turtles to climate change, the speed of decline that turtle populations are now suffering will probably accelerate to the point where extinctions occur.

First, let us look at the changes in sand temperatures that are affecting turtle sex ratios. Sand temperatures on natural beaches are influenced by air temperature and the intensity of solar radiation, as well as the sand's depth, specific heat, and degree of light absorbency (or color). The amount of shade afforded by plants growing in the sand and the sand's moisture content also play a role. For instance, it is usually assumed that sand temperatures on Okinawan beaches, in the southern part of the Japanese Archipelago, must be higher than those on beaches on the Japanese mainland. However, because Okinawa's beaches are composed of coral-derived white sands, they tend to be cooler. Also, areas of beaches that are shaded by plants will receive less direct sunlight and will consequently be cooler than other sections of the same beach.

As such, simply looking at natural sand temperatures shows how extremely varied the sea turtles' environment is. Earlier in this chapter we gave the example of sex ratio changes due to seasonal temperature differences on beaches on the Atsumi Peninsula. Tetrapods have been placed on the inland side of these beaches (Figure 19.7). For this reason, turtles going onto the beaches run into the tetrapods and deposit their eggs close by them. Very few plants grow on beaches where barriers such as tetrapods have been placed, so sand temperatures are essentially uniform. If, on the other hand, the back section of the beaches were characterized by pine forests flowing into a band of beach plants and finally into open sand, the sex ratio of the hatchlings would undoubtedly be different. Therefore, even if sand temperatures rise due to global warming, the preservation of varied plant life on beaches would ensure a broad range of sand temperatures and this would mitigate the effect of any temperature rise on sea turtle sex ratios. From this perspective, it is vital to protect turtles' breeding beaches, particularly their plant life.

Further, it is often thought that sea level rises will lead to a loss of beach area. However, as beaches are created by the pounding of the sea on the land, as long as there is enough sand available, beaches will simply form further inland and will not disappear. The problem here is coastal protection works. Coastal protection works prevent the encroachment of beaches further inland and lead to the shrinkage or complete disappearance of beaches suitable for nesting. Most beaches used for breeding by turtles have some form of coastal protection works on their inland side. Consequently, if sea levels rise as a result of global warming, many beaches currently used for breeding will decrease in size and turtle hatchability will doubtless fall as a result. It is vital, therefore, to exercise caution when building coastal protection works in the future and to consider the removal or improvement of those already in place.

Turtles are highly flexible and adaptable and will be able to respond to a certain degree of environmental change. The problem is that human activities, such as the building of coastal protection works, stand in the way of this adaptability and may well push turtles further down the road toward extinction.

References

Bowen, B. W., N. Kamezaki, C. J. Limpus, G. R. Hughes, and A. B. Meylan. 1994. Global phylogeography of the loggerhead turtle (*Caretta caretta*) as indicated by mitochondrial DNA haplotypes. Evolution 48: 1820-1828.

Bowen, B. W., F. A. Abreu-Grobois, G. H. Balazs, N. Kamezaki, C. J. Limpus, and R. J. Ferl. 1995. Trans-Pacific migrations of the loggerhead turtle (*Caretta caretta*) demonstrated with mitochondrial DNA markers. Proceedings of the National Academy of Sciences USA 92: 3731-3734.

IUCN, 1996. *1996 IUCN Red List of Threatened Animals*. IUCN, Switzerland and Cambridge, 368pp.

Kamezaki, N. and K. Kuroyanagi. 1991. On the TSD of *Caretta caretta* from Japan. Umigame Newsletter 7:8-10. (in Japanese)

Kamezaki, N. and M. Matsui. 1997. A review of biological studies on sea turtles in Japan. Japanese J. Herpetol. 17(1): 16-32.

Mrosovsky, N. 1994. Sex ratios of sea turtles. J. Exp. Zool. 270: 16-27.

Chapter 20

What Will Happen to the Birds ?

Nobuo Takeshita and Masayuki Kurechi

Birds are endotherms, and maintain their internal body temperature at a relatively constant value by metabolic means, a process also described as homoiothermy. Because they are incapable of perspiring, when their body temperature rises excessively due to flying or other vigorous activity, birds radiate the excess heat through respiration (Schmidt-Nielsen, 1972). The feathers are an excellent insulator. Birds can also vary the angle between their feathers and skin using feather muscles to control the degree of insulation provided by the feathers (Welty, 1975).

Homoiothermy makes it possible for birds to remain active irrespective of the ambient atmospheric temperature. Most birds can fly and move about within a large area in order to forage. There are a number of birds that migrate over long distances to change their habitat according to the season. Nestlings are usually very small and sensitive to cold, however, and must be carefully raised by their parents for a long period.

Birds are relatively better equipped to cope with the effects of global warming on account of their homoiothermy, flying ability, and reproductive patterns. In general, the body temperature and fatal temperature in birds (40 - 42°C and 45 - 47°C, respectively) are higher than in mammals. Accordingly, birds may be able to survive in their present habitats by making the most of their homoiothermic abilities. They can also resort to their flying ability to migrate to higher or colder locations (more northerly regions in the case of the Northern Hemisphere) to cope with the warmer climate. Hence, birds have a number of different ways to survive global warming.

The effects of global warming will not be confined to rising temperatures, however. The sea level will rise on a global scale and regional climate drying and dampening will become more pronounced due to changes in local precipitation as well as to an increase in the frequency of tropical storms. In addition, the increase in temperature will not occur homogeneously. Birds, depending on their environments, may be seriously affected when these environments change.

The negative influence of environmental changes on birds is highly likely to be compounded by the effects of chemical pollution and other impacts of economic activity. For example, DDT, a pesticide that has been banned in industrialized countries since the 1970s, but is still in widespread use in the developing world, impedes calcium metabolism and causes female birds, especially raptors, to lay eggs with thin eggshells. DDT accumulates in fat tissues of animals and is released into the bloodstream when fat stores are consumed. An increase in the level of DDT in the bloodstream of female birds as a result of decreased food consumption during the brooding period can prove fatal, particularly in pheasant species.

There are approximately 9,000 bird species on Earth, about 1,000 of which are in serious danger of extinction. Approximately 550 bird species are found in Japan. How will they cope with global warming and the phenomena related to it?

An earlier laying season

Since 1931, the British Trust for Ornithology has accumulated more than a million items of data concerning the nesting of 225 bird species in Britain. When the data covering 65 species over the most recent 25 years (between 1971 and 1995) were analyzed, it emerged that the initial egg-laying day (the day on which the first eggs of the season are laid) of 20 species had shifted to an earlier period. The birds in question were laying their eggs between 4 and 17 days earlier (8.3 days on average) than they had done previously. Thirty-one other bird species also showed the same tendency. The remaining 14 species tended to lay their first eggs later than before, but only one species provided statistically significant data (Crick et al., 1997). Although it has not been proven that the tendency toward an earlier initial egg-laying day is due to climate warming, no other reason has been suggested.

When eggs are laid earlier, a longer period is available for raising nestlings. Among individuals of

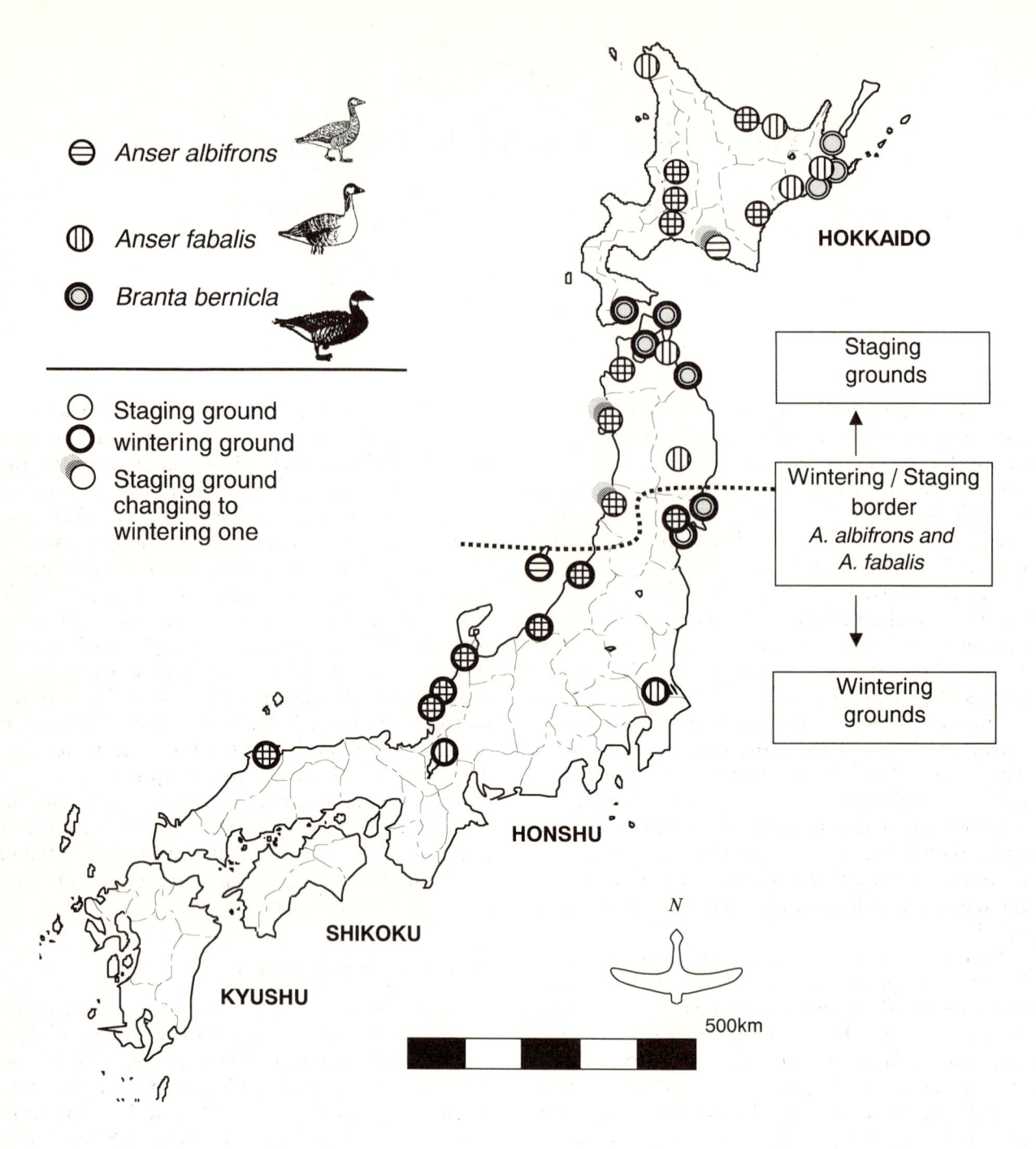

Figure 20.1.
Main staging and wintering grounds of three major species of geese in Japan (JAWGP, unpublished data). Staging grounds are changing to wintering grounds.

the same species, the earlier the eggs are laid, the larger the number and the size of the eggs. This may be because adult birds with the previous experience of reproduction tend to prepare for the subsequent reproduction earlier. Young birds that are raised by parents over a longer period can better survive the winter season, during which mortality rates tend to be high. Earlier egg laying also gives parent birds more time to produce two or more clutches within a year.

The 20 species that have managed to make the most of climate warming by laying their eggs earlier surely benefit by producing more offspring. Even if climate warming escalates further, they should be able to reproduce further north. On the other hand, those

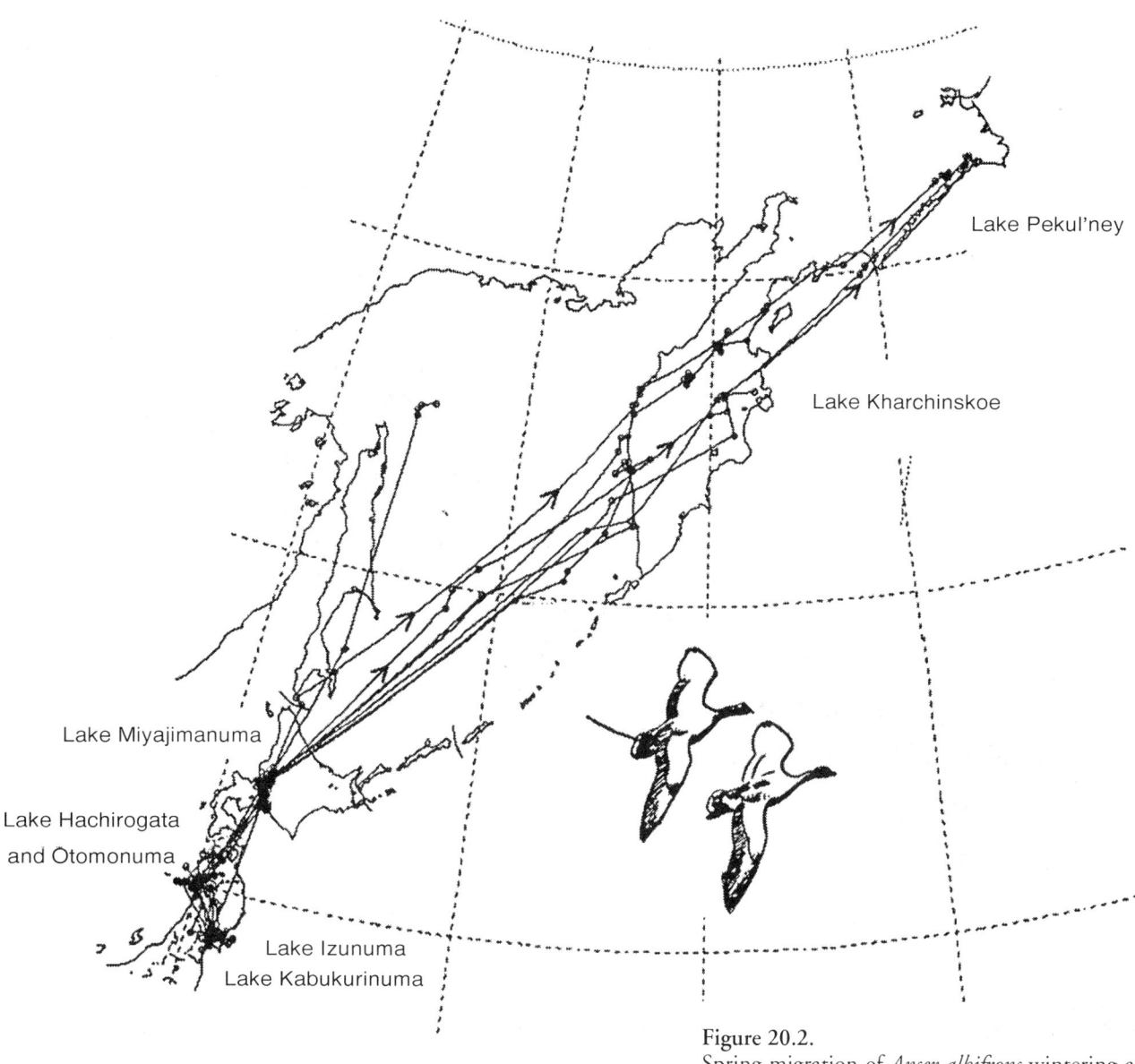

Figure 20.2.
Spring migration of *Anser albifrons* wintering at Lake Izunuma, as obtained by satellite transmitter tracking in February - July, 1994 (Kurechi et al., 1995).

species that cannot lay their eggs earlier may be left behind in inter-species competition.

White-fronted geese and snow cover

The most important reason for bird migration to the south for the winter is to avoid excessive cold, and in the course of migration to Japan migratory birds try to move as short a distance as possible. In Japan, larger birds like the Whooper swan *Cygnus cygnus* pass the winter in relatively northerly locations and smaller ones like the Bewick's swan *Cygnus columbianus* prefer to overwinter at locations further south (Environment Agency, from 1970 to 1999).

Figure 20.1 is a distribution map of the main staging and wintering grounds of the three major species of wild goose in Japan - the White-fronted goose *Anser albifrons*, the Bean goose *A. fabalis*, and the Brent goose *Branta bernicla*. Staging grounds are places where migratory birds stop off during the course of migration. Of these three, *B. bernicla* is the only species that winters along the coast, in estuaries and in other locations near the sea. The border between the wintering grounds and staging grounds of *B. bernicla* lies across southern Hokkaido (Figure 20.1). *B. bernicla* lives near the sea, which is not frozen, so its wintering grounds are located further north than those of *A. albifrons* and *A. fabalis*. The

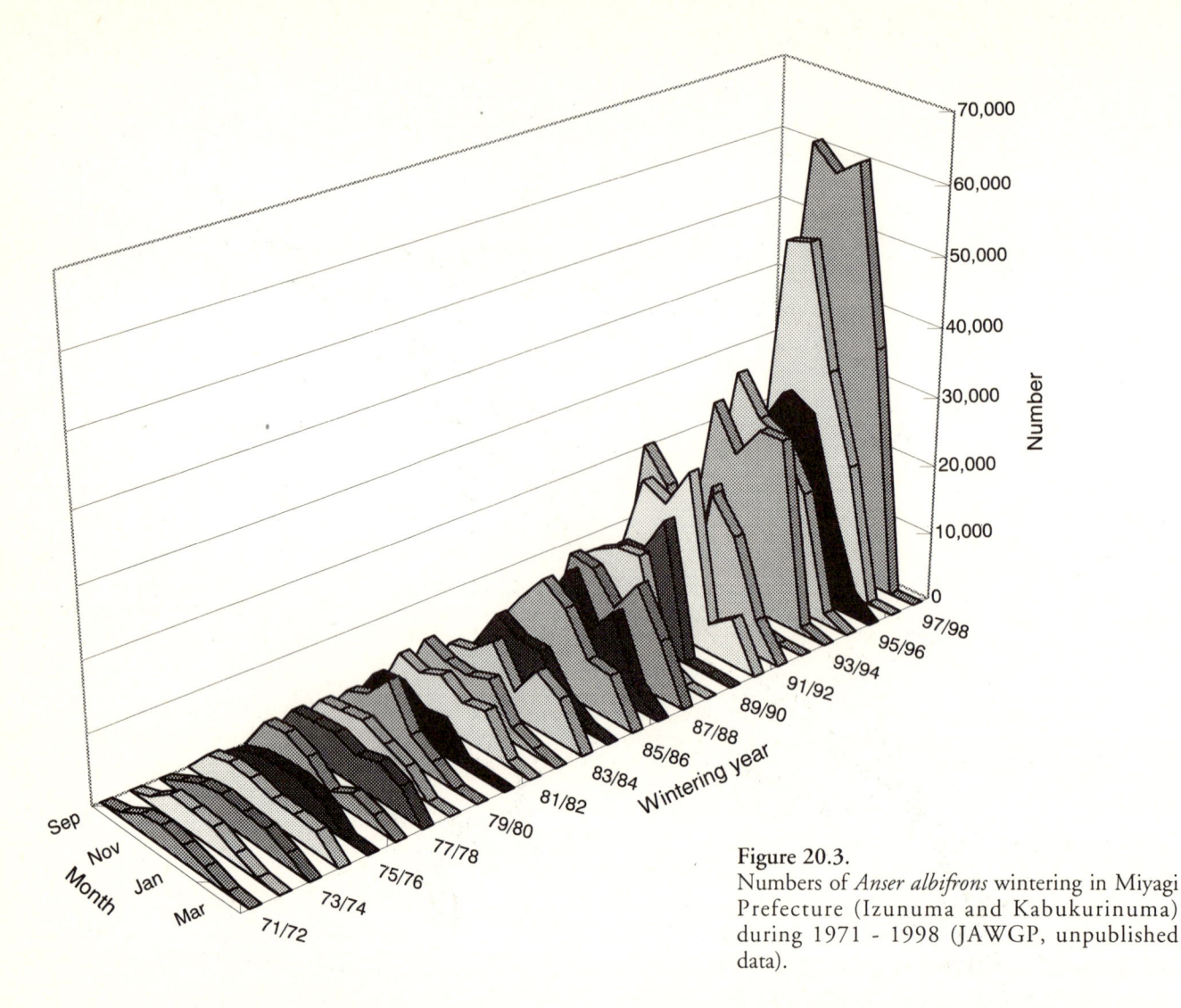

Figure 20.3.
Numbers of *Anser albifrons* wintering in Miyagi Prefecture (Izunuma and Kabukurinuma) during 1971 - 1998 (JAWGP, unpublished data).

wintering grounds of *A. albifrons* and *A. fabalis* are inland wetlands, which are more easily frozen than the open sea. Therefore, both species come to relatively southern places to pass the winter.

The flyways of *A. albifrons* were obtained by satellite transmitter tracking (Figure 20.2) (Kurechi et al., 1995). *A. albifrons* breeds around Lake Pekul'ney (177° 10'E, 62° 40'N) facing the Bering Sea near the Arctic Circle, and migrates to Japan crossing Kamchatka en route. It appears first in Hokkaido and then continues on to wintering grounds in Honshu as autumn advances and snow cover increases. Its Japanese wintering grounds are very restricted in area and number, and the northernmost location in which this species overwinters along the Pacific side of the country is in Miyagi Prefecture. Only Miyagi meets the imposing conditions of being as northerly as possible, not being severely cold in winter, and remaining relatively free from heavy snow. Nearly 80% of the total population of geese in Japan stay through the winter around Lakes Izunuma and Kabukurinuma in Miyagi Prefecture.

For its wintering grounds, *A. albifrons* prefers large, shallow and safe lakes and marshlands, and broad rice-paddy areas. It cannot feed itself if the ground is completely frozen or covered with snow. *A. albifrons* is especially fond of fallen rice grains remaining in the fields after the harvest, but also eats the seeds, leaves, roots, and stems of true grasses when fallen rice is unavailable.

The *A. albifrons* population overwintering in Miyagi was much larger prior to 1971. Over many years the population continued to decline steeply due to excessive hunting and habitat loss. Hunting of *A. albifrons* in Japan was banned in 1971, and since that year the population has steadily increased, at first gradually in the 1970s and 1980s (Miyabayashi, et al., 1994), and then rapidly in the 1990s (Figure 20.3). There are several possible reasons for its rapid increase in numbers. First of all, its population naturally increased due to the legal protection given to this species. Second, it shifted its wintering ground to Japan. That is, flocks that used to overwinter in countries other than Japan have been forced by hunting to change their migration routes toward Japan. Third, the region near the Arctic Circle facing

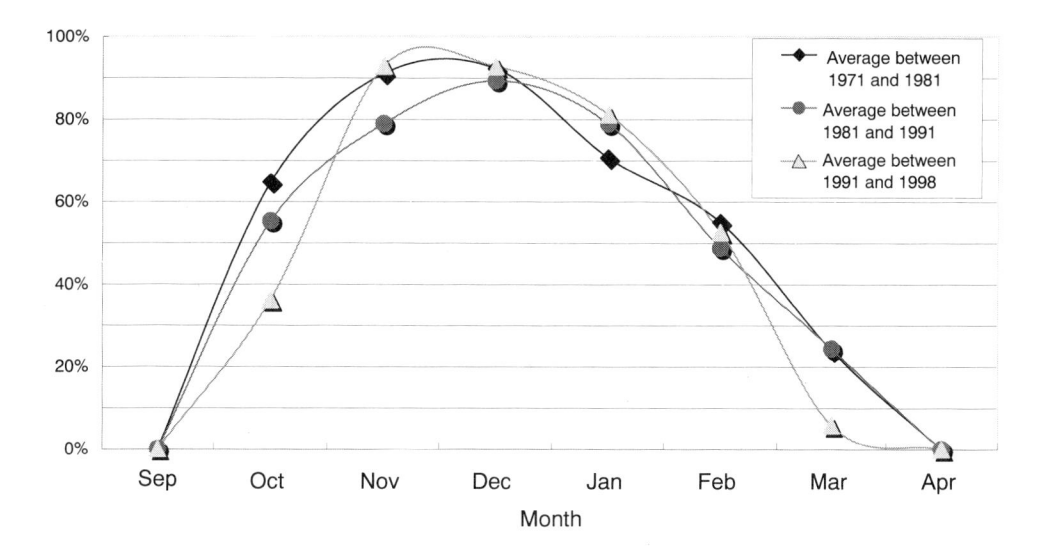

Figure 20.4.
Relative monthly peak of *Anser albifrons* wintering in Miyagi Prefecture (Izunuma and Kabukurinuma) during 1971 - 1998. The data shown in Figure 20.3 were used.

the Bering Sea is one of the areas most strongly affected by global warming (IPCC, 1996; Frontispiece 6 and 7). The climate may have warmed in the breeding areas of *A. albifrons*, leading to an increase in its breeding population.

Shift of wintering grounds toward the north

Figure 20.4 shows the timing of arrival at and departure from wintering grounds in Miyagi (Lakes Izunuma and Kabukurinuma). In the 1990s, *A. albifrons* tended to arrive in Miyagi later on average than was the case in the 1970s and 1980s. The timing of its departure from Miyagi has tended to occur nearly one month earlier in recent years.

Data for the 1970s shows that the numbers of wild geese sometimes declined during January, the winter of 1976/77 being a typical example (Figure 20.5). This occurred because of a period of unusually cold weather. From December 1976 to February 1977, there was heavy snow and the wetlands were frozen. Consequently, the geese disappeared from Lake Izunuma and flew as far south as the Kanto Plain. During the 1970s, wild geese migrated to areas further south than Lake Izunuma in the winters of 1973/74, 76/77, and 77/78 (Yokota et al., 1979). Since the 1980s, however, migration to locations south of Lake Izunuma has rarely been observed. Instead, wild geese have tended to stay around the lake throughout the winter.

In a reversal of the situation that persisted until the 1980s, Miyagi in the late 1990s is in some years no longer the most northerly location that satisfies the wintering requirements of *A. albifrons*. The major portion of the flock of more than 30,000 birds that overwinters in Miyagi used to leave there around mid-February, but now does so about one month earlier.

Wild geese depart from Lake Izunuma and travel to Akita Prefecture, northwest of Miyagi. The number of *A. albifrons* at Lake Otomonuma in Akita during each wintering season from 1987/88 to 1996/97 shows that the lake was a typical staging ground until the late 1980s (Figure 20.6) because the wetlands around the lake were frozen in winter. Geese appeared there in autumn, left for places further south in winter, and arrived again on their way back north in the spring. In recent years, however, the period during which geese are not found at the lake has become much shorter, and the number of geese overwintering there is increasing because wetlands around the lake have not tended to freeze. The pattern of migration at Lake Otomonuma in the 1990s is similar to that at Lake Izunuma in the 1970s. That is, only when it becomes unusually cold do geese migrate further south and when it becomes a little warmer, they quickly return. Lake Otomonuma, which is about 170 km north of Lake Izunuma, is essentially now a wintering ground for geese.

There are some flocks that overwinter in Hachirogata, Akita, located about 20 km south of Lake Otomonuma. Hachirogata was formerly a staging ground in autumn and spring (Figure 20.2). In Yamagata Prefecture, just to the south of Akita, geese that used to stop over in the course of their autumn and spring migrations have recently begun to overwinter. In the past, wild geese never overwintered in Hokkaido, the northernmost main island. In Shizunai Town in southern Hokkaido, however, a

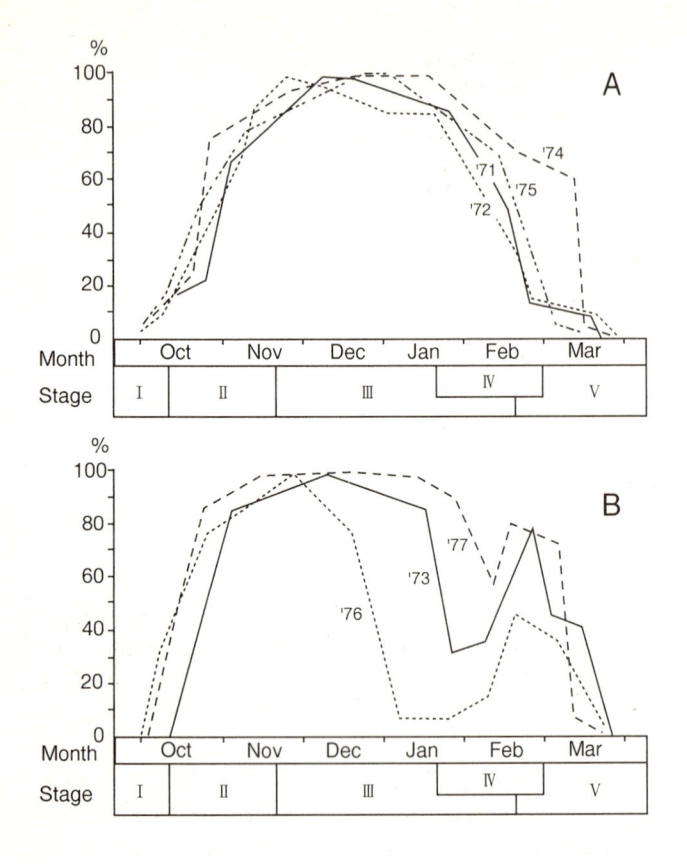

Figure 20.5.
Relative monthly-peak-numbers of wild geese at different stages of the wintering period (annual peak-number is 100%). A: Cap type (1971, 1972, 1974, 1975), B: Two-peak type (1973, 1976, 1977). Stage I: arrival stage, II: increasing stage, III: staying stage, IV: dispersal stage, V: departure stage (Yokota et al., 1979).

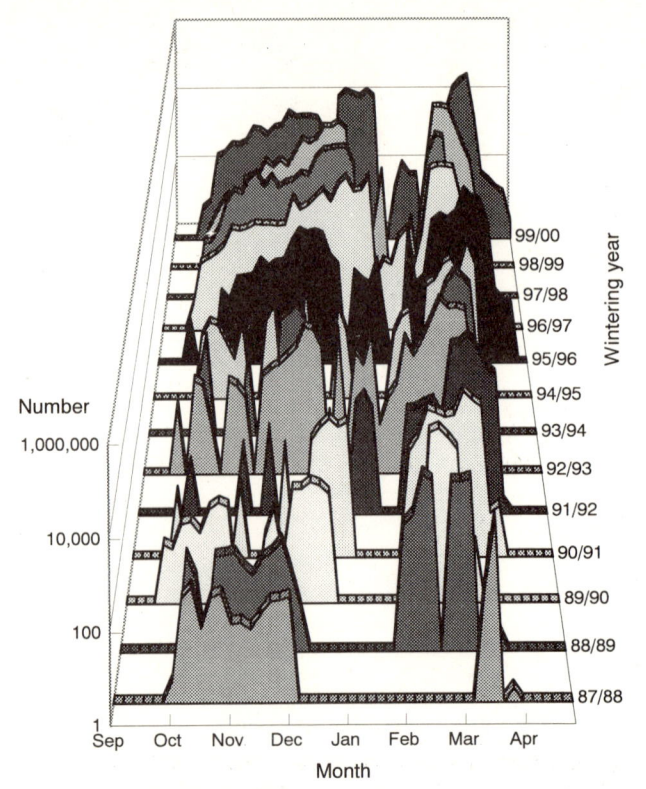

Figure 20.6.
Change in the staging pattern of geese at Lake Otomonuma, Akita Prefecture during 1987 - 2000. (Hatakeyama, unpublished data)

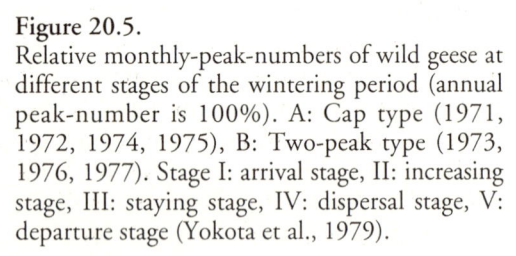

small flock of *A. albifrons* has been spotted passing the winter since the winter of 1995/96. This flock arrives in Shizunai in early December or in early January and remains in grasslands where there is not much snow (Figure 20.1) (Kurechi, 1998).

Japan has been experiencing relatively warm winters in recent years and the warmer weather has had an influence on the wild geese overwintering in Japan. Wild geese used to overwinter at locations throughout Japan. In recent years, however, they have stopped visiting a number of locations where they previously overwintered. They have gone further north due to changes in the environment. If the 0°C isotherm in mid-winter moves north, the wintering grounds of wild geese and their patterns of migration can be expected to change accordingly. The northward shift in the wintering habitats of *A. albifrons* will accelerate in the future due to climate warming. A more precise understanding of the influence of global warming-induced changes on wild geese will allow us to grasp the extent to which the general influence of global warming has advanced.

Darwin's finches and climate drying

Some types of birds exhibit changes in body size in response to drier or wetter climatic conditions. In the Galapagos Islands, there are 14 Darwin's finch species. One of these is *Geospiza fortis* which eats seeds on the ground. The beaks of different individuals of this species living on the same island have long been known to vary greatly in size (Figure 20.7).

Detailed research on *G. fortis* has been conducted since 1973 on Dafnet-Majole Island, which is only about 40 ha in size. Almost all the individuals of this species have been captured for measuring and subsequently released with an identification ring on their leg. The island was hit by a severe drought beginning in 1976, during which time it barely rained for a year and a half. Over the course of the drought, many plants lost their leaves. Large numbers of *G. fortis* died, with only 15% surviving the drought. Curiously, many of the surviving individuals were relatively large, and their beaks were also large. Moreover, in the years following the drought they

Figure 20.7.
Large and small individuals of the same species of *Geospiza fortis* (two on the left). Another species, *G. magnirostris*, that has an especially large beak (right) (from Harris, 1974).

often passed these features on to their offspring. The same phenomenon has been observed in subsequent droughts. The average size of the birds' beaks became 4% larger after each drought. On the other hand, the number of individuals with small bodies and beaks increased after years of heavy rain (Grant, 1991).

The reason for this transformation appears to be as follows. Many kinds of plants produce many relatively small seeds, while a few plants produce a small number of relatively large seeds. *G. fortis* prefers to eat small seeds and turns to larger seeds only after the supply of small seeds is exhausted. Individuals with relatively large body and beak sizes can eat large seeds that their smaller relatives cannot eat. This gives them an advantage when the overall supply of seeds is reduced due to drought.

If the climate of Dafnet-Majole Island becomes drier due to global warming and if the Galapagos Islands experience drought conditions once every ten years, individuals of *G. fortis* will tend to become larger. Moreover, if there are no counterbalancing factors at work, it is possible that within only 200 years *G. fortis* will become as large as *G. magnirostris*, another Darwin's finch which is currently 50% larger than *G. fortis*.

G. fortis may be able to adapt to a considerably drier climate. Nevertheless, if the island experiences continuous drought conditions, the species' rate of reproduction will decline and the probability of nestlings surviving to maturity will decline significantly. Overall, the consequences of drought appear to be negative for *G. fortis*.

The fate of rock ptarmigans in Japan

In the North Japan Alps and other ranges in the high mountain regions of central Honshu, the Rock ptarmigan *Lagopus mutus*, the Alpine accentor *Prunella collaris*, the Japanese accentor *P. rubida*, and the Nutcracker *Nucifraga caryocatactes* are a common sight in summer. The latter three descend from the mountains in autumn and pass the winter in warmer locations, while *L. mutus* does not migrate. *L. mutus* lives on plants and prefers areas where *Picea pumila* and alpine flowers grow above the tree line. *L. mutus* is usually found in the arctic and sub-arctic zones of the Northern Hemisphere and does not migrate. As a relic species from the most recent glacial, its distribution ranges in Japan are completely separated from those of other populations elsewhere in the world.

L. mutus is thought to have been widely distributed even in the present northern temperate zone around 18,000 years ago. This was the peak of the most recent glacial, which in total extended from about 100,000 to about 10,000 years ago. When the climate became warmer after the glacial, its distribution was narrowed down to more northerly regions. In Japan, however, some individuals of this species responded to the warmer climate by migrating to higher altitudes. Their descendants now inhabit alpine areas in the central high mountains of Honshu. They are found only at elevations of 2,400 m or higher above sea level, which is the altitude of the tree line in this region (Environment Agency, 1991).

Let us assume that the suitable environment for *L. mutus* will shift upwards by 200 m to locations at elevations of 2,600 m or higher (where the temperature is 1.3°C lower) due to global warming. In the North Japan Alps, where about 2,000 individuals of *L. mutus* are thought to live at present, the area of suitable habitat available to them will be reduced from about 250 km^2 to about 140 km^2. In the South Japan Alps, where the population is about 2,700, the available habitat area will shrink from about 290 km^2 to about 110 km^2.

If we assume that the present population density of *L. mutus* is maintained irrespective of small differences in their habitat, we can expect there to be 1,100 individuals living at elevations of 2,600 m or higher in the North Japan Alps and 270 in the South Japan Alps. Moreover, ranges that are now connected will be fragmented and the flocks will become more isolated. Consequently, there will be locations in which *L. mutus* will become extinct and which will not subsequently be re-colonized by other members of the species. The 270 individuals projected to remain in the South Japan Alps would be the bare minimum necessary to maintain the viability of the population.

The increase of 1.3°C in atmospheric temperature upon which this assumption is based is a relatively moderate figure in the context of the climate warming that has been projected to occur before the end of the 21st century. A global average increase of 2°C, with larger increases at higher altitudes, has been forecast. If such a scenario were to become reality, the area in which *L. mutus* could survive would be even smaller. The climate warming projected for the years to come will create a very difficult situation for *L. mutus* in Japan, a species that has already been forced to retreat into high mountain areas.

Other birds inhabiting high mountains throughout the world's temperate zones will also have to move to higher elevations to cope with the effects of global warming. The previously mentioned *N. caryocatactes* and *P. rubida* in Japan can utilize forests, so these species will be able to survive. However, *P. collaris*, which prefers rocky areas and overwinters at such locations in lower mountains, will face difficulties in the 21st century.

Birds in tidelands

According to the Environment Agency (1997), if the sea level rises by 30 cm due to global warming, the area of sandy beaches along the coast of Japan will shrink by 56.6%. If the rise is 65 cm the area of sandy beaches will become 81.7% smaller, and in the case of a rise of 100 cm the loss will be 90.3%. The present rise in sea level is caused by an increase in the total amount of seawater due to glacial and icecap melting and to the thermal expansion of the surface sea water layer. Tidelands, both muddy and sandy, which currently exist near the mouths of Japanese rivers will be totally submerged as the sea level rises. Above these tidelands are beaches and marshlands that are not currently inundated by seawater. Such places could potentially turn into tidelands when the sea level rises. Most tidelands, however, are separated from these higher beaches and marshlands by embankments.

Tidelands are important habitats for snipes and plovers, which eat lugworms and crabs. Some birds increase their body weight by up to 50% in a week when they stop by at a tideland during migration. Here they accumulate energy in the form of fat which enables them to fly over long distances. The distances that birds migrate can be immense, so it is important that tidelands exist not only at their wintering grounds, but also at points along their migration routes. The loss of even one such tideland can have a significant negative impact on the migratory birds that utilize it. Since the 1960s, Tokyo Bay and other tidelands in Japan have been rapidly developed with the aid of large machinery, and a large number of wintering and staging grounds of great importance to migratory birds have been lost. Nevertheless, a survey conducted at about 200 locations throughout Japan in the spring of 1997 recorded still 54 species of snipes and plovers, including *Calidris alpina*, *Numenius phaeopus* and *Charadrius alexandrinus*, and approximately 100,000 birds in total (Fujioka et al., 1997).

References

Crick, H. Q. P., C. Dudley, D. E. Glue, and D. I. Thompson. 1997. UK Birds are laying eggs earlier. Nature 388:526.

Environmental Agency Japan, from 1970 to 1999. The report on the annual census of waterfowl (ANATIDAE) in Japan. Environment Agency, Tokyo. (in Japanese)

Environment Agency (ed.). 1991. *Red Data Book: Vol. Vertebrate animals*. Tokyo. (in Japanese)

Fujioka, E., J. Fujioka, K. Inada, and K. Kuwabara. 1997. National count of shorebirds in Japan, Vol. 3, Spring 1997. Shorebird Committee - JAWAN (Japan Wetland Action Network), Toyohashi.(in Japanese)

Grant, P. R. 1991. Natural selection and Darwin's finches. Scientific American 265-(4):60-65.

Harris, M. 1974. *A Field Guide to the Birds of Galapagos*. Collins, London. 160pp.

IPCC, 1996. *Climate Change 1995*. Cambridge University Press, Cambridge.

Kurechi, M., Y. Sabano, S. Iwabuchi, E. Syroechkovsky, V. V. Baranyuk, A. Andreev, A. Kondratyev, J. Y. Takekawa, N. Mita. 1995. Study on the restoration of Lesser Snow goose to northeast Asia using miniature satellite transmitter. The Telecommunication Advancement Foundation Research Report No.9: 518-541. (in Japanese)

Kurechi, M. 1998. Global warming makes White-fronted goose begin to stay further north in winter in Japan. SCIaS 31: 70-71. (in Japanese)

Miyabayashi, Y. (ed.) 1994. *Inventory of Goose Habitat in Japan*. JAWGP, Wakayanagi, Japan. 316pp.(partly in English)

Schmidt-Nielsen, K. 1972. *How Animals Work*. Cambridge University Press, Cambridge.

Welty, J. C. 1975. *The Life of Birds* (2nd ed.). Pp.127-

133. W. B. Saunders Company, Philadelphia. 623pp.

Yokota, Y., M. Kurechi, and M. Kosugi. 1979. Studies on the behaviour of wintering geese 1. Numbers of geese wintering at Lake Izunuma. Bulletin of the Ornithological Society of Japan (Tori) 28: 29-52. (in Japanese with English summary)

Chapter 21

Can Pikas on High Mountains Survive the Greenhouse Effect?

Takeo Kawamichi

The Japanese pika *Ochotona hyperborea yesoensis*, confined to the mountains of Hokkaido is considered a relic of the glacial period. The alpine ecosystem, including pikas, is doubtless going to be influenced directly by the greenhouse effect in the future. In this paper, I attempt to estimate the influence of the greenhouse effect on pikas and other alpine mammals.

The Order Lagomorpha is divided into two families, Leporidae (hares and rabbits) and Ochotonidae (pikas). Pikas, unlike leporids, have small round ears and short legs (Frontispiece 11), which make them well suited for walking around in narrow spaces such as between rocks or in underground burrows (Kawamichi, 1996). Only one genus, *Ochotona*, is extant in the Family Ochotonidae. Twenty-five species belonging to this genus are distributed in the Northern Hemisphere (Wilson and Reeder, 1993). They occur in high mountain regions like the Himalayas, the Tien Shan, the Altai, and the Rocky Mountains, and also in steppe regions such as the Tibetan Plateau and the Gobi Desert.

Pikas can be divided into three types based on habitat preference (Smith, 1988). One type includes those species living in rocky areas and which are said to be "rock-dwelling". These rocky areas in mountain regions include talus debris, moraines, and lava flows. There are at least eight "rock-dwelling" species including *O. hyperborea yesoensis* (Kawamichi, 1969). Another is the "steppe-dwelling" type of pika which excavates burrows beneath the grasslands. These burrows extend in extensive networks. Six species in this type range across the steppes from China, into Russia, central Asia, and Mongolia. There is also an "intermediate" type (Kawamichi, 1994). They live in the rocks if there are any, but excavate burrows underground if there are no rocks. Two species of this type occur in Afghanistan and Mongolia. In this way, pikas have developed small-scale radial adaptation to enhance their survival within the simple environments found at high altitudes and high latitudes.

Pika fossils suggest climate changes

Living pikas are adapted to the cold climates that characterize higher altitudes and higher latitudes. Throughout the Pleistocene (1.6 million to 10,000 years ago), glacials have alternated with interglacials over a cycle lasting on the order of 100,000 years. The climate alternately grew colder and warmer, and the changes it brought had a major influence upon the evolution and migration of life. Fossils of pikas provide an excellent indicator of the climate changes of the past.

Ochotonids first appeared in the mid-Oligocene (30 million years ago) in Asia and Europe (see Dawson, 1967). During the Miocene (23.3 to 5.2 million years ago), a total of 13 genera appeared in the Family Ochotonidae, ranging from Eurasia to North America and Africa. At this time, the number of genera of ochotonids reached its peak and their geographical range was at the widest. In the Pliocene (5.2 to 1.6 million years ago), the ochotonids diminished to four genera. The genus *Ochotona* first appeared in Eurasia and North America during the Pliocene. Today the other three genera which survived into the Pleistocene are already extinct and only one genus, *Ochotona*, continues to exist.

Why does only one genus remain? The tectonic activity of the Earth's crust and the large changes in climate provide the explanation. The Indian subcontinent collided with the Asian Continent causing the upheaval of the Tibetan Plateau and the building of the Himalayas during the Miocene (Andel, 1985). The upheaval of the Rocky Mountains was also proceeding in North America. These events opened up large areas to cold climates. It is supposed that modern pikas are the descendants of ochotonids that moved into these cold regions. Other genera which lived in warmer climates may have had to compete against ground-dwelling rodents and were ultimately unsuccessful (Kawamichi, 1994).

Periods of glaciation occurred cyclically throughout the Pleistocene. It is probable that pikas migrated to lower altitudes and spread out into wider ranges during these glacials, and retreated to the alpine areas during the interglacials. Species differentiation in the genus *Ochotona* is assumed to have been promoted by the cyclical growth and decline of glaciers or alternation between colder and warmer climates, as speciation may occur when a population is split in two, or when some populations adapt themselves to a new environment.

Pikas have not changed much in terms of form, however, and consequently, many pika fossils from the late Pleistocene are included as members of the same species that exist today. This is because their skull form has been extremely "conservative", making it possible to work out the range that today's pika species occupied in the past. For example, the steppe pika *O. pusilla* ranged throughout Europe during the late Pleistocene, but after the last glacial, gradually retreated from the west to Kazakhstan (Smith et al., 1990).

Huge amounts of water accumulated on land in the form of ice during the glacial periods. As a result, the sea level fell and some land bridges opened to connect islands and continents with each other. The only living pika species which occurs on islands today is the northern pika, found on Sakhalin and Hokkaido. Japanese pikas, a subspecies of the northern pika, are the descendants of pikas that migrated from Siberia through Sakhalin to Hokkaido along glacial-period land bridges. These land bridges are now submerged and straits separate these islands now. Small mammals like pikas would have had no opportunity to migrate to Hokkaido had it not been for such land bridges.

The temperature warmed when the last glacial period came to an end. Pikas that had been living in mountains at lower latitudes had to migrate toward higher altitudes. Glaciers had eroded the ground and left moraines behind them as they retreated, which made excellent habitat for "rock-dwelling" species. Pikas that ascended to high altitudes became restricted within each mountain range and have been isolated from each other since. Many small populations have therefore had no further opportunity for cross-fertilization. For example, *O. princeps* ranges extensively from Canada to California, mainly around the Rocky Mountains. This species is divided in 36 subspecies, some of which are very different in terms of body size and color (Smith, 1988). These differences suggest that each isolated population has distinct genetic characteristics.

The Mongolian pika *O. pallasi* has steadily decreased in numbers in the Gobi Desert during the last few thousand years. The bones of *O. pallasi* accounted for 23.6% of all the excavated bones of small mammals deposited 3000 to 4500 years ago, but this percentage decreases to 7.3% for the period 1500 to 2000 years ago, and to just 0.4% for bones deposited over the past 200 years (Smith et al., 1990). The same story is told by owl pellets (pellets disgorged by owls). *O. pallasi* bones accounted for 38% of pellet contents from 1100 years ago, falling to 21% of pellet contents from 600 years ago. The region in question is at the southern margin of the pikas' range, where few of these animals are found today. This may be taken as evidence that the Gobi Desert is becoming steadily warmer or more arid (Smith et al., 1990).

The influence of temperature change

The rate at which temperature rises or falls in accordance with the alternation between glacials and interglacials is incomparably slower than the global warming phenomenon dealt with this volume. However, past changes in fauna and migration patterns provide useful information for predicting the changes that present animals may experience under the influence of the greenhouse effect.

When their environment becomes warmer or colder, the biotic community is forced to migrate. Among terrestrial vertebrates, amphibians, reptiles, and mammals (excluding bats) encounter barriers to migration in the form of the sea and mountains. Migration is easier when the temperature is colder if this leads to lower sea levels and the appearance of land bridges. But in cases where no such land bridges exist, mammals that are adapted to warm climates have to remain in colder areas, and only those that can adapt themselves to the colder climate survive. Examples of this phenomenon in contemporary Japan are the Japanese macaque *Macaca fuscata*, the Japanese serow *Capricornis crispus*, and the Japanese giant flying squirrel *Petaurista leucogenys*. Japan is at the northernmost range for the genera to which these animals belong, and other species of these genera belong to the fauna of the Oriental Region (Kawamichi, 1996).

High mountains are also a barrier to migration, with mountain ranges extending in an east - west direction having an especially large influence. In Europe, the east - west barriers of the Alps and the Mediterranean Sea inhibit the migration of life forms in a north - south direction. This has led to the extinction of many species, and, as a result, Europe has rather poor biodiversity despite its present warm climate. The same thing has happened in the case of the Himalayas, which also lie in an east - west direction. The northern side of the Himalayas experienced an upheaval and became the Tibetan Plateau. Life forms adapted to a warm and moist climate were completely eliminated from these regions due to the cold and arid climate. Many primitive animal and plant are preserved in Sichuan and Yunnan in China, which lie on the eastern edge of the Himalayas (Editorial Committee of Biogeography in

China, 1979). This is presumably because this mountain range changes its orientation to north-south in this region, so that life forms were easily able to migrate north or south across the border between the Palaearctic sub-region and the Oriental Region (Kawamichi, 1993).

It is easy for lowland life forms to migrate north and south in response to climate change in regions where mountain ranges extend in a north-south direction. Large mountain ranges which extend over several thousand kilometers, such as the Rocky Mountains, also become corridors for alpine life forms to migrate south toward lower latitudes when the climate becomes colder. When the climate becomes warmer, however, many small populations remain isolated in the southern high mountains as glacial relics. Since the end of the last glacial period, these animals have maintained themselves in small populations.

Where one species ranges extensively in a north-south direction, the environment tends be more severe in the southern alpine areas than in the lower-altitude northern areas of its range. One of the reasons for this is that daytime hours in the summer are not as long at low latitudes as at high latitudes. Lower temperature reduces the number of days in the year for potential photosynthesis, regardless of latitude, but the total time available for photosynthesis will be shorter at lower latitudes within a range. This is a harsh environment for plants, and the amount of plant life available in the form of food influences herbivores. Other reasons include the increased strength of the westerly winds in high mountains located between latitudes 40 to 60°.

The areas suitable for glacial relics in the high mountains within the temperate zone are small, and their respective ranges are isolated from each other. The opportunity for cross-fertilization between isolated populations is therefore very small. Consequently, over long periods of geological time, differentiation takes place. Each mountain area may, to some extent, developed its own subspecies, if not an entirely new species. Small and isolated populations exhibit little genetic variation. Such populations can easily be threatened with extinction as a result of disease or by a climatic change that would present no danger for larger populations.

What will happen to the Japanese pika and other mammals?

Let us now consider what will happen to the Japanese pika due to global warming. Its range is presently restricted to central Hokkaido (Figure 21.1). In altitude, this species ranges from 400 m to nearly 2290 m (the highest point in Hokkaido) above sea level (Kawamichi, 1969).

As global warming progresses, it is estimated that within a given geographic region, areas of a given temperature will eventually be located at an altitude of approximately 400 m higher than they are today. In Hokkaido, the lower limit of the Japanese pika's range is currently about 400 m above sea level (Onoyama and Miyazaki, 1991). This limit will rise to about 800 m if it is determined by temperature alone. The upper border, on the other hand, is currently almost at the highest point in Hokkaido (Mt. Asahidake) so it will remain the same. As a result, the pikas' vertical range will be cut back, and consequently their horizontal area will shrink. Onoyama and Miyazaki (1991) surveyed pika distribution and found that of the total of 570 locations inhabited by these animals, 18.6% are located at elevations below 800 m. This fact indicates that approximately 20% of the pikas' range will disappear. The influence of climate change will be more serious in the Kitami Mountains and southern Hidaka Mountains, where most of their habitats are below 1000 m above sea level (Figure 21.1). There most of habitats will disappear, and many isolated ranges will appear as larger ranges are fragmented.

There are some populations of other Japanese mammals whose ranges are considered to be restricted to colder areas. These include the ermine *Mustela erminea* in central Honshu, the least weasel *M. nivalis* in northern Honshu, the large red-backed vole *Clethrionomys rex* in Hokkaido, the Azumi shrew *Sorex hosonoi* in central Honshu, and Ikonnikov's whiskered bat *Myotis ikonnikovi* in Honshu (Mammalogical Society of Japan, 1997). Much the same thing is expected to happen to them as to the Japanese pika. Furthermore, Daubenton's bats *M. daubentonii* and whiskered bats *M. mystacinus*, which live only in northern and eastern Hokkaido even today, may disappear completely within Hokkaido. The small Japanese flying squirrels *Pteromys momonga* and the Japanese squirrel *Sciurus lis*, both of which prefer a cold climate, are already close to extinction in Kyushu, and will surely become extinct there.

The homoiothermy of mammals may allow them to adapt to temperature increases of a few degrees. Their specific food sources, however, may decrease or disappear at the altitudes they inhabit in response to the increased temperature. When a food range shifts to a higher altitude, the animals that consume it will have to follow.

Expected temperature increases will be larger in winter than in summer. Snowfall will decrease and the area covered with snow in winter will also decrease. Snow cover is thought to be an important factor in determining the ranges of some animals. The Japanese deer *Cervus nippon* and wild boar *Sus scrofa* range only in the western part of Honshu and along the Pacific Coast, where periods of snow cover are short. These animals will probably extend their ranges to the Sea of

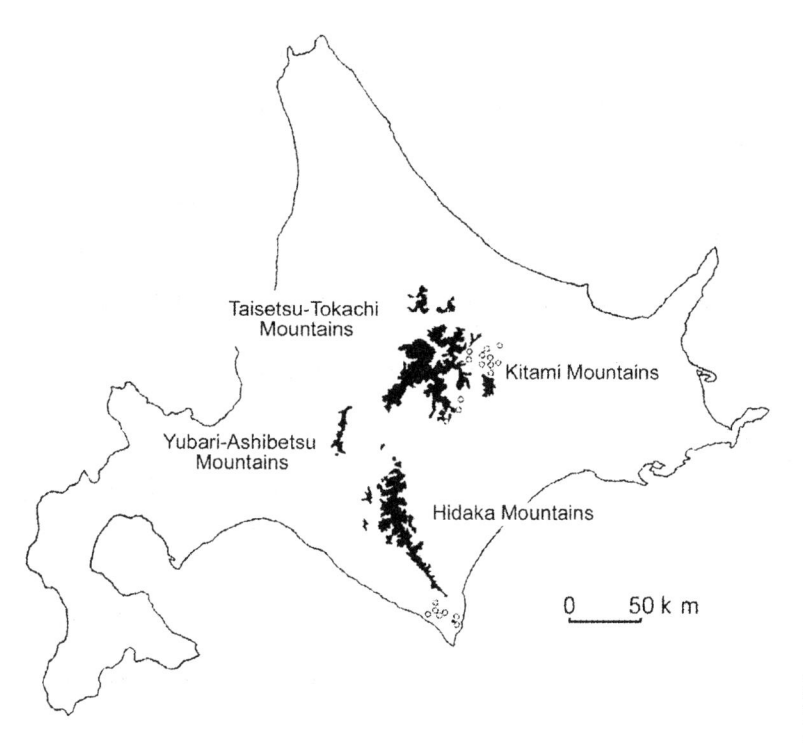

Figure 21.1.
Expected range of the Japanese pika in the near future. The solid black areas represent the range at elevations of 1000 m or more above sea level where pikas are widespread. Hollow circles represent their range today below 1000 m. Global warming will reduce their range to within this solid black area.

Japan side of the country. The population of Japanese deer has been increasing at many localities for the past ten years (Japan Wildlife Research Center, 1997). One possible reason is that calves have lower winter mortality due to warmer winters. Temperature increases in winter will result in a further increase in the population of this species.

Biogeographically speaking, the mammals of Hokkaido differ markedly from those in Japan's other three main islands of Honshu, Kyushu, and Shikoku (Kawamichi, 1996). Many species in Hokkaido are the same as those in Sakhalin and Siberia. At present, in the case of terrestrial mammals, excluding bats, cross-fertilization between members of different populations located on the different main islands within Japan, or likewise, on the Asian Continent and the Japanese Archipelago, is not possible in the wild. There is no opportunity for mammals outside Japan to reach Japan by themselves in response to a temperature increase. Neither, for instance, can the mammals of Honshu move into Hokkaido.

There will be a greater risk than before, however, that foreign animals brought in by humans will become established in Japan. The Japanese marten *Martes melampus*, for example, was brought from Honshu into southwestern Hokkaido and became established. It is possible that this species will expand its range eastward and eject the native sable *M. zibellina* as the climate warms. As for Honshu and other southern islands, naturalized animals such as the house shrew, masked palm civet, Pallas squirrel, coypu, and mongoose prefer a warmer climate, so they can be expected to expand their ranges. Pet animals of subtropical origin will, if released, have a greater opportunity than before to establish themselves in the wild in Japan. Once they are established, they will tend to adapt themselves to the Japanese climate and then expand their range further north toward colder areas. One example is the masked palm civet *Paguma larvata*, which has been rapidly expanding its range recently, even into the snow covered regions.

References

Andel, T. H. van. 1985. *New Views on an Old Planet.* Cambridge University Press. (Japanese translations by T. Uda, 1987. Tsukiji Shokan, Tokyo)

Dawson, M. R. 1967. Lagomorph history and the stratigraphic record. In: (E. L. Yochelson, ed.) *Essay in Paleontology & Stratigraphy.* Pp.287-316. University Press of Kansas, Lawrence.

Editorial Committee of Biogeography in China. 1979. *Zoogeography.* Science Publisher, Beijing. (Japanese translation by M. Asahi et al., 1981. Japan-China Publisher, Tokyo)

Japan Wildlife Research Center. 1997. *Present Status and Challenges for Management of Sika Deer: Report of the Workshop on Sika Deer Management in 1996.* Japan Wildlife Research Center, Tokyo, 91pp. (in Japanese)

Kawamichi, T. 1969. Behaviour and daily activities of the Japanese pika, *Ochotona hyperborea yesoensis.* J. of the Faculty of Science, Hokkaido University. Series VI, Zoology 17: 127-151.

Kawamichi, T. (ed.) 1993. Polar regions and mountains. In: *Animals on the Earth.* No.114. Pp.162-192. Asahi Shinbunsha, Tokyo. (in Japanese)

Kawamichi, T. 1994. *Trails Lagomorphs Left Behind: their Behavior, Ecology, and Evolution.* Kinokuniya-Shoten, Tokyo, 270pp. (in Japanese)

Kawamichi, T.(ed.) 1996. *Mammals. Vol. I. The Encyclopedia of Animals in Japan.* Heibonsha, Tokyo, 156pp. (in Japanese)

Mammalogical Society of Japan (ed.) 1997. *Red Data in Japanese Mammals* (compiled by T. Kawamichi). Bunichi Sogo Shuppan, 279pp., Tokyo. (in Japanese with the red list in English)

Onoyama, K. and T. Miyazaki. 1991. The distribution of the Japanese pika in Hokkaido . In: *The Present Status of Japanese Pikas.* Pp.25-55. (in Japanese)

Smith, A. T. 1988. Patterns of pika (Genus *Ochotona*) life history variation. In: (M. S. Boyce, ed.) *Evolution of Life Histories: Theory and Patterns from Mammals.* Pp.233-256. Yale University Press, New Haven.

Smith, A. T., N. A. Formozov, R. S. Hoffmann, C. Zheng, and M. A. Erbajeva. 1990. The pikas. In: (T. A. Chapman and J. E. C. Flux, eds.) *Rabbits, Hares and Pikas.* Pp.14-60. IUCN, Gland.

Wilson, D. E. and D. M. Reeder. 1993. *Mammal Species of the World.* 2nd ed. Smithsonian Institution Press, Washington DC, 1207pp.

Chapter 22

Global Warming and Increases in Human Infectious Diseases

Takayuki Ezaki

The end of the 20th century saw the re-emergence in different forms of several infectious diseases that had nearly been forgotten, and the discovery of new infectious diseases. Globally, part of the explanation lies with the large movements of people that are taking place. In Japan, the increase in food imports has also played a role, contributing to an increase in the contamination of food with pathogens.

It is not quite as easy to predict or understand the impact of global warming on the incidence of infectious diseases. Would a situation develop under global warming in which tropical diseases would spread through Japan? Many people will doubt that this could happen in Japan where hygienic conditions have greatly improved in recent decades. However, higher temperatures do have important effects on the spread and rate of reproduction of pathogens. Here, I will limit my remarks to how changes in temperature relate to increases in infectious diseases, and the role global warming may have in this process.

Re-emerging infectious diseases

The Center for Disease Control (CDC) in the United States has become acutely aware of the dangers posed by the spread of re-emerging diseases, and has started restructuring its research program to strengthen research into emerging and re-emerging diseases. The same fears prompted the National Infection Research Institute in Japan to initiate new research in 1997. Important newly emerging diseases in the world include tropical and endemic diseases that have spread from certain limited areas. Most are viral infections (Figure 22.1). There are also, however, pre-existing diseases that have re-emerged in a changed form. These are largely bacterial diseases such

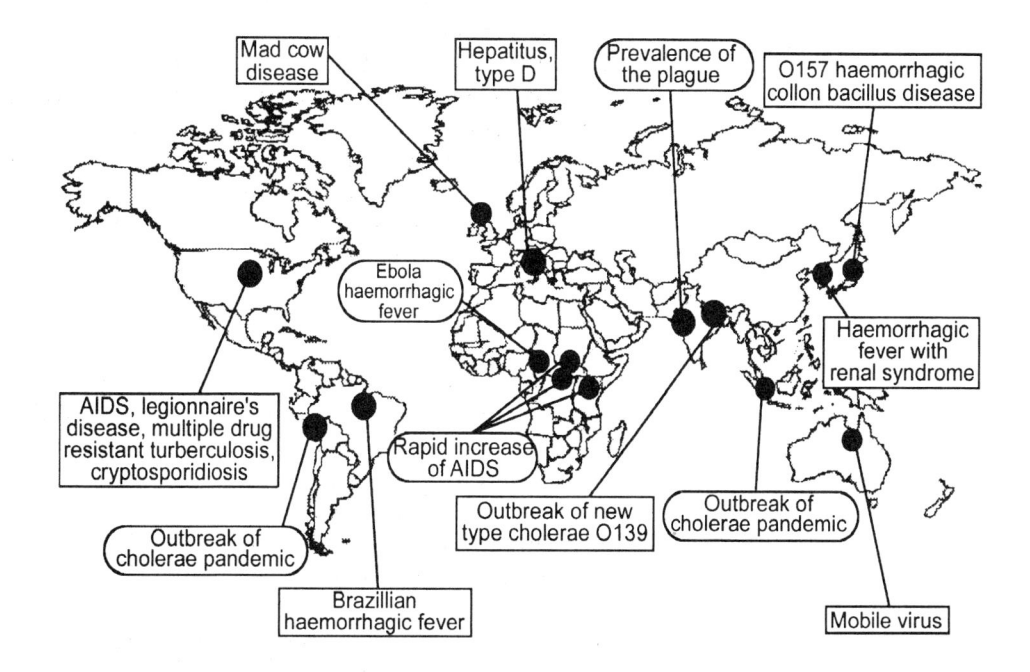

Figure 22.1.
Examples of emerging and re-emerging diseases in the latter half of 20th century.

as tuberculosis, staphylococcus and streptococcus infections. In the half century after the advent of antibiotics, these bacterial diseases seemed to be in eclipse, but today their pathogens have gone through various transformations, and are no longer affected by ordinary antibiotics. The diseases raging through hospitals today are pathogens that have become resistant to antibiotic drugs. Patients particularly vulnerable to these infections include those with immunodeficiency, those who have had operations or organ transplants, those undergoing cancer treatments, the aged with chronic diseases, and children.

Increased temperature and wider distribution of vector organisms

A great sensation has been created by the idea that infections of the tropics and subtropics will spread to the temperate zone with global warming. Today, from 300 to 500 million people are infected by malaria annually, and several million of them die from it. It is estimated that 2.4 billion people are living in areas where there is a danger of being infected by malaria. If the distribution of the anopheles mosquito that transmits malaria expands as a result of global warming, the area contaminated with malaria will spread into the temperate zone and a great many more

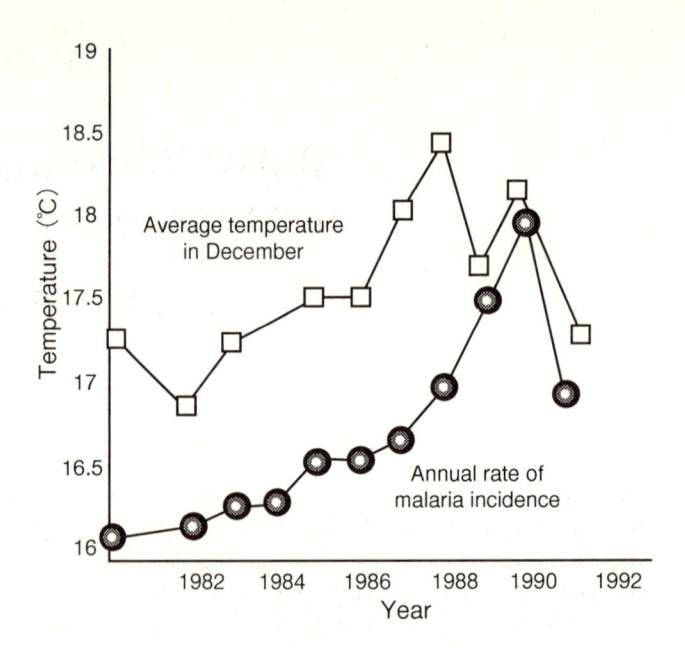

Figure 22.3.
Rise in temperature and occurrence of malaria (modified from Bouwmann et al., 1994).

people will be exposed to the risk of infection. The protozoan which causes malaria cannot complete its life cycle when temperatures fall below 15°C, as propagation becomes difficult (Figure 22.2). Based on fluctuations in the number of patients and the average temperature in December in Pakistan from 1982 to 1991 (Figure 22.3; Bouwman et al., 1994), it can be concluded that rates of infection increase with a rise in winter temperatures. Malaria used to break out sporadically in Japan before World War II, but these outbreaks have declined dramatically due to spraying with insecticides such as DDT. All present occurrences of malaria in Japan result from the patient having been infected overseas. The number of patients is gradually rising as more people travel abroad. It would seem reasonable to foresee that an epidemic could be suppressed by controlling populations of mosquitoes, but the following example shows that this alone cannot guarantee success.

Mosquitoes are also the vector in the spread of Japanese encephalitis. The number of patients of this disease in Japan decreased rapidly through vaccination and the elimination of mosquitoes. However, the virus that causes Japanese encephalitis has not yet been exterminated from the country. As Figure 22.4 shows, the frequency of positive reactions to Japanese encephalitis in pigs shifts from south to north in summer. If global warming proceeds, pigs will be exposed to vector mosquitoes over a larger area and from spring to autumn. Because nearly 70% of children in Japan are vaccinated against this disease, most of the population has antibodies against

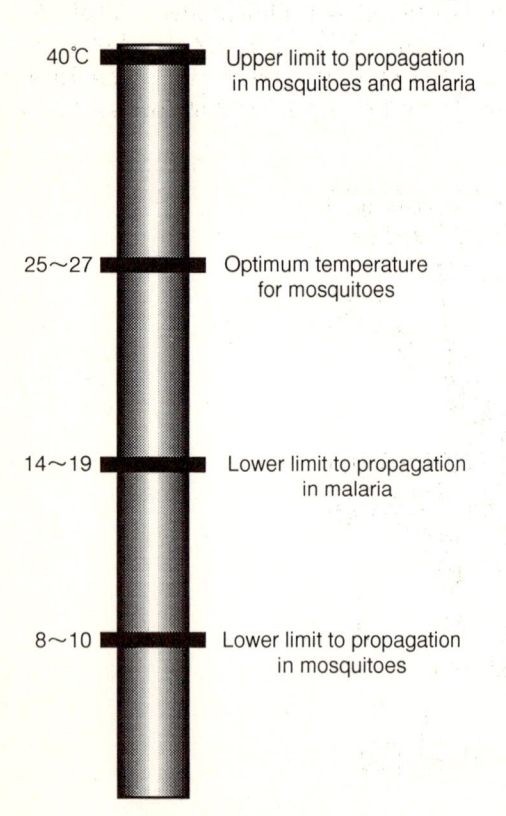

Figure 22.2.
Propagation temperatures of malaria and malaria-carrying mosquitoes.

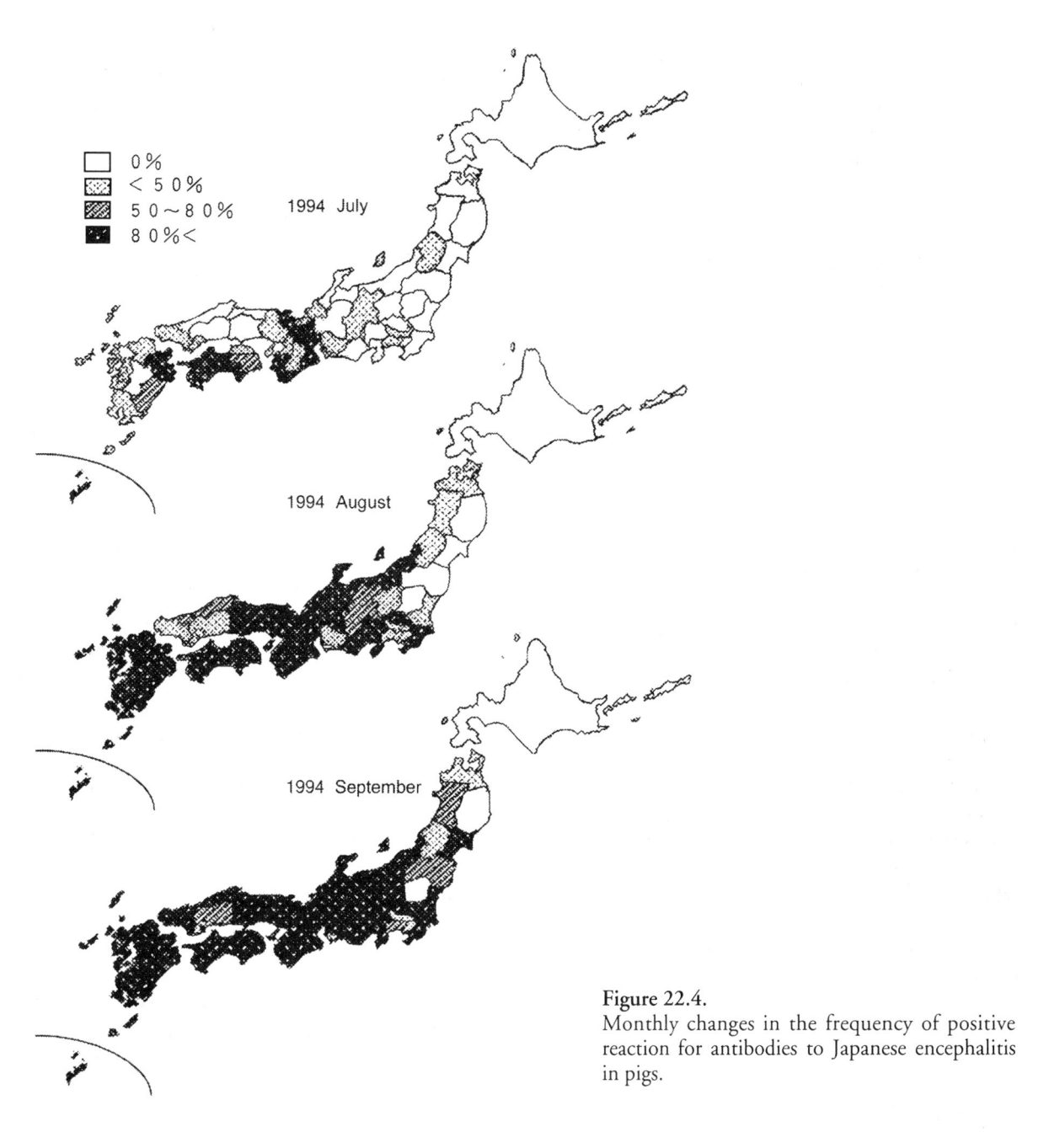

Figure 22.4.
Monthly changes in the frequency of positive reaction for antibodies to Japanese encephalitis in pigs.

Japanese encephalitis. If vaccination levels become lower, the disease could easily re-emerge. Since no vaccine exists for malaria, this kind of preventive suppression will not be feasible.

Expansion of contaminated areas through global warming and food contamination

Because Japan imports more than half its food, we must be aware that epidemics in areas of supply will lead directly to the contamination of imported food. For example, when there are outbreaks of typhoid fever and cholera in Southeast Asia, the number of patients in Japan also increases. Since a case of cholera was diagnosed in Arita in 1977, there have cases in Nagoya in 1988 and in Tokyo in 1991. In 1995 there was an epidemic of cholera in Bali, Indonesia, and many Japanese tourists were infected.

There is a positive relationship between rising temperatures and incidences of food poisoning. The epidemic of infections involving the colon bacillus *Escherichia coli* O-157 that raged through Japan in 1996 suggests the expansion of the area affected by food contamination. Table 22.1 shows major pathogens found in foods and the food items they infect. The O-157 bacillus has been thoroughly studied, but there are no sensitive detection methods available, and its frequency of detection in meat is low (0.1% to several percent). When we consider that haemorrhage-causing colon bacilli other than O-157 cannot be detected at all, we can estimate that the incidence of such bacilli is higher than shown in the

Table 22.1. Examples of pathogens and foods causing food poisoning

Pathogens related to the food	Number of cases ($\times 10^3$)	Foods with high incidence
Campylobacter spp.	4,000	Chicken, fresh milk, water
Salmonella spp.	2,000	Eggs, chicken, milk
Enterohemorrhagic E. coli (O157:H7)	25	Beef, fresh milk, water
Listeria spp.	1.5	Cheese, dairy products
Vibrio (V. cholerae and V. parahaemolyfius)	10	Marine products (fish, shellfish)

table. The *E. coli* O-157 bacteria causes infections with a toxicity equal to that of the dysentery bacillus. It causes haemorrhaging diarrhoea and haemolytic urine poisoning and may lead to death in infants, and is officially considered an epidemic-causing organism. As colon bacteria inhabit the feces of humans and animals, great care is needed in handling both domestic and imported food supplies.

Salmonella is another troublesome pathogen that causes food poisoning. Contamination of chicken and eggs by *Salmonella* has been an international concern, and the incidence of *Salmonella* food poisoning is also apparently on the increase in Japan (Figure 22.5). In Japan, where food is often served raw, contamination with *Salmonella* in chicken and eggs and *Vibrio enteritis* and cholera in seafood is of particular concern.

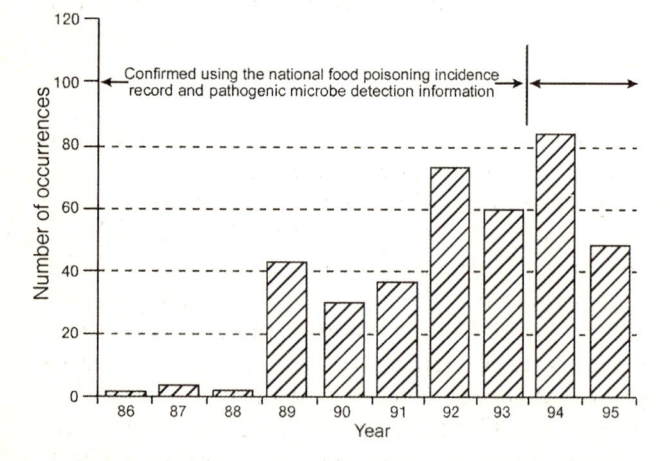

Figure 22.5.
Annual changes in the incidence of salmonella food poisoning in Japan (Information on Pathogenic Microbe Detection, National Institute of Infectious Diseases, 1997).

Multiplication of pathogenic bacteria depends on temperature

Compared to viruses that can only propagate in the body cells of humans and vector organisms, pathogenic bacteria can propagate in artificial media, food, or in bodies of water. Human pathogenic bacteria can affect humans because they propagate rapidly at temperatures of 30 to 37°C, the normal human body temperature range. When cultured in the laboratory at 35°C, a single bacillus of many of these species can multiply into a hundred million bacilli just overnight. In the case of *E. coli* O-157, 100 individual bacteria are said to be enough to cause a clinical infection in a human. It takes only 20 min for a colon bacillus to double, which means that 3 hours suffice for it to multiply to 100. Thus we can clarify why there is a high frequency of food poisoning in summer; high temperatures create an environment which encourages rapid multiplication of pathogenic organisms.

Given satisfactory temperature and nutritional conditions, a single *E. coli* or cholera bacillus can multiply to 100 million overnight. Once the bacteria have propagated, they will not perish if refrigerated at 4°C. When conditions for propagation are unfavorable, the bacteria remain in a suspended state, waiting for better conditions to start multiplying again. Even freezing does not kill these pathogens. Pathologists use this characteristic to preserve bacteria by freezing them at -20 to -80°C. Bacteria preserved at -80°C can be revived even after 10 or 20 years.

However, most pathogenic bacteria are vulnerable to high temperatures. Except for bacteria that have spores, such as the one that causes botulism, most die when exposed to 60°C for 30 min. Thus food poisoning can be prevented by boiling the food. (*Clostridium botulinus* survives even at 100°C).

Temperature and the eutrophication of rivers

The level of contamination in rivers and the sea is determined by the rate of growth of colon bacteria found in the water. Generally, human pathogens including colon bacteria cannot propagate in rivers that are oligotrophic (poor in nutrients and organic matter). Unlike industrial pollution, however, domestic sewage contains plenty of the nutrients necessary for propagation of colon bacteria. Thus, when the amount of domestic sewage increases, rivers act as ideal environments for colon bacteria. This is why the number of colon bacteria is used to assess the cleanliness of the water at bathing beaches.

Rivers into which little domestic sewage is discharged have low nutrient levels and, in general, human pathogens cannot propagate. Slow-growing microbes such as photosynthetic bacteria and algae contribute to purifying the water, using up the small amount of nutrients available. However, when nutrient levels become higher and the temperature rises to around 30°C, bacteria that propagate in a eutrophic (nutrient-rich) environment start to multiply rapidly. Colon bacteria and the bacillus that causes cholera are of this type. Eutrophic rivers can support the rapid growth of these bacteria in the same way laboratory cultures do. If the temperature rises to over 30°C, this will lead to explosive propagation of the bacteria, causing contamination over a wide area.

Infectious disease and houses built to be comfortable in summer

In the latter half of the 20th century, our living environment has become much more comfortable thanks to a myriad of electrical appliances. Legionnaire's disease is an example of an infection resulting from an urban environment made comfortable by air conditioners. In 1976, a number of pneumonia-like infections occurred among people attending a Legionnaire's party in the US. The organism that causes this disease is called Legionnaire's bacillus. In nature it inhabits soil and water, but it is blown by the wind into artificial cooling towers that function as a part of air conditioning systems. When the cooling tower is in full operation, the water temperature in the tower rises and the bacteria multiply. At low temperatures, predatory amoebae in the cooling tower eat the *Legionnaire's bacilli*, and because the bacteria propagation rate is slow, they die out. However, in summer when the water temperature starts to rise with the operation of the cooling tower, the propagation rate of the *Legionnaire's bacilli* exceeds the predation rate, and bacilli which have been ingested by amoebae continue to multiply, killing the amoebae. The upper graph in Figure 22.6 shows that the rate of division of the bacteria in a cooling tower increases in summer. The number of patients suffering from this disease is also larger in summer (lower graph in Figure 22.6).

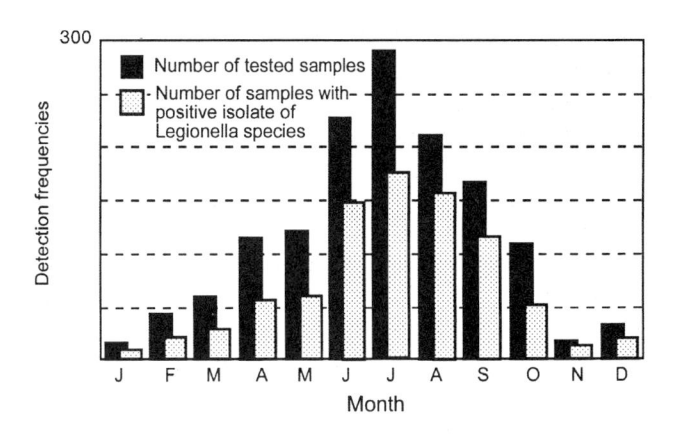

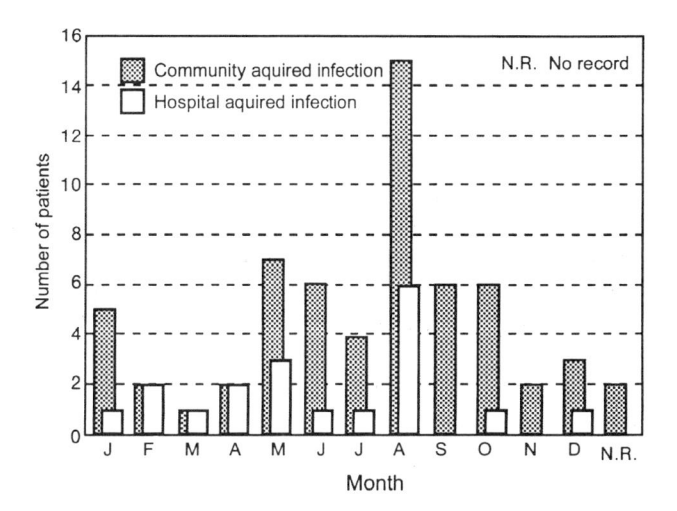

Figure 22.6.
Frequencies of detection of *Legionnaire's bacilli* from cooling towers (above) and the cases of Legionnaire's disease (below) by month (from the Guide of Preventing Legionnaire's Disease, Building Management Education Centre).

According to our research data, these bacteria contaminate 70% of cooling towers in Japan. It has also been reported that 70% of the so-called 24 hour public baths, where the bath water temperature is kept at about 40°C, are also contaminated with *Legionnaire's bacilli*. When bath water is kept at 40°C for a long period, *Legionnaire's bacilli* start to appear from about the third day. Here again, amoebae are likely to be supporting the propagation of the bacteria.

Legionnaire's bacilli cause pneumonia but do not infect the digestive organs. This is because the bacteria cannot propagate within the intestines where the nutrient level is very high. People who directly absorb contaminated water into their lungs contract pneumonia. In general, Legionnaire's disease is falsely regarded as a opportunistic disease which only affects people with lowered immunity, but even healthy people become ill when they absorb the bacteria directly into their lungs through the medium of water droplets. When normal bacteria enter the lungs, the phagocytes in the lungs engulf and destroy them. However, *Legionnaire's bacilli* can propagate within the lung phagocytes in the same way as in the predatory amoebae. Therefore, normal antibiotics are not effective. It is a dangerous infection that can lead to death. Unlike colon bacteria, these bacteria can survive for a long time in distilled oliogotrophic water (water with no nutrients) or even in clean rivers with little domestic sewage, once the water temperature is warm enough. For this reason as well, it is a pathogen which requires a renewed strategy.

At present there is no analytical method to simulate the changes in pathogen density in the environment given a rapid rise in temperature. Thus there is a lack of data that can quantitatively point to increases in infections with a rise in temperature. However, for pathologists who are witnessing a real-life increase in re-emerging diseases, the offensive and defensive mechanisms of pathogens are nothing short of astonishing. Multi-drug resistant staphylococci and tuberculosis bacilli that used to be susceptible to penicillin and streptomycin 50 years ago now inhabit hospitals. Pathogens with no available antibiotic cures are being reported one after the other in hospitals. Pathogens give birth to a new generation every 20 min, and in the 50 years since the discovery of antibiotics, they have acquired defense mechanisms in the form of multi-drug resistance. Microbes have been adapting to various environmental changes over the past 4 billion years, and there are many successful species which can propagate under diverse environmental conditions. They survive aggressively, undergoing repeated mutations or importing useful genes from other bacteria until favorable conditions for their propagation return. A counter-attack by microbes is now steadily under way, and they may be waiting for humans to provide them with even more favorable environmental conditions, namely through an increase in temperature.

Figures in this text are extracted from information on pathogens distributed via the Internet from the National Infectious Disease Research Institute. Additional data is from the Building Management Education Center [both of Japan].

Reference

Bouwman, H. et al. 1994. Bulletin of WHO 72: 921-930.

Chapter 23

Global Warming and the Dynamics of Biodiversity

Kunio Iwatsuki

The world leaders and citizens groups that gathered at the Earth Summit in Rio de Janeiro in 1992 recognized that a global consensus on how to sustainably use biodiversity and stabilise global warming was needed in order to ensure a decent future for humanity in the 21st century and beyond. To maintain the earth's environment optimally now and in the future, all people on earth need to be aware of the problems to be faced and act positively to protect and conserve the environment. No one can forsake his or her individual responsibility in this, from the scientists who work on the regulation of carbon dioxide emissions, to the economic leaders who maintain the world's economy in order to keep the earth clean and sustainable, to the policy-makers who carefully monitor decisions pertaining to the earth's environment. We must place the responsibility upon ourselves to save our earth from an environmental crisis. If there are those who do not realise the importance of environmental issues, even though they carry on vitally important work, the earth's environment may suffer because of their lack of knowledge.

It is disconcerting to note that biodiversity is not treated very seriously on the global level. This book was, therefore, compiled to discuss the dynamics of biodiversity in relation to global warming. We hope this book will provide an impetus for scientists, business leaders, policy-makers, and all human beings to participate in conservation efforts connected with biodiversity and global warming.

Successes in science and technology

The 20th century was the century of the sciences, especially of natural sciences. Considering the great successes in science, we might even be led to believe that there is nothing that cannot be overcome by the power of science today. This is especially true if we consider the power of modern technology, which developed rapidly during the last century in conjunction with rapid progress in the natural sciences.

Science in the 20th century was especially successful in its particular method of reductionism, namely the analytical method. All events were understood through experimental evidence and modern technology, which allowed for rapid progress in the natural sciences. Scientists contributed papers to recognised international journals and reported the causalities of events with carefully analysed experimental evidence. Modern human beings are proud of these scientific successes. The scientific method is understood, especially in the natural sciences, to provide proper evidence for the understanding and interpretation of nature through physical-chemical analysis and mathematical logic.

Standing at the turn of the century, however, we often are amazed to see that so much is still unknown about natural phenomena. It is obvious to everyone that we cannot yet perfectly predict the weather or earthquakes, though there have been great efforts to do so by scientists and policy-makers alike. During times of rapid scientific development, scientists have had a general tendency to be proud of their successes but to be less than willing to discuss what we are not yet able to understand. The public also feels that scientists should analyse the facts and present precise conclusions. Most scientists will, therefore, report only the facts they have analysed by scientific procedures and will not report on anything that lacks sufficient evidence. Thus, we are aware of many natural phenomena appropriately analysed by science, but have few opportunities to gain a sense of how many unanalysed problems remain in nature.

With respect to the earth's climate, we can offer a good example of a relatively unknown phenomena. Fully applying our advanced technology, we cannot produce a perfect weather forecast. How, then, can we predict the earth's climate one century or ten centuries into the future? On the issue of global warming, therefore, we have to discuss the subject even though there are still many uncertainties.

Biodiversity is yet another of those unknown natural phenomena about which it is very difficult to make predictions. There are some 1.5 million known species on earth. The number that actually exists, however, has been estimated to be anywhere from several million to hundreds of millions, depending on the method of estimation. Some scientists estimate that currently known species may be only about one per cent of all the species actually living on earth. And, we have to confess that the term 'species' is still a controversial one. There is no definition of species which is generally agreed upon by biologists. Of the 1.5 million known species, most of them are only named and little is understood about their specific features. Even with respect to *Homo sapiens*, we cannot overcome a variety of diseases, as we know little about many characteristics of this species.

When we act on a natural phenomenon about which we know everything in detail, we can judge what kind of effects will be invited by our actions. But how can we judge the impacts of our actions when we have only a limited understanding of the underlying natural phenomena? In an area where we can estimate the effect of an action correctly, or scientifically, we can act with a certain level of confidence. When we cannot expect to have a correct estimation of the influence of our actions on a natural phenomenon, however, we should keep any change to a minimum.

However, few people consider the global environment as their own responsibility. They have a tendency to believe that scientists, economic leaders, policy-makers, or other such leaders will take care of the future of our global environment. Individuals tend to believe that any action they take will have little, if any, effect on an environment so great as the earth's. They prefer to think that their particular actions are insignificant, with no lasting influence. Modern technology has given us a deep-seated sense of power, but in so many respects it is a false sense; we can influence the global environment greatly without fully understanding the effects invited by such actions. If we continue on this path, many people will forget that there are still great gaps in our knowledge of the natural world.

In this book, most chapters show that biodiversity has been, and will continue to be, greatly influenced by global warming, which results from human activities. It is not easy to demonstrate the general effect of climate change on biodiversity. Examples from various taxa, from various areas, using various methods, indicate that global warming does have an influence on the dynamics of the earth's biodiversity. More simply stated, global warming is one of the key threats to biodiversity.

Our daily lives and the earth after several centuries

A major earthquake could occur in central Japan in the very near future. Most people in the region take this threat seriously. In contrast, the crisis of global warming and its threat to biodiversity will not severely affect people's lives within the next few years. It will be at least several decades until the average temperature on the earth's surface rises by 2°C.

Few people are willing to sacrifice their lifestyles for the sake of future generations. They usually feel that their present lives should be enjoyable. Most people consider the lives of unknown descendants much less carefully. The problem we are faced with at the moment is that people do not have a sense of crisis in their personal lives. They optimistically believe that the wonders of modern technology will work to provide a prosperous future for human beings, without any sound basis for such an assumption. This attitude can only be described as irresponsible.

It will be too late to take care of the earth if we wait until we are in the midst of an actual crisis. It takes greater effort to cure people of disease if they are in the midst of an epidemic than to encourage a better lifestyle while they are still in good health. We need not have a crisis to teach us the importance of maintaining sustainability in our global environment; we need only to take care to sustain our natural world for future generations. We should not attempt to avoid this painstaking task, which is an honourable duty for the lord of all creatures.

We have to be careful not to consider our global environment only in terms of our individual lives and in the time frame of today. The future of the earth should be considered on a global scale, in the time frame of centuries, and by all human beings living on the earth. Life has actually inhabited the earth for 3.8 billion of years.

Some facts found in plant distribution

Some examples of changes in plant distribution observed recently in Japan are introduced below to give more supporting evidence to the relationship between the dynamics of biodiversity and recent climate change on earth.

Naturalisation of Trachycarpus fortunei in the Tokyo area

Trachycarpus fortunei (Hook.) H. Wendl. is the only species of Palmae known on the main islands of Japan, and its northern limit of natural distribution is central Kyushu. This palm has long been cultivated in central Japan, but while cultivated stocks flowered and produced fruit there, germination did not occur naturally.

Since some 20 years ago, we have observed a number of germinations of *T. fortunei* in the Botanical Gardens at the University of Tokyo. *T. fortunei* is cultivated quite commonly in the Tokyo area and the seeds are carried by birds, resulting in an extended distribution area. This type of plant is often seen in city areas, and its presence was easily explained by increasing urbanisation. In large cities such as Tokyo, introduced plants growing vigorously in unexpected places are removed in order to keep the areas clean. Thus, *T. fortunei* is seen in Tokyo only where man has allowed it to continue to grow.

Recently, there has been an increase in the natural germination of *T. fortunei* in the Tokyo area. Under bushes or in greener areas of Tokyo, germinations of *T. fortunei* are very common now, and if we fail to maintain these areas for only a short while, *T. fortunei* becomes one of the dominants in the undergrowth there.

T. fortunei was introduced into central Japan due to human activities. In the past in the Tokyo area, however, it often germinated but seldom grew to the adult stage. Only recently has *T. fortunei* begun to grow with the same habits as in its native habitat in southern Kyushu. A variety of factors are necessary to favour its growth, and higher temperatures are one of the most important among them.

T. fortunei has been seen in various places in the Kanto Region and in the greater Tokyo area in recent years, even in Oume and Okutama semi-natural forests. We cannot say that urbanisation is solely responsible for the spread of *T. fortunei* in the Tokyo area. Even in semi-natural vegetation around Tokyo, it is now very commonly naturalised and grows easily to the adult phase.

As yet, we have no sound evidence to show that *T. fortunei* has become naturalised in the Tokyo area as a result of global warming. Still, its naturalisation appears to be supported by global warming. The equilibrium in vegetation already established in northern areas will be upset by the introduction of particular species such as *T. fortunei*. Every species reacts differently to climate change; this is a most important factor of biodiversity, and natural equilibrium will be upset by a rapid change in environmental conditions.

Distribution of ferns in Japan

Adiantum capillus-veneris L. was native to southern Kyushu. Within the last few decades, many naturalised plants have been observed and reported in various parts of Honshu (Iwatsuki, 1992; Iwatsuki et al., 1995); we usually explained them as having escaped from cultivation, for this species is commonly cultivated in greenhouses. However, there are many examples of this species growing outside of greenhouses, and it makes sense that this species can grow easily in various parts of Honshu if its regular life cycle can occur. Slight warming of the climate on Honshu supports the completion of the life cycle of *A. capillus-veneris* there.

Pteris vittata L. is another species of fern which was known only in southern Kyushu and has now been found on many occasions in the Kinki District. This is another greenhouse species, and is easily cultivated if a higher temperature is maintained. Global warming seems to favour this species, which has expanded its distribution area farther north than it was a few years ago.

Thelypteris dentata (Forsk.) St. John is widely distributed in the tropics where it is a very common wayside fern. In Japan, it was found until recently only in a few particular habitats, especially in caves and in artificial wells where the temperature was not very low even in winter. In a record from Wakayama Prefecture, southern Honshu, this species was found in the 1950s and was a very rare species there. In the 1980s, however, this species was widely distributed throughout the prefecture, and recently has become common in village areas (Iwatsuki, 1992; Nakajima, 1998). Such a common tropical species may be able to grow in various areas if the lowest temperature there is over its threshold. We can refer to this particular species as one which extended its distribution northward under the influence of global warming.

There are other examples of Japanese ferns which were observed only in more southern areas in the past but which are now extending their areas northward. At least some of them must be influenced by global warming, but not all species move northward. Thus the transposition of distribution areas differs according to the species concerned.

Examples observed in Kyoto and Wakayama Prefectures

Murata recently reported on a southern species newly recorded in Kyoto Prefecture (Murata, 1998). *Epipogium roseum* (D. Don) Lindl. was known in Nagasaki Prefecture and Miura Peninsula in Kanagawa Prefecture and southward. In the Kinki District in central Honshu, this species was first found in the Old Kyoto Palace in 1991, and then in the mid-1990s in Kashiwara shrine in Nara Prefecture, and in Kinugasa, Momoyama tomb, Takaragaike Park, and the Higashiyama mountain area in Kyoto Prefecture.

Dioscorea bulbifera L. was not recorded in Kyoto Prefecture until 1992. Thereafter, it became rather common in Kyoto, and flowering has been observed on many stocks. *Dichondra micrantha* Urban was also first recorded in Kyoto Prefecture in 1993, although no observation has yet been made of the flowering of this species in Kyoto.

Nakajima reported several examples from Wakayama Prefecture (Nakajima, 1998). In addition to the ferns *Pteris vittata* L. and *Thelypteris dentata*

(Forsk.) St. John as noted above, he has also reported examples of flowering plants. *Persicaria chinensis* (L.) Nakai was a rare species in Wakayama Prefecture, and is now very common in the southern part, being a vigorous weed in cultivated areas. *Talinum crassifolium* Willd. was introduced from tropical America into Wakayama Prefecture; it escaped from cultivation and has become a weed since the mid-1980s. Another species escaped from cultivation is *Lilium formosanum* Wallace, seen rather commonly in the wild since the 1970s. This is still extending its area, and is common even in the northern part of Nara Prefecture.

These are only a few examples of recent changes in distribution areas, and even from these few examples, we realise that the distribution of some plant species is changing rapidly. This means that there is a rather sudden change in the dynamics of biodiversity, and global warming must provide some influence on these distributional changes.

Is there any possible benefit to biodiversity from global warming ?

With respect to biodiversity, we should remember that human activities have led not only to a decrease in diversity but also to changes in diversification. There are signs of plant species diversification under the influence of human activities. Biodiversity is remarkable in village areas or in so-called man-made vegetation at the edge of virgin forests, and these areas are heavily influenced by human activities (Iwatsuki, 1997).

Some have suggested that global warming could be utilised for human benefit. Wasteland, such as tundra and heath, may become useful land under increased temperatures and may sustain agricultural production. The current cold Temperate Zone may become subtropical under global warming, and this may result in much more diverse vegetation in these areas. Should not we evaluate such beneficial changes? In the past, periods of warming and glacial epochs occurred repeatedly on earth. Even with the present warming of the earth, the earth and its organisms will continue to evolve. There were several periods of great extinction of species in the past, and we may expect to have further prosperity after another such cycle of extinction. These ideas seem to be constructive in considering the future of the earth, and we have to test them carefully.

We have to remember one important fact, however. The great extinctions in the past took place over several hundreds of thousands of years. The present extinction of species is occurring in the space of tens of years, about ten thousand times more rapidly than in the past. What can we expect for the future evolution of organisms? In their natural environment, speciation of sexually reproducing organisms usually occurs on a time scale of a million years; even in such unique places as oceanic islands with a smaller scale of isolated populations, completion of speciation takes several hundreds of thousands of years. The great extinctions of the past took a long time to complete, allowing enough time for recovery from the loss of diversity. The extinction of species at the moment is taking place over a few decades, and no organisms can speciate rapidly enough to make up for these high rates of extinction. In what way, then, can biodiversity be maintained tomorrow ?

We may say that global warming will contribute to the lives of human beings in particular ways, although the individual positive contributions are limited in scope. What will happen if warming is global? We must always consider the impact on the whole earth, even if there are some particular places where warming will produce beneficial effects to the people living there.

We may be able to enumerate some benefits of global warming in particular places and in particular times. In considering the total effects, however, we should examine these carefully on a global level and on the time scale of evolution. For instance, some organisms can migrate following a change of temperature, but other species cannot adapt to such rapid changes and will become extinct. Those organisms that migrated successfully may not be able to survive without the species with which they were previously associated. We need a longer interval for an entire ecosystem to be transferred in accordance with a climatic change, and partial immigrants are usually unable to establish a new stable ecosystem in the short term. Evolution on the earth has been a long process; speciation occurred over millions of years, and current climate change is proceeding on the time scale of centuries. Changes on the time scale of centuries are quite rapid in evolutionary terms, and we must consider the effects on biodiversity as a whole. The global ecosystem will be badly damaged by rapid global warming. Sustainability of biodiversity will thus be threatened, and because of this we have to focus our attention carefully on the influence of climate change.

There is much we do not know about the present status of nature, and there is much we misunderstand. We focus our eyes only on our present lives, forgetting to consider the consequences of today's actions on tomorrow. It is important for us to see the facts as they are. We should consider the earth today and tomorrow with the facts we have at hand.

Conclusion and proposal

Most scientists usually do not want to discuss the facts without having sound evidence to support them.

They always wish to keep close at hand evidence to understand nature's phenomena. However, it is problematic if scientists tell the public only those facts that are well understood. If scientists are willing to speak only with absolute conviction, they will make recommendations only when science has elucidated everything and completed its role. We are faced with various crises on earth at present, and we need to make estimates for the future now, based on the limited facts we have, in order to protect ourselves. Many suggestions and proposals will be based on speculation, but even with this uncertainty, scientists should speak out. Their contributions should be in scientific journals as often as possible.

The examples presented in this book consist of those not fully elucidated by scientific evidence but based largely on indirect evidence. We still need to have additional information if we wish to discuss the relationship between global warming and the sustainability of biodiversity on a scientific basis. At the moment, however, we can discuss the future of the earth based on an enumeration of the facts presently available, even though they are not fully understood.

It is a given that we must adhere to facts fully elucidated by the scientific method, but we have to recognise that there are many phenomena not fully explained. We can not expect to conquer the unknown overnight, so we must consider it with respect and a healthy curiosity. This is a basic principle in mankind's long history, but it is one which has been all but forgotten recently. Thus, we can summarise our understanding of biodiversity and global warming as follows:

1) The climate change as observed recently is caused by human activities and is proceeding very rapidly compared with natural climatic changes in the past. This artificial change may greatly influence biodiversity relative to the natural evolution of organisms during the past 4 billion years. It may even lead to the extinction of the human race.

2) Although this crisis in biodiversity is the result of a number of factors, one of the important ones is without doubt the global warming we are experiencing. We can see great changes in biodiversity on the local level and in some particular taxa. Expansion of these to the global level will lead to a crisis in biodiversity.

3) This warning is based not on proven scientific facts but on estimations by scientists; we can only point out that such a crisis may occur. We need more advanced scientific research both on global warming and on biodiversity. These are different subjects belonging to different scientific disciplines but are closely related to each other, and interdisciplinary investigation should be promoted. Such research must be conducted by specialists, and the results should be made available to the public in easily understood language.

The Convention on Biological Diversity was opened for signature in 1992, and many countries throughout the world are in favour of the sustainable use of biodiversity. To promote such an idea, it is vitally important to regulate the present climatic changes resulting from human activity. The control of climatic change is one of mankind's most urgent tasks at the moment, and all human beings should consider seriously the future of the earth.

We have as yet not fully elucidated the actual relationship between a crisis of biodiversity and global warming; we can enumerate at the moment only the facts observed to date in our scientific experience. More accurate understanding of biodiversity is urgently needed, and both basic research and dissemination of information should be promoted. A new organisation, including facilities for both basic research and social education, should be established quickly to respond the crisis with which we are faced.

References

Iwatsuki, K. (ed.) 1992. *Ferns and Fern Allies of Japan*. Heibonsha, Tokyo. (in Japanese)

Iwatsuki, K. 1997. *The Species Diversification of Plants Induced by Human Activities*. University of Tokyo Press, Tokyo. (in Japanese)

Iwatsuki, K., T. Yamazaki, D. E. Boufford, and H. Ohba (eds.) 1995. *Pteridophyta and Gymnospermae. Vol. 1 of Flora of Japan*. Kodansha, Tokyo.

Murata, G. 1998. Are they influenced by global warming? Puranta 58: 13-15. (in Japanese)

Nakajima, A. 1998. The tropical and subtropical species recently wide-spread in Wakayama Prefecture. Puranta 58: 16-17. (in Japanese)

Postscript: Global Warming and Biodiversity

The Situation in Japan

Harufumi Nishida

Otomono Yakamochi who was involved in the compilation of the Manyoshu, the oldest collection of Japanese 31-syllable poems, composed the following poem: "I never tire of looking at the snow on Tateyama in summer. It must be a gift of the gods".

More than 1,200 years have passed since Otomono wrote those words and Tateyama, a mountain rising 3,015 m above sea level in Toyama Prefecture, is still snow covered in summer. We cannot be sure, however, if in a hundred years future generations will be able to enjoy the same mountain scenery in summer as we do now.

Everybody seeks wealth of some kind or other. Even those who disdain material riches aspire to the possession of spiritual wealth. The driving forces in our development as human beings are our endless curiosity and our unrelenting search for wealth. A diverse world with a rich variety of living things such as flowers and animals has provided spiritual support for people in their pursuit of wealth. This diversity is now being rapidly lost. We have a responsibility to preserve this diversity for future generations. At all costs we must avoid losing an Earth that is rich in life and on which our descendants can continue to experience a strong sense of spiritual wealth.

Although the importance of biodiversity is now generally accepted, the response of Japanese society to global warming has been characterized by a lack of concern regarding its serious implications for biodiversity and ecosystems. When the impact of global warming on biodiversity and the countermeasures that can be taken against it are examined, however, two perspectives tend to emerge: an optimistic and a pessimistic one. The optimists argue that living things have undergone repeated cycles of extinction and emergence throughout the long history of life on Earth. That, after all, is how the planet's present biological richness was produced. Therefore, life on Earth will recover despite the extinction of many species and the consequent reduction in biodiversity. On the contrary, pessimists assume that human beings will become extinct anyway, and that we can do nothing about this. These people also tend to think that the problems confronting the world have been caused by human beings' high intelligence and desire for domination and possession, qualities unique to our species. These factors, they argue, make the situation irreversible. What the thinking of both optimists and pessimists has in common is the notion that events will take their own course.

Concern over problems related to climate warming is growing in Japan, however, and more and more people think that climate change can actually be reversed. Unfortunately, concerns about impacts on biodiversity are rarely expressed. Perhaps because Japanese corporations possess excellent technologies, they seem to believe that climate warming and CO_2 reduction can be tackled by technological means alone. Their actions are confined to specific facilities and regions, and no comprehensive view is taken as to what should be done with respect to the global environment as a whole.

Advanced technologies are capable of producing what can be described in purely statistical terms as "ecological" products. In an ideal environmentally friendly city, for instance, dependence on fossil fuels for energy is eliminated as far as possible and waste is disposed of in as clean a fashion as possible. We cannot, however, sustain the global environment simply by keeping the places we live in clean. We must also take into consideration the maintenance of biodiversity in development, urban construction, and many other human activities. What plants and animals will live on the clean concrete banks of rivers in an ideal city? What kinds of forests will surround such a city? What insects will fly into lighted windows on summer nights? A truly "ecological" world can be created only when these factors are taken into consideration.

What is happening to animals and plants in Japan?

Research results and data are being accumulating around the world on how biodiversity is affected by global warming. In Japan, however, attention has only just begun to be paid to this issue, largely because the seriousness of the warming and danger it presents to biodiversity are not yet fully understood by Japanese people.

Geographically, the Japanese Archipelago extends for more than 2,000 km in a northeast-southwest direction, with a complex topography and a large number of islands which together provide a diverse range of environments. A moist oceanic climate has been maintained since the Cretaceous Period (146 to 65 million years ago). In response to past climatic changes, and especially changes in temperature, species have been able to migrate to the south or north. This has made it possible for unique species to survive in various places as relicts. Alpine animals and plants in the high mountains of Honshu have survived since the most recent glacial. The islands of Japan are also surrounded by a wide range of marine environments that support an extremely rich diversity of life forms. These environments include continental shelves, deep sea areas, warm and cold currents, inland and open seas, as well as complex and diverse coastal features. Additionally, Japan is an important base for many kinds of migratory birds in the middle latitude areas of the Northern Hemisphere.

We do not yet have sufficient information about the impact of climate change on the rich biodiversity of Japan. An accurate understanding of what is going on in the natural world is necessary, however (Environment Agency, 1996). Efforts by Japan's Environment Agency to forecast changes in forest distribution as a result of climate change (1994) are an example of the type of research that needs to be done (Figure 1).

Tsunekawa et al. (1996) divided Japan into a grid of 386,950 squares and examined the distribution of eight types of vegetation within each square. They found that in 59,786 squares, or 15.4% of the total, natural vegetation remained. An increase in temperature of 1°C would change the vegetation in 23% of all squares, and an increase of 3°C would affect 62%. This is a forecast based solely on horizontal distribution. In practice, there will be greater vertical changes in the alpine and sub-alpine regions. Omasa et al. (1996) summarized forecasts of the following phenomena: the blooming of *Prunus yedoensis* and *Camellia japonica*, the autumn colors and leaf shedding of *Ginkgo biloba* and *Acer palmatum*, changes in climate and vegetation in Asia, and the impact on alpine plants of changes in the amount of snow cover.

Phenological and other types of field research on various species need to be conducted urgently and with geographic accuracy. To begin with, numerical data as well as information on potential risks need to be collected. In light of such research, effective

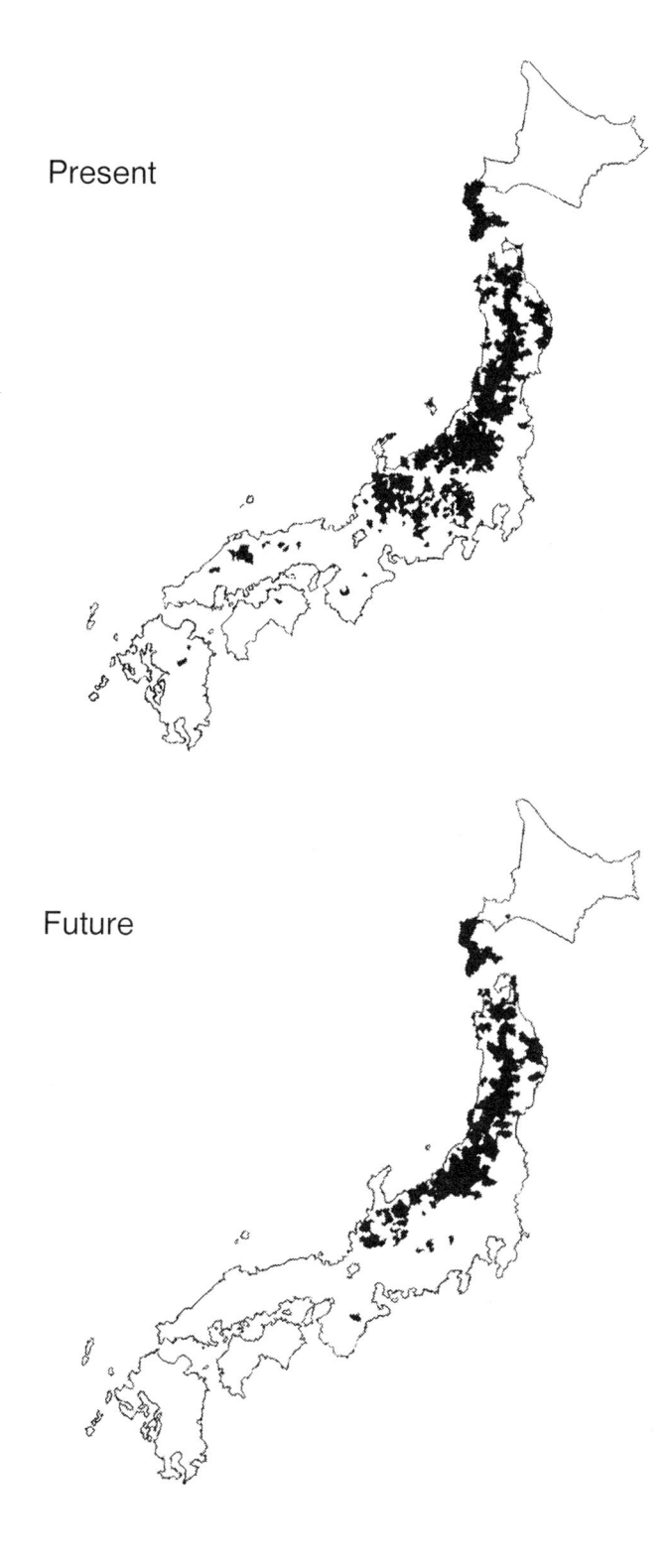

Figure 1.
Predicted change in distribution of Japanese beech *Fagus crenata* based on NOAA's GFDL model (modified from Environment Agency, 1994). Above: present distribution of *Fagus*. Mixed forest with *Fagus* and *Cyclobalanopsis/Quercus* is excluded. Below: predicted distribution of Fagus is based on the model under doubled CO_2.

measures to minimize changes in biodiversity can and must be proposed.

Climate warming is not entirely a negative phenomenon. Bio-productivity may increase, and living things may actually become more diversified. Climate warming and increases in the atmospheric CO_2 concentration may contribute to increasing plant productivity.

In practice, however, things are not expected to take such a favorable turn. For instance, Horie et al. (1996) forecast that a rise in the CO_2 concentration will increase yields in rice production. However, this will be offset by an increase in temperature of 2°C. If rice is exposed to high temperatures during the pollination period, the rate of fertility decreases. The size of the rice crop depends on the local climate, the method of cultivation, and the variety of rice planted. Thus, predicting the response of rice to climate change will be difficult. This is also true of other cultivated and wild plants.

It is far from easy to predict either the influence of environmental changes on biodiversity or the resulting feedback. A number of scientists engaged in research on biodiversity are saying that we should not leave climate warming to take its own course, but should take countermeasures against it. It should be noted that their arguments are not grounded simply in a nostalgic desire to recover white sandy beaches and green forests, but are based on the long-term viewpoint that we have a responsibility to our descendants to sustain the future existence of human beings.

Countermeasures

Human beings have always had an impact on biodiversity in the course of securing food and energy and carrying out commercial activities. Climate warming has now been added to the list of ways in which this damage is being done. We are now deeply ensnared in the dilemma of having to carry out both economic activities and the protection of the global environment. Appropriate management to cope with this situation is needed.

Regarding biodiversity, it is difficult to make detailed predictions concerning the influence of climate change on entire ecosystems. First, establishing the facts concerning what is actually happening is necessary. Following the seasonal changes in flora and fauna using key species as examples is an important tool for measuring the extent of climate warming impacts. For example, in Japan we have the research basis necessary to predict the blooming of *Prunus yedoensis*, and we can also select key species that will allow more precise forecasts to be made. Forecasts should be precise enough to allow us to distinguish between the "heat island" phenomena in cities and the effects of global warming. To this end, a system for observing the situation of various species over the course of many years at a given locality on a small grid scale is urgently required.

In addition to elucidating the facts, technological countermeasures against climate warming need to be improved. Schneider (1997) has produced a proposal for the creation of environmental policies from the perspective of comprehensive sciences, or the science of the global system. Protection of biodiversity is a concept that runs counter to the conventional thinking behind economic activities. It has become clear that the Earth's biological resources are not inexhaustible. As Schneider (1997) stresses, it is necessary to form groups of experts including those who have embraced a new economics (that can be called "environmental economics") which goes beyond the empirical economics of the past. These groups, consisting of people from different sectors and departments of central and municipal governments, researchers, private companies and NGOs, should be organized to cooperate with each other. They will be a crucial means of conducting a dialogue between "economy first" and "environment first" advocates in such a way as to produce more practical solutions. Moreover, individual Japanese people will have to modify their activities in a way that takes the care of the Earth into account. The future of biodiversity is also the future of humanity.

References

Environment Agency. 1994. *Implications of Climate Change for Japan*. Working group on implications of climate change, 181pp. (in Japanese)

Environment Agency. 1996. *Evaluation of the Global Warming Effects on Plants*. Global Environmental Research Fund. (in Japanese with English summary)

Environment Agency. 1997. *Implications of Climate Change for Japan-Produced in 1996*. Working group on implications of climate change. (in Japanese)

Horie, T., et al. 1996. Effects of elevated CO_2 and global climate change on rice yield in Japan. In: (K. Omasa et al., eds.) *Climatic Change and Plants in East Asia*. Pp.39-56. Springer-Verlag, Tokyo.

Omasa, K. et al.(eds) 1996. *Climatic Change and Plants in East Asia.* Springer-Verlag, Tokyo.

Schneider, S. 1997. *Laboratory Earth.* Harpercollins, New York.

Tsunekawa, A. et al. 1996. Prediction of Japanese potential vegetation distribution in response to climatic change. In: (K. Omasa, et al., eds.) *Climatic Change and Plants in East Asia.* Pp.57-65. Springer-Verlag, Tokyo.

Genus Index

Abies 77
Abis 78
Acer 153
Acomastylis 46, 47
Acropora 95, 96, 97
Acytolepis 65
Adelges 77
Adiantum 149
Aeshna 64, 66
Aethes 73
Agriocnemis 65
Agrotis 67, 72, 73, 74
Alnus 39
Alternanthera 54
Anabaena 103, 104, 107
Anarta 66, 67, 73
Anax 63, 64
Ancylis 73
Andromeda 71
Anguilla 117
Anomogyna 67, 73
Anser 128, 129, 130, 131, 132
Apamea 67
Aphelia 72, 73, 74
Apotomis 73
Appias 61
Archilestes 64
Arcterica 46
Argyreus 62
Arnica 46
Artemisia 49
Asarum 65

Betula 39
Bosmina 106
Brachythemis 63
Branta 128, 129
Brasenia 54, 55

Cabomba 52
Calidris 134
Camellia 153
Campanula 49
Campylobacter 144
Capricornis 137
Caretta 120, 121, 122, 123, 124, 125
Carex 46, 47
Castanopsis 39
Catostomus 111
Ceriagrion 65
Cervus 138
Cetraria 46
Chamaedaphne 71
Chamaepericlymenum 46
Chaoborus 104
Charadrius 134
Chelonia 120, 121, 122
Chrysobasis 64
Cinara 77, 78
Cladonia 46
Clepsis 73
Clethrionomys 138
Clossiana 66, 67
Clostridium 144

Coenagrion 64
Coregonus 111
Cotesia 79
Crepis 50
Crocothemis 64, 65
Cryptomeria 39
Cyclobalanopsis 39
Cygnus 129
Cymodocea 59
Cymolomia 73
Cyrestis 61

Daemilus 73
Daimio 65
Daphnia 103, 104, 105, 106, 107
Dasya 59
Dendrolimus 79, 80
Dermochelys 120, 121
Deschampsia 46
Diapensia 46
Dicentra 47, 74
Dichondra 149
Dioscorea 149

Ecklonia 57
Egeria 52, 53
Eichhorinia 52
Eisenia 57
Elodea 52, 53
Empetrum 46, 71, 72, 74
Enhalus 57, 59
Entephria 73
Enterohemorrhagic 144
Epinotia 73
Epipogium 149
Eretmochelys 120, 121, 122
Erigeron 50
Eriopsela 72, 73, 74
Erythemis 64
Escherichia 143, 144
Euphrasia 46
Euphydryas 62, 63
Eupitheoia 73
Everes 65

Fagus 39, 65, 153
Favia 95, 97
Favites 95, 97
Flaxinus 40
Fungia 99, 100

Gasterosteus 115
Gentiana 46
Geospiza 132, 133
Ginkgo 153
Glyptapanteles 79
Goniastrea 95, 97
Grammia 73
Graphium 65
Gynacantha 65
Gynaephora 73
Gypsonoma 73

Hada 73

Halodule 59
Halophila 57, 59
Hemicordulia 65
Heterothera 72, 73
Homo 148
Hydrilla 52, 53
Hydrobasileus 63
Hyphantria 76
Hypochoeris 50
Hysterosia 73

Ictinogomphus 63, 64
Idea 61
Indolestes 65
Ips 78, 79
Ixeris 47

Jesogammarus 104

Kobresia 46

Ladoga 62
Lagopus 133, 134
Larix 66
Ledum 71, 72, 74
Legionnaire's 145, 146
Leontopodium 46, 47
Lepidobalanus 39
Lepidochelys 120, 121
Lepomis 114
Libythea 62
Lilium 150
Listeria 144
Lozotaenia 72, 73, 74
Luehdorfia 65, 68
Lymantria 77
Lyriothemis 65

Macaca 137
Martes 139
Megisba 61
Melanitis 61
Micrathyria 64
Micropterus 110, 111, 114
Millepora 97
Minuartia 47
Miscanthus 50
Montipora 95, 96, 97
Mortonagrion 65, 68
Mustela 138
Mycalesis 65
Mycrosystis 103, 104, 106, 107
Myotis 138
Myriophyllum 53
Mysina 107

Natator 120
Narathura 62
Nebria 67
Nehalennia 64
Neomyces 104
Neptis 65
Notocrypta 61
Nucifraga 50, 133, 134

Numenius 134
Nymphaea 54, 55
Nymphoides 54, 55

Ochlodes 67
Ochotona 136, 137
Oeneis 66, 67
Olethreutes 72, 73, 74
Oncorhynchus 104, 105, 110, 111
Oncotympana 67
Oreochromis 112
Orthemis 64
Orthetrum 65, 68
Oscillatoria 103, 104
Oxytropis 46

Pachnobia 67, 73
Pagothenia 110, 111
Paguma 139
Pantala 63
Papilio 61, 62
Parnassius 62, 66, 67
Persicaria 150
Petaurista 137
Phiaris 72, 73, 74
Phormidium 103, 104
Phyllodoce 46
Phyllospadix 58, 59
Picea 40, 133
Pinus 46, 50, 66, 72, 74, 81
Pistia 54
Plantago 62
Plecoglossus 117
Pocillopora 96, 97, 98, 99
Polygonia 62, 65
Polygonum 49

Polytrichum 46
Porites 95, 96, 97
Porphyra 59
Precis 61
Pristiphora 77
Prunella 133, 134
Prunus 153, 154
Psammocora 95, 96, 97
Pseudothemis 63
Psodos 73
Pteris 149
Pteromys 138
Pterostichus 67

Quercus 39, 40
Quercusia 65

Rhododendron 46
Rhopobota 73, 74

Salmo 111, 114, 117
Salmonella 144
Salvelinus 104, 105, 115
Salvinia 54, 55
Schzocodon 46
Sciurus 138
Selenodes 72, 73, 74
Seriatopora 96, 97, 98, 99
Shizocodon 46
Sieversia 46
Somatochlora 66, 67
Sorex 138
Sphagnum 71, 74
Standella 38
Stellaria 47
Strymonidia 65

Stylophola 96, 97, 98, 99
Sus 138
Sympetrum 64
Sympistis 66, 67, 73
Syngrapha 73, 74
Syringodium 59

Talinum 150
Tegillarca 38
Tellinimactra 38
Thalassia 59
Thamnolia 46
Thelypteris 149
Tholymis 64, 65
Tokunagayusurika 104
Trachycarpus 148, 149
Tramea 63, 64
Trichodesmium 87
Trithemis 63
Tsuga 65

Udara 61

Vaccinium 46, 71, 72, 74
Vaccinnina 66
Vallisneria 54
Verarifictorus 67
Veronica 50
Vibrio 144

Xanthorhoe 73
Xestia 67

Yezognophos 73

Zostera 57, 58, 59, 60

Subject Index

acidification 32
ad hoc working group 3
adaptability 113
adaptive radiation 113
aggregative pheromones 79
AIDS 141
AIM-model 20, 21
algae 95, 102, 103, 104, 145
algae-bloom 102
alpine ecosystem 136
alpine flora 51
alpine insects 66
alpine mammals 136
alpine meadow 46, 47, 50
alpine moths 67, 71, 72, 73, 74, 75
alpine plant 46, 47, 48, 49, 50, 51, 74
alpine species 49
alpine zone 50, 66
amount of snowfall 35, 36, 37
amphipoda 104
Antarctic 15, 83, 86, 87, 92
anthropogenic global warming 84
antibodies 142, 143
ants 65
aphids 77

aquarium 54
aquatic plant 52, 54, 55
aquatic species 107
Arctic 48, 83, 86, 87, 92
Arctic zone 46, 133
artificial change 151
artificial structures 107
Assessment Report 4

bacteria 28
banana plant 54
beetles 65, 67, 77, 79
Bellagio Conference 4
benthic fishes 117
benthos 103, 120
bio-productivity 154
biodiversity loss 4, 7
biogeography 66
biological invasion 52
biological pump 27
biomass 50, 87, 88, 89
biospheric carrying capacity 28
bleaching 95, 96
breeding population 131
buffer effect 26

butterfly 61, 62, 65, 66, 67, 68

C3 plant 32
C4 plant 32
calcification 100
CAM plant 32
carbon cycle 24, 25
carbon intensity 20
carbon tax 23
Cartagena Protocol on Biosafety 5
catfish 114
CBD 1, 4, 5, 6, 7, 151
Cenozoic Era 113
chlorosis 85
cholera 141, 143, 144
circulation model 19
CITES 6
Clean Development Mechanism 5
clean type glaciers 43
Climate models 14, 15, 16
closed freshwater systems 114
CO_2 emission 15, 19, 20, 21, 22, 23
CO_2 partial pressure 28
coastal protection works 126
cod 112, 113

commercial activities 154
competitive exclusion 52
competitors 66
concrete jungle 65
contaminated water 146
contamination 143
CONTROL 19
coral 7, 85, 86, 95, 96, 97, 98, 99, 100, 121
corridors 138
coypu 139
Cretaceous Period 120, 153
crisis 148, 151

daily compensation 59
Darwin's finches 132, 133
Data Deficient species 60
DDT 106, 127, 142
debris-covered type glacier 44
decreasing beach areas 123
defoliators 79, 81
deforestation 25, 31, 86
degradation 9
desert 91
desertification 83
diatoms 91
Diptera 104, 106
discoloration 85
disease 10
dispersal ability 66
dissolved oxygen 35, 36, 37, 102, 103, 107
diversity of fish 117
dragonfly 63, 64, 65, 66, 67, 68
driving force 22
drought 32, 62

earlier initial egg-laying day 127
Earth Summit 4, 147
Ebola 141
ecological niches 113
Ecosystem 24, 65, 74, 86, 88, 89, 91, 106, 115, 152, 154
El Niño 17, 18, 85, 87
embryo 112, 123
emission scenario 19, 22
endangered 123
energy service demands 21
ENSO 87
Environment Council 4
environmental economics 154
equilibrium line altitude 42, 43, 44
estimations 151
euphotic zone 26, 27, 28
eutrophic lakes 103
eutrophication 36, 37, 53, 60, 86, 102
evaporation 117
evolution 113
exotic plants 54, 55
extinction or drastic reduction 115, 120, 125
extinction rate 63

fall webworm 76
fauna 137, 154
First National Report 4
floating ice 92, 93, 94
flora 154

flyways 130
follow-up 5, 7
food chain 105
food poisoning 144
foreign species 53
fossils 136
fragmentation 10, 12
fresh water fish 112, 116
freshwater 110
freshwater ecosystem 102, 107
future trends 22

GEF 1
genetic variation 66
germination 148, 149
glacial 39, 47, 136, 137, 153
glacial fluctuations 42
glacial lakes 44, 45
glacial-interglacial cycles 38
glaciation 38, 136
glacier outburst floods 42
glaciers 38, 43, 44, 45, 47
Global 2000 Report 3, 4
Global Biodiversity Assessment 3
Global Biodiversity Forum 6
Global Biodiversity Strategy 6
global level 151
global ocean circulation 83
Global Warming Projection 14
GLOF 42, 43, 44
Gobi Desert 136
GPP 25, 28
green corridor 65
green deserts 65, 66
green highways 68
greenhouse effect 2, 14, 136
greenhouse gases 13, 14, 19, 61
growth rate 110, 111, 112, 113
habitat destruction 9, 12
habitat fragmentation 68

Haemorrhagic fever 141
hatchling 123
Hepatitus typeD 141
herbivores 138
hibernate 115
Himalayas 136
holistic revision 5
Holocene 38, 39, 40
homoiothermy 127
house shrew 139
human activities 33, 106, 148
hunting 130
Hypsithermal 38, 67

IBP 24
ice algae 87, 88, 91, 92
ice cap 83
immediate threats 12
implementation 4, 6, 7
Industrial Revolution 15
infectious diseases 141
insect pests 76, 77, 81
inter glacials 40, 113, 137
introduced species 10
invading plant 50
invasion 78
IPCC 2, 4, 5

IPCC estimates 25
iron 91
ITEX Plan 48, 49

Japanese encephalitis 142, 143
Japanese waters 120, 121
Jomon Period 39
juveniles 112

key species 154
keystone species 105, 107
Khumbu district 42, 43
killifish 113, 115
Kyoto Conference 21
Kyoto Protocol 1, 5

lack of synergy 2
Lake Pekul'ney 130
land bridge 68, 137
larvae 112
last glacial 38, 40, 137, 138
layer 83, 84, 86, 87, 91
Legionnaire's disease 145, 146
life cycle 65, 123, 124, 125, 142
life-cycle regulation 66
lifestyles 148
linkages 1, 7
litter fall 30
LMOs 5
longicorns 77

Mad cow disease 141
malaria 142
marine fish 112
marine flora 57
marine macrophytes 57
marine organisms 83, 86
masked palm civet 139
meta-population 62
microorganisms 77, 103, 104
migrate 77, 127, 131, 133, 137, 138, 150
migrating insects 65
migration 125, 129, 131, 132, 134, 137
migration corridor 11
migration routes 130
Miocene 136
Mobile virus 141
modern technology 147, 148
molluscs 120
mongoose 139
mortality 111
mosquito 142
most recent glacial 66, 68, 74, 133
moth 77, 79, 81
mud flats 84

native habitat 149
native species 10
natural disaster 45
natural enemies 66, 77
natural phenomena 147, 148
natural sciences 147
natural selection 111, 112
natural vegetation 153
naturalise 55, 148, 149
naturalized exotic species 52
Nature Conservation Bureau 5
Nekton 87

NEP 31
Nepalese Himalayas 42, 44, 45
nesting 121, 122, 124, 125
nestlings 128
new production 26
NON-CONTROL 19, 20
northward expansion 61
northward shift 132
NPP 28

O157 141, 143, 144
OECD 20
oligoaerobic layers 103
Oligocene 136
oligotrophic 145, 146
optimal temperature 59
Oriental Region 137, 138
OTC 48, 49
outbreak 12, 76, 77, 78, 79, 80, 81, 141
over-harvesting 10, 12
overwintering 130
oxygen concentration 35, 37
oxygen consumption 111

Palaearctic sub-region 138
Pallas squirrel 139
parasites 77
parasitic wasps 79
pathogenic bacteria 144
pathogens 144
pest-induced damage 81
phenological characteristics 76
photoperiodism 76, 77
photosynthesis 28, 57, 91, 95, 100
photosynthetic bacteria 145
phsiological stress 79
physiological characteristics 110
physiological resistance 77
phytoplankton 24, 25, 26, 27, 28, 87, 88, 91, 92, 105, 107
PIC 27
pika 136, 138, 139
plague 141
plankton 86, 88
Planning and Coordination Bureau 5
planulate 98, 99
Pleistocene 38, 136, 137
pleumonia 145, 146
Pliocene 136
plovers 134
POC 27
polar ice 95
Polar Region 26, 48, 83, 84, 87
policy-makers 147
pollination period 154
pollinator 54
pollution 12, 13, 107, 145
polygon 47
polyps 99
population changes 121
precipitation 15, 17, 31, 36, 37, 42, 55, 72, 74, 80, 84, 110, 117, 127
predators 77
predatory amoebae 146
preferred temperature 113

primary production 86
protect biological diversity 12, 13
protected areas 7
protozoan 142
Psychrophilic fish 104, 107

Quaternary Period 40

radiative dryness index 31, 32
raised bogs 71, 72, 74, 75
Ramsar Convention 6
range shift 63
re-emerge 141, 143
Red List 52, 60, 68, 120
Redfield ratio 26
reef-building corals 95
relic 66, 71, 74, 115, 138
reproduction 27
reproduction and mating 111
reproduction rate 111
rice 154
rock area plant community 47
Rocky Mountains 136

salmon 92, 93, 94, 105, 113, 114, 117
saltwater ecosystem 102
sand accumulation 124
sand temperature 123
sandy beaches 134
sapsucking insects 77
satellite transmitter tracking 130
sawfly 65, 77, 79
scenario 3, 4, 19, 20, 22, 67, 110, 115, 123, 134
scientific experience 151
sea grass 84
sea ice (zone) 17, 86, 87, 88
sea level 2, 17, 38, 40, 67, 68, 83, 84, 85, 95, 123, 124, 126, 127, 134, 137
sea turtles 120
sea water temperature 83, 85, 86
seagrass 57, 59, 60
seaweed 84, 91
sex ratio 123, 125
shift 114
simulation models 19
sinks 5
snipes 134
snow line 36
snowbed plant 46
social-structural change 23
solar radiation 14
solubility pump 26
spawning season 99
species at risk 11
species interactions 105
species migration 11
Species Preservation law 5
species-area curve 66
SPOT 43
spring-fed waterbodies 115
springtails 65
staging ground 128, 129, 131
staphylococcus 142
stratification of water 103

streptococcus 142
structural changes 43
sub-arctic 66, 133
survival rate 111
sustainability 150
swimming ability 111
synergies 2, 4, 5, 7

taiga 66
TDS 123
technology 21, 22
tectonic activity 136
temperate zone 33, 48, 61, 68, 111, 113, 115, 117, 133, 134, 142, 150,
temperature coefficient (Q10) 112
temperature preference 113
terminal fluctuation 43
tetrapods 126
thermocline 25, 26, 27, 59
thermohaline circulation 113
thin eggshells 127
threespine stickleback 115, 116
tidelands 134
todo fir 77, 80
tolerable temperature range 112
Toxic chemicals 106
transgression of the sea 116
tree's resin 79
tropical aquatic plant 53, 54
tropical rain forest 28, 29, 30, 31, 32, 85
tropical regions 85
tropical zone 112
tuberculosis 142
typhoons 17, 124

unanalysed problems 147
UNFCCC 1, 4, 5, 6, 7
United Nations Development Program 6
upwelling zone 26
UV irradiation 96, 99

vector organisms 142
vertical mixing 83

warmth index 75
water hyacinth 53, 54
water lettuce 54
water resources 45
water stratification process 88
water temperature 35
weevils 77
wetlands 3, 7, 12, 131
wind-shaped plant 46
winter air temperature 36
wintering 128, 129, 131, 132
wood boring insects 77

Younger Dryas 38

zooplankton 27, 87, 88, 102, 103, 104, 105, 106, 107
zooxanthella 95, 100
Zosteraceae 57

Location Index (see MAP of JAPAN and Figures)

Abashiri (Map 2) 93
Akan Mountains (Map 5) 67, 73
Akita (Prefecture) (Map B) 131, 132
Akkeshi Town (Map 8) (Fig. 13.1) 71, 72, 74
Amakusa (Map 25) 96
Amami Island (Map 23) (Fig. 11.1) 58
Aomori Prefecture (Map A) 76
Asahidake (Map 10) 47
Ashibetsu Mountains (Map 16) (Fig. 21.1) 139
Atsumi Peninsula (Map 26) 123, 125, 126
Awajishima Island (Map 21) (Fig. 12.5) 63

Bihoro (Map 5) 80
Boso Peninsula (Map 24) 38

Cape Nosappu (Map 16) 65
Cape Soya (Map 16) 65
Central Alps (Map F) 48
Chugoku (Fig. 12.5) 53, 61

Fukuoka Prefecture (Map V) 63
Funakoshi Bay (Fig. 11.1) 58

Gifu Prefecture (Map H) 115

Hida Mountains (Map F) 67
Hidaka mountains (Fig. 21.1) 50, 66, 67, 73, 138, 139
Hidaka Region (Map 13) 65
Hiroshima Prefecture (Map S) 61, 68
Hokkaido (Fig. 20.1) 47, 48, 50, 52, 65, 66, 67, 68, 71, 76, 77, 78, 81, 92, 93, 115, 128, 129, 131, 132, 137, 138, 139
Hokuriku Region (District) (see Map) 65
Honki (Map near 5) 80
Honshu (Fig. 20.1) 47, 52, 61, 65, 66, 67, 128, 133, 138, 139, 149, 153
Hyogo Prefecture (Map O) 53, 54, 55, 61

Ibaragi Prefecture (Fig. 11.1) 57
Ibi River (Map 18) 117
Iriomote Island (Map 27) 67, 125
Ise Bay (Map near 26) 38
Ishigaki Island (Map 27) 67
Iwate Prefecture (Map C) 15
Izu Peninsula (Fig. 11.1) 57, 59

Kagoshima Prefecture (Map Y) 54
Kanagawa (Prefecture) (Map E) 149
Kanto Plain (see Map) 131
Kanto Region (see Map) 38, 39, 40, 65, 149
Kii Peninsula (Map 28) 64, 65
Kimobetu (Map Hokkaido) 78
Kinki (District) (Fig. 12.5) 53, 54, 63, 149
Kirigamine (Map Nagano) 47

Kiritappu Marsh (Map 7) (Fig. 13.1) 71
Kiso Komagatake (Map Nagano) 47
Kiso River (Map 18) 117
Kitami Mountains (Fig. 21.1) 138, 139
Kitami Region (Map 4) 80
Kobe City (Map Hyogo) 53, 55
Kuroshio (Current) (see Map) 38, 57, 71, 72, 74, 120, 124, 125
Kushiro marsh (Fig. 13.1) 71
Kyoto (Prefecture) (Map K) 149
Kyushu (Fig. 20.1) 52, 57, 65, 68, 96, 128, 138, 139, 148, 149

Lake Biwa (Map J) (Fig. 17.1) 35, 52, 53, 64, 102, 103
Lake Hachirogata (Fig. 20.2) 129, 131
Lake Izunuma (Fig. 20.2) 129, 130, 131
Lake Kabukurinuma (Fig. 20.2) 129, 130, 131
Lake Kasumigaura (Fig. 17.1) 103, 104
Lake Miyajimanuma (Fig. 20.2) 129
Lake Otomonuma (Fig. 20.2) 129, 131, 132
Lake Yunoko (Fig. 17.1) 103

Makkari Stream (Fig. 17.1) 103, 104, 105
Mie Prefecture (Map L) 61, 63
Miura Peninsula (Map Kanagawa) 149
Miyagi (Prefecture) (Fig. 11.1) 57, 130, 131
Miyako Island (Map 27) 57, 96
Miyazaki (Map X) 121, 122, 124
Mt. Apoi (Map 13) 50
Mt. Asahidake (Map 10) 138
Mt. Ashibetsudake (Map 14) 67
Mt. Atosanupuri (Map Hokkaido) 74
Mt. Fuji (Map 17) 48, 49
Mt. Gozadake (Map 27) 67
Mt. Ishikari (Map 10) 73
Mt. Muine (Map 16) 73
Mt. Nipesotsu (Map 14) 73
Mt. Niseikaushuppe (Map 9) 73
Mt. Omotodake (Map 27) 67
Mt. Rishiri (Map near 15) 73
Mt. Shokanbetsu (Map near 14) 73
Mt. Yatsugatake (Map Nagano) 67
Mt. Yotei (Map near 16) 73
Mt. Yubari (Map 16) 73
Mutsu Bay (Fig. 11.1) 58

Nagano Prefecture (Map F) 47, 48
Nagara River (Map 18) 117
Nagasaki (Map W) 149
Nagoya (Map 18) 143
Nakaumi (Fig. 11.1) 58
Nansei Islands (see Map) 61, 120, 121
Nara (Map M) 149, 150
Nemuro (Map 7) (Fig. 13.1) 71, 72, 74, 75
Niigata Prefecture (Fig. 11.1) 58
Nobi Plain (Map 18) 115, 116, 117
Nopporo (Map near 16) 78
Noto Peninsula (Map 19) 57

Odawa Bay (Map near Tokyo) 60
Ogasawara Islands (Map Tokyo) 121
Okayama Prefecture (Map P) 61, 63, 64
Okhotsk (see Map) 17, 92, 93
Okinawa (Map Z) 95, 96, 97, 99, 125, 126
Okutama (Map Tokyo) 149
Osaka (Prefecture) (see Map) 61, 64
Oshima Peninsula (Map Hokkadio) 65
Otsuchi Bay (Fig. 11.1) 57
Oume (Map Tokyo) 149
Oyashio Current (see Map) 57

Ryukyu Islands (Map Okinawa) 38, 68, 121

Sanin Region (District) (see Map) 62
Sanriku (Fig. 11.1) 58
Sea of Japan (see Map) 68
Sesoko Island (Map Okinawa) 95, 96, 97
Seto Inland Sea (Map 20) 64
Shiga Prefecture (Map J) 115
Shikoku (Fig. 20.1) 38, 52, 61, 63, 65, 128, 139
Shimane Prefecture (Map R) 61
Shimoda Bay (Fig. 11.1) 57
Shiranuka Town (Fig. 13.1) 71, 74
Shiretoko Mountains (Map 1) 73
Shiretoko Peninsula (Map 1) 92
Shizuoka (Prefecture) (Map I) 121, 122, 124

Taisetu mountains (Fig. 21.1) 47, 48, 66, 67, 73, 78, 139
Tateyama (Map Toyama) 48
Tateyama City (Map near 24) 38
Teshikaga (Map 5) 74, 80
Teshio Mountains (Map near 9) 73
Tohoku District (see Map) 53
Tokachidake Mountains (Fig. 21.1) 73, 139
Tokai Region (see Map) 65
Tokoro (Map near 4) 80
Tokushima (Map U) 121, 122
Tokyo (see Map) 143, 148, 149
Tokyo Bay (Fig. 11.1) 39, 57, 59, 134
Tomakomai (Map near 13) 78
Tottori Prefecture (Map Q) 59
Toyama (Prefecture) (Map G) 48, 152
Tsubetsu (Map Hokkaido) 80
Tsushima Current (Map Kuroshio Current) 38, 39, 57
Tsugaru Strait (see Map) 38

Wakayama (Prefecture) (Map N) 61, 121, 122, 124, 149, 150

Yaeyama Islands (Map 27) 96
Yakushima Islands (Map 22) 121, 124
Yamada Bay (Fig. 11.1) 58
Yamagata (Prefecture) (Map B) 131
Yamaguchi Prefecture (Map T) 61, 63
Yubari Mountains (Fig. 21.1) 139

MAP OF JAPAN

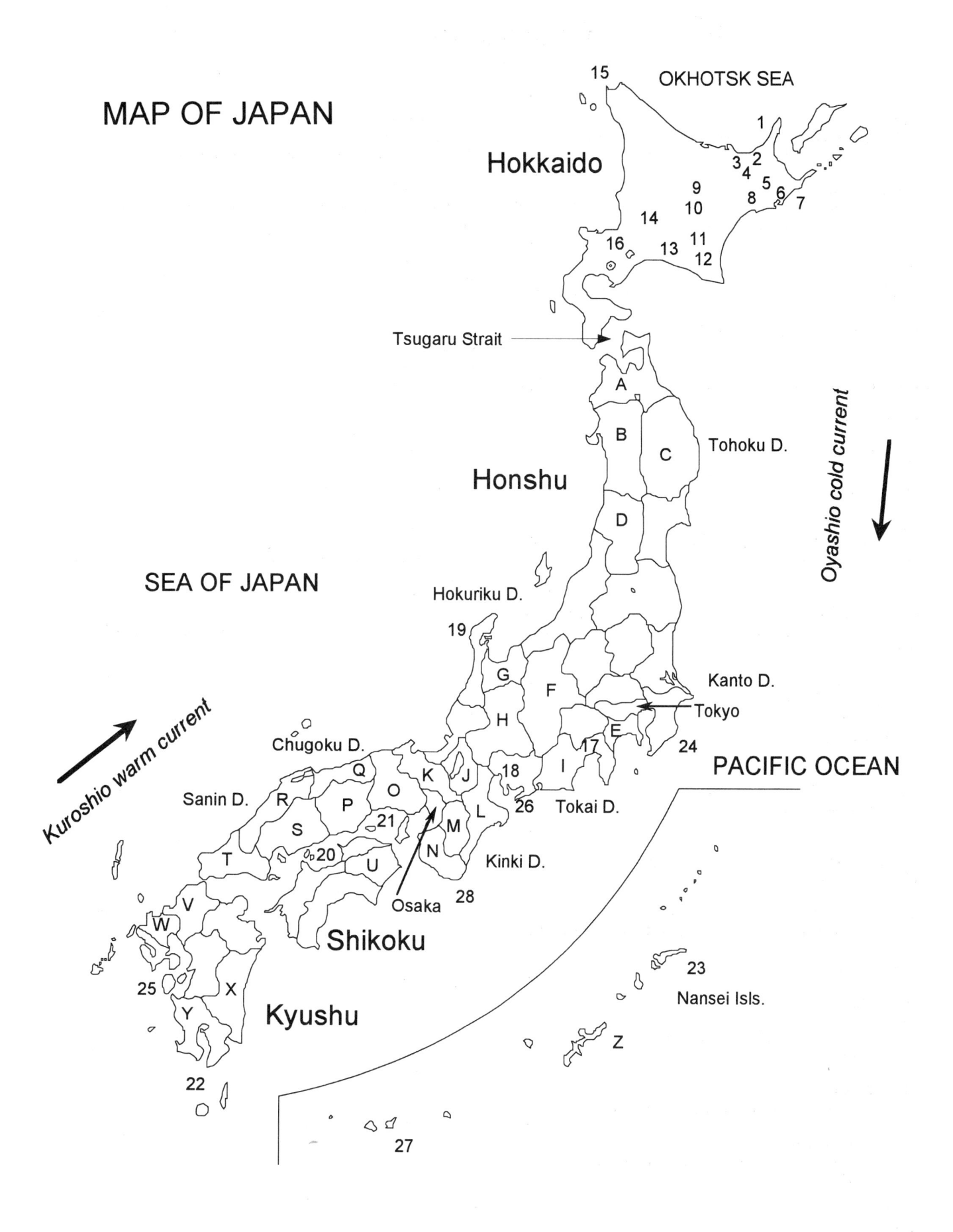

OKHOTSK SEA

Hokkaido

Tsugaru Strait

Honshu

Tohoku D.

Oyashio cold current

SEA OF JAPAN

Hokuriku D.

Kanto D.
Tokyo

Kuroshio warm current

Chugoku D.

Sanin D.

Tokai D.

PACIFIC OCEAN

Kinki D.

Osaka

Shikoku

Kyushu

Nansei Isls.

Contributors

Keiko Aioi
Assistant Professor at the University of Tokyo, Ocean Research Institute Ph.D. in Science

Akiko Domoto
House of Councilors, GLOBE Japan President, IUCN-World Conservation Union Councilor and IUCN Vice President

Takayuki Ezaki
Professor of microbiology in the Faculty of Medicine at Gifu University.
M. D. and Ph.D. in Medical Science

Kenji Fukuyama
Counselor for Research Planing, Forestry Agency, Japanese Government
Ph.D. in Agriculture

Hiroji Fushimi
Professor at the University of Shiga Prefecture
Ph.D. in Science

Nobuo Gouchi
President of the Library of Shari Town
M. Sc.

Kunio Iwatsuki
Steering Committee member of the Species Survival Commission of the IUCN, President of the International Association of Botanical Gardens, and President of Biodiversity Network Japan

Yasuro Kadono
Associate Professor in the Department of Biology at Kobe University
Ph.D. in Science

Mikiko Kainuma
National Institute for Environmental Studies
Ph.D in Applied Mathematics and Physics

Naoki Kamezaki
Director of the Sea Turtle Association of Japan
Ph.D. in Human and Environmental Studies

Takeo Kawamichi
Associate Professor in the Department of Biology at Osaka City University
Ph.D. in Science

Hiromi Kobori
Associate Professor in the Faculty of Environmental and Information Studies, the Musashi Institute of Technology
Ph.D. in Marine Microbial Ecology

Masayuki Kurechi
President of the Japanese Association for Wild Geese Protection

Takehiro Masuzawa
Professor at the Faculty of Science, Shizuoka University
Ph.D. in Science

Yuzuru Matsuoka
Professor in the Department of Environmental Engineering, Graduate School of Engineering, Kyoto University

Jeffrey A. McNeely
Chief Scientist with the headquarters of the IUCN, Director of the IUCN's Biodiversity Program.

Arata Momohara
Associate Professor in the Faculty of Horticulture at Chiba University
Ph.D. in Science

Seiichi Mori
Associate Professor of biology at Gifu Keizai University
Ph.D. in Ecology

Tsuneyuki Morita
Professor at Tokyo Institute of Technology

Masahiko Nakatani
Officer of Hokkaido Government, Division of Nemuro District

Hiroshi Nirasawa
Head of the Climate Information Section in the Climate Prediction Division, Climate and Marine Department, Japan Meteorological Agency, Japanese Government.

Harufumi Nishida
Professor in the Department of Science and Engineering at Chuo University
Ph.D. in Science

Takehisa Oikawa
Professor of Biological Science at the University of Tsukuba
Ph.D. in Science

Yuji Omori
Curator at the Natural History Museum of Yokosuka City

Richard B. Primack
Professor in the Department of Biology at Boston University
Ph.D. in Botany

Masayuki M. Takahashi
Professor at the Graduate School of Arts and Sciences, University of Tokyo
Ph.D. in Science

Nobuo Takeshita
Expertise in bird ecology

Hidenori Ubukata
Professor at Hokkaido University of Education
Ph.D. in Science

Kiyoshi Yamazato
Professor Emeritus of the University of the Ryukyus
Director at the Subtropic Research Institute, Okinawa
M. Sc.